Tourism Policy and Planning: Case Studies From the Commonwealth Caribbean

Paul F. Wilkinson, Ph.D.
Professor, Faculty of Environmental Studies
York University
4700 Keele Street
North York, Ontario, Canada M3J 1P3

tourism dynamics

Cognizant Communication Corporation

New York   Sydney   Tokyo

Tourism Policy and Planning: Case Studies From the Commonwealth Caribbean

Cognizant Communication Offices:

U.S.A.   3 Hartsdale Road, Elmsford, New York 10523-3701
Australia   P.O. Box 352 Cammeray, NWS, 2062
Japan   c/o OBS T's Bldg. 3F, 1-38-11 Matsubara, Setagaya-ku, Tokyo

Library of Congress Cataloging-in-Publication Data

Wilkinson, Paul F., 1948–
      Tourism policy and planning : case studies from the Commonwealth
    Caribbean / Paul F. Wilkinson.
         p.   cm. — (Tourism dynamics)
      Includes bibliographical references and index.
      ISBN 1-882345-12-6 (hardbound). — ISBN 1-882345-13-4 (soft)
      1. Tourist trade and state—Caribbean Area.   I. Title.
    II. Series.
    G155.C35W5   1997
    338.4'791729—dc21   97-18753
                                                                CIP

Printed in the United States of America

Printing: 1 2 3 4 5 6 7 8 9 10 Year: 1 2 3 4 5 6 7 8 9 10

Dedication

For Doh, Chris, and Melanie
and our many Caribbean friends.

Contents

List of Maps

List of Figures

List of Tables

Acknowledgements

This project was funded by research grants from the Social Sciences and Humanities Research Council of Canada. Support was also received from many members of the Faculty of Environmental Studies, York University, most notably Ms. Judie Cukier, who served as research assistant for that part of the project related to Barbados, Dominica, and St. Lucia. Ms. Lisa-Ann Hurlston's research is also acknowledged in providing recent material on the Cayman Islands. Appreciation is also extended to the Governments of the Cayman Islands (GOCI), Commonwealth of the Bahamas (GOCB), Barbados (GOB), Commonwealth of Dominica (GOCD), St. Lucia (GOSL); Caribbean Tourism Organization (CTO); Caribbean Conservation Association (CCA); and Canadian International Development Agency (CIDA) for their assistance. Many individuals—researchers, government and regional agency officials, private sector personnel—were generous in providing both time for interviews and valuable information, including:

- *Ms. Lissa Adams*, President, Cayman Islands Hotel and Condominium Association; Manager, Victoria House, George Town, Grand Cayman
- *Mr. W. Ken Alleyne*, General Manager, National Development Corporation, Roseau, Dominica
- *Mr. Arthur Archer*, Project Director, South and West Coasts Sewerage Project, GOB, Bridgetown, Barbados
- *Mr. Andrew Armour*, Manager, Anchorage Hotel; former Member, Executive Committee, National Development Corporation, Roseau, Dominica
- *Mr. Isaac Baptiste*, Senior Physical Planner, Physical Planning Division, Ministry of Finance and Planning, GOCD, Roseau, Dominica
- *Mr. Joe Bergasse*, Executive Secretary, St. Lucia Hotel Association, Castries, St. Lucia
- *Mr. Erik Blommestein*, United Nations Economic Commission on Latin America and the Caribbean, Port of Spain, Trinidad
- *Mr. Clem J. Bobb*, Deputy Chairman, Development Control Authority, GOSL; Chair, Soufriere Development Committee; former Deputy Chairman, St. Lucia Tourist Board, Castries, St. Lucia
- *Mr. Norman Bodden*, Director, Cayman Travel Services; former Member Responsible for Tourism, GOCI, George Town, Grand Cayman
- *Mr. Eudes Bourne*, Assistant Secretary, Ministry of Trade, Industry and Tourism, GOSL, Castries, St. Lucia
- *Mr. Brian Boxhill*, Chief Statistician, GOCI, George Town, Grand Cayman

- *Mr. Dick Burch*, Small Hope Bay Lodge, Andros, Bahamas
- *Mrs. Patricia Charles*, Executive Director, National Research and Development Foundation, Castries, St. Lucia
- *Mr. Allen Chastenet*, Marketing Manager, Windjammer Landing Resort, St. Lucia; Director, St. Lucia Tourist Board, Castries, St. Lucia
- *Mr. David C. Coathup*, Consultant, CIS Conference and Incentive Services Ltd., Castries, St. Lucia
- *Mr. Victor Curtin*, Statistical Advisor, CTO, Christ Church, Barbados
- *Mr. Graham Dann*, Reader, Department of Sociology and Government, University of the West Indies, Cave Hill, Barbados
- *Mr. Ausbert d'Auvergne*, Permanent Secretary of Planning, Personnel, Establishment, and Training, GOSL, Castries, St. Lucia
- *Mr. Krispin d'Auvergne*, Cadet, Ministry of Fisheries, GOSL, Castries, St. Lucia
- *Mr. E. John Deleveaux*, Executive Vice-President, Bahamas Hotel Association, Nassau, Bahamas
- *Dr. Oscar Pérez De Tagle*, Acting Chief Statistical Officer, Central Statistics Office, GOCD, Roseau, Dominica
- *Mr. Robert Devaux*, Director, St. Lucia National Trust, Vigie, St. Lucia
- *Mr. Eisenhower Douglas*, Chief Economist, Ministry of Finance and Development, GOCD, Roseau, Dominica
- *Mr. Noel Drakes*, Research Officer, Ministry of Tourism and Sports, GOB, Bridgetown, Barbados
- *Mr. Kenneth Ebanks*, Deputy Director of Planning, Ministry of Tourism, Environment and Planning, GOCI, George Town, Grand Cayman
- *Ms. Marie-José Edwards*, Director, Dominica Tourist Board, GOCD, Roseau, Dominica
- *Ms. Agnes Francis*, Product Development Manager, St. Lucia Tourist Board, Castries, St. Lucia
- *Mr. Raphael Francis*, Physical Planner, Physical Planning Division, Economic Development Unit, GOCD, Roseau, Dominica
- *Mr. Oliver Georges*, Manager, Housing Division, Economic Development Unit, GOCD, Roseau, Dominica
- *Mr. Felix Gregoire*, Director, Division of Forestry and Wildlife, Ministry of Agriculture and Environment, GOCD, Roseau, Dominica
- *Ms. Hadassah Guillaume*, Ministry of Tourism, GOCB, Nassau, Bahamas
- *Mr. Cliff Hamilton*, General Manager, Xanadu Beach Resort and Marina, Freeport, Grand Bahama, Bahamas
- *Mr. John Hastings*, Systems Caribbean Ltd., Bridgetown, Barbados
- *Dr. James Hepple*, Director of Research and Planning, Ministry of Tourism, GOB, Nassau, Bahamas
- *Mr. Jean Holder*, Executive Director, CTO, Christ Church, Barbados
- *Mr. Lennox Honychurch*, Consultant and Author, Roseau, Dominica
- *Mr. Calvin A. Howell*, Executive Director, CCA, Barbados, St. Michael, Barbados
- *Mr. Tim Hubbell*, Deputy Director, Department of Tourism, GOCI, George Town, Grand Cayman

- *Mr. Hudson Husbands*, Executive Director, Barbados Hotel Association, Bridgetown, Barbados
- *Mr. Arlington James*, Forester, Division of Forestry and Wildlife, Ministry of Agriculture and Environment, GOCD, Roseau, Dominica
- *Sir Stansilaus James*, Governor-General, Castries, St. Lucia
- *Mr. Thomas Jefferson*, Member Responsible for Tourism, Environment and Planning, GOCI, George Town, Grand Cayman
- *Mr. Philip Jules*, Chief Economist, Central Planning Unit, GOSL, Castries, St. Lucia
- *Mr. Ravi Kapoor*, Director, Tourism Council of the Cayman Islands; Member, Chamber of Commerce of the Cayman Islands; Realtor, George Town, Grand Cayman
- *Ms. Cheryll Lay*, Social Planner, Central Planning Unit, GOSL, Castries, St. Lucia
- *Mr. Edward Layne*, Permanent Secretary, Ministry of Tourism and Sports, GOB, Bridgetown, Barbados
- *Ms. Theresa Louis*, Economist, Ministry of Agriculture, GOSL, Castries, St. Lucia
- *Mr. Wolsey P. Louis*, Permanent Secretary, Department of Trade, Industry and Tourism, GOCD, Roseau, Dominica
- *Mr. Brian Louisy*, Planning Officer, Central Planning Unit, GOSL, Castries, St. Lucia
- *Mr. Barry McInnis*, Managing Director, Bahamasair, Nassau, Bahamas
- *Mr. Stephen D. McNamara*, Chairman, St. Lucia Tourist Board, Castries, St. Lucia
- *Mr. Keith Miller*, Tourism Officer, Ministry of Trade, Industry and Tourism, GOSL, Castries, St. Lucia
- *Ms. Annie Multon*, Member, Tourism Advisory Council of the Cayman Islands; Manager, Casa Caribe, George Town, Grand Cayman
- *Mr. Lionel Nurse*, Chief Town Planner, Ministry of Planning, GOB, St. Michael, Barbados
- *Mr. Basil O'Brien*, Permanent Secretary, Ministry of Education and Culture; former Permanent Secretary, Ministry of Tourism, GOCB, Nassau, Bahamas
- *Mr. Francis Pappin*, Economist, Central Planning Unit, GOSL, Castries, St. Lucia
- *Ms. Arthurlyn Pedley*, Director, National Trust of the Cayman Islands, George Town, Grand Cayman
- *Dr. Philip Pedley*, Director, National Archives, GOCI, George Town, Grand Cayman
- *Dr. Auliana Poon*, former Economic Research Officer, CTO, Christ Church, Barbados
- *Mr. Rudyard Robinson*, Chief Economist, GOCI, George Town, Grand Cayman
- *Ms. Norma Rolle*, Project Development Officer, Tourism Division, National Development Corporation, GOD, Roseau, Dominica
- *Mr. Giles Romulus*, Projects Coordinator/Planner, St. Lucia National Trust, Vigie, St. Lucia
- *Mr. James Salton*, General Manager, Pointe Seraphine Complex, Castries, St. Lucia

- *Mr. Robert Sands*, Senior Vice-President Operations, Carnival's Crystal Palace, Cable Beach, Nassau, Bahamas
- *Mr. Andrew Satney*, Marketing Specialist, Ministry of Agriculture, GOSL, Castries, St. Lucia
- *Mr. Rudi Selzer*, Director, Department of Tourism, GOCI, George Town, Grand Cayman
- *Mr. David A. Simmons*, Programme Coordinator, CCA, St. Michael, Barbados
- *Mr. Arley Sobers*, Statistical Officer, CTO, Christ Church, Barbados
- *Mr. Clairvair Squires*, Chief Project Officer, Tourism Division, Caribbean Development Bank, Bridgetown, Barbados
- *Mr. Darrell Theobalds*, Principal Assistant Secretary, Ministry of Trade, Industry and Tourism, GOSL, Castries, St. Lucia
- *Mr. Nicholas Thomas*, Director, St. Lucia Tourist Board, Castries, St. Lucia
- *Mr. Vincent Vanderpool-Wallace*, Director-General of Tourism, Ministry of Tourism, GOCB, Nassau, Bahamas
- *Mr. David Vousden*, Director of Natural Resources, Ministry of Tourism, Environment and Planning, GOCI, George Town, Grand Cayman
- *Ms. Cicely Walcott*, Research Director, Tourism Office, GOB; and Board Member, Barbados Board of Tourism, Bridgetown, Barbados
- *Mr. Walling Whitaker*, Director, Department of Environment, GOCI, George Town, Grand Cayman
- *Mr. Gregor Williams*, Acting Director, St. Lucia National Trust, Vigie, St. Lucia
- *Mr. Mervin Williams*, Executive Director, Coastal Zone Management Project, Organization of Eastern Caribbean States; former Town Planner, GOSL, Castries, St. Lucia
- *Mr. Ray Wilson*, Managing Director, Cayman Airways Ltd., George Town, Grand Cayman
- *Mr. Gary Young*, Director of Planning and Research, Ministry of Tourism, GOCB, Nassau, Bahamas

Chapter 1

Introduction

Tourism is at the top of the food chain of human consumption sensitive to the actions of all other sectors which influence the availability and quality of the product which it sells. (Manning, 1993, p. 8)

The Importance of Tourism

By 1987, travel and tourism constituted the world's largest economic sector (Anonymous, 1991c). The sector accounted for:

- US$2.9 trillion or 12.3% of the world's aggregate consumer spending by 1991 (Caribbean Tourism Organization [CTO], 1994);

- 25% of all international trade in services by 1990;

- 112 million employees or 6.5% of the global workforce by 1991;

- US$350 billion per annum in new facilities and capital equipment or 7.3% of worldwide capital investment by 1991 (Wharton Econometric Forecasting Associates [WEFA], 1991).

Moreover, continued expansion of the sector seems likely. For example, the World Tourism Organization (WTO) projects that international tourist arrivals will grow by approximately 4.2% per annum during the 1990s (Gayle & Goodrich, 1993a). If so, the number of international tourists will grow from 528.0 million in 1994 to approximately 675.8 million in 2000. In addition, there are probably 10 times more domestic tourists globally than international tourists (WTO, 1983), with much of their impact not yet having been studied (D. G. Pearce, 1987).

With the past growth of tourism, the economy of many countries has come to depend greatly, and in some cases almost exclusively, on tourism—particularly in the developing world (although the tourism sector is also probably the largest single component of the economies of many developed countries, e.g., Canada). Much debate on the costs and benefits of tourism for developing countries has resulted, but "in many communities and areas, whether tourism is beneficial to the area is academic. The area may have almost no other options" (Lundberg, 1980, p. 156). This is particularly so in the case of small islands (Walker & Duffield, 1984); given the current world economic system, for many islands tourism is almost inevitable (Wilkinson, 1989b) because a variety of factors (e.g., lack of natural resources, poor infrastructure, poverty, lack of trained personnel in sufficient numbers, lack of investment capital) may virtually preclude economic alternatives. Such nations should, therefore, examine their tourism industry and begin to plan both for its future and for alternative economic prospects (Wilkinson, 1987b).

Tourism in the Caribbean

One region where tourism has come to dominate much of the economy is the Caribbean[1] (see Map 1.1). Tourism in the Caribbean has grown in parallel to worldwide patterns: there was a 213% increase in stay-over arrivals in the Caribbean from 4.34 million in 1970 to 13.03 million in 1993, compared to a 221% increase worldwide from 159.6 million to 528.0 million in the same period (Anonymous, 1995; CTO, 1994). It has been estimated that tourism expenditures accounted for 25% of the region's exports in 1988 (European Economic Community [EEC], 1990) and approximately 420,000 jobs or 8–10% of total employment in 1990 (Mather & Todd, 1993). With visitor expenditures in the region in 1993 being estimated at US$11.1 billion (CTO, 1994), "There is probably no other region in the world in which tourism as a source of income, employment, hard currency earnings and economic growth has greater importance than in the Caribbean" (Mather & Todd, 1993, p. 11).

Map 1.1. The Caribbean.

However, there has been a great deal of debate on tourism centered on arguments about the supposed exaggeration of its positive economic impacts, with the Caribbean being the primary focus for research. The role of tourism as a potential economic force in the region was first voiced strongly by the Anglo-American Caribbean Commission (AACC) (1945) in its examination of potential postwar development alternatives. The debate was later fueled by the Tripartite Economic Survey (Great Britain Ministry of Overseas Development [GBMOD], 1966), financed by the governments of Canada, United Kingdom, and United States, which argued that tourism and light industry were the types of labor-intensive industries on which the small islands of the Caribbean could base their economies. This view was supported by the Zinder and Associates (1969) report, which had a great deal of influence on international aid agency policies. Zinder, however, was soon severely criticized by many authors because of what were considered to be overly optimistic cost–benefit ratios and economic multipliers (e.g., Bryden, 1973; Levitt & Gulati, 1970) and overly low leakage rates (e.g., R. A. Britton, 1980; Perez, 1974). Such criticisms have had a great impact on opinion throughout the development literature through the extension of their conclusions to other islands. There are few reliable and consistent studies of these issues, but it appears that (a) a large proportion of tourist revenues (even after multinational corporations [MNCs] such as airlines and hotels take out their costs and profits) is lost through the purchase of foreign products (e.g., liquor, food, hotel equipment) and through profits being exported; and (b) the multiplier effect on the rest of the economy is not as high as is often predicted or reported (Wilkinson, 1989b).

The growth of Caribbean tourism is largely related to the presence in a very small area of a range of tourism destinations as interesting and as diverse as any other region in the world, complemented by a favorable climate, areas of exceptional beauty, and diverse cultures.

> Amid this beauty, and despite its glamorous image as one of the world's primary playgrounds for the (relatively) rich, however, it is easy to overlook the fact that many of the Caribbean territories are poor, overpopulated, underdeveloped countries in which population growth generally exceeds the rate of growth in employment. There are some islands in which children still grow up poor and hungry and, at its worst (in countries such as Haiti and in some of the rural parts of the small Windward Islands in particular), the region presents development problems every bit as intractable as those in Africa. Because of the small scale, however, many of these problems remain hidden and the casual visitor may get little or no impression of the difficulties faced by many of the region's inhabitants. (Mather & Todd, 1993, p. 9)

Such poverty is not, however, universal in the Caribbean. Some rank among the wealthiest societies worldwide (e.g., Cayman Islands' gross domestic product [GDP] per capita of US$22,700), whereas others (e.g., Anguilla: US$7,500) have in recent years risen from poverty to increasing prosperity. For both of these examples, the main source of that prosperity has been tourism. Nevertheless, while not faced with the dire problems confronting Haiti, other states remain quite poor (e.g., Jamaica: US$1,400; Dominica: US$2,500). Yet, they too are seeing tourism becoming increasingly more important in their economies.

In fact, a common characteristic of most Caribbean states rich or poor is an important and growing tourism sector, with its impacts becoming a major factor in not only the economic environment, but also the social and biophysical environments. Moreover, as traditional economic activities (e.g., plantation agriculture, fishing, mining) wane, it seems likely that tourism and other service activities will become even more predominant in the region.

Tourism is not a recent phenomenon in the Caribbean, but it was only with the advent of mass tourism in the late 1950s and of inexpensive jet air travel in the early 1960s that tourism swiftly and dramatically became a major economic activity in the region. In the 1960s, the great optimism for the potential of tourism led to the rapid expansion in (largely foreign) investment in tourism facilities, generous financial incentives by national governments (many of whom were newly independent of their "Northern" colonial masters or looking toward imminent independence) wanting to attract foreign investment, and government provision of infrastructure (financed in large part by foreign aid). Growth in visitor arrivals and expenditures, which, although dangerously simplistic, are the most frequently used tourism statistics worldwide continued into the 1970s. The first energy "crisis" of 1973, worldwide recession, and some strong nationalistic expressions (which many tourists perceived to have racial overtones) led, however, to a temporary decline in the middle part of the decade. After 1975, there was renewed optimism about the vitality of the sector, as a result of such factors as improved economic conditions in North America, better marketing and promotion, the opening of new markets (e.g., Europe), and increasingly successful promotion of summer (low-season) vacations. The second energy "crisis" of 1979 caused another temporary slump, but the 1980s ushered in a period of overall growth for the region (contrasted by serious problems for particular destinations) halted only briefly by global uncertainty related to the Gulf War of 1991.

Despite this almost continuous growth in visitor arrivals and expenditures, numerous decision makers and researchers have expressed concern about Caribbean tourism for many years, citing problems related to such factors as obsolete facilities, overcrowding, environmental impacts, and "the need to apply long-range planning strategies based on accurate market and product information" (Spinrad, Seward, & Bèlisle, 1982, p. 15). The point about strategies or the lack of them was clearly stated long ago by Tinsley (1979), who contends that the state of the Caribbean tourism sector up to that point was "the result of twenty-five years of non-planning" (p. 310). (Tinsley's conception of "planning" is much more general than that adopted here [see Chapter 2] and can be taken to include both policy and planning.)

The focus of this book is on tourism policy and planning in the Caribbean (specifically, a subset of the region's states drawn from the Commonwealth Caribbean) in an attempt to determine whether Tinsley was correct and whether the situation has changed since then. The basis for exploring this topic is admittedly simplistic and seemingly straightforward: given that tourism, like any other economic activity, has both positive and negative impacts, a goal for these states should be to minimize the negative impacts and maximize the positive impacts of tourism.

That is a normative goal, but what exactly has happened in practice? Have Caribbean island states really taken an active role in trying to guide the course of tourism development to the benefit of their people and their islands? The underlying rationale for exploring the problem is also quite simple. Basic to making informed decisions that would guide the future is an understanding of how the current situation came to be. With a better knowledge of the past, perhaps there is a greater opportunity to influence the future, not just of individual Caribbean states or the Caribbean region as a whole, but also of other societies that are part of the global tourism system. This is not to say that tourism in other areas is directly comparable to the Caribbean; rather, tourism in the Caribbean provides examples of both similarity and diversity that might be applicable to other situations.

Goal and Objectives

Most research to date on island tourism has focused on the analysis of macroscale or regional data (e.g., tourism destination trends), single-sector effects (e.g., economic impacts, effects on agricultural employment or local food production), and single case studies. There have, however, been calls for the development of comparative case studies focusing on the spectrum of tourism impacts, decision-making processes, and alternative tourism development models. Similarly, with tourism's potential for both positive economic benefits (e.g., direct and indirect employment) and negative economic, social, and environmental impacts being well documented (Mathieson & Wall, 1982), many writers propose the adoption of models of tourism development other than traditional mass tourism in order to avoid many of these negative impacts and to increase the positive impacts. Such models have been variously termed "indigenous tourism" (Pigram & Cooper, 1980), "alternative tourism" (Dernoi, 1981), "soft tourism" (Krippendorf, 1982), "New Tourism" (Rosenow & Pulsipher, 1979), or "integrated development" (Jenkins & Henry, 1982). Key features of each of these models are alternative styles of government involvement in tourism decision making and high levels of local community involvement. There are few examples in the literature of states that have even attempted to implement such a policy. In fact, there are few examples of the detailed examination of island tourism policy and planning in general, although it seems logical to suggest that tourism policy and planning or, again, the lack of them has the potential for important effects on tourism development in a particular island.

In contrast to tourism's almost constant growth at world and regional levels, detailed analysis of data on Caribbean island microstates shows a range of patterns in tourist arrivals in recent years, including fluctuation, dramatic growth, stagnation, and even decline (Wilkinson, 1987b, 1989a). Although the pattern of tourist arrivals in individual destinations is consistent with various stages of tourist cycle models (e.g., R. W. Butler, 1980; de Albuquerque & McElroy, 1992; Lundberg, 1980), examination of only regional patterns does not reflect this high degree of variability within the set of islands (Wilkinson, 1987b). Moreover, regional approaches are simply descriptive and provide little explanatory power as to the factors influencing such variations. Therefore, the dramatic variety of patterns among these islands suggests that past descriptive studies now need to be supplemented by more detailed, comparative, on-site case studies seeking interpretation and a stronger focus on policy and implementation (Steed, 1988). Healy (1992) agrees, noting that

> A key need . . . is for retrospective studies of tourism development over relatively long periods of time. . . . Such studies should identify key policy choices at national, regional and local levels, both within the tourism sector (e.g. policies to subsidize investment) and outside it (transportation systems). Particular attention should be paid to how policy choices have affected environmental impacts and the three classes of economic impacts . . . —linkages, locations and beneficiaries. (p. 32)

Therefore, the focus of this book is on tourism policy and tourism planning (the latter as an indicator of implementation of policy). It attempts to search for evidence of the implementation of alternative development models (as articulated in tourism policies and plans) that could assist island governments in the formation of policies and plans aimed at more effective routes to sustainable national development.

The book's overall goal is to encourage island states to examine their tourism sector in a clearer perspective, to understand how past tourism policy and planning have resulted in current patterns of tourism development, to assess how policy and planning can be used in the future to secure a more sustainable form of development, and to recognize the potential for sharing experiences with other similar states. Additionally, there may be lessons that larger countries can learn from this examination of island microstates because "the combination of smallness and insularity produces spatial structures and development processes which are more evident there than in most mainland countries and destinations" (D. G. Pearce, 1989, p. 54).

The book has two objectives. First, it provides both quantitative and qualitative analysis of the varying nature of a set of case study islands as tourist destinations in order to account for their diverging patterns of tourist development that, to date, have received attention only in the form of research on theoretical descriptive models usually focused on visitor arrival or expenditure statistics alone. Data include each case study's history of tourism policies and plans, detailed visitor statistics, the nature of the tourism infrastructure and superstructure, economic indicators, degree of local involvement, and employment.

Second, a comparative analysis is presented in which the alternative styles of local government and local community involvement in tourism decision making and modes of tourism development are examined.

The research was undertaken from 1989 to 1995 through a multimethod approach: literature review; on-site investigation of both tourism policies and plans;

discussions with local academics, consultants, politicians, public servants, and private sector decision makers; and analysis of existing tourism data provided by individuals, island governments, and regional agencies. With respect to the last approach, reanalysis of existing tourism statistics has not been a common feature of tourism research to date, but Dann, Nash, and Pearch (1988) argue that there is a wealth of information collected that is often poorly reported by government sources and that contains much valuable information. Similarly, much information that is gathered is never published or made available to researchers (P. Pearce & Moscardo, 1985). Draft reports of findings were distributed to persons and public and private organizations who assisted with the project; their comments and criticisms were incorporated and are gratefully acknowledged.

Outline

Chapter 2 focuses on theoretical background and definitions of key concepts, including tourism and tourist, current research on tourism, policy, policy analysis, tourism policy and planning, development, sustainability, and government involvement. Chapter 3 follows with an overview of previous studies that have evaluated Caribbean tourism, concluding with the use of the tourist cycle of evolution as the rationale for selecting the particular case studies. Chapters 4 through 8 are the five case studies, presented in the order explained in Chapter 3: Dominica, St. Lucia, Cayman Islands, Barbados, and Bahamas. Finally, Chapter 9 provides conclusions and recommendations for policy and research.

On Studying Islands

Despite the growing literature on island development in general and island tourism in particular, Lowenthal's (1992) tongue-in-cheek comment on the hazards of being a researcher interested in islands is worth repeating:

> Students of islands have two strikes against them. One is that islands instantly connote having a good time getting away from it all on tropical shores among friendly and leisure-loving primitives. From Darwin in the Galapagos to Malinowski in Melanesia, island scholars have had trouble in being taken seriously. Referring to one study, The Times [14 March 1987] found it "absurd to imagine worthwhile research could be carried out in an exotic island setting." So goodbye Darwin, Wallace, Malinowski, and all the rest. . . . A second disadvantage is that islands connote smallness, hence unimportance. It is weighty continental states that shape our fates; islands are minute, peripheral, remote, uninfluential. (pp. 18–19)

It is hoped that this book will convince the reader otherwise: that while small in population and land area, the islands of the Commonwealth Caribbean are intimately connected with each other and with the metropolitan world in the global tourism system, which could be called the largest migration of people the Earth has ever witnessed—a system that has profound economic, social, and biophysical implications for both the islands as destinations and the metropoles as origins of the tourists. To assume that the Caribbean peoples are uninfluential in this process is to refute Richardson's (1992) forceful contention that, throughout the past 500 years, they have been active shapers of their region and therefore are actively a "part of the global economy's overall trajectory" (p. 3).

Note

[1]The *Caribbean* is a term at once both simple and complex. Richardson (1992), for example, argues that, as in the delineation of any large culture region, the vague boundaries of the Caribbean are fuzzy, permeable, and somewhat arbitrary. The term *Caribbean* is used here to include the islands that begin in an arc at the Yucatan Peninsula of Mexico, stretch across the Greater Antilles and north and east to the Bahamas and the Turks and Caicos, curve through the Lesser Antilles to Trinidad and Tobago, and then curl back to Isla Margarita (Venezuela) and the ABC islands (Arbua, Bonaire, and Curaçao).

Chapter 2

Tourism Policy and Planning

International tourism is simultaneously the most promising, complex, and understudied industry impinging on the Third World. (Turner, 1976, p. 253)

Introduction

Chapter 2 focuses on theoretical background and definitions of key concepts, including tourism and tourist, current research on tourism, policy, policy analysis, tourism policy and planning, development, sustainability, and government involvement.

Tourism and Tourist

A *tourist*, whether international (visiting another country) or domestic (visiting own country), is a person traveling for a variety of reasons, such as education, religion, health, sports, business, recreation, and so on (International Union of Official Travel Organizations [IUOTO], 1968) staying at least one night (United Nations Commission of Trade and Development [UNCTAD], 1971). Two different definitions provide a picture of *tourism*.

> "Tourism" is a sum of the . . . elements (travel, destination areas, tourist), resulting from the travel of non-residents (tourist, including excursionist) to destination areas, as long as their sojourn does not become a permanent residence. (Murphy, 1985, p. 9)

> Tourism may be defined as the sum of phenomena and relationships arising from the interaction of tourists, business suppliers, host governments, and host communities in the process of attracting and hosting these tourists and other visitors. (McIntosh & Goeldner, 1986, p. 4)

The former has the advantage of emphasizing the travel aspect, whereas the latter highlights the terms *business* and *host*.

At its most basic conceptualization from the point of view of the tourist, tourism follows the seemingly linear pattern described by Clawson's model of the recreation experience (Clawson & Knetsch, 1963): anticipation → travel to → on-site experience → travel from → recollection. Such a picture, however, is too simplistic and one-sided. More completely, tourism includes a complex pattern of people, decisions, artifacts, and effects:

- **anticipation** and **preparation** as alternative routes, destinations, and activities are examined and weighed by potential tourists;

- **involvement of intermediaries** (national travel organizations, travel agents, multinational airline and hotel companies, etc.);

- **choices** about travel times, dates, locations, activities, etc.;

- **the movement of tourists** (*guests*) from **origins** (usually their permanent homes);

- various forms of **transportation** (car, plane, ship, etc.);

- various **routes** (highways, air, sea, etc.);

- a **destination** (a temporary residence) or destinations (e.g., enclave beach resort on a tropical island, five-star hotel in a major city, campground in a desert or mountain national park);

- **interaction** economically and socially with local people (*hosts*);

- **participation** in particular activities (forms of recreation, e.g., shopping, scuba diving, gambling, sunbathing) in a variety of **human-made and natural environments** (e.g., hotels, restaurants, shops, theaters, casinos, beaches, coral reefs, mountains);

- **social, economic,** and **biophysical impacts** on the destination and the hosts;

- **movement back** to the **origin** via the same or another form of **transportation** and **route**;

- **recollection** as the experience lives on in the form of pictures, stories, and souvenirs;

- perhaps **anticipation of future travel** to the same or another destination.

Clearly, tourism involves more people than merely tourists and hotel-keepers, restaurant staff, and souvenir sellers. It includes travel agents, airline and ship crews, recreational equipment and clothing manufacturers, wholesalers and retailers, medical personnel and insurance agents, construction crews, bankers, farmers and fishers, politicians, planners, and many others. Moreover, international tourism involves people in countries other than just the tourist's origin country and the destination country. For example, a Canadian visiting Barbados may fly on a plane built in the United States, drink Dutch beer (produced under licence in St. Lucia) and French wine (imported via Martinique), dine on lobster from Guyana, tour the island in a Japanese-built bus, and go scuba diving on an American-built boat with a Canadian dive-master. All are involved in the complex global system that is international tourism.

Current Research on Tourism

Tourism has been the focus of research in many disciplines. For example, geographers have produced many excellent books on tourism, including reviews of past research (e.g., D. G. Pearce, 1987, 1989), analytical methods (e.g., S. L. J. Smith, 1989), and impacts (e.g., Mathieson & Wall, 1982), and collections of papers on a range of tourism destinations, notably in the developing world and especially islands and microstates (e.g., S. G. Britton & Clarke, 1987; Huetz de Lemps, 1989; Marsh, 1986). There has also been research in many other disciplines, including anthropology (e.g., V. L. Smith 1989), economics (e.g., Seward & Spinrad, 1982), international relations (e.g., English, 1986), political science (e.g., Richter, 1989), psychology (P. Pearce, 1982), etc.

Despite this vast literature, however, "there exists no all embracing theory of tourism, since tourism, like any other field of human endeavour, is a target field, comprising many domains and focuses, to which various theoretical approaches can be appropriately applied" (Dann & Cohen, 1991,p. 167). In the absence of this lack of a theory *of* tourism, one would expect that researchers from various disciplines would have developed a great deal of theory *in* tourism, but this has not been the case.

S. L. J. Smith (1989) argues that, given the complexity of the field of tourism, the "relatively poor state of theoretical development in tourism" (p. 152) across disciplines is not surprising. The problem is compounded by the "(1) a lack of credible information about the importance of tourism; and (2) a tradition in tourism that places little emphasis on the high-quality research that would produce the necessary credible information" (S. L. J. Smith 1989, p. 1). Moreover, tourism research as a recognized specialty has only a very recent history, with most of the literature dating since the early 1970s—a point in time that followed soon after the advent of jets, charter flights, and mass tourism. As a result, most tourism research does not have a satisfactory blend between theory and method, or, in Weberian terms, sophistication at the level of both adequacy of meaning (theory) and causal adequacy (method) (Dann et al., 1988).

This theory–method problem is reflected in the fact that much of the tourism literature focuses only on the first level of S. L. J. Smith's (1983) typology of research: descriptive, explanatory, predictive, normative. This is not to denigrate the importance of description, for *descriptive research*, the basic level of scientific inquiry, is "the process of answering questions about where, what, who, and when" (S. L. J. Smith, 1983, p. xiv). However,

> It is common to hear some research criticized because "it is merely descriptive." This type of criticism misses the point. The problem is often not that the research is descriptive, but rather that the description is not informative or detailed enough to be useful. Description works best when it is tied to another problem. Description for its own sake is rarely sufficient in any social science, and that includes tourism analysis. It must be undertaken with the spirit of trying to uncover some new, hidden relationships or patterns

that will teach us new, useful things about the world. (S. L. J. Smith, 1989, p. 194)

The other types of research are also very important for tourism. *Explanation* is "the answering of questions about how" or why (S. L. J. Smith, 1983, p. xiv). There is a wide variety of qualitative measures of interest, many of which are directly related to this book (e.g., development policies, land availability, political influences, user conflicts, public–private joint use of facilities and resources).

Prediction can be based on either forecasting future patterns through the extension of explanatory models or projecting future events based on observing statistical regularities and assuming that these will hold into the future (S. L. J. Smith, 1983, p. xv). Many past predictions about Caribbean tourism by both governments and consultants have proven to be wildly unrealistic, a fact that supports S. L. J. Smith's (1989) comment about the difficulty of successful forecasting.

> The challenges of successful forecasting are more than just the technical difficulties of developing an accurate model. Forecasting models must be developed with a clear understanding of both the nature of the problem for which forecasts are desired and of the resources available to the analyst charged with making the forecast. Stynes (1983) identifies four factors that should be considered when developing a forecasting model: (1) the organizational environment; (2) the decision-making situation; (3) existing knowledge; and (4) the nature of the phenomenon being studied. (p. 96)

Too often, attempts to forecast tourism seem to have been conducted in almost total ignorance of all four of these factors, as is demonstrated in some of the case studies presented here.

Normative research—research that attempts to say what should be or that is employed to guide policy decisions—builds on the other types: "To be able to do normative research a researcher needs to be able to describe what exists, explain how it came to be, predict future trends and consequences, and to apply value judgements to the analysis" (S. L. J. Smith, 1983, p. xv). Normative research on travel ultimately deals with the context of change and what has been termed elsewhere the "limits to growth"; however,

> Research on the promotion or limitation of recreational travel is scarce in the social sciences . . . due, in part, to the complexity of issues that must be considered before one can suggest the optimal level of tourism and travel development. The information shortage is also due to the fact that decisions about desirable levels of travel-related development must be made by civil and political leaders responding to the values and needs of society, rather than in response to a scientific analysis of travel impacts. (S. L. J. Smith, 1983, p. 169)

It is these decision-makers' judgements about their society's values and needs that guides their decisions. In tourism, that judgement is most frequently expressed in and most easily researched through the historical record of such documents as legislation, tourism policy statements, tourism plans, and national development plans that state (albeit to a varying degree of clarity) the normative goals of successive administrations.

Adequate analysis of tourism policy and planning, therefore, requires each of these types of research. Yet, the little analysis of tourism policy and planning that does exist tends to be only descriptive or predictive, with few attempts to be critical, let alone explanatory or normative—characteristics that are necessary if one assumes that a major purpose of research is to assist decision makers in formulating enlightened choices that might lead to improved quality of life for their people.

This suggests the need for an inductive or basic research approach to the problem at hand, involving a variety of methods as the research proceeds through descriptive, explanatory, predictive, and normative analysis. Therefore, the complex relationships involved in tourism policies and planning are examined here through a logical research framework that moves inductively from *description* of past and current patterns and processes, through *explanation* of how they came to be, to *prediction* of future trends and consequences, and finally to apply value judgements to the analysis—the goal being at least an initial attempt at *normative* theory. (It is recognized, however, that there is a strong degree of overlap among topics and that the material cannot be presented in this way.) Such an approach is consistent with Steed's (1988) belief that past descriptive studies now need to be supplemented by more detailed, on-site case studies seeking interpretation and a stronger focus on policy and implementation.

Research on Tourism Policy and Planning

Little attention has been paid in the tourism literature to the analysis of tourism policy and its subsequent implementation through tourism planning. An outstanding exception to this lack of research on tourism policy and planning is political scientist Linda Richter, who argues that "where tourism succeeds or fails is largely a function of political and administrative action and is not a function of economic or business expertise" (1989, p. 11). She calls for more research on the tourism policy-making process.

> Many governments, especially in developing nations, either by ignorance, neglect, or inexperience, lack planning, personnel or data independent of marketing biases (Richter 1985 . . ., [Richter & Richter, 1985]). Relatively few have staff or skills to monitor more than very crude tourism indices like arrivals, bed-nights, surveys of tourist expenditures, and gross receipts (Richter [1983a]). Rarely do governments, developed or developing, attempt net receipt figures, social impact studies, or systematic independent appraisals of market needs (Richter [1984, 1985]). Surprisingly the host country almost never attempts to assess the expectations or reactions of its own citizens (Hoivik and Heiberg 1980) to what has been described as "the most successful agent of change (short of political or military agents) active in the contemporary world" (Nunez 1978). (Richter, 1987, p. 218)

What is known about tourism policy suggests that it shares many commonalities with other policy sectors within a nation (Richter, 1989, p. 13).

In explaining the absence of theoretical perspectives on tourism policy, Richter (1983b) argues that "one of the reasons tourism policy has been neglected by students of the policy process . . . [is that] [t]ourism is a policy where there appears to be substantial rewards and few interests to placate or offend" (p. 318). Unlike policies such as agrarian reform, language policies, and some industrial policies forced upon a reluctant regime by political pressures, tourism is a *chosen policy* (Hirschman, 1976) that frequently creates little apparent conflict in its initial stages. Consequently, it tends to become a subject of political debate late in the implementation process when major social, economic, or environmental costs become apparent. Richter contends that seldom are tourism policies and plans scrutinized in terms of what Lasswell (1958) describes as the core issues of politics: who gets what, when, where, why, and how. As a result, when it is adopted as a development strategy, tourism is often assumed by policy makers to be simple or certain.

In an attempt to begin to fill this policy research gap, the analysis presented here shows that the pattern of tourism development in a particular country cannot be understood without an examination of that country's policies toward resources and the environment, in general, and tourism, in particular. There are both cause and effect relationships here. For example, the nature of international tourism (e.g., the volume and type of demand from particular origins) is a factor in shaping tourism policy (e.g., visa requirements). Similarly, a country's development policies in general (e.g., foreign ownership, tax incentives) affect the nature of tourism development (e.g., MNC vs. domestic ownership of hotels). A comparative policy analysis approach is used, therefore, to situate tourism policy within the context of overall national development policy.

National development policy, however, can only be understood in the light of development theory. There is a vast literature in the development field and a wide range of models, a topic that is explored briefly later in this chapter. An essential argument that arises out of the examination of such theoretical models is that tourism cannot be viewed in isolation, but rather must be considered in the broader context of national and/or regional development.

> Consideration of contextual characteristics—the nature of the place in which tourism develops—is important, for the context will influence the way in which tourism evolves and will condition the impact which tourism will have. These impacts will in turn modify the places concerned and contribute to a redefinition of their character and geography. (D. G. Pearce, 1989, p. 52)

This need to appreciate context implies that

> . . . tourism is a highly political phenomenon, the implications of which have been only rarely perceived and almost nowhere fully understood. Furthermore, it matters a great deal whether the public and key policymakers are able to grasp the fact that, although tourism may have a frivolous carefree im-

age, the industry is huge, intensely competitive, and has acute social consequences for nearly all societies. (Richter, 1989, p. 2)

The approach taken here, then, is grounded in consideration of the nature of national development in the developing world, in general, and the overall role of
tourism in that development, in particular.

The Nature of Tourism Policy

. . . the political interests are such that leadership does not ask policy ana-
lysts or outside consultants, "is it wise to develop tourism?" but rather "how
can we develop it quickly to showcase our nation's attractions and bring in
big bucks?" (or yen, or francs). . . . (Richter, 1989, p. 19)

Policy and Policy Analysis/Research

A simple definition of policy is that it is a course of action adopted and pursued by
a government. Steed (1988), however, warns that policy

. . . has both a micro-component, referring to pre-decision and decision
stages, and a macro-element, relating to power and the means, subjects, and
objects of coercion. Policy types differ along substantive lines, such as loca-
tional, urban, regional, or environmental, and each policy arena, as indeed
each policy instrument (taxes versus grants, for instance), develops its own
special political context, closely associated with the perception of winners
and losers (Leone 1986). (p. 5)

As a type of research, *policy analysis* (or *policy research*) has followed many—often conflicting—methodological models, reflecting the varying issues of concern
and perceived social realities of the researchers, communities, and problem sets involved (Heintz & Jenkins-Smith, 1988). A common thread appears to be an implicit
definition of policy that is vague and interpreted in many ways, but is viewed as
having some value-laden interpretation of how the dynamics of the multidimen-
sional realms of society (e.g., economic, social, biophysical) operate (Marden,
1992).

Ritchie (1987) defines *policy research* as "analysis of overall organizational situations with a view to formulating major policy proposals and establishing their priorities" (p. 16). Its common procedure is to seek a better understanding and direction for policy creation, evaluation, and structure and, in turn, an improved
understanding and direction of social reality through asking Lasswell's (1958) basic questions of who, what, when, where, why, and how. The implication, therefore, is that policy guides society—society does not guide policy (Goulet, 1993).
Thus, there is an implicit separation between policy research and social reality, a
separation that is necessitated by the requirements of objectivity in research.

Steed (1988, p. 4) notes that, over the previous three decades, the social sciences
came to play a variety of multifaceted roles in the policy-making process, including the development of *public policy analysis* (Dunn, 1981), a field that Torger-

son (1986) describes as a jungle of diverse and conflicting modes of inquiry, full of inconsistent terminologies, divergent intellectual styles, and perhaps incommensurable paradigms. Public policy analysis is essentially comprised of three broad paradigms: positivist, humanist, and radical (Johnston, 1983). The first—which, in simplistic terms, implies an "if . . . then . . ." rationality—has dominated the field of policy analysis as a whole since the 1960s, its main contribution being based on the technocratic (Torgerson, 1986) ideal of replacing politics with knowledge. The 1970s and 1980s, however, brought a realization that the technocratic orientation of conventional policy analysis was blinded to the nature of its political context and thus failed to understand the dynamics of the policy process, which is an exercise of political thought and application of power (Steed, 1988, p. 4).

Tourism Policy

Acerenza (1985) defines *tourism policy* as "the complex of tourism related decisions which, integrated harmoniously with the national policy for development, determines the orientation of the sector, and the action to be taken" (p. 60). He sees tourism policy as providing the broad guidelines that shape the development of the sector, whereas the development strategy constitutes the means by which resources are used to meet the objectives defined. Drawing on the work of Gunn (1979, pp. 191–194), Acerenza suggests that three fundamental elements underlie all tourism policy: visitor satisfaction, environmental protection, and adequate rewards for developers and investors. (His lack of consideration of positive impacts on the host population, other than "environmental protection," is noteworthy.)

Edgell (1987) describes *tourism policy decision making*: "A policymaker deciding on a present or future action or program based on specific goals and objectives from among alternatives and in light of given conditions" (p. 24). He argues that tourism policy development is a decision process that is a function of three elements:

- **economic, sociocultural, and environmental conditions**: political, economic, and social factors[1];

- **goals and objectives**: organizational survival, service to community, realization of economic return, etc.;

- **available resources**: human, financial, and material/physical.

Describing the state of the art of tourism policy analysis as being in its infancy, Edgell (1987) contends that the focus has been on a very limited set of goals and objectives: "(1) maximizing tourist arrivals and (2) improvement in the balance of payments through international tourism receipts" (p. 28). To broaden the analysis, S. L. J. Smith (1989) argues that six major themes should be addressed:

> (1) marketing and tourist-demand questions; (2) identification of opportunities for development, especially in the context of site selection and regional development priorities; (3) definition of the geographic structure of the industry; (4) description and evaluation of tourism destination regions; (5) determi-

nation of the value of public resources used in tourism; and (6) estimation of the economic magnitude of the industry. (p. 14)

These themes are the subject of *strategic research*, a recent field of research that is neither well-defined nor understood:

> Policy research relates to the strategic analysis and planning activities of a tourism organization . . . on the tourism system as a whole. It appears to be composed of three elements: research which studies how policy formulation occurs with a view to understanding and improving the process; research which is designed to analyze situations at the strategic level and to formulate overall policy proposals; and research which systematically evaluates the priorities to be accorded to conflicting/contemporary policy alternatives (Bauer and Gergen, 1968). (Ritchie, 1987, p. 16)

The complexity of this dynamic process is underscored by Atkinson and Chandler (1983), who suggest four broad strategies of policy analysis that offer separate routes into understanding the policy process by posing distinctive initial problems:

- **the determinants of policy making**: to examine how political, social, and economic forces shape policy outputs which emerge as successive political bargains are struck by various participants;

- **how processes vary across policy fields**: to see whether or how policies might ultimately be related to the policy-making process through, for example, the degree of coercion, the nature of distribution, and the extent of systematic impact;

- **the choice of policy instruments and what prompts government to prefer some over others**: to understand the consequences that flow from this choice on, for example, the policy makers' personal goals, the type of political process required to implement the choice, and the implications for both equity and efficiency;

- **appraisal of policy effects and program evaluation**: the former to understand the spatial impact or the effects of policy on political behavior and public institutions, and the latter for positivist reasons related to the technocratic ideal noted above.

Tourism can be seen as appropriate subject matter for each of the above four strategies of policy analysis:

- Tourism policy is affected by political (e.g., the United States embargo on tourism to Cuba, which resulted in great increases in American tourists to other Caribbean destinations), social (e.g., historical reactions against tourism in some parts of the Caribbean because of its overtones of continuing plantation relationships), and economic (e.g., the impacts of global recession) forces.

- Agricultural and industrial policies (and their failures in some cases) have affected tourism policy (e.g., Jamaica's increasing emphasis on tourism as world agricultural and mining markets have softened).

- Governments have adopted a wide range of policy instruments (from tax incentives to national airlines) to promote tourism.

- Evaluative research is needed to compare and contrast the successes or failures that can be related to this variety of policies.

In the context of national policy, Ritchie (1987) defines *policy research requirements* as "primarily macrolevel data related to the present values and anticipated trends of the major economic, social, technical, and political factors which have a present or potential bearing on tourism" (p. 17). (An omission is the natural environment.) Two of the three types of measures that Ritchie (1987, p. 17) describes as the major data sources for policy research are used here: longitudinal or time-series measures of the major indicators related to the complex phenomena that constitute tourism; and expert judgement focused on specific strategic questions that are not well-explained by longitudinal data. (The third type of measure— large-scale system simulation such as that of econometric and industrial dynamics models—is not included because that type of data on Caribbean tourism does not exist to create such models.)

This brief outline of the complexity of tourism policy analysis suggests that such policy can only be understood if the broad social, economic, and biophysical environment in which the policy exists is examined. This environment has been termed the *policy context*.

Policy Contexts

> At the national level . . ., policies tend to be the product of both the political system and the policy-making process itself. (Steed, 1988, p. 5)

It is important for researchers to address policy contexts and to come to grips with the nature of changeable and changing goals and objectives, which reflect the variety of constraints in existence (Steed 1988, p. 6). Doern and Aucoin (1971) contend that policies vary between the two major policy structures, the Cabinet (the "Executive") and the bureaucracy—the boundaries of which are not precise:

> . . . policy-making within the executive-bureaucratic arena is continuously and increasingly a contest between the on-going and new policy structures. The new policy structure operates primarily in and around the Cabinet in the conversion of new policy issues into outputs. The on-going policy structure operates primarily in and around the bureaucracy in the continuing conversion of the manifest or latent support for existing programs into outputs. (pp. 267–268)

If this picture of the nature of policy and the realities of the policy context is accepted, then it becomes clear that it is necessary to break away from the legacy of positivism and its associated model of technical rationality and to accept the importance of understanding, explanation, and practice of troublesome phenomena such as complexity, uncertainty, instability, uniqueness, and value conflict (Schon, 1983). As Steed (1988) notes, "These phenomena simply do not fit the model of technical rationality, with its emphasis on practice as a process of solving well-structured problems and on choice of the best means to achieve established ends" (p. 7).

Ackoff (1979) uses the seemingly unscientific term *mess* to describe the realistic nature of the policy context.

> Managers are not confronted with problems that are independent of each other, but with dynamic situations that consist of complex systems of changing problems that interact with each other. I call such situations messes. Problems are abstractions extracted from messes by analysis. . . . Managers do not solve problems: they manage messes. (pp. 99–100)

In order to manage messes, it is necessary not only to solve a problem, but first to define the context and conceptualize the problem (Steed, 1988, p. 7). The necessary condition for any subsequent technical problem solving is the art of recognizing a problem setting, making sense of an uncertain situation, and developing perspectives (Schon, 1983). In most real-world problems, however,

> . . . ends are confused and conflicting, thereby leaving no "technical problem" to be solved, for technical rationality depends on agreement on fixed and clear ends. It is hardly surprising, therefore, to find severe difficulties in relating the key paradigm of social science to much policy practice. (Steed, 1988, p. 7)

This view of problems is reminiscent of Wittgenstein's (1958) definition of a *problem* as "a rough tract of unknown ground" (p. 123). The analogy suggests the need to do more than collect facts for theoretical purposes; instead, one needs to personally find a way around the problem or question (i.e., to interpret the context).

The Interpretive Approach to Policy Analysis

If this view is accepted as an accurate description of the reality of the policy process, it leaves the researcher in the position of having to search for an alternative approach to policy analysis other than positivism. Steed (1988, p. 9) suggests that an *interpretive approach* is appropriate because it is able, with a broad-based understanding of the social sciences (Christensen, 1982; Hahn, Bellah, Rabinow, & Sullivan, 1983), to tackle the selection of ill-structured problems, for which there are competing interpretations of the problem domain, let alone the solution space. He argues that the aim of interpretation is not to uncover universals or laws, but rather to define contexts and relative perspectives on real problems in the lived world (Rabinow & Sullivan, 1979). This is achieved by:

- developing adequate descriptive narratives and creating texts that capture the interpretive roles of actors within a social structure and of the social scientist with regard to the data (Duncan, 1985);

- trying to understand what people understand, mean, or intend by their actions (Sayer 1982);

- incorporating theory into the narrative itself, so that it is part of the enterprise and of the interpretation, designed to illuminate and help emancipate (Gould, 1985a; Rabinow & Sullivan, 1979).

The interpretive approach views human beings as acting subjects, not behaving objects, and recognizes that no single interpretation or explanation is likely to be complete.

> The interpretive mode requires creativity, insight, and judgement. It focuses on action, intention, and convention. It emphasizes style, rhetoric, and persuasion. It relies on symbol, metaphor, and analogy. And it is drawn toward interdisciplinarity. . . . [R]esearch in this mold of interpretive social science can make a significant contribution to policy analysis and lead to a more democratically participatory form of policy-making (Jennings 1983). It may also have practical value in helping governments to reduce costs, spark investment, and work toward improving community well-being. . . . (Steed, 1988, pp. 9–10)

It is ultimately engaged in story telling based on convincing interpretations of text, where both technical text creation and interpretation are informed and shaped by the values of the inquirer and where critical self-reflection exposes and perhaps modifies the shaping values.

An interpretive approach, when linked to policy considerations, requires detailed attention to at least the five following themes as necessary if not sufficient conditions (Steed, 1988, pp. 10–11):

- **effective social knowledge** that identifies the consumers of the research and establishes its relevance for the many parties involved;

- **realistic expectations** achieved in part by deliberating with stakeholders and pointing out the limitations to intervention and the long time scale that may be necessary;

- **reconceptualization** of the role of research in the policy process and the raising of consciousness of how and where research can contribute in the policy-making process;

- **reflection-in-action** as an epistemology of practice that seeks collaboration and partnership between researchers and practitioners;

- **interdisciplinarity, cases, and interpretations** in order to move away from a laws-and-instances ideal of explanation toward one that is sensitive to time, place, actors, and organizations (Winkler, 1985).

Steed (1988, p. 12) summarizes the three critical aspects of the new paradigm of the interpretive approach as follows:

- the properties of the parts can be understood only through the dynamics of the whole; this is the opposite to the mechanistic, classical scientific paradigm, which considered that in any complex system the dynamics of the whole could be understood from the properties of the parts;

- it involves a shift from thinking in terms of structure to thinking in terms of process;

- the metaphor of knowledge as a building with solid foundations is replaced by a metaphor of interconnected and dynamic networks of relationships in which no part is primary or secondary or more fundamental than any other; as a result, researchers deal not with truth, but with limited and approximate descriptions of reality.

As a means of utilizing the interpretive approach recommended by Steed, this book therefore adopts a *comparative case study approach* that attempts to tell the story of tourism in five case studies.

The Case Study Approach

Case studies are thorough examinations of specific social settings or particular aspects of social settings (Black & Champion, 1976, p. 90) that constitute in-depth investigations of a given social unit resulting in a complete, well-organized picture of that unit (Isaac & Michael, 1971, p. 20). Their major characteristic is that they usually examine a small number of units (sometimes even one) across a large number of variables (Pizam, 1987, p. 70). They may have advantages over other types of research designs: they are flexible with respect to data collection methods used; they may be conducted in practically any kind of social setting; and they are inexpensive (Black & Champion, 1976, p. 91). On the other hand, case studies have limitations: they may have limited generalizability, they are time consuming to undertake, and they may be vulnerable to subjective biases (Pizam, 1987, p. 70).[2]

The use of a case study approach is common in the tourism literature, but few researchers have focused on more than one case study or attempted a *comparative approach* (Dann et al., 1988, p. 24; D. G. Pearce, 1993, p. 20) in an effort to search for broader patterns. In particular, D. G. Pearce (1989) notes that "little attention has been paid to exploring differences between and within the wide range of developing countries which are to be found throughout the world . . . " (p. 87). He (1989, p. 282) goes on to argue that the value of case studies could be enhanced if they were set in a broader conceptual context and if a more systematic approach was adopted in carrying them out, thus increasing understanding of the nature of tourist development through cumulative research, identification and pursuit of general issues, and explicit links being made between different areas of research and the methods employed in them. D. G. Pearce (1993) later states that the question of what constitutes a comparative approach in tourism research has received little attention in the literature (with Richter's [1989] comparative analysis of Asian tourism policies being a notable exception), but defines it simply as "the analysis of a problem in two or more places, usually but not exclusively, in a cross-national context" (pp. 20–21).

Feldman (1978, p. 87) believes that comparative public policy analysis is valuable for three reasons:

- it can explore the range of choice available to societies whose perception of choice may be bound by institutions, economics, social structure, and culture;

- it promises insight into the role of institutions by exploring parallel institutions operating in other systems;

- it promises embracing theory for politics, as well as policy, beyond the boundaries erected by the details of systems because comparison helps establish norms for judgement and helps distinguish the essential from the trivial.

Noting that "Comparison in its broadest sense is the process of discovering similarities and differences among phenomena," Warwick and Osherson (1973, p. 7) argue that comparison involves more than the mere juxtaposition of cases studies, for to be comparative the analysis must draw out and attempt to account for similarities and differences.

Recognizing a deficiency of many tourism case studies, D. G. Pearce (1989, p. 288) believes that a fuller assessment of tourism's contribution to development requires a more thorough evaluation of tourism's performance against that of other sectors or what he later terms as "contexts" (D. G. Pearce, 1993, p. 30). He describes many studies as dealing solely with the impact of tourist development, but providing no touchstone against which tourism might be compared; in contrast, those studies that have had a comparative element have generally been more restrained in their evaluation of tourism's contribution to development. An attempt is made here, therefore, to examine tourism within the political context of the other sectors of the economy in each case study.

The Political Economy Approach

Consistent with Steed's (1988, p. 111) call for interdisciplinarity, a *political economy*[3] approach is used here.

> [E]conomy is understood in its broad sense as social economy, or way of life, founded in production. In turn, social production is viewed not as a neutral act by neutral agents but as a political act carried out by members of classes and other social groupings . . . [W]hile political economy refers to a broad spectrum of ideas, these notions have focus and order: . . . as part of a general, critical theory emphasizing the social production of existence. (Peet & Thrift, 1989, p. 3)

A benefit of a political economy approach is the focusing of attention on the formative political, economic, social, and institutional processes that influence societal organization (Potter & Binns, 1988, p. 279).

A political economy approach goes beyond the usual concerns of tourism research to include a consideration of institutions, notably those related to tourism policy and planning:

> . . . the character and performance of national institutions are specific to each country's economic history, social composition, and class structure. These factors are only on the level of appearances of underlying, less observable social mechanisms. It is important to go beyond these appearances. The political economy of tourism encompasses the ways in which the industry manifests the division of labour, class relations, ideological content, and social distributions specific to a social formation. . . . (S. G. Britton, 1987, p. 171)

In effect, this political economy approach attempts to go beyond the "developmentalist paradigm" (Browlett, 1980), which has been the focus of much tourism research; in that paradigm, "Researchers interpreted their findings through the lens of apolitical, ahistorical social-science perspectives" (S. G. Britton, 1987, p. 185). In that sense, this approach is influenced by underdevelopment theory and neo-Marxian social science, which call for consideration of the underlying political, ideological, economic, and class dynamics that structure small developing countries—thus requiring an *historical approach* to study the evolution of those dynamics.

An Historical Approach

An *historical approach* is not common in the tourism literature, but attention to the temporal dimension of tourism is described by Dann et al. (1988) as "an exciting direction for future research" (p. 24). The historical approach adopted here is that of a social scientist, rather than that of an historian. Towner (1988, p. 51) clarifies the different aims: mainstream historical tourism research might be undertaken to understand the role of that phenomenon in a certain society at a *particular* time; social science historical research might primarily seek examples that would contribute to a dynamic model or concept of the role of tourism in societies in general. That is, the historian aims to reconstruct the reality of a particular past period or event, whereas the social scientist aims to develop more general concepts of society where the specific historicity of the data is not of central importance (Towner, 1988, p. 51). In each of the case studies, therefore, the history of tourism is examined to understand the changing role of the sector in national development, thus setting the stage for recent policy and planning activities.

Summary

This book on tourism policy and planning, therefore, follows Steed's call for an interdisciplinary and interpretive case study approach conditioned by a consideration of both political economy and history. The next section places tourism planning into that perspective.

The Nature of Tourism Planning

Planning

At its simplest, *planning* is the implementation of policy. Basically a sociopolitical process (Graycar, 1979), policy implementation is essentially a bargaining exercise that meshes political and social acceptability with economic and technical feasibility and with administrative reality (Pigram, 1992, p. 81). Policy making itself is clearly a difficult task, but de Kadt (1992, p. 65) argues that the difficulties of tourism policy implementation are even more greatly underestimated, for too often policy is made without instruments being in place for its management. Moreover, the context within which policies are to be implemented is of fundamental importance because conflicts and resistance can emerge as a result of the nature and complexity of the policy, the way it is perceived by the target groups and the implementing organizations, and the environmental conditions—physical, sociocultural, political, and economic—that prevail (T. Smith, 1973). For the purposes of this book, the instruments of policy implementation that are of interest are the processes and organizations involved in *tourism planning*.

Green (1987) provides a conventional definition of *planning*: "the implementation, supervision, and review as well as the formulation of plans . . .; [it] covers private as well as governmental and public enterprise" (p. 95). Murphy's (1985) definition is more detailed:

> Planning is concerned with anticipating and regulating change in a system, to promote orderly development so as to increase the social, economic and environmental benefits of the development process. To do this, planning becomes "an ordered sequence of operations, designed to lead to the achievement of either a single goal or to a balance between several goals" (Hall, 1970, p. 4). (p. 156)

Such definitions, however, seem to place emphasis on a straightforward approach that accepts the (positivist) possibility of comprehensive rationality. Such a process assumes several factors: consensus on objectives, lack of uncertainty, known alternatives, a high degree of centralized control, and ample time and money to prepare a plan (Lang, 1986a). Clearly, such factors rarely exist in any planning situation, let alone tourism planning.

Tourism Planning

Although the general planning literature provides few references to *tourism planning*, Inskeep (1988) argues that it is a sufficiently specialized and different form that demands special attention on its own. Getz (1987) defines it as "A process, based on research and evaluation, which seeks to optimize the potential contribution of tourism to human welfare and environmental quality" (p. 3). Mathieson and Wall (1982) provide a very succinct statement on its main objectives: "to ensure that opportunities are available for tourists to gain enjoyable and satisfying experiences and, at the same time, to provide a means for improving the way of life of residents of destination areas" (p. 186). In applying a strategic planning approach to tourism planning, Acerenza (1985) develops a simple model of tourism planning which is consistent with Getz's definition: analysis of previous tourist development → evaluation of position of tourism from different perspectives → formulation of tourism policy → definition of development strategy → elaboration of action program → recycle.

A *plan* is a document that has been the focus of political debate and is publicly available; it provides the details why and how this implementation, supervision, and review is to take place, in the context of the country's social, economic, and environmental setting. The WTO (1980) describes five types of plans related to tourism:

- **general national plan**: a national development plan including tourism;

- **national infrastructure plan**: a plan establishing guidelines for the development of infrastructure at a national level, including tourism;

- **national tourism development plan**: a specific plan for the development of tourism at a national level;

- **tourism infrastructure plan**: a plan establishing guidelines for the development of tourism infrastructure at a national level;

- **national promotion and marketing plan**: a plan or program of promotion and marketing of tourist products at a national level.

In a study of over 1,600 tourism-related plans, the WTO (1980) finds that: approximately one third were not implemented, few integrated tourism with socioeconomic development objectives, plans where social aspects were given priority over profitability were even rarer, few made firm and specific provision for environmental protection, and most were not supported by specific legislation. The WTO (1980) concludes that "*a desire to plan* exists in the tourism sector, but . . . few countries have been in a position to follow a policy of continuity regarding tourism development. Furthermore, the virtual absence of legislation seems to prejudice applying a directive plan" (p. 22).

A significant problem for tourism planning is that most economists and compilers of industrial classifications agree that a tourism industry per se does not exist because it does not produce a distinct product (Chadwick, 1981). As Murphy (1985) notes, "certain industries, such as transportation, accommodation, and entertainment, are not exclusively tourism industries, for they sell these services to local residents as well" (p. 9). The result is that tourism is not "properly" an industry, but more a cross section or sector of a regional or national economy (Davidson, 1994; Kaiser & Helber, 1978). Therefore, tourism must be planned on a cross-sectoral basis taking into account the connections between tourism and all other aspects of the national social, economic, and environmental context.

The implication is that tourism planning needs to be directed by national policy that weaves tourism into the overall development context. The problem, however, is how to do this, as "genuinely successful small island development embracing reasonable external assistance and support, local democratic participation, and economic and social developments matching the 'developed country aspirations' of the island's inhabitants, is a little understood process" (Marlow, 1992, p. 42). A brief discussion of the meaning of development is therefore needed at this point.

The Nature of Development

Development

The meaning of *development* remains either obscure or contested in much of the literature—but this is not the place to enter the fray fully.[4] The main point of contention is the distinguishing of *economic growth* from *development* (Gayle & Goodrich, 1993a, p. 3). C. A. Lewis (1955) clearly states that *economic growth* implies the constant creation of enhanced capacity to produce wealth. Measured in terms of GDP levels and rates of increase, such growth is generated by product and service innovation, employment, export expansion, and increased investment. Uphoff and Ilchman (1972), in contrast, argue that *development* emphasizes productivity and distribution, or the creation of optimal capacity to challenge human abilities, as well as to satisfy human needs and desires, over time.

Building on the latter conception, a Lasswellian political economy view of development is adopted here, following D. M. Smith's (1977) argument for development as "welfare improvement . . . [which] means a better state of affairs, with respect to who gets what where"[5] (p. 207). In that sense, therefore, the major goals of development are sustenance of life, self-esteem, and freedom—each broadly defined (G. Goulet, 1968). Similarly, writers such as Seers (1979) and Bromley and Bromley (1982) adopt a set of socially and politically oriented criteria of development: improvement, modernization, increasing welfare, and the enhancement of the quality of life.

When the mainstream development literature deals with tourism, it tends to focus on the relationships between tourism and development in terms of the "impacts of tourism":

> Such studies commonly examine issues of tourism-generated revenue or employment, social changes induced by the expansion of tourism or the environmental impacts of tourist projects. These issues are seen in terms of the impacts of tourism but such impacts . . . are not usually set in any broader context of development, however defined. For a variety of reasons, most studies also only focus on a limited range of impacts and few pretend to be exhaustive or comprehensive. Moreover, these impacts are often divorced from the processes which created them. Many writers speak of the impact of tourism without considering the type of tourism or the way in which tourism has developed. (D. G. Pearce, 1989, p. 15)

Otherwise, the development literature generally ignores tourism (D. G. Pearce, 1989, p. 10), except for criticizing it as a tool of continued colonialization. Erisman (1983, p. 339) argues that such harsh comments against tourism are symptomatic of the hostility that, among others, many Caribbean nationalists harbor toward the externally controlled tourism sector. For example, Perez (1975) states that

> The travel industry in the Caribbean may very well represent the latest development in the historical evolution of the neocolonial context of the West Indian socio-economic experience. Through tourism, developed metropolitan centers, . . . in collaboration with West Indian elites, have delivered the Caribbean archipelago to another regimen of monoculture. (p. 1)

Heavily influenced by Latin American *dependencia* theorists (e.g., Cardosa, 1972; Frank, 1972, 1981), these critics have been mainly concerned with tourism's economic ramifications (particularly increased dependency on the United States). *Dependence* is "a situation in which a certain group of countries have their economy conditioned by the development and expansion of another economy to which the former is subject" (Dos Santos, 1972, pp. 71–72). In the tourism literature, the most commonly adopted form of dependency theory is that of the plantation model (e.g., Weaver, 1988), which uses an analogy of tourism being similar in effect to monocrop export agriculture.

Development Constraints Facing Island Microstates

> I see islands as special and different, unlike continental areas in their societal, cultural, and psychological makeup. One difference is that even seemingly beneficial changes can have catastrophic effects in highly vulnerable island societies. Hence despite the environmental and economic handicaps under which most island peoples labour and the profound diseconomies of scale they suffer, they do well to view development options with grave reservation, if not to shun them altogether. (Lowenthal, 1992, p. 19)

First applied to small countries by Harrigan (1974), the term *microstate* has been used to describe a variety of types of political units. It usually refers to independent nations with populations under 1 million, but has also been used to include various other forms of government, including associated states, territories, and dependencies. These latter areas are not independent and therefore not completely autonomous in decision making, but are at least potentially involved to some greater or lesser degree in determining policy and implementing policy (e.g., tourism policy and planning). There are approximately 87 microstates in the world, of which 53 are island microstates (Wilkinson, 1989b, p. 154).

Connell (1988, pp. 2–8) provides a detailed review of the vast literature on the development constraints facing island microstates, which can be summarized briefly as follows:

- no advantages of economies of scale (which are reduced further by fragmentation);

- a limited range of resources;

- a narrowly specialized economy, based historically primarily on agricultural commodities;

- small, open economies with minimal ability to influence terms of trade or to manage and control their own economies;

- limited ability to adjust to changes in the international economic environment;

- dependence for key services on external institutions such as universities, regional training facilities, banking institutions;

- a narrow range of local skills and problems of matching local skills and jobs (often exacerbated by a brain and skill drain);

- a small GDP (hence problems of establishing import substitution industries) yet alongside considerable overseas economic investment in key sectors of the economy, and especially commerce;

- high transport, infrastructure, and administration costs;

- cultural domination by metropolitan countries;

- geographical constraints (e.g., soils, climate);

- vulnerability to natural hazards;

- vulnerability to externally influenced illegal activities.

Clearly, many of these problems also face larger countries. Moreover, not all small states have all of these problems. For example, in the Commonwealth Caribbean, there are several regional and national development banks, three campuses of the University of the West Indies, etc. On the whole, however, most Caribbean islands are faced with many of these constraints. Although the picture varies among the islands, the result is that many Caribbean states are characterized by rapid population growth, high population densities, low agricultural productivity, unequal land distribution, high rates of inflation, and relatively large foreign debts (Marshall, 1982, p. 452).

De Kadt (1979) cautions that "tourism planning is no different from planning for other activities" (p. 22) in terms of these constraints. A microstate might, for example, equally lack the capability to plan adequately for implementing an oil entrepôt as for tourism. The case of tourism is particularly worthy of study in small islands, however, because tourism appears to be "nearly inevitable for island microstates as long as international tourism continues to expand" (Wilkinson, 1989b, p. 171). The fact that tourism plays a major role in so many island economies underlies this view of "inevitability." For example, using the criterion of tourism receipts accounting for more than either 10% of export earnings or 5% of GNP (Bryden, 1973), at least 22 Caribbean island states (CTO, 1994) have "tourism economies"—including all of the case studies presented here.

Liew (1980, p. 13) has noted that the ability of smaller, less-developed nations to earn foreign exchange through the growth of a tourism sector is often severely restricted by the inherent economic, social, and political characteristics associated with their smallness and isolation. The most significant characteristic is the *macrostate emulation syndrome* (Harrigan, 1974); that is, attempts by such states to try to get all of the benefits of big countries. In the process, they ignore the consequences of such "mimicry" to a small society by trying to attain the impossible. They try to replicate a full range of government functions, public services, commercial activities, and professions associated with nationhood. However, they face a lack of trained personnel in management, planning, design, administration, science, technology, and industry needed for development; educational systems that emphasize academic subjects rather than job training; lack of qualified teachers; and a lack of program integration into national development goals (Morley & Wilkinson, 1985, p. 39).

This situation is compounded by *microstate reality imperception* (Harrigan, 1974); that is, the refusal to recognize that they are small islands, unique in many ways, limited in natural resources, with a set of peculiar characteristics, some of which require change (e.g., education systems), and others reinforcement (e.g., local culture). As a result, such island microstates appear to have little choice other than tourism due to their lack of human, institutional, and natural resources. When they observe comments that international tourism on a world scale will continue to grow strongly in the foreseeable future (e.g., English, 1986, p. 7; Gayle & Goodrich, 1993a, p. 2; WTO, 1981, p. 21), it is not surprising "that the idea of permanent growth in tourism became firmly planted in many minds" (Tinsley, 1979, p. 298). Tourism development, therefore, becomes an "obvious" economic policy choice.

Because they lack power and wealth, microstates are ripe targets for *exogenous decision making* (Harrigan, 1974); that is, many decisions governing their lives, even those dealing with local matters, are made elsewhere by other countries, MNCs, airlines, etc.

> When a Third World country uses tourism as a development strategy, it becomes enmeshed in a global system over which it has little control. The international tourism industry is a product of metropolitan capitalist enterprise. The superior entrepreneurial skills, resources and commercial power of metropolitan companies enables them to dominate many Third World tourist destinations. (S. G. Britton, 1982, p. 331)

This high degree of metropolitan control also occurs because the metropolitan enterprises are in direct contact with the majority of tourists (i.e., those who live in the metropoles). They, therefore, control the key links in the tourist flow chain—information, advertising, transportation, tour groups, hotels, etc. (IUOTO, 1976). The question arises as to whether a microstate can avoid a situation of "comprehensive dependency" that occurs when a country's three major subsystems—economic, political, and cultural—are all dominated by a foreign metropole (Erisman, 1983, p. 343). Both R. A. Britton (1980) and S. G. Britton (1980) argue that the tourism sector, because of the predominance of foreign ownership, imposes on peripheral destinations a development mode that reinforces the characteristics of structural dependency on and vulnerability to developed nations.

With the exception of the Cape Verde Islands (which, as a result of the absence of economic alternatives, has reversed its postindependence policy of restricting tourism [Reaud-Thomas & Lesourd, 1989]), island microstates do not appear to have adopted policies that discourage tourism on economic, cultural, or political grounds. Perhaps this is because the decision whether to encourage or discourage tourism is more in the hands of MNCs—airlines, hotels, travel agents, tour operators—than in those of the local government; in fact, the relative economic strength of MNCs is often greater than many developing countries. For example, there have been few, if any, cases of an island government blocking tourism development when an international airline decides that it wants to include a particular island on its regular schedule. This dependence of island microstate tourism on international airlines has been demonstrated for a wide variety of islands, including the Cook Islands (S. G. Britton & Kissling, 1984), other South Pacific islands (King, 1984), Réunion (Cousty, 1984), and Martinique and Guadeloupe (Chardon, 1983). Indeed, Huetz de Lemps (1989) argues that, rather than particular government decisions, the construction of an international airport is usually the "take-off" point for island tourism. Island microstates without a significant tourism sector are simply not on scheduled airline routes, or near international airports that can be reached by local feeder airlines.

Tourism Development and the Sustainability Debate

> . . . political leaders tend to be the last to recognise formally the importance of tourism in their development strategies. (Mather & Todd, 1993, p. 10)

There is, of course, another meaning for development, in the sense of *tourism development*, a sector-specific term that might be narrowly defined as the provision or enhancement of facilities and services to meet the needs of tourists (D. G. Pearce, 1989, p. 15). Pearce argues that, in a broader sense, tourism can also be seen as a means of development, the path to achieve some end state or condition. In this light, the impacts of tourism are reexamined in terms of how these impacts contribute to national, regional, or community development and how the state of development in any area depends on the way tourism there has developed. In these terms, therefore, development can be considered as both a process and a state.

In general, the literature agrees with S. L. J. Smith's (1983) contention that there is never a single, right answer about the desirable level of tourism development or the capacity of a destination region to host tourists. Rather, limits and capacities are best obtained by policy reviews and evaluation whereas development is allowed to proceed slowly and incrementally: "Only through cautious, deliberate evaluation of on-going development and policy applications can intelligent decisions be made regarding what is best for host and guest" (p. 182). Such a conclusion leads into the current debate on blending tourism with sustainable development in the Brundtland sense (World Commission on Environment and Development [WCED], 1987).

Given the lack of a widely accepted definition of "sustainable tourism," the World [Brundtland] Commission on Environment and Development's (WCED, 1987) definition of sustainable development is presented as a beginning point: development that meets the needs of the present generation without compromising the ability of future generations to meet their own needs. The concept has been the subject of much debate, but it is not the purpose here to enter that debate.

R. W. Butler (1993) provides a "working" definition of *sustainable development* in the context of tourism:

> . . . tourism which is developed and maintained in an area (community, environment) in such a manner and at such a scale that it remains viable over an indefinite period and does not degrade or alter the environment (human and physical) in which it exists to such a degree that it prohibits the successful development and wellbeing of other activities and processes. (p. 29)

R. W. Butler (1993) argues, however, that this is not the same as *sustainable tourism*: "tourism which is in a form which can maintain its viability in an area for an indefinite period of time" (p. 29).

He states that the notion of tourism being an evolutionary process is widely held; similarly, it is also broadly recognized that tourism is extremely dynamic and that the processes and impacts associated with it are susceptible to change. This element of change is a crucial factor, particularly when tourism is being considered in the context of sustainable development because sustainable development implies some degree of stability and permanence, at least in the very long-term view. R. W. Butler (1993, p. 30), therefore, argues that this does not blend well with a highly dynamic and constantly changing phenomenon such as tourism. For this reason, the view taken here is that sustainable development in terms of tourism is an heuristic concept (i.e., an organizing concept), rather than an operational one.

Criteria are necessary against which to measure sustainability, however, so Ascher and Healy's (1990, p. 10) definition of sustainable development as a process that achieves the following goals will be used here:

- high per capita consumption, sustainable over an indefinite period (rather than "increasing consumption");

- distributional equity;

- environmental protection, including protection of biological diversity and the continued functioning of complex natural systems;

- participation of all sectors of society in decision making.

There could be many surrogate measures of these goals, but the ones used here because of availability of data include: the consequences of tourist numbers and expenditures such as growing GDP per capita and employment; level of local involvement in the tourist sector; environmental impacts; and the presence of politically debated tourism policies and plans. In this sense, therefore, it is clear that the goal is not to sustain tourism per se through "increasing consumption" in the sense of continuously growing numbers of tourists, but rather to use tourism as one means of achieving sustainable development for a country (B. Farrell, 1993, personal communication).

McElroy and de Albuquerque (1989, p. 4) take another approach to sustainability, arguing that without strong policy intervention, the contemporary island tourism economy system is nonsustainable because of "the basic incompatibility of the imposition of an expanding, open, tourist-consumption-biased throughput economic system upon a closed, fragile, finite environment" (McElroy, 1975, p. 48). They provide five dimensions underlying this structural dysfunction:

- the large international tourist economy interacting upon the delicate, tightly bound insular environment generally produces wide sectoral income disparities and resource imbalances (Beller, 1987);

- impacts are created that cannot be absorbed by the fragile socioeconomic and ecological environments of islands;

- seasonality in tourism demand both stresses the environment at peak times and leads to pressures for year-round tourism;

- preoccupation with increasing the number of tourist arrivals leads to a growth bias (Holder, 1988) among island decision makers;

- to satisfy overhead and profit criteria of MNCs, the number of visitors continues to expand beyond social and ecological limits (McElroy & de Albuquerque, 1989, p. 5–6).

The result is an environmentally incompatible growth process that is not sustainable:

> This overgrowth propensity exemplifies what steady-state advocates have called the inability of the throughput economy to self-impose an optimum scale of operation consistent with ecosystem stability that maximizes long-run natural resource returns and avoids intergenerational inequities in the distribution of income and resource access (Daly, 1984; Goodland and Ledec, 1987). (McElroy & de Albuquerque, 1989, p. 5)

Following McElroy and de Albuquerque's contention that strong policy intervention is needed if tourism is to be a viable route to sustainability that avoids the environmentally incompatible growth process, it appears that government has to select a form of involvement in tourism policy and planning that is consistent with its development goals. There is a variety of forms of such involvement in both theory and practice.

Government Involvement in Tourism

> Because of the particular type of organization and the structure of the [tourism] industry prevailing in many countries . . . the net benefit [of tourism] is often far smaller than is frequently thought to be the case. This is particularly

so in developing countries where tourism has sprung up outside of any planning framework and has assumed features at variance with the requirements of national welfare and long term development. (Ramsaran, 1979, p. 75)

It is widely argued that local control and the extent of policy and planning practices are two key factors in the political arrangement of tourism destination areas (e.g., R. W. Butler, 1992; D. G. Pearce, 1992). Jenkins and Henry (1982), for example, hypothesize that "For each developing country, the degree of active involvement by government in the tourist sector will reflect the importance of tourism in the economy" (p. 506). As measures of tourism's economic importance, they use contribution to GDP and national income, foreign exchange earnings, employment and income generated, and contribution to government revenues: "Using these four indicators, one would expect government to intervene actively in the tourist sector either when tourism is of major economic significance or where government follows a system of centrally-planned economic activity" (Jenkins & Henry, 1982, p. 506).

Jenkins and Henry (1982) define *active involvement* as "a deliberate action by government, introduced to favour the tourism sector" (p. 501). It implies not only a recognition by government of the specific needs of the tourism sector, but also of the necessity for government's operational participation to attain stated objectives.

There are two types of active involvement:

- **managerial**: a government not only sets out tourism objectives (e.g., in a tourism development plan), but also induces necessary organizational and legislative support to attain the objectives; involvement, therefore, is essentially selective and specific (e.g., legislation favoring foreign nationals seeking employment in tourism, tourism investment incentives legislation, bilateral air services agreement with specific tourist arrangements);

- **developmental**: a government undertakes an operational role in the tourism sector, either for ideological reasons or because of the inability or unwillingness of the private sector to become involved in tourism (e.g., government financing or ownership of hotels, government training facilities for the tourism sector).

In contrast, *passive involvement* occurs when a "government undertakes an action that may have implications for tourism, but is not specifically intended to favour or influence tourism" (Jenkins & Henry, 1982, p. 501). There are two types of passive involvement:

- **mandatory**: legislation is introduced that relates to the country as a whole and is not intended to discriminate in favor of the tourism sector, although it may have implications for tourism (e.g., legislation relating to the employment of foreign nationals, investment incentives legislation, bilateral air services agreement);

- **supportive**: a government does not deliberately inhibit the development of tourism, but neither does it encourage it, essentially "benign neglect" (World Bank, 1972) (e.g., approving a private sector "national" tourist board, providing educational services that may or may not have relevance to the tourism sector).

Arguing that "It is probable that most governments would be involved in policy-making in each area, if only in a passive role," Jenkins and Henry (1982, p. 506) discuss five general "areas of concern" in the formulation of tourism policy:

- **foreign exchange earnings**: minimization of leakages caused by tourism-related imports through import substitution (Demas, 1965) in the form of either import replacement (e.g., locally made furniture) or import displacement (e.g., local fruit juices);

- **foreign investment**: attraction of foreign capital to support development efforts through incentives legislation with specific objectives (e.g., attracting investment, encouraging reinvestment of profits or domestic participation);

- **employment in tourism**: whereas foreign nationals might be needed at the initial stages of tourism development, long-term policy should be to replace foreign employees by local people;

- **land use policies**: because it has the responsibility to consider the impact of any proposed development on the environment and society, government is in the unique position of being able to exercise the necessary factual and value judgements required in the allocation and use of land [and water];

- **air transport and tourism**: establishment of a national airline, involvement in a regional airline, designation of a "national" carrier, bilateral air agreements.

"Even a necessarily brief consideration of each area will indicate the need for active government involvement" in order to avoid what Jenkins and Henry (1982) describe as a progression that has become all too familiar in developing countries:

> Unspoiled place with unique character attracts tourists; new buildings and amenities necessary to house tourists bring about change; more tourists produce more change; loss of initial attractive character becomes an element responsible for departure of tourists; and final result is economic, social and financial disaster. (p. 506)

This progression suggests that potential conflicts between short-term benefits and longer term objectives have not been recognized or anticipated and that, to achieve these objectives, it will be necessary to monitor and control the nature and pace of tourism development: "As in most government decisions, evaluation [of means to achieve the objectives] should be seen in terms of political economy rather than mere economic rationale" (Jenkins & Henry, 1982, p. 506).

Tourism has, to varying degrees, played an important role in the national development of each of the states examined here. If Jenkins and Henry's hypothesis holds, therefore, one would expect that they would all be involved in their tourism sectors in each of the five "areas of concern." Although the forms of government involvement that are of interest to this book are tourism policy and planning—clearly, modes of active managerial involvement—there are many other forms of involvement that are possible. Jenkins and Henry's hypothesis, therefore, will be tested for each case study and demonstrated in the form of a matrix of types of involvement by areas of concern.

Summary

The prime focus of the book is on relating the positive and negative impacts of tourism on the island microstates of the Caribbean to the tourism policy and planning directions that they have developed, the objective being the supplementing of the past emphasis on descriptive case studies with explanatory, predictive, and normative approaches.

In adopting this form of analysis, the book follows Cohen's (1979) recommendation that tourism research should optimally be:

- **processual**: be longitudinal in nature;

- **contextual**: take into account the prevailing economic, political, and sociocultural circumstances of the situation;

- **comparative**: be related to other studies;

- **emic**: be conducted from the perspective of the participants (P. Pearce, 1982, p. 19).

To do otherwise would be to provide an overly simplistic and static picture of the incredibly complex set of phenomena and actors that have roles in the play of international tourism.

Notes

[1]Environmental factors are omitted by Edgell from this list of factors for an unknown reason, despite their later inclusion (Edgell, 1987, p. 32).

[2]Having undertaken these five case studies over a period of five years, this author particularly agrees with Pizam's time-consuming argument—but rejects Black and Champion's inexpensive one!

[3]An alternative label might be "political ecology," a perspective that combines political economy and cultural ecology. Grossman (1993, p. 348) describes the emphasis in this approach as follows. Human–environment relations can be understood only by analyzing the relationship of patterns of resource use to political–economic forces. Inquiry, therefore, is directed to how patterns of resource use have been influenced historically by state policy, penetration of the market, and patterns of surplus extraction, accumulation, and differentiation (M. Watts, 1978). Whereas the phrase "political ecology" dates only from the 1980s, Grossman (1993) argues that it has a longer lineage than some recent articles (e.g., Bassett,

1988; Zimmerer, 1991) suggest, with other previous research displaying the characteristics of the approach, but not the phrase (e.g., Franke & Chasin, 1980; Kjekshus, 1977; P. W. Porter, 1979; Yapa, 1979). The more common term, political economy, however, will be used here.

[4]There are many theories of development, including dependency, advanced Third World, basic needs, decolonization, evolutionism, functionalism, grass roots, positivism, modernization, and structural adjustment. The literature is vast and the reader is directed to, among other writers, Amin (1974), Barnett (1988), Bourguinon and Anderson, (1992), S. G. Britton (1982), Corbridge (1986, 1989a, 1989b), Doyle and Gough (1991), Rostow (1960), Ruffing (1979), and Warren (1989).

[5]Note the similarity in the concern with ''welfare'' in Getz's (1987, p. 3) definition of tourism planning presented above.

Chapter 3

Caribbean Tourism Policy and Planning— From Overview to the Case Studies

> . . . [P]robably the most appropriate generalization concerning the landform geography of the Caribbean realm is that it is characterized by surprising diversity, surprising because of the monotonous sun-and-sand television advertisements beamed into mid-latitude households portraying the Caribbean region simply as a beach. (Richardson, 1992, p. 15)

Introduction

The review of the literature in Chapter 2 presents a very daunting picture. Although there is a strong argument to be made for the importance of tourism policy and planning, their successful implementation is both difficult and apparently rare. This would be a problem even for relatively large and wealthy "developed" states; for example, neither Canada nor the United States appears to be very successful in either tourism policy or planning. With "developing" states—particularly island microstates—these tasks are even more difficult, particularly given the development constraints facing them.

This chapter, therefore, begins with a review of past evaluations of tourism policy and planning in the Caribbean to compare the region's "state of the art" with the broader picture presented in Chapter 2. This review is used to provide a basis for comparing the tourism policy and planning experiences of the case studies. The final part presents the method used to select specific Commonwealth Caribbean states to serve as case studies for detailed analysis.

Evaluations of Caribbean Tourism Policy and Planning

> . . . tourism [is] generally treated as a minor interest in government policies and plans. (Likorish, 1988, p. 151)

There have been several earlier evaluations of tourism policy and planning in the Caribbean, but the published reports have usually only produced general conclusions without specific reference to particular countries (the exception being Mather & Todd, 1993), and many of the reports are not widely available. The most significant conclusions of some of the major recent ones are briefly summarized below.

Lack of Commitment to Tourism Policy and Planning

Arguing that "Caribbean commitment to tourism as a long-term vehicle of development is weak and, in some cases, absent," Holder (1988, p. 12) believes that the dilemma is caused by the Caribbean having grown dependent on a sector to which it often seems to have a deep-seated resentment based on tourism's past performance and the unhappy associations that Caribbean tourism tends to evoke in societies recently emerging from a colonial past. Tourism, therefore, was seen during the 1960s by Black majority populations as "an alien industry, where non-Caribbean personnel, managing low-level Caribbean staff, catered to a non-Caribbean clientele." As a result, tourism was widely perceived as an extension of the colonial syndrome traditionally associated with sugar plantations (Holder, 1993, p. 21). Moreover, the governments of the time saw tourism as a private sector product supported, but not directed, by government. Therefore, tourism

> . . . was not included in their economic planning processes. There was no manpower development plan for indigenous personnel; no physical zoning plan geared towards environmental protection; no research activity. They were, in fact, timid about supporting a sector that attracted criticism from a vocal, newly independent intelligentsia, and from some international development agencies, because of socio-cultural factors. In spite of significant changes and great improvements in these aspects during the 1970s and 1980s, even today Caribbean tourism suffers from this legacy of negative social perceptions and unplanned growth. (Holder, 1993, p. 21)

Similarly, Blommestein (1988) argues that many Caribbean states demonstrate "a weak commitment to formal comprehensive planning" (p. 58) because of a lack of realism in terms of constraints and barriers to achieve stated goals. Moreover, because many plans have been formulated by experts without much participation by other national, economic, and social agents, these do not reflect the aspirations of the larger community or even those of the political directorate.

Consequently, many plans never go beyond the status of a mere technical document. While recognizing that many Caribbean countries do have "development plans," Ramsaran (1989, p. 256) makes the distinction between a plan as a document and planning as a process, the latter being the pursuit of policies through the implementation of projects in a framework consistent with stated goals. This failure of implementation is at the heart of the development problems in many countries and largely results from the public sector's lack of a clear structure of authority and delineation of decision-making areas; in effect, the civil service has tended to be more oriented to routine than to development.

Lack of Integration With National Development

> The lack of commitment towards planning has had its consequences on tourism planning as well as its integration with national development, environmental protection and cultural development. The lack of policy directives

> makes it difficult to plan the development of the sector in an effective man-
> ner taking into account national needs and national resources. (Blommestein,
> 1988, p. 61)

Because tourism planning should be part of comprehensive development and land-
use planning, the problem in the Caribbean has not been solely a lack of planning,
but also one of limited coordination and integration of sectoral planning efforts
(United Nations Economic Commission on Latin America and the Caribbean
[UNECLAC], 1988). Past and present policies have for the most part consisted of
an ad hoc response to tourism development proposals; as a result, there has been
relatively little commitment to integrated planning at the national level and, as a
consequence, to multisectoral issues such as tourism and the environment. This
has led to:

- **a lack of information and inadequate dissemination of existing information** regarding tourism's contribution to development, intersectoral linkages, natural resource policies, environmental impacts of developmental options, and market and technology trends;

- **institutional weaknesses**, which are reflected in an incapacity to formulate
  and implement effective policies and programs (UNECLAC, 1988, pp. 110–
  111).

As a consequence, many countries lack clearly defined and communicated objectives relating to tourism and the environment in order to clarify choices and strategies, identify conflicts and resolve them at an early stage, provide the basis to moti-
vate people to implement policy, and evaluate and monitor performance.

Weak Institutional Arrangements

Girvan and Simmons (1988) conclude that policy and institutional frameworks for
integrating tourism development and environmental protection are deficient in
most of the Caribbean. Although the problem begins with lack of political will—itself both product and cause of insufficient public understanding of tourism's economic value and its dependence on the environment—it is manifested in an absence of guidelines for tourism development, criteria for appropriate siting and
design of facilities, environmental legislation, and effective enforcement of standards. Efforts to integrate tourism and environment are hampered by poorly developed coordinating mechanisms, a weak commitment to integrated planning, insufficient resources, limited institutional capabilities (particularly on smaller islands)
to apply accepted methods for assessing and planning tourism projects, and national tourism strategies.

Preoccupation With Tourist Numbers
Rather Than Benefits

Ramsaran (1989) argues that too many Caribbean states are preoccupied with simply increasing tourist numbers rather than maximizing benefits. While some governments are beginning to focus on benefits,

The type of tourism the various states wish to encourage remains a controversial issue. . . . Certain states which feel that benefits have declined while numbers have grown are giving consideration to what they call quality tourism. The idea here is to attract the "big spenders" desiring high quality accommodation, transport and food. Exactly how this is to be done, however, remains a problem, since providing only high cost hotel rooms could also result in less tourists being attracted. (Ramsaran, 1989, pp. 90–91)

Lack of Regional Cooperation

At the February 1992 CARICOM Summit on Tourism held in Jamaica, CARICOM heads of government highlighted the lack of regional cooperation in three vital areas: marketing, air carriers, and cruise ships (Mather & Todd, 1993, pp. 23–24).

Recognizing the intensification of competition throughout the world and recession in major tourism markets, the Summit supported regional marketing as an important element in maintaining the region's international profile. There is, however, varying opinion in the Caribbean as to whether the public sector or the private sector should be responsible for marketing. Moreover, although there are some grounds for regional marketing on a cooperative basis, it may not be entirely consistent with the maintenance of individuality or with the promotion of the attractions of specific destinations (Mather & Todd, 1993, p. iv).

Also acknowledged were the changes taking place in the world of air transport, the need for the Caribbean to avoid overdependence on foreign carriers, and the need for better regional air transport cooperation. Although most islands are well-served by international carriers (Jemiolo & Conway, 1991), there have been two notable patterns over the past few years. First, deregulation of the airline industry in the United States resulted in the bankruptcy of several airlines with only some of their Caribbean routes being assumed by other carriers. Second, because the region's air carriers are small, almost entirely state owned, often underequipped, and at the mercy of MNC airlines, Caribbean airlines must cooperate more and become less dependent on state aid and more aggressively competitive (Mather & Todd, 1993, p. iii). The major concern is that MNC airlines will completely dominate the Caribbean market, particularly because of their control over computer reservation systems and the increasing tendency to form cross-border groupings. Such near-oligopolies have the capacity to benefit from economies of scale and scope that are far beyond those that could ever be achieved by small regional carriers. There are three possible future strategies open to the region: continued subsidization by government for operating losses of the regional airlines, strategic alliances with international carriers, or some form of regional cooperation or merger (Mather & Todd, 1993, p. 59).

On cruise ship tourism, the Summit agreed that the region should seek to levy a standard minimum charge on all cruise passengers. The industry is the subject of much debate about its costs and benefits, related to four concerns: low local expenditure per passenger, increasing competition to onshore shopping facilities from on-board shops, low direct government revenues from landing fees, and impacts of the ships on the marine environment (Mather & Todd, 1993, p. 68). Whereas cruise passengers clearly account for large expenditures on particular islands, their per capita spending is much lower both absolutely and relatively in comparison with stay-over visitors. Moreover, there are concerns about the social impacts of huge numbers of cruise passengers being unloaded for short periods of time on very small islands and about the environmental impacts caused by pollution of water and reefs and by the construction of major port facilities.[1]

The Need for Investment

The CARICOM Summit saw investment in both tourism infrastructure and plant as essential to remain competitive, a task that would require better cooperation between the public and private sectors. Specific concerns include upgrading infrastructure and hotels, diversifying facilities and services, special consideration by regional investment organizations being given to tourism, maximizing job opportunities for Caribbean nationals, improving training, maintaining high environmental standards, and cooperating regionally on security matters, especially the control of drugs. There are three main investment and development issues: investment in tourism facilities and supporting infrastructure, employment opportunities and promoting intersectoral linkages, and environmental protection and enhancement (Mather & Todd, 1993, pp. 23–24).

Despite calls for regional development banks to become involved in tourism, one area that has not received attention is the accommodation sector. Caribbean hotels—which range from some of the most exclusive hotels in the world to mass market resorts to small, locally owned inns—are characterized by an apparent contradiction: the ability to charge high prices, because the region is viewed by tourists as being expensive, and high operating costs resulting from high supply and labor prices, high taxes, and a tradition of small, intimate hotels, resulting in profitability being among the lowest in the world (Mather & Todd, 1993, p. iv). Prospects are hampered by low efficiency levels and the lack of interest in local financial institutions in the sector, thus retarding much-needed refurbishment.

Pannell Kerr Forster (1991, pp. 10–12), in summarizing the operating performance of hotels worldwide, demonstrate that the Caribbean (based on the Bahamas, United States Virgin Islands, Puerto Rico, and Aruba) has the highest average room rate per room sold (US$146.20 compared to a worldwide average of US$94.45 in 1990) and the highest average room occupancy (71.3% vs. 67.2% worldwide), but also the lowest percentage of income before fixed charges[2] (22.3% vs. 30.3% worldwide). Thus, although Caribbean hotels on average can generate the most revenue per room, the cost of doing business is the highest worldwide, resulting in the lowest profitability of any group of hotels anywhere. In fact, whereas income before fixed charges per room for the Caribbean overall was US$15,199 in 1990, the figure for the Bahamas was a *loss* of US$29 (Pannell Kerr Forster, 1991, p. 46). There are several reasons for such high operating costs: high levels of imports; bureaucracy; wage rates; staff training; inadequate standards; slow adoption of new technology; utility costs; limited availability and cost of capital; and taxes (Mather & Todd, 1993, pp. 87–89).

Hepple (1992, personal communication) concludes that, from the perspective of an external investor examining the Caribbean, there is no point in investing in the construction of a hotel because the chance of getting an adequate return on that investment is nil; thus, there has been little private sector construction in hotels in the region recently. Consequently, governments faced with the need for jobs and tax income borrow money they cannot afford to build hotels that cannot operate profitably; moreover, government hotels often lead the way in reducing room rates to build market share, thus jeopardizing the financial viability of private sector hotels.

Conclusion

> . . . [F]ew Caribbean territories have any tourism policy beyond that of unlimited growth, and many of their sporadic plans are often idealistic. (Dann, 1992, p. 162)

Taken as a whole, these concerns paint a rather dismal picture of both the past and present; moreover, they provide only glimmers of optimism for the future. They present an overwhelming image of small, vulnerable islands with limited natural resources, constrained expertise and institutions, and policies and plans that are either nonexistent or not implemented, doomed to suffer all the costs of tourism and to realize few of the benefits—situations that might be adequately described by Ackoff's (1979) term *mess*.

The Tourist Area Cycle of Evolution and the Choice of Case Studies

Is it really the case that all Caribbean islands fail to have effective tourism policy and planning processes? If so, how did it come about? Can anything be done to improve the chances of a better future? Is it possible for states in the early stages of tourism development (as described by the life cycle concept examined below) to learn from the experience of others and avoid past mistakes? Can states with troubled tourism development learn similar lessons and turn the situation around?

As argued in Chapter 2, questions such as these are best addressed through a case study approach that interprets the political economy of tourism geography in an historical policy context. The problem arises, however, of how to select a set of case studies that reflects the potentially wide range of varying experiences of Commonwealth Caribbean states. An obvious assumption is that tourism development, its impacts, and the experience of host nations vary over time and, therefore, case studies should be selected at various stages of tourism development—an assumption that is at the heart of the concept of the tourist area cycle of evolution.

The Life Cycle Concept

Rooted in theories of population ecology and diffusion processes (Hannan & Freeman, 1977; Haywood, 1990), the life cycle concept has been employed in tourism research as an *explanatory* tool of destination area development. In marketing, the product life cycle describes the evolution of a product as it passes through stages of introduction, maturity, and decline (Cooper, 1993, p. 146). In applying the concept to tourism, R. W. Butler (1980) notes that

> There can be little doubt that tourist areas are dynamic, that they evolve and change over time. This evolution is brought about by a variety of factors, including changes in the preferences and needs of visitors, the gradual deterioration and possible replacement of the physical plant and facilities, and the change (or even disappearance) of the original natural and cultural attractions which were responsible for the initial popularity of the area. (p. 5)

He compares this pattern of change in the number of tourists visiting an area to the concept of the product cycle, "whereby sales of a product proceed slowly at first, experience a rapid growth, stabilize, and subsequently decline; in other words, a basic asymptotic [S-shaped] curve is followed" (R. W. Butler, 1980, p. 6). He describes a hypothetical tourist area cycle of evolution, which consists of six stages:

1. **Exploration**: a small number of "explorers" (Cohen, 1972) make individual travel arrangements and follow irregular visiting patterns; no specific facilities are provided for tourists.

2. **Involvement**: as numbers of visitors increase and assume some regularity, local residents begin to provide facilities for visitors.

3. **Development**: a well-developed "institutionalized" (Cohen, 1972) tourist market area is shaped in part by advertising in tourist-generating areas; local involvement and control of development declines rapidly, being replaced by larger, more elaborate and more up-to-date facilities provided by external organizations.

4. **Consolidation**: the rate of increase in visitor numbers declines, but a major part of the area's economy is tied to tourism.

5. **Stagnation**: the peak number of visitors is reached and capacity levels for many variables have been reached or exceeded, with attendant environmental, social, and economic problems.

6. **Decline/rejuvenation**: the area may not be able to compete with new attractions and so will face a declining market, both spatially and numerically; or there may be an increase in tourists if efforts are made either to add human-made attractions or to take advantage of previously untapped natural resources.

Various authors argue that particular tourist destinations experience this cycle, for example, Atlantic City (Stansfield, 1978), Grand Isle, LA (Meyer-Arendt, 1985), Isle of Man (Cooper & Jackson, 1989), Lancaster County, PA (Hovinen, 1981), Laurentians, Québec (Lundgren, 1982), Malta (Oglethorpe, 1984), Mexico (R. W. Butler, 1980), Northwest Territories, Canada (Keller, 1987), Paradise Island, Bahamas (Debbage, 1991), Vancouver Island (Nelson & Wall, 1986).

Lundberg (1980) develops a somewhat similar six-phase model of tourism development:

1. Governmental incentives for development, promiscuous location of projects, no identification of land qualities requiring protection, and highly optimistic feasibilities.

2. Short-run success—a halcyon period for all concerned that may last from 5 to 10 years.

3. The beginnings of the awareness of some realities: less economic impact than anticipated, labor unrest, local resistance, and environmental errors.

4. A tourism recession resulting from overbuilding, high labor costs, and a backlash against poor service.

5. The exposure of even deeper difficulty: local conflict, erosion of natural and cultural resources, further decline in visitors.

6. A reflective phase in which investors, developers, managers, local society, and political leadership reassess the entire tourism development pattern and wish they had planned.

This model has attracted less attention than that of Butler, perhaps because it presents a more pessimistic and deterministic view, with little hope being held out at the end for recovery.

The life cycle concept outlines both the physical development of a destination and its market evolution, as changing provision of facilities and access is matched by an evolving clientele in both quantitative and qualitative terms (Cooper, 1993, p. 147). The most important phases of both of these models, however, are the later stages, because of their implications for tourism in general and for the planning and arrangement of particular tourist areas:

> The assumption that tourist areas will always remain tourist areas and be attractive to tourists appears to be implicit in tourism planning. Public and private agencies alike, rarely, if ever, refer to the anticipated life span of a tourist area or its attractions. Rather, because tourism has shown an, as yet, unlimited potential for growth, despite economic recessions, it is taken for granted that numbers of visitors will continue to increase. (R. W. Butler, 1980, p. 10)

Similarly, the later phases of Lundberg's model suggest that, after tourism has begun to decline and serious structural problems are recognized, planners and decision makers will realize that much of the situation is attributable to lack of planning and might take the opportunity to reassess how they are going to deal with the future.

De Albuquerque and McElroy (1992, p. 620) develop a version of Butler's model that postulates three stages in the tourism growth process: emergence or initial discovery, followed by the transition to rapid expansion, and culminating in maturity as defined by visitor saturation. The characteristics of each stage are as follows:

Stage I: Emergence. A slow and irregular stream of long-staying explorers, seeking pristine and exotic natural surroundings and unusual cultural experiences, tend to be satisfied with modest lodging and eating facilities. This low-density, environmentally benign phase is typified by small-scale local entrepreneurial participation and resident–visitor interaction. Often lacking major airport and harbor infrastructure, such quiet destinations frequently become retirement hideaways for North Americans and Europeans.

Stage II: Transition. Rapid change, increased foreign investment and control, and rising international visibility is reflected in expanded transport facilities, large-scale hotels, liberal hotel tax incentives, and aggressive visitor promotion. Marked winter seasonality often spawns summer specialty tourism substyles based on unique natural amenities (e.g., fishing, diving, wind surfing, sailing). The cruise ship trade may be significant.

Stage III: Maturity. The mass-market mature destination is characterized by the economic dominance of tourism, growth stagnation, short-stay visitors with a taste for the familiar, international chain hotels and restaurants, high densities and crowding that alter the visitor experience and disturb the host population, and the substitution of artificial attractions (e.g., casino gambling, duty-free shopping, golf courses) for degraded natural assets. Resident–visitor resource competition becomes commonplace, and local cultural identity and participation in tourism decline. There is some environmental impact mitigation, but most of the energy goes into intensive advertising for high-volume visitors: conventions, cruise ships, packaged charters, and all-inclusives.

This model is basically compatible with that of Butler, but it has greater detail in terms of impacts, changes in types of tourists (e.g., cruise passengers), seasonality, and government involvement.

Noting that the only (previously published) test of the life cycle model in the Caribbean context involved four small islands (Antigua, Aruba, St. Lucia, and the United States Virgin Islands) and confirmed an evolutionary fit "at least up to the later stages" (Wilkinson, 1987b, p. 144), de Albuquerque and McElroy (1992, p. 623) classify 23 Caribbean microstates into the three stages based on examination of wide range of data (see Figure 3.1).

Arguing that the life cycle model has strong policy implications, de Albuquerque and McElroy (1992, p. 630) believe that tourism tends to move through these dynamic stages, despite the many differences among the islands, with the current Stage III destinations having been in Stage II in the 1960s and 1970s and in Stage I in the 1950s; similarly, the current Stage II islands were just emerging on the tourist horizon in the 1960s and 1970s. Although implications are most immediate for late Stage III islands faced with stagnation of the tourist sector and environmental problems, this dynamic model also suggests that destinations in the earlier stages need to consider now ways to avoid serious medium- and long-term problems.

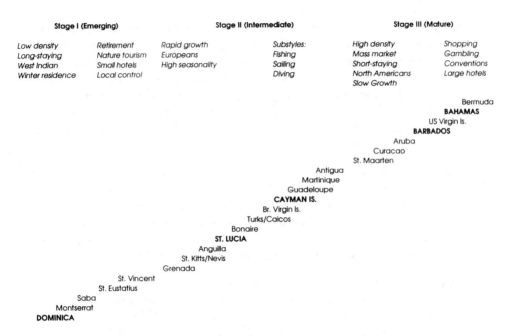

Figure 3.1. Caribbean small-island tourism stages and styles. Case studies are shown in bold capitals. Source: de Albuquerque and McElroy (1992).

Problems With the Cycle Concept

The cycle concept is not without limitations. For example, Cooper (1993, p. 149) notes that the cycle is destination specific, with each stage varying in length and the curve displaying different shapes and patterns (Hovinen, 1981) depending upon supply factors (access, rate of development, government policy, competing destinations) and factors on the demand side (such as the changing nature of clientele) as the destination's market evolves along with supply-side developments. Cooper (1993, pp. 149–150) discusses the main problems of the concept:

- **identifying turning points in the curve**: several indicators could be used, e.g., growth rate of visits, level of visits compared to market potential, percentage of first-time visitors, number of competitors, emergence of new destinations meeting customer needs more effectively, levels of prices and profits, advertising, price elasticity (Day, 1981; Doyle, 1976; Haywood, 1986; Rink & Swan, 1979);

- **identifying stages**: a variety of possible shapes of the curve and acceleration/delay due to external factors make it difficult to identify the stage reached by a destination, although it can be done by plotting the rate of change of visitor numbers, type of tourist, visitor expenditure, market share, or profitability; however, Jones and Lockwood (1990, p. 7) argue that shape is less relevant than different types of growth (slow, medium, high, constant, declining);

- **differing lengths**: the length of each stage and of the cycle itself is variable depending on the nature of the destination (e.g., newly or well-established); as well, there is a variety of types of cycles (e.g., a scalloped pattern where a sequence of developments at the destination prompts a revival of visitor arrivals [Buttle, 1986]);

- **level of aggregation and geographical scale**: the unit of analysis is crucial as the cycle for each country is made up of a mosaic of resorts and tourist areas (which in turn contain cycles for hotels, theme parks, etc.), with each element perhaps being at a different stage in the cycle (Brownlie, 1985; Kotler, 1980; Rink & Swan 1979).

Cooper (1993, p. 156) argues that the life cycle concept does have utility as a descriptive tool because it integrates the disparate factors involved in developing a destination (e.g., demand, supply, organization, investment, scale, impact, planning). He raises the question, however, as to whether the concept can be used as a forecasting tool, a use that Butler's original conceptualization did not envisage. Accurate forecasting requires the ability to isolate and predict the forces driving it (Onkvisit & Shaw, 1986), the use of strict assumptions (e.g., a constraint on long-run growth, an asymptotic diffusion curve, homogeneity of customers), and no explicit consideration of marketing decisions or the competition (Cooper, 1993, p. 150). Moreover, successful forecasting demands long runs of visitor arrival data to give stable parameter estimates (Brownlie, 1985). Although these are lacking for most types of destinations (R. W. Butler, 1980), commonly only island destinations are able to provide such data sets (Cooper, 1993, p. 150)—as can be seen below for these case studies.

Sceptics, therefore, believe that

> . . . the cycle, at best, can assist general trend projection rather than causal forecasts. In terms of its use for strategic planning, some argue that rather than being an independent guide for strategy, or forecasting, the cycle is simply an outworking of management decisions and heavily dependent on external factors such as competition, the development of new destinations, swings in consumer taste, government legislation and regional policy (Dhalla and Yuspeh, 1976). (Cooper, 1993, p. 156)

Emphasizing its strength for integration, however, Cooper (1993, pp. 156–157) concludes that the concept provides tourism researchers with a glimmer of the elusive unifying concept or generalization of tourism. He argues that its logical and intuitive appeal deserves greater attention among tourism researchers, who should not be swayed by those who criticize the life cycle for its lack of operational value:

> By regarding destinations as dependent upon the actions of managers, the tourist industry and their markets, the life cycle provides an integrating medium for the study of tourism, a promising vehicle for future research, and a frame of reference for emergent themes in tourism, such as sustainable tourism. (Cooper, 1993, p. 157)

Thus, despite some weaknesses, the life cycle concept does have utility, both as a means by which to select case studies and as a measure against which to compare their tourism developments.

The Choice of the Commonwealth Caribbean

Clearly, there are too many states in the Caribbean for an analysis of all of them. This study, therefore, is limited to the islands of the Commonwealth Caribbean, that is, islands that historically have been administered by Great Britain. These are of two types:

- **independent nations** that are full members of the international organization known as the Commonwealth of Nations (previously termed the British Commonwealth) (and other international organizations such as the United Nations): Antigua and Barbuda, Bahamas, Barbados, Dominica, Grenada, Jamaica, St. Kitts and Nevis, St. Lucia, St. Vincent and the Grenadines, Trinidad and Tobago;

- **colonies or dependent territories** of Great Britain that are not full Commonwealth members, but are strongly associated historically and politically with their Commonwealth neighbors: Anguilla, British Virgin Islands, Cayman Islands, Montserrat, Turks and Caicos.

The Commonwealth Caribbean was chosen for reasons related mainly to the need for conceptual equivalence and equivalence of measurement (Warwick & Osherson, 1973), especially in cross-cultural studies (D. G. Pearce, 1993, p. 30):

- Although varying in size and complexity, their governments have a similar structure based on the British Westminster model (unlike, e.g., Puerto Rico's ''Commonwealth'' status with the United States).

- Their policy and planning environments have common bases, for example, land-use planning based on Britain's Town and Country Planning Act (in contrast, e.g., to American, Dutch, French, and Spanish traditions elsewhere).

- Although some islands have local dialects (e.g., St. Lucia's French-based *Kwéyol*), the language of government and business is English.

- With exceptions (e.g., Grenada), their recent histories have been characterized by social and political climates that are conducive to tourism (unlike, e.g., Haiti).

- They are open economies that have the potential to receive tourists from any other nation (unlike, e.g., Cuba, which under United States law cannot be visited legally by American tourists).

- In addition to ties to Britain and the Commonwealth, they have various internal regional ties, for example, organizations such as CARICOM, Organization of Eastern Caribbean States (OECS), Caribbean Development Bank (CDB); joint ownership of Leeward Islands Air Transport (LIAT); campuses of the University of the West Indies on Jamaica, Barbados, and Trinidad, etc.

Case Study Selection

For reasons related to research funding, the case studies were selected in two phases. For the first phase, a trend analysis of the basic tourism statistics of stay-over arrivals and visitor expenditures in the previous decade was undertaken in 1987 to compare the patterns to the models formulated by Butler and Lundberg, but particularly the former (Wilkinson, 1990). The goal was to select case studies representing as wide a range as possible of the types of tourism development. The states chosen were:

- **Dominica**: low but fluctuating levels of tourism, followed in recent years by growth, with tourism being only a minor component of the national economy—Stage 2 (Involvement) of Butler's model.

- **St. Lucia**: following serious declines in the early 1980s, continuous growth with tourism becoming a major economic sector—Stage 4 (Consolidation).

- **Barbados**: fluctuations, but tourism levels at the end of the period being similar to those at the beginning—Stage 5 (Decline).

In the second phase, two further case studies were sought, the intention being to broaden the range of types along the cycle's curve. At that time, McElroy and de Albuquerque (1989) presented their model (later published as de Albuquerque & McElroy, 1992). Although their model used a wider range of data than in the selection of the first three case studies, those islands appeared to fit approximately similar locations as suggested above. Two states were chosen as filling out the range of stages of development:

- **Cayman Islands**: rapid growth to high levels, with tourism being a major force in the economy and a sector characterised by large-scale development, aggressive marketing, niche marketing (scuba diving), and a major cruise ship presence—late Stage II (Transition).

- **Bahamas**: a mass market destination with tourism dominating the economy, growth stagnation, short average lengths-of-stay, international hotel chains, high densities, casinos, packaged charters, cruise ships—late Stage III (Maturity).

The five case studies, therefore, are located in the following order on the model (and in the subsequent case study chapters): Dominica in the early phases of Stage I; St. Lucia and Cayman Islands in Stage II; and Barbados and Bahamas in Stage III.

A common format will be used in the presentation of each case study:

- a brief description of their physical and cultural geography, probably the major factors "pulling" tourists to each island;

- an overview of the state's history, with an emphasis on historical economic development;

- a more detailed analysis of the recent economic context, to situate the tourism sector's importance;

- a quantitative and qualitative analysis of the tourism sector;

- a detailed history of the evolution of tourism policy and planning;

- a concluding section that synthesizes the situation and speculates on the future.

Following the case study chapters is a concluding chapter, which compares and contrasts the case studies.

Notes

[1]In response to these concerns, the Caribbean Hotel Association (CHA) formed in 1993 the Caribbean Tourism Development Task Force, chaired by former Jamaican Prime Minister Michael Manley, to examine tourism's environmental impacts, training and education, infrastructural development, taxation issues, and growth—although it is the latter subject that has elicited the most attention (Anonymous, 1993d).

[2]Income before deducting depreciation, rent, interest, amortization, income taxes, property taxes, and insurance.

Chapter 4

Dominica

Dominica is one of the fayrest Islands of the West, full of hilles, and of very
good smell. (Richard Hakluyt [1552?–1616], 1904, in Murray, 1991, p. 59)

Introduction

Situated between Guadeloupe and Martinique in the Windward Islands, Dominica
has an area of 751 km² and maximum dimensions of 50 × 22 km (see Map 4.1). A
mountainous volcanic island (with a maximum elevation of 1730 meters above sea
level at Morne Diablotin), deep incised valleys, and a narrow coastal shelf, it is the
most rugged island in the Caribbean, with only about 30% of the total area being
suitable for agriculture (Government of the Commonwealth of Dominica [GOCD],
1985). Throughout the center of the island, there is considerable evidence of recent volcanic activity, with numerous small geysers, hot springs, and waterfalls;
the most notable feature is the "Boiling Lake," the second largest boiling lake in
the world. There are six major watersheds containing numerous rivers that flow
all year. Humid tropical marine in climate, the island has higher temperatures and
lower rainfall (1,800–3,000 mm) on the leeward (west) side than the windward
side (3,000–4,000 mm); some interior areas have as much as 10,000 mm of rain.

With over 60% (520 km²) of the island covered by the finest forest in the Caribbean (Evans, 1986), the vegetation includes swamp-plains, secondary forests, mon-
tane-woodlands, rainforests, and elfin woodlands. The flora and fauna are diverse:
166 species of birds (of which 50 are resident) including the endangered Sisserou
and Jacquot parrots, over 1,000 species of flowering plants, and forests with up to
60 tree species per hectare (Caribbean Conservation Association [CCA], 1991a).
There are very few beaches and most that do exist have dark, volcanic sand and/or
are located on the harsh eastern windward coast. The CCA (1991a:1) presents a be-
guiling picture of the island:

> . . . Dominica has, with justification, been heralded as the region's premier
> nature island. With its very rugged terrain, perennial streams, rivers and wa-
> terfalls, and its great diversity of flora and fauna, Dominica's mostly un-
> spoiled landscape is considered by island aficionados to be among the most
> dramatically beautiful and pristine in the world. The country's undisturbed
> vegetation is more extensive than on any other island in the Lesser Antilles.

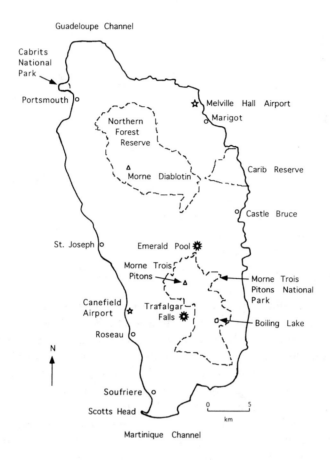

Guadeloupe Channel

Cabrits National Park

Portsmouth

Northern Forest Reserve

Melville Hall Airport

Marigot

Morne Diablotin

Carib Reserve

Castle Bruce

St. Joseph

Emerald Pool

Morne Trois Pitons

Morne Trois Pitons National Park

Canefield Airport

Trafalgar Falls

Boiling Lake

Roseau

N

Soufriere

Scotts Head

Martinique Channel

Map 4.1. Dominica.

. . . Its forests have been extolled as undoubtedly the finest in the Caribbean, even comparing favorably with those of Central and South America.

In promotional literature designed to lure visitors and tourists, Dominica is described as an island of rainbows, a place where mists rise gently from lush green valleys and fall softly over blue green peaks, where trees sprout orchids, and where rivers framed by banks of giant ferns rush and tumble to the sea. Along mountain slopes, fields of broad-leafed bananas contrast with cocoa and citrus trees, and cattle graze in the feathery shade of coconut palms. . . . (CCA, 1991a, p. 1)

Dominica was settled first by the Ciboney (not a tribal name, but a term designating a subservient class), a Meso-Indian, preceramic, fishing culture perhaps as early as 400 BC, and later by the Arawaks, with their strong agriculture, fishing, and hunting society, sometime before 100 BC. War-like Caribs, who overran the Arawaks around 1200 AD, inhabited the island they called *Waitukubuli* ("Tall is her body") (Honychurch, 1991, p. 3) when Columbus sighted it on Sunday, November 3, 1493 and renamed it Dominica after the day of the week. Although Spanish ships often stopped in Dominica before or after cross-Atlantic voyages during the 16th century, there were apparently no serious attempts by Spaniards to colonize the island, perhaps because of the unfriendly response of the Caribs (Boromé, 1972a).

Several attempts to bring the island under British and French control in the 17th century failed because of fierce Carib resistance. Even though Dominica had been included in the land patent of the British Crown to the Earl of Carlisle in 1627 to encourage settlement, by 1660 Britain and France agreed to abandon Dominica and St. Vincent to the Caribs (Boromé, 1972b). Interest in settlement was later revived several times by both nations, but in 1748 through the Treaty of Aix-la-Chapelle, Britain and France declared Dominica and St. Vincent "neutral," existing for the "sole benefit" of the Carib populations (CCA, 1991a, p. 21). Such neutrality was short-lived, however, for in the late 18th century the British and French traded control several times both through invasion and by treaty, with Britain finally being ceded the island in 1783 by the Treaty of Versailles; a subsequent French invasion in 1805 ended when a ransom was paid.

By that time, the Caribs had been driven from the more hospitable Caribbean coast to the mountains and the more rugged Atlantic coast. The modern result is a unique legacy for Dominica: the 1480-hectare Carib reservation—officially called the Carib Territory—was formally established in 1903 on the northeastern part of the island.[1] The Territory maintains a system of communal land tenure—probably the only substantial remnant of communal land in the Caribbean region today—which has existed since pre-Columbian times. Although much of the Carib culture (e.g., language, religion, most rituals) has been lost, there has been a growing ethnic consciousness among the Caribs since about 1970 (CCA, 1991a; Honychurch, 1984, 1988). Frequent government proposals to change the Carib's communal land tenure system to one based on private property have strained the relationship between the Caribs and the Government; such an approach could render the Caribs landless within a short period of time (Gregoire & Kanem, 1989).

In terms of European-initiated settlement, colonial domination and its plantation-based socioeconomic system never took hold in Dominica the way they did in most of the other islands of the Eastern Caribbean because of the barriers presented by the climate and terrain (Trouillot, 1988). Although African slaves were used in attempts at plantation agriculture, many were set free, long before Emancipation in 1834, to fend for themselves. The result was a strong tradition of peasant, village-based farming, a fact that spared the country much of the labor and political strife characterizing more-developed Caribbean islands in the 20th century.

About 90% of the population[2] of approximately 72,900 (1993) lives along the coast, primarily (70%) in a narrow coastal strip along the leeward (western) Caribbean side, which offers more protection from prevailing winds. The population is largely concentrated in the capital of Roseau in the south and Portsmouth in the north. Dominica's cultural roots are varied: Caribs, African slaves, and English and French colonizers. In fact, there is more French than English influence; the effect of French is everywhere in the dominant Afro-Créole culture and the local patois

(*Kwéyol*), whereas the British left their primary mark on the country's system of government (Honychurch, 1984, 1988). Above all are the values of a deeply religious and overwhelmingly agrarian society (CCA, 1991a, p. 24).

The Commonwealth of Dominica[3] became an associated state in 1967 with full internal self-government, and an independent republic (a status different from any of its Commonwealth neighbors) within the British Commonwealth on November 3, 1978—the 485th anniversary of the sighting of Dominica by Columbus. It is governed by a President appointed by the Dominican Government (not a Governor-General appointed by the British Crown) and an elected legislative assembly, with a legal and legislative system based on that of Britain.

The Economy

In the last three decades, the only sector that has flourished has been the service sector, with most of that growth having been fueled by tourism. For example, in 1993 tourist expenditures accounted for 22.6% of the GDP, compared to 3.9% in 1980.[4] Traditionally, the economy has been based on export agriculture: coffee, sugar, limes, cocoa, vanilla, and bananas in succession. Commercial-scale banana production, which began only in 1949, brought Dominica its first real cash economy in 1954 when British-owned Geest Industries developed a virtual export monopoly and spurred expansion (L. Honychurch, 1989, personal communication). Agriculture, however, has declined seriously in relative terms since 1960. Between 1960 and 1970, the number of agricultural employees dropped a third, from 11,693 to 7,720 (GOCD, 1976). A decade of relative stability followed, with approximately 8,183 agricultural workers in 1981 (GOCD, 1985). This, however, represented a decrease in the percentage of the active population involved in agriculture from 38.1% in 1970 to 30.8% in 1981; similarly, the percentage contribution of agriculture to GDP at factor cost dropped from 35.0% in 1974 to 30.2% in 1983 (UNECLAC, 1984).

Since then, the non-banana sector has been increasing and there have been continuing attempts at agricultural diversification in coconuts, tropical fruits, exotic vegetables, rice, aquaculture, and ornamental flowers. Whereas diversification helps to decrease imports, exports are hindered by difficulties in transportation to international markets (CCA, 1991a, p. 34; Caribbean Development Bank [CDB], 1989b, p. 7; J. Taylor, 1989; World Bank, 1990, p. 49). Bananas, however, now predominate, accounting for 70% of total exports and 40% of the total area under cultivation (CCA, 1991a, pp. 65–66; Welch, 1991). The CDB (1989b, p. 7) warns, however, about the uncertainty of continuing preferential tariff arrangements with Britain after the formation of the single European market in 1993 and urges efforts to increase competitiveness in banana production.[5] The World Bank (1990, p. 53) predicts that agriculture's share of GDP will drop from an average of 24.9% in 1985–1988 to 15.0% in 2000.

There has been a serious decline in the industrial sector for several reasons: inadequate airport facilities, banana boom, tax incentive structure, and regulatory framework (World Bank, 1990, p. 83). Manufacturing (which is dominated by a single factory processing copra into soap, edible oil, and cosmetic products) accounts for 7% of GDP (E. Douglas, 1989, personal communication).

Fueled by a GDP bolstered by increasing banana revenues, per capita income growth was substantial in the 1980s and early 1990s (averaging over 5% per annum), rising to US$2,500 in 1993—still, however, one of the lowest in the Eastern Caribbean. McElroy and de Albuquerque (1991) describe Dominica's economy as being "premodern." That is, the processes of diversifying the economy away from a monocrop base and of rapid urbanization and suburbanization have only just begun in Dominica; it is still predominantly an agricultural country, with a relatively low rate of net population growth (partially due until recently to out-migration), a small tourism sector, and no other "modernizing" sector (e.g., as with banking in the Cayman Islands or insurance in Barbados). The CCA (1991a, p. 30) argues, however, that the premodern designation is a positive factor for Dominica because it means that many of the crucial choices about future development paths have not already been foreclosed.

The Government's Structural Adjustment Program, which began in 1986, sought to increase real growth to about 4% per annum and reduce fiscal and external imbalances; it consistently exceeded targets, with real growth averaging over 6% per annum. The overall economic picture is not strong, however, with the long-term debt being US$88.4 million in 1993 (CTO, 1994) and a growing problem with a deficit on the current account balance of payments—US$25.8 million in 1990 (Mather & Todd, 1993).

Among developing countries, such figures are not necessarily disastrous, but McElroy and de Albuquerque (1991) warn that conditions among small Eastern Caribbean countries seem to lead to payment difficulties at relatively low debt levels. They suggest that the extreme openness of these economies, plus poor or inelastic revenue collection mechanisms, make OECS nations more prone to defaulting on foreign debt than has been assumed in the past. This implies that future economic policy must devote considerable attention to reducing the rate of growth of foreign-held debt and increasing foreign exchange earnings, through higher returns on export agriculture, more exports from small industry, and more tourism development (CCA, 1991a, p. 37). Given the picture presented above concerning agriculture and manufacturing, such a conclusion suggests that tourism—the only real growth sector—will have to receive more attention.

But who will lead in the push to increased development: the private or public sector? The indigenous entrepreneurial class is small; as a result, private investment has contributed less to economic growth than has public sector investment. Moreover, there are problems in the private sector (e.g., lack of technical, productive, and managerial skills; capital; information). Given the small size of the private sector, therefore, the Government may be required to maintain relatively high levels of investments in all sectors (CDB, 1989b, p. 7). If that is the case, the Government will have to increase its direct involvement, particularly in tourism.

The Tourism Sector

Dominica's tourism product is not typical of most other Caribbean destinations, perhaps most significantly because of the limited availability of white sandy beaches which North American and European visitors generally prefer. On the other hand, the island does offer a variety of unique attractions (e.g., spectacular scenery, rain forest hikes, hot springs, good diving, and national parks) which, when marketed as a "package," have earned Dominica its reputation as the region's "nature island." (CCA, 1991a, p. 134)

Dominica has many characteristics of de Albuquerque and McElroy's (1992) Stage I (Emergence): a slowly growing stream of long-staying visitors interested in the natural and cultural environments, staying in and eating at modest, mainly locally owned facilities, and arriving by small plane at minor-scale airports. Modest expansion of the tourism plant is occurring and cruise ship tourism is increasing—both drawn by the growing advertising of and interest in nature tourism.

The Beginnings

The travel literature has consistently characterized Dominica as a remote, rugged, verdant, undeveloped, and somewhat offbeat destination infrequently visited by tourists (Weaver, 1991). Moreover, most historical sources, while praising the island's physical beauty, recognized that its physical geography and limited facilities (e.g., accommodations, transportation) hindered its prospects for large-scale tourism development. For example, before the 1956 completion of the Transinsular Road, the principal link between Portsmouth and Roseau was by boat. Similarly, prior to the 1958 completion of Melville Hall Airport, air transport was limited to sea planes whose landing was often prevented by inclement weather (Honychurch, 1984, pp. 141–142).

Dominica had approximately 2,000 tourists in 1959 (Caribbean Tourism Association [CTA], 1960), a figure that rose slowly but steadily to 13,000 in 1970 (Gilles, 1980). Just as tourism was going beyond this very modest scale, the international press highlighted a vocal "Black Power" movement that developed in the late 1960s and early 1970s, thus fostering a negative image of Dominica as a tourist destination. This was followed by anti-White protests, the murder of a tourist in 1974, and the violent activities of the anti-White "Dreads" (named after their Dreadlock hairstyle) in the late 1970s. As Weaver (1991) notes, "The fact that such incidents did not reflect the attitudes or activities of most Dominicans attests to the vulnerability of tourism to the unrest generated by a relatively small minority of agitators" (p. 419).

The situation was further complicated by an image of instability associated with the political regime of then Prime Minister Patrick John. A scandal erupted in 1979 over a proposed scheme to lease a fifth of the island to an American businessman; the land was to be taken from small farmers to set up a free port (including oil refineries, casinos, etc.), which would have constituted a virtual ministate within a state. Public protest led to the plans being dropped, but Government attempts to curtail the press and trade unions led to a period of heated civil disobedience that ended only with the resignation of the Government. This was followed by two coup attempts in 1981, including one involving the arrest in New Orleans of American and Canadian mercenaries about to invade the island to overthrow the new Government with the support of disgruntled members of the disbanded Dominica Defence Force and to restore the former Prime Minister to power (Honychurch, 1984, 1988).

The problem was compounded by the impact of Hurricane David on August 29, 1979, which killed 37 people, injured 5,000, and destroyed much of the country's infrastructure, including electricity, telephone system, harbor, etc. Within the next year, there were two more serious hurricanes, Frederick and Allen. As a result, the number of tourist arrivals fell from 20,300 in 1979 to 14,400 in 1980, thus discouraging investment, both local and international, in the sector.

Stay-Over Tourist Arrivals

Since then, the number of stay-over arrivals to Dominica, although still relatively small compared to many other Caribbean destinations (rising in rank only from 28th to 27th out of 30 destinations in the region from 1980 to 1993), has increased dramatically, rising to 51,900 in 1993 (see Table 4.1). At 260.4%, Dominica had the sixth highest rate of growth in the period 1980–1993 in the region. This was matched or exceeded by increases in the number of arrivals per 1,000 local population per year from 196 to 712, the penetration ratio from 4.19 to 15.22, and the density ratio from 0.39 to 1.48 in the same period. All of these measures, however, are extremely low, in fact among the lowest in the Caribbean region and the lowest among the case studies, thus confirming Dominica's status as Stage I.

An unusual characteristic is that 24,000 tourists (46.2% of the arrivals) came from the Caribbean region in 1993 (compared to a proportionately similar 6,000 or 42.9% in 1980). The large proportion of regional visitors probably accounts for the reason why Dominica spends much less (US$25.15 in 1992) than the governments of any of the other case studies in marketing terms for each stay-over visitor. Such a regional pattern has both advantages and disadvantages. Regional tourists share many cultural traits with Dominicans, thus lessening possible cultural conflicts; they are able to take advantage of off-peak travel; and they may be more interested in staying in locally owned and smaller establishments. However, they have generally lower expenditure levels than other market sources and have shorter average lengths of stay. For example, in 1991 Caribbean tourists stayed an average of 9.9 nights, compared to 11.8 for Americans, 12.3 for Canadians, and 13.5 for Europeans (CTO, 1992).

Dominica's French heritage represents a major drawing card for the Francophone market, a factor reinforced by the proximity of Martinique and Guadeloupe, both having international airports and direct air connections to France. Over one third (35.5%) of the stay-over tourists in 1993 had French origins: 14,581 (28.1%) from the French West Indies—making the French West Indies the major single market for Dominica—and 3,877 (7.5%) from France. These are particularly important

Table 4.1. Dominica: Tourism Statistics

Year	Stay-Over Tourists		Excursionists		Cruise Passengers		Total Tourists		Visitor Expenditure		Tourist Rooms		
	No. (000s)	% Annual Change	No. (000s)	% Annual Change	No. (000s)	% Annual Change	No. (000s)	% Annual Change	US$ (M)	% Annual Change	No.	Av. LOS (No. Nights)	No. Tourist Nights/Yr. (000s)
1980	14.4	−29.1	3.1	−35.4	7.4	NA	24.9	NA	2.1	−8.7	157	7.8	112.3
1981	15.9	10.4	2.2	−29.0	5.5	−35.7	23.6	−5.2	3.0	42.9	187	8.2	130.4
1982	19.0	19.5	1.5	−31.8	2.4	−56.4	22.9	−3.0	4.0	33.3	263	8.2	155.8
1983	19.6	3.2	2.7	80.0	6.1	154.2	28.4	24.0	7.3	82.5	280	9.5	186.2
1984	22.2	13.3	1.9	−29.6	3.2	−47.5	27.3	−3.9	8.6	17.8	343	10.7	237.5
1985	21.5	−3.2	0.9	−52.4	6.6	106.3	29.0	6.2	8.7	1.2	405	11.9	255.9
1986	24.4	13.5	0.7	−22.2	11.5	74.2	36.6	26.2	11.2	28.7	405	10.9	266.0
1987	26.7	9.4	1.5	114.3	12.1	5.1	40.3	10.1	12.8	14.3	405	11.9	317.7
1988	31.8	19.1	1.9	26.7	9.0	−25.6	42.7	6.0	12.0	9.4	412	11.0	352.0
1989	35.2	10.7	2.5	3.6	7.3	−18.9	45.0	5.4	18.5	32.1	412	7.8	349.8
1990	45.1	28.1	7.3	192.0	6.8	−6.8	59.2	31.6	25.0	35.1	531	9.0	405.9
1991	46.3	2.7	9.0	23.3	65.0	855.9	120.3	103.2	28.1	2.4	547	7.8	361.1
1992	47.0	1.5	7.8	−13.3	89.8	38.2	144.6	20.2	30.3	7.8	603	7.8[a]	366.6[a]
1993	51.9	10.4	5.6	−28.2	87.8	−2.2	145.3	0.5	33.2	9.6	757	7.8[a]	404.8[a]

NA: not available.

[a] Estimated.

markets because they are relatively wealthy ones compared, for example, to other Caribbean markets. As *départements* of France and not *territoires*, Martinique and Guadeloupe have "developed"—albeit within a colonial heritage—economies with GDP per capita in 1991 of US$4,223 and US$4,539, respectively.

Dominica remains a minor destination in the region for European, American, and Canadian tourists, ranking near the bottom of the list of 30 countries in the region for each of these market sources. Nevertheless, growth in each of these market sources has been considerable in the period 1980–1993, with American, Canadian, and European tourists more than doubling.

This broad mix of origins means that Dominica has the lowest market concentration ratio (53.0) among the case studies (i.e., the French West Indies, United States, and United Kingdom accounted for only 53.0% of stay-over tourist arrivals in 1993). Undoubtedly, this reflects the lack of direct international air connections, which would otherwise enable a country such as the United States to be more dominant. On the one hand, this mix is a healthy situation in that Dominica is not overly dependent on one market and the consequences of its political and economic situation; on the other hand, it creates economy of scale problems in terms of marketing and promotion.

Despite the slow but constant growth in the number of tourists, it is unlikely that Dominica will ever make the transition to mass-market tourism, for obvious reasons: the limited hotel stock, the lack of white-sand beaches, and the small airports. Access into Dominica is still a bottleneck to the further development of tourism, particularly stay-over tourism. Jemiolo and Conway (1991, p. 29), for example, describe Dominica as having insufficient airline connections within the Caribbean and with Europe via connecting flights, although they argue that there are sufficient connections with North America via connecting flights.[6] There are two airports, neither of which can be extended to handle jets: Melville Hall (which currently is greatly underutilized), 58 km and a 1.5-hour drive from Roseau in the northeast, with a 5,200-foot runway located between a mountain and the sea; and Canefield, 5 km north of Roseau, with a 2,600-foot runway located on a narrow coastal plain next to a steep mountain. As a result, there are no direct scheduled international air connections outside of the region. The introduction of competition for LIAT into Canefield (e.g., Nature Island Express) has the potential to lower the relatively high air fares and to increase access.

There has long been speculation (e.g., GOCD, 1976, p. 142) about the potential for an international jet port north of Melville Hall Airport on the northeast coast, but the difficult terrain would make such an enterprise extremely expensive. The Government has attempted, without success, to obtain external funding for such an airport. Laventhal and Horwath's (1986c) negative comments on the economic viability of such airports in the Eastern Caribbean are worth noting:

> . . . it is not evident that the increased tourism contribution justifies the considerable expenditure involved, possibly even if it is measured simply in terms of the recurrent cost burden and, certainly, if the capital and recurrent expenditures involved are valued at the cost of opportunities foregone. . . .

> One may conclude, as far as any future action in this area is concerned, that the Leeward and Windward Islands possess sufficient airport facilities for the foreseeable future. (pp. 22, 41)

The estimated cost of construction of an airport capable of handling wide-body jets (i.e., 10,000-foot runway) would be at least US$760 million and of one handling medium-range jets (i.e., 6,000-foot runway) at least US$400 million (L. Honychurch, 1989, personal communication). Such costs do not include massive expenditures within the public sector (e.g., roads, electricity) nor in the private sector (e.g., hotels). Given the magnitude of these costs in light of questionable benefits (to say nothing of the potential negative environmental impacts of airport construction), the notion does not seem to be viable.

Accommodations

Although Dominica is still one of the smallest destinations in the Caribbean in terms of accommodation stock, growth in that stock has been steady, with the number of rooms increasing 382% from 157 in 1980 to 757 in 1993. There remain, however, relatively low rates of number of tourist rooms per 1,000 local population (2.1 in 1980 and 10.4 in 1993) and of number of rooms/km^2 (0.2 and 1.0)[7]—again, measures that are among the lowest in the Caribbean region and the lowest among the case studies. Most of the rooms are in relatively small hotels, the largest hotel having 76 rooms (many of which are rented out on a long-term basis to students of an adjacent offshore medical training university). About two thirds of the tourist rooms are located in or near the capital of Roseau, with about one fifth being north of Roseau on the west coast, and the rest in the interior (Weaver, 1991).

Weaver (1991, p. 422) notes that there is a high degree of local ownership, with Dominicans in 1989 wholly controlling 62% of facilities and 70% of units and partially controlling another 19% of facilities and 15% of units; this pattern of local control extends to the largest facilities, unlike most small Caribbean destinations. Because of the small size of the hotels, there is no ownership by MNCs; also, there is no domination by any single source, with the 19% of the accommodations that are wholly owned by foreign interests being dispersed among German, Canadian, American, and Swiss holdings.

In 1988 (the only year for which a figure is available), the average occupancy rate was an estimated 32.5%, resulting in a low tourist occupancy function (rooms) of 1.9. Although occupancy rates are not available by type of accommodation, hotels appear to have very low occupancy rates as only a small proportion of tourist arrivals (e.g., 28% in 1993) indicate their intention to stay in a hotel. Such a pattern may suggest why the formal hotel and restaurant sector's value-added contribution was only 3.3% of GDP in 1993.

Given the apparently low occupancy rates, significant increases in tourist arrivals could easily be accommodated in existing hotels (World Bank, 1990, p. 67). Upgrading of these hotels, however, would be needed to offer the facilities and standards that the international travel market expects. This excess capacity is available even in the high season as Dominica has very low seasonality: its seasonality index of 1.025 in 1989 (de Albuquerque & McElroy, 1992, p. 627) was the third lowest of 23 countries in the region—and remained virtually the same at 1.051 in 1993.

Concerns have frequently been expressed about the adequacy of services (e.g., electricity, water, sewerage) for further significant tourism development (CDB, 1989b, p. 4). The country has an expensive energy system given its small scale, high capital costs for hydroelectric power, high diesel fuel costs, and the need to maintain, at present, both the diesel and hydroelectric systems (CCA, 1991a, p. 30). Completion in 1991 of a new 3.5-MW hydroelectric plant at Trafalgar Falls above Roseau, however, means that two thirds of the country's electricity is water supplied, thus substantially decreasing the need for importing diesel oil. There is also geothermal potential of unknown quantities at Trafalgar and Soufriere; however, tapping such resources would be extremely expensive and has been tried unsuccessfully elsewhere in the region (e.g., St. Lucia). The water supply problem is a function of the limits of the distribution system and not lack of rainfall, as is the case in other islands (e.g., Anguilla).

There has been a bell-shaped curve in the average length of stay, which rose from 7.8 nights in 1980 to 11.0 in 1988 and then fell to 7.8 in 1993. Perhaps this is a result of increased numbers of short-stay visitors taking brief trips from other islands as Dominica's nature tourism becomes better known. Increases in the number of tourist arrivals as noted above have resulted in the annual number of tourist nights increasing from 109,000 in 1980 to 404,800 in 1993.

Excursionists

With the continued marketing of Dominica as the "Nature Isle" and the growth in the ecotourism[8] market, the number of day excursionists visiting the island grew dramatically (e.g., from 1,485 in 1987 to 8,898 in 1991), but has significantly decreased recently (5,600 in 1993), for reasons related to instability among tour operators. The arrivals per 1,000 local population (77), penetration ratio (0.21), and density ratio (0.02) are quite low, put present the possibility of rapid increases. Major factors in encouraging this type of visitor were the introduction in 1990 of expanded air service as competition for LIAT and increased marketing of the island as a day destination for nature tours. Little information, however, is available on excursionists, including their spending patterns and travel behavior.

Cruise Passengers

Cruise passenger arrivals exhibited an erratic pattern in the 1980s, with the numbers of ships and passengers fluctuating wildly (e.g., lows of seven ships and 2,400 passengers in 1982, and highs of 38 ships and 12,080 passengers in 1987). Dominica remained a minor cruise destination throughout this period, dropping from 20th to 24th in rank of number of passenger arrivals among 24 countries in the Caribbean region and being 21st in rank of change in number of arrivals. There were many reasons for this low level of performance and eroding position, including lack of suitable berthing facilities (including on the Roseau waterfront where a dock was destroyed by the 1980 hurricane), shopping and restaurant facilities, and local tour companies capable of handling large influxes of arrivals.

The completion of a new cruise ship facility at Cabrits National Park, however, appeared to be turning the picture around. There were 87,800 passenger arrivals in 1993, the highest growth rate in the Caribbean, bringing Dominica up to 16th of 24 countries in the region in total arrivals. Although still having the lowest number of arrivals among the case studies, in 1993 Dominica exceeded the next highest, St. Lucia, in terms of passenger arrivals per 1,000 local population (1,205) and passenger penetration ratio (3.30). If the trend continues, even these smaller absolute number of arrivals will begin to exert relatively greater pressure on the island's smaller population and cruise facilities. Significant improvements in both facilities and services, therefore, are needed to meet the needs of these short-stay visitors. Moreover, there is evidence that cruise ship dockings at Cabrits are decreasing, with docking preference going to Roseau because the capital is closer to inland nature attractions (e.g., Emerald Pool and the national park) (Sharkey, 1994).

Even if the number of passenger arrivals continues to grow significantly, however, the effect on overall tourist expenditures will undoubtedly be much lower than would occur with similar increases in tourist arrivals. No data are available on passenger expenditures for Dominica, but this pattern is very clear for other Caribbean islands. It has been estimated, for example, that a passenger in St. Lucia spends only about US$44 during a short stay of only a few hours, compared to a stay-over tourist who spends US$68 per day for an average stay of over 10 days (CCA, 1991b, p. 225).

Total Visitors

When all three types of visitors are aggregated, Dominica's position as a Stage I destination remains clear. Between 1980 and 1993, the number of total visitors has shown a dramatic 483.5% increase (highest among the case studies) to 145,200. There have been similar increases in arrivals per 1,000 local population (1994), penetration ratio (18.73), and density ratio (1.82). Nevertheless, these latter measures are still the lowest among the case studies.

Expenditures

In terms of estimated visitor expenditures, Dominica remains one of the most minor destinations in the Caribbean region. Despite significant increases in the recent past, it only ranks 27th in 1991 among 30 countries in the region, up only slightly from 28th in 1980. With visitor expenditures estimated at US$33.2 million in 1993, tourism, however, now ranks as the second highest foreign exchange earner for the country after bananas. While increasing dramatically in terms of the proportion of GDP since the early 1980s, tourism seems to becoming more important in relation to total GDP, accounting for 22.6% of GDP in 1993. Tourism's secondary position to bananas is also demonstrated by the low ratio of estimated visitor expenditures to merchandise exports at 0.7 in 1993; however, this ratio has risen significantly since 1980, again indicating tourism's relative and absolute growth. This trend may also be related to the recent growth in estimated visitor expenditures as a percentage of external debt that, while still very small compared to other countries in the region, rose to 37.6% in 1993.

In comparison with other Caribbean countries and despite impressive increases since the 1980s, tourist expenditures are absolutely and relatively low. For example, visitor expenditure per capita of local population was US$455 in 1993, the lowest among the case studies. This is partly related to low average room rates; for example, in 1987–1988, Dominica ranked the lowest among 31 countries in the region, with average winter rates of US$41.70/night and summer rates of US$42.10, the (insignificant) seasonal difference being also the lowest in the region (Curtin & Poon, 1988). The high proportion of regional tourists, with their low average expenditure, and the high proportion of tourists staying in private, unregistered, or other accommodation are other factors in lowering overall tourist expenditures.

The recent past has seen expansion of the tourism sector (e.g., ground tour operators, car rental agencies). Increases in cruise ship arrivals are likely to foster expansion in these and related services, but the economic impact will probably be highly concentrated in a relatively small number of operators, rather than being spread across the broader tourism sector, including the hotel and restaurant sector, because of the tight scheduling constraints required for cruise tourists. Handicraft sales are likely to increase, but it is not clear whether local production is capable of meeting expanded demand in terms of quality, quantity, or variety. One result could be an erosion of Dominica's reputation for high-quality crafts (e.g., Carib woven baskets), albeit of a limited range.

There are several conflicting figures available on recent tourist-related employment. For example, the Dominica Tourist Board's (1987, p. 13) estimate of 1,000 jobs in total in 1986 contrasts with the 1991 Tourism Sector Plan's 500–600 in 1990 (Tourism Planning and Research Associates, 1991, p. 22). Similarly, the World Bank's (1990) figure of 748 direct jobs in 1989 contrasts with the CTO's (1994) 409 in 1993. The World Bank (1990, p. 67) argues that, although figures on indirect employment are unavailable, they may be higher than expected, given the fact that the "local value added" to tourism expenditures is estimated to be twice as much as other Eastern Caribbean islands. This contention is consistent with Laventhal and Horwath's (1986a, p. 21; 1986b, p. 10) estimates of 43.4% as the leakage rate in Dominica for tourist-generated foreign exchange, a figure much lower than for other islands in the Eastern Caribbean and of the multiplier being 0.73, a figure somewhat higher than the other islands.[9]

Given tourism's growing contribution to GDP and a comment in the same report that by the year 2000 agriculture's share of GDP would drop to 15.0% (World Bank, 1990, p. 53), a somewhat unusual conclusion is reached by the World Bank (1990): "Dominica is unlikely to become a major tourism destination in the next decade, but effective promotion of tourism assets would generate steady development of the sector. . . . However, the existing base is so low that the sector will not be a large contributor to the economy even by 1999'' (p. 67). Between 1989 and 1999, the World Bank (1990, p. 67) predicts that available rooms will rise to 672, "gross receipts" from US$12.7 million to US$16.9 million, and direct employment from 748 to 1,143—but it does not predict the number of tourist arrivals.

Tourism Policy and Planning

Although until recently tourism has played a relatively minor role in the Dominican economy, it has received considerable attention from past and current Governments. Therefore, it is appropriate to analyze the specific policy and planning framework that has been adopted to carry out the goal of increased dependence on tourism.

The Policy and Planning Context

Whereas policy is Cabinet's prerogative, development planning is the responsibility of the Economic Development Unit (EDU) of the Ministry of Finance and Economic Development, consisting of the Economic Development Planning Division (EDPD) and the Physical Planning Division (PPD), the former being responsible for economic issues and the latter for physical planning.[10] The PPD is responsible for the administration of the Town and Country Planning Act (TCPA) (1975)[11] and enforcement of land subdivision and building regulations. It also provides advice to government authorities on land use, building control, and environmental protection and enhancement.

The TCPA requires the preparation of national plans and written statements of national planning and development policy. It also requires land-use zoning, but this has never been implemented (L. Honychurch, 1992, personal communication). Nor have the two National Structure Plans (GOCD, 1976, 1985) received official approval. Nevertheless, Bourne (1989) contends that the Plans are referred to and used as a basis for planning judgements and decision making; in contrast, Soler (1988) claims that the 1985 Plan is neither used as a reference nor as a basis for policy recommendations. The CCA (1991a, p. 165) suggests that both may be correct, with the Plans being used more by technical planners than by political decision makers. The result is that most major developments (which are usually in the public sector [Lausche, 1986] because of the small private sector) tend to get approval first at the political level, with the PPD being relegated to reviewing subdivision plans and performing site-level planning functions (CCA, 1991a, p. 167). The problem is compounded by the PPD's small staff and lack of enforcement capability (I. Baptiste, 1989, personal communication).

From the point of view of tourism, the lack of strong environmental controls is particularly significant given that environmental quality is in fact a resource that is particularly important to tourists in general and certainly to tourists visiting Dominica. Failure to maintain the environment, both urban and nonurban, could result in decreased tourist demand: ". . . Dominica's relatively pristine environment can only become of growing economic importance as an attraction to visitors—but only if developments are sensitive to aesthetics'' (CCA, 1991a, p. 168). Moreover, the current Government's emphasis on ecotourism appears to have potential for serious conflict with this absence of strong environmental controls.

The following is an analysis of policies, plans, and legislation that relate to tourism.

Unfulfilled Dreams

Spurred by the arrival of modest numbers of tourists following World War II, the 1958 Hotels Aids Ordinance was the first tangible attempt by the Government to promote tourism. It offered a 10-year income tax holiday for hotels with 10 or more rooms and waived customs duty on goods and equipment required for construction of such hotels. Little use was made of these incentives, however, for within the next decade little hotel development took place and doubts began to surface that Dominica was suited to large-scale tourism—doubts that became a matter of public record with the eventual rejection of virtually all of the major recommendations of a 1971 consultants' report.

Prepared for the British Overseas Development Agency (ODA), the Shankland Cox (1971b, p. 7) tourist development strategy for Dominica was based on the assumption of an annual growth rate of 10% in the number of tourists in the Eastern Caribbean.[12] The consultants' optimism was based on phenomenal growth rates in worldwide tourism during the 1960s, particularly as a result of jet charters. In 1969, according to the report, Dominica had an estimated 8,246 stay-over tourists,[13] or 2% of the total 419,000 tourists in the Eastern Caribbean. Shankland Cox (1971b, p. 97) felt that this proportion could be increased to 3% or even 5% with more intensive and sustained promotion. Assuming 10% annual growth rate as a base, forecasted numbers of stay-over tourists in Dominica in 1990 were 124,120 for a 2% share, 186,180 for a 3% share, and 310,300 for a 5% share. Clearly, reality did not match the forecasts: the actual 1990 figure was 45,100. The implication of this wide discrepancy can be understood in light of the proposals made in the report, largely based on three problematical points.

The first problem is *the conflict between preservation and use of the natural environment*. Shankland Cox (1971b) recognize that "the most important tourist attraction the island has to offer is the entire unspoilt expanse of mountainous forest and coastline when these are made suitably accessible" (p. 79). Utilization of this resource is seen as requiring two priorities: most of the interior to be demarcated as a national park; and visitor access to the mountains and forests to be allowed (Shankland Cox, 1971a, p. 15). Other than a caveat about "international standards" of resource management, however, the report does not deal with the issue of how "the unspoilt expanse" is to remain unspoilt with the introduction of the massive numbers of tourists forecast in the report itself.

Second, *growth was predicated on the rapid and massive construction of both infrastructure and accommodations*. It was assumed that the capacity of Melville Hall Airport would be upgraded dramatically (which is not feasible given the location of the runway between the ocean and a mountain ridge) and that the road network would be greatly improved (which did happen in the late 1980s as part of a British aid-supported agricultural feeder road system, but which does not match the requirements for massive tourist traffic). The report also notes the need for regional water and sewerage schemes, a hotel school, restoration of historical resources, and other tourist attractions and facilities. The accommodation target for 1990 was to be 5,200 beds—a far cry from the actual total of 412 rooms in 1990. The number of direct tourism jobs in 1990 was to be 3,000, with 2,250 indirect jobs. Indeed, there would have been considerable external contracting due to a projected labor shortage in the construction industry (Shankland Cox, 1971a, p. vi). Little mention is made of the environmental, social, or economic impacts of such a level of development—other than the positive projections concerning employment.

Third, *the tourists did not materialize in the numbers projected.* For a number of reasons (e.g., "energy crises," worldwide recessions, high inflation rates, and access problems), stay-over tourism in the Caribbean as a whole only approached or exceeded the 10% growth rate used in the Shankland Cox forecasts twice between 1971 and 1993. Although faring better than the rest of the region in growth rates, Dominica still had only 0.4% of total Caribbean stay-over tourist in 1993.

It would appear, therefore, that the consultants basically took an approach that forecast a particular growth pattern for the region and then worked backwards to calculate the level of development needed in Dominica to support such figures. The exactness of the projections is hedged by several further convoluted caveats, for example:

> There is no magic in these figures. They are consistent with the objectives established for the development of the strategy and are related to the capacity of the airport at Melville Hall to absorb additional visitors without a major investment in coastal works and based on certain assumptions of occupancy rates and lengths of stay. Neither can they be regarded as particularly precise. They are indicative of the order of the amount of tourist accommodation which should be planned for now, bearing in mind the state of the development of the country. Much can happen over 20 years that cannot be foreseen and which might suggest a lower or higher figure. This is unlikely to happen over the next ten years but the figures should be reviewed in 1980, 1985 and 1990. (Shankland Cox, 1971a, p. 3)

The review did not take that long. For reasons related to projected development costs, lack of aid funding, and energy costs, the report's structural proposals were formally rejected in the course of the development of the (unapproved) 1976 National Structure Plan.

The Island's Environment—A Shift From Liability to Asset

Just as the Government was embarking on a search for an alternative strategy of tourism development, there was growing interest both in Dominica and internationally in nature conservation and national parks. During the 1960s, the lumbering activities of a Canadian company, Dom-Can Timbers Ltd., in an area of mountain rain forest resulted in widespread erosion—and public outcry. The lumber project itself soon turned out not to be financially viable, partly as a result of the difficult cutting conditions (Prins, 1987) and partly through undercapitalization and mismanagement (May, 1981), but it did spur public interest in environmental conservation.

In the early 1970s, Morne Trois Pitons National Park was established and in 1975 the National Parks and Protected Areas Act was passed. The park, covering 65 km^2 of some of the last relatively undisturbed tracts of tropical rain forest in the Caribbean[14] in an area near the former Dom-Can site, includes both rain forest and montane forest, the Boiling Lake, two freshwater lakes, and many fumaroles and hot springs (James, 1988; Thorsell, 1984; Thorsell & Wood, 1976). Although not created because of its tourism potential, the park includes facilities for a low level of visitation (Wright, 1985).

Competing demands for the use of the Park's resource base have, however, intensified recently (e.g., hydropower, geothermal power, power transmission, roads, agriculture). Such uses are often in direct conflict with the more traditional objectives of national parks (e.g., conservation, enhancement of biodiversity, "wilderness" recreation) (CCA, 1991a, pp. 53–54). The "preservation vs. use" controversy is, of course, not unique to Dominica, but it does raise particular problems in light of Dominica's current nature-oriented tourism policy.

Coincident with the parks act was the United Nations Development Program (UNDP)-sponsored Kastarlak (1975) report clearly delineating the limitations of Dominica's tourism development potential and recommending that the focus not be on the development of major beach-oriented hotels, but on lower scale developments focused on the island's environment, particularly the interior, and its attraction to specialized market segments (e.g., environmentalists). This new approach entailed a shift in perception and a basic redefinition of Dominica's tourism resource base: whereas its physical geography had previously been seen as a tourism liability, it was now to be marketed as a tourism asset (Weaver, 1991). Government quickly adopted this theme and it soon came to dominate virtually all plans and policies that related directly or indirectly to tourism.

Plans—But Not Approvals

Under the 1975 Planning Act (which calls for regional, local, and structure plans), the Government (GOCD, 1976) formulated—but did not officially approve—a National Structure Plan for 1976–1990. The Plan emphasizes agriculture (including forestry) and related industries (GOCD, 1976, p. 3). In contrast to the Shankland Cox recommendations, the Plan sees tourism as playing "a modest role keeping in view the realities of the regional market and available resources" (GOCD, 1976, p. 83), to be tied closely to the natural and cultural environment, notably to agricultural, forestry, and natural resources development and conservation programs and to the Carib Reserve (GOCD, 1976, p. 83).

Recognizing that tourism could not be based on beach facilities, the Plan proposed a dispersed pattern of development with a number of components: beach-oriented hotels; locally owned cluster hotels and residential tourism areas; resort subdivisions of modest scale integrated with the cluster hotels; development of historic areas in Roseau and the Cabrits; development of the National Park and Forest Reserve areas (with proposed conservation areas covering 30% of the island's total area); and a Carib Centre in the Territory, including a tourist restaurant, handicraft workshop, and shopping area (GOCD, 1976, pp. 112–125). A number of problem areas were noted: poor quality of roads, long and expensive taxi rides from Melville Hall Airport (then the only airport), and poor services by LIAT (GOCD, 1976, p. 41).

Although not solely tied to tourism, a detailed environmental protection strategy was proposed, including protection and conservation measures related to beach pollution, forest conservation and utilization, national parks, scenic and recreational resources, environmentally critical areas, historic structures, water catchments, fisheries, and wildlife (GOCD, 1976, p. 105).

Although rejecting the tourism development recommendations of the Shankland Cox report, the Government did adopt many of its organizational recommendations. For example, the Development Corporation was put in charge of physical planning and development of tourism projects and the Tourist Board was given responsibility for marketing (GOCD, 1976, p. 41).

None of the tourism development plans proposed in the 1976 Plan were subsequently implemented, largely due to the lack of finances and of tourist demand. However, the Plan did enshrine the concept of Dominica as a nature-oriented tourism destination.

Although the 1976 Plan was intended to be operative until 1990, significant changes in development policies and the availability of improved socioeconomic data from the 1981 census led to a revised National Structure Plan (GOCD, 1985) being prepared in 1985—but, again, not officially approved. The Plan continues the Government's commitment first to agriculture and then to fisheries, forestry, and manufacturing. Agriculture is still seen as the mainstay of the economy, although its share of GDP dropped from 40% in 1979 to 24% in 1983; nevertheless, agriculture "provides a living for more than 70% of the population" (GOCD, 1985, p. 29). Manufacturing is viewed as "increasingly becoming an important sector of the economy" (GOCD, 1985, p. 30), accounting for 7.5% of GDP in 1983, compared to 4.7% in 1979. Tourism is predicted to remain a minor force (GOCD, 1985, p. 31). Like the earlier Plan, this document clearly states a policy of tying tourism to the natural environment, but links it more strongly to other sectors of the economy: "Tourism will be developed on the basis of the country's natural and historical assets such as rivers, mountains, forests, lakes and . . . [a] high level of linkage will be encouraged between tourism and other sectors" (GOCD, 1985, p. 90).

Recognizing that the tourism development programs proposed in the 1976 Plan had not been implemented and that tourism facilities remain concentrated on the west coast while attractions are located throughout the country (e.g., Forest Reserve, National Park, Cabrits, Carib Territory), this Plan (GOCD, 1985, p. 126) endorses a general policy of dispersal of tourism facilities and destination points. Access to many of these destinations being seen as a barrier, a program of road and hiking track construction is recommended, along with facility upgrading for beaches (e.g., washrooms, restaurants) in conjunction with the private sector. Several short-term developments are recommended: the restoration of Fort Shirley, feasibility studies for a cluster of 50-room hotels in the Cabrits area, a Carib Centre (also proposed in the 1976 Plan), and health spas at the Soufriere sulphur springs. In the longer term, major resorts are suggested for the Portsmouth Bay area. There are also proposals for marketing plans (including the targeting of the Caribbean market that, as described above, has been quite successful), licensing and quality control powers for the Tourist Board, and staff training for hotels and restaurants. Finally, improvements are suggested in LIAT's scheduling of connecting flights to avoid overnight stays at regional hubs and in the handling of trans-shipped baggage—problems that remain.

The Plan (GOCD, 1985, pp. 139–141), recognizing the "relatively fragile ecology" of the country, reiterates the strategic aims developed by the 1976 Plan for environmental conservation and protection. In particular, attention is directed at national park, watershed, and forestry planning. Environmental impact assessments (EIAs) are recommended for all development proposals and an Environmental Protection Unit is suggested (GOCD, 1985, p. 141). If the proposals had been implemented, the area devoted to "conservation" would have risen from 178 km^2 (22.4% of the land area of the country) to 357 km^2 (45.1%) by the year 2001. This would have resulted from increasing forest reserves from 92 to 145 km^2, national park units from 65 to 160 km^2, and water catchment areas from 2.1 to 5.2 km^2 (GOCD, 1985, p. 150).

The CCA (1991a, p. 172) notes that many of the Plan's recommendations were not implemented (e.g., those concerning EIA legislation, improvements in institutional capacity, an Environmental Protection Unit). However, some problems are recognized by the Government (e.g., lack of staff for enforcement, regulations requiring an EIA for all projects are in the draft stage) (R. Francis, 1991, personal communication).

Towards a Tourism Policy and Institutional Innovation

Whereas plans both realized (the National Park) and unrealized (the National Structure Plans) were signaling strong Government support for a form of tourism firmly rooted in the environment, there was still a tourism policy vacuum. The first major call for such a policy occurred in 1982, when the Dominica Tourist Board (1982) prepared a series of recommendations focused on five basic tenets:

- tourism developed in harmony with natural and historical attractions;

- upgrading of facilities;

- appropriate markets (e.g., bird-watchers, hikers, scuba divers);

- small to medium-sized hotels, under Dominican or joint ownership, constructed of local materials, and classified as to quality;

- linkages with the agricultural sector for the production of local produce, with education to increase public and tourist awareness and to train sector personnel, with industry to produce appropriate arts and crafts, and with cultural organizations to establish relationships between tourists and traditional cultural activities.

Although some of the points are still outstanding (e.g., education, arts and crafts), these policies continue to be echoed.

In a widely distributed document, the Government (GOCD, 1987)[15] clearly states its Tourism Policy to "provide the basic conditions necessary for lasting growth of tourism so as to optimize the sector's contribution to the national economy in terms of net value added" (p. 1). The benefits to Dominica of such development are seen as improved quality of life, increased employment, increased foreign exchange, improved balance of payments, enhanced cultural heritage, resource conservation and environmental protection, regional distribution of benefits, and revival of national arts and crafts.

Within this general framework and given the sector's current performance, the competition, and general economic conditions, the following specific objectives are stated:

- increased tourist arrivals, revenue, employment, and market share in existing and new (particularly upscale) markets;

- revived cruise ship and yachting arrivals;

- emphasis on occupancy rates, length of stay, repeat business, year-round tourism, ethnic tourism, and better value-for-money for customers by adjusting products to market demand;

- linkages with agriculture and related sectors;

- protection of natural resources (GOCD, 1987, pp. 1–2).

Several constraints on achieving these objectives are noted: price, standards, and organization of the tourism product; effectiveness of current marketing programs; inadequacy of financial and human resources and skills; lack of integrated teamwork by the public, private, and airline sectors; and weakness of trade and investment confidence in Dominican tourism. To meet the objectives and to overcome the constraints, a series of mechanisms, already supported by the World Bank (1985a), is proposed for the next 5 years:

- providing and upgrading infrastructure (e.g., roads, air links);

- establishing and enforcing standards (e.g., hotels, restaurants);

- developing a marketing strategy based on natural and cultural resources;

- identifying human and financial requirements (e.g., internal and external sources of finance, private/public sector training needs;

- encouraging both local and foreign private investment (GOCD, 1987, p. 3).

Using this policy as a directive, the Dominica Tourist Board (1987) states specific objectives—all of which were exceeded by 1991. A target of 67,000–72,000 foreign tourists—a doubling within 6 years—is set, consisting of 42,000–44,000 stay-over visitors, 19,000–21,000 cruise ship passengers, and 6,000–7,000 other excursionists (i.e., interisland excursionists, yacht passengers).

In a report to the Government, Giersch (1987) provides the basis for a marketing program to support these directions. Recognizing that Dominica's tourism potential is not typical of other Caribbean islands because of limited white-sand beaches, he proposes a tourism concept based on a combination of the natural (aimed at naturalist, hiker, mountain climber, photographer, and scuba diver markets), cultural (focused on the Caribs and Carnival), and historic (concentrated on Fort Shirley and the Cabrits area) environments, and on the exploration of development problems (e.g., agriculture).

A series of detailed actions—ranging from the development of facilities to the opening of banks and post offices on Saturday to a set of possible tour programs—is proposed which, it is suggested, if implemented would mean that the existing accommodation facilities could accommodate up to 44,000 stay-over visitors per year at higher occupancy rates. (This target of 44,000 stay-over visitors was indeed achieved by 1990.) Giersch (1987, pp. 14–38) concludes that major changes are needed in marketing: increased budget, more research, greater availability of information materials for tourists, more emphasis on the Caribbean market, the development of a strategy for day visitors, the improvement of smaller facilities. Some of his recommendations have been implemented, including training programs, upgrading sites, and participation in foreign trade shows.

Giersch's report remains the basis of the country's marketing focus—a focus that must be judged a success given the increase in tourist and cruise ship arrivals (although problems in the latter are noted above) since it was formulated. Much of this increase is related to Government attempts to increase the range of tourist attractions including historic resources and infrastructure needed to encourage cruise ships through the development of Cabrits National Park.

Restoration of the British Fort Shirley was outlined originally in a 1984 report for CCA (Eastern Caribbean Natural Area Management Programme [ECNAMP], 1984) and financed by funds from CIDA and Geest Industries (L. Honychurch, 1992, personal communication). A second national park, Cabrits National Park, was established in 1986, focusing on the 100 hectares of historical ruins of the fort, nestled in dry woodlands adjacent to a wetland area on the Cabrits peninsula, and 430 hectares of marine park (Dominica Port Authority, 1989). The development is apparently unique: cruiseship tourists walk straight off a ship, proceed through customs and immigration formalities, visit an interpretive center and shops, and then walk directly to the fort. There is also the potential for recreational use of an adjacent underwater area. The spread of the economic impact into nearby Portsmouth, however, will require major upgrading of local services, particularly roads (L. Honychurch, 1991, personal communication). There are, nevertheless, concerns that the influx of large numbers of tourists visiting the area will create a "shock loading" effect and cause social disruption (F. Gregoire, 1989, personal communication). Honychurch's (1991) description of Portsmouth highlights the potential for negative "host–guest" relations: "This is very much a seaport town of schooner hands, captains of tramp steamers, hucksters and street-wise youth, and therefore has a jaunty, buccaneering air about it" (p. 76).

The Government also seemed to recognize that an improved administrative structure was needed to implement its tourism policy. Therefore, as a result of the National Development Corporation Act of 1988, the institutional arrangements for public sector activities in tourism underwent a radical change with the Dominica Tourist Board being merged with the Industrial Development Corporation (IDC) into a single National Development Corporation (NDC) comprising two divisions, one for industry and one for tourism. Such an arrangement is rare, with few, if any, equivalents elsewhere (World Bank, 1990, p. 67). The NDC is responsible for development planning, with the Physical Planning Department using the Town and Country Planning Act to approve individual development plans; this legislation provides a great deal of leeway to blocking development on environmental, structural, or design grounds (I. Baptiste, 1989, personal communication).

The Tourism Division has functions similar to any other national tourist organization: market promotion, supervision of operational standards, liaison with airlines and shipping, training, hotel classification, and improvement and collection of tourism statistics. Through the NDC's unusual structure, however, it is linked with the Industry Division for the purpose of investment promotion and evaluation of investment proposals. Project evaluation is particularly necessary because approvals are required in the granting of fiscal incentives under the Hotel Aids Ordinance. Although all hotel projects are exempt from customs duties on materials and equipment required for the investment, only approved hotel projects of 10 or more rooms benefit from a 10-year income tax holiday for a new establishment and pro rata for extensions to existing establishments. There are no tax concessions for renovations and refurbishments. The range of tourism investment subsidies includes assistance with project financing, tax holiday, investment and other tax credits, double tax relief, and infrastructure aid (Arthur Young Ltd., 1988) and customs exemption on scuba and snorkeling equipment and on power boats, as an incentive to the growing underwater sports market (World Bank, 1990, p. 68).

Since the formation of the NDC, however, no new hotel construction has actually been started. Several hotel projects have been proposed, including a 100-room hotel/condominium and marina development with an adjacent industrial park south of Portsmouth being proposed by British-owned Guinness Management (R. Francis, 1991, personal communication) and a 50-bed hotel and a marina near Portsmouth (Tourism Planning and Research Associates, 1991).

Ecotourism

> *The Uncut Emerald of the Caribbean.*
> *The Nature Island of the Caribbean.*
> (Tourism advertising slogans for Dominica)

Despite many continuing problems, local interest in environmental concerns appears to be increasing. Examples include the institution of the second national park,[16] the rejuvenation of the private sector Dominica Conservation Association in 1990, and the designation of the years 1989–1990 as the "Years of the Environment and Shelter (YES)" by then Prime Minister Mary Eugenia Charles, along with the establishment of a broadly based public and private sector committee to provide institutional support for YES activities (CCA, 1991a, p. 182). This increasing environmental concern has grown in parallel with the official Government tourism marketing policy of nature tourism and the worldwide interest in "ecotourism." Indeed, Weaver (1991, 1993) concludes that Dominica is the Caribbean destination most closely associated with comprehensive ecotourism and that it has developed a "deliberate" form of ecotourism based on conscious policy direction, as opposed to other destinations with "circumstantial" ecotourism, or the mere appearance of alternative tourism in the exploitation phase of development.

Although still extremely small in relative terms compared to mass tourism, ecotourism represents the fastest growing international tourist market segment. This trend is reflected in the expanding literature on the subject (e.g., Boo, 1990a, 1990b; Lindberg, 1991; McNeeley & Thorsell, 1988; Thorsell, 1990). In fact, some of this literature has focused partly on Dominica, with the island being one of Boo's case studies. There is also a growing interest in ecotourism in the travel and tourism press. For example, quoting the Smithsonian Institution's description of Dominica as "a giant plant laboratory, unchanged for 10,000 years" and the United Nations Food and Agriculture Organization's statement that "The island of Dominica has the greatest expanse of undisturbed tropical rain forest remaining in the Caribbean," Okey (1987, p. 8) presents a glowing picture of Dominica's ecotourism potential in a major international travel magazine. Similarly, in 1991, *Skin Diver* magazine labeled Dominica as the best scuba diving island in the Eastern Caribbean (Gleason, 1991).

As support for such a nature-based tourism policy, a study by the Organization of American States (OAS) (Lynn, 1990) concludes that, in general, tourists expressed overall satisfaction with the Dominican tourism product, especially its "nature" aspects. Similarly, the CCA (1991a, pp. 136–137) strongly endorses nature-based tourism as the only viable route to tourism development, but issues warnings about competition from within the region, the need for marketing, and environmental protection. These concerns are backed by Boo (1990a), who identifies four major obstacles to the growth of nature tourism in Dominica: funding for park maintenance, tourism infrastructure in the Morne Trois Pitons National park, trained guides, and international promotion of tourism. She also points out that it is difficult to calculate the exact economic contribution of nature tourism, partly because of the lack of adequate statistics on current levels of use.

An even more fundamental point, however, is the total lack of reliable information about the size and nature of the international ecotourism market. The research that has been done to date is based on exit surveys and not market research (i.e., the respondents are existing customers and not potential customers).[17] The problem is compounded by the growing number of countries that have both established (e.g., Costa Rica) and proposed (e.g., Montserrat [Reynolds, 1992]) ecotourism focuses. There are two seemingly simple, but unaddressed, questions: how big is the international ecotourism market pie? and into how many slices of what size can the pie be cut? Research on these questions is fundamentally important, lest too many destinations (particularly small developing countries with little financial room for mistakes, such as Dominica)—to mix metaphors—put all their eggs into too small a basket.

Although not addressing these questions directly, the Government accepted the EEC-funded 1991–1994 Dominica Tourism Sector Plan (Tourism Planning and Research Associates, 1991), which clearly designates the basic framework of its tourism policy: a focus on the "nature island" image (although the plan argues that there is a greater potential for traditional beach-based tourism than has been generally acknowledged), small-scale developments, integration with the rural community, strong economic linkages to other sectors, orientation on conservation, and tourism at a level within the "absorptive capacity" of the island.

Reinforcing this policy, the Plan suggests that tourism planning in the medium term should be directed to:

• creating a dispersed high-quality pattern of tourism activity focusing on small hotels using local materials and products;

• targeting a broad mix of both regional and international tourists;

• using tourism to encourage environmental and cultural conservation;

• maintaining future tourism development in scale with the human and other resources available to service the sector;

• raising standards of all aspects of the sector.

It also details an urgent need for detailed physical and land-use planning, so that both the short-term and longer term needs of the tourism sector are met, noting that "the principal beneficiary of such planning would be the people of Dominica, whose physical and cultural heritage is currently under considerable pressure" (Tourism Planning and Research Associates, 1991, p. 2). Given the current low level of tourism, however, it is unclear in this Plan to what extent this "pressure" is caused by tourism, as opposed to such factors as increased levels of education, economic uncertainty, and modern communications systems (e.g., television, films).

The Plan proposes several action programs: improved government tourism structure related to public awareness, education, training, product development, marketing, sales, and promotion; cruise ship management for Cabrits National Park; better information for tourists; accommodation upgrading and development; and conservation of natural, historical, cultural, and tourism resources. The report concludes that a reasonably attainable target for stay-over tourist arrivals in 1994 would be 60,000. Despite minor disagreement on details, this plan appears to have met with general approval and is being implemented.

There are, however, concerns about the ability of Dominica to compete with other destinations (because of the lack of white-sand beaches) and about the potential negative impacts of tourism on cultural, social, and moral values (Anonymous, 1989a, p. 12). In recognition of increasing environmental consciousness throughout the world and of Dominica's unique natural features, the Government's policy of nature-based tourism has gathered considerable support. Another form of diversification would be increased emphasis on historical tourism, particularly the further development of fortress ruins at Cabrits National Park (Arthur Young Ltd., 1989b; Christian, 1989; James, 1985).

Such an increased emphasis on nature and historical tourism—when coupled with projections of relatively large increases in tourists and cruise passengers—is not without potential problems.

First, Dominica is a complex mix of the most fragile of natural environments: a small tropical island, coral reefs, and tropical forests—all of which provide a wide array of attractive tourist resources. Increased use of such resources will, however, inevitably result in some level of environmental destruction, through both development (e.g., construction of access roads and trails) and use (e.g., trampling of vegetation, destruction of trails).

Second, no matter how interested in seeing natural or historical features, most visitors are not likely to travel far off the beaten path, let alone far from the tour bus parking lot, particularly in a steep, harsh, hot, humid environment. This is an almost universal phenomenon of tourist behavior and there is no reason to suspect that Dominica will be able to avoid it. Most visitors will limit their activities to the more easily accessible sites, resulting in the spatial concentration of serious impacts on, for example, the Emerald Pool, a small, fragile waterfall just a few minutes' walk from the main road.

Third is the problem of temporal concentration, relating to the "shock loading" effect of large numbers of visitors descending on a small number of relatively fragile sites for very short time periods.

These problems combine to form a "worst-case scenario." As the literature on visitor impacts clearly demonstrates, the most serious negative impacts on fragile natural environments are related to the initial use of the site (and do not increase significantly with the length of time that a visitor spends at the site), increasing numbers of users, and spatial concentrations of use (Graefe, Kuss, & Vaske, 1990a, 1990b). Minimization of these impacts will require careful planning, training of guides and tour operators, and site preparation and management—all of which will require increased levels of Government support in the form of both financial resources and personnel.

Conclusion

Since the Government quickly and wisely rejected the Shankland Cox report's call for mass tourism, Dominica's approach to tourism policy has been relatively successful. There has been slow but steady growth in numbers of tourists and tourist expenditure (with the exception of downturns caused by political problems in the 1970s and by hurricane damage in 1979 and 1980). Such success is a result of a realistic and pragmatic recognition of the country's lack of suitability for mass tourism (largely related to the absence of white-sand beaches and an international airport) and its potential to attract a small but growing number of tourists who mainly are interested in its natural environment.[18] And that success has been fueled by a marketing program that, while relatively low key and modest in scale, presents a clear and honest picture to the potential market niche.

On the other hand, occupancy rates appear to be generally very low—but that is a complex problem requiring action simultaneously on a number of fronts: expanded marketing, upgrading of facilities, and improved air access (in terms of the number of flights and routes, but not necessarily of an international airport).

In the area of tourism planning (in the sense of planning as a deliberate intervention that results in the carrying out of a program of action), Dominica has not been as successful as on the policy front. There are notable exceptions, particularly in terms of the two national parks, but their exceptionality lies mainly in their potential, which will require careful management and substantial improvements in related infrastructure to become major tourism magnets and to avoid serious environmental degradation—the universal problem of use vs. preservation of fragile natural environments. Land-use and site development planning do exist with respect to particular hotel development proposals, but that is a reactive process and not one of deliberate government involvement in development (e.g., the often-proposed Carib Centre). (Again, the Cabrits cruise ship project is an exception, but it appears to be having problems.)

It is difficult, however, to criticize the Government for taking such an approach given its emphasis on agriculture as the backbone of the economy and given its financial position. Nevertheless, economic diversification is the goal of the Government and, because of the internal and external problems with agriculture and manufacturing, tourism appears to be the only viable economic alternative—the opinion of the World Bank notwithstanding. The question, however, of who would fund increased tourism development (on the assumption that the Government cannot afford to do so) remains. It is Government policy—a wise and realistic policy—to encourage small-scale development and local participation, yet local capital and expertise are limited. Moreover, involvement from foreign investors on anything beyond a modest scale is unlikely without a major improvement in access. Finally, international aid agencies are not interested in the tourism sector and, apparently, in international airport construction, despite the long history of such aid in the Caribbean until recently.

It appears reasonable that the Government should continue its current realistic and pragmatic policy, which fosters steady but incremental growth in tourist numbers and expenditures through improved and targeted marketing focused on the island's environment, coupled with improved services (e.g., roads, information, tour guides) and upgraded accommodations. Moreover, if a marketing goal is to attract more tourists from the upper end of the market, then greater attention has to be given to the quality of existing and new accommodations, in terms of location, design, and services, largely through the strengthening of the planning process.

Notes

[1]A much smaller population of Caribs can be found in St. Vincent, but it does not have its own territory.

[2]An estimated additional 80,000 Dominicans live in Great Britain, the United States, and Canada (L. Honychurch, 1989, personal communication).

[3]The name was selected to avoid confusion with the Dominican Republic. The fact that the problem still exists is highlighted by the chapter in Honychurch (1991) titled "We Are Not the Dominican Republic!".

[4]A note is in order on the tourism statistics presented here. No single source, whether published by governments, tourist boards, or other organizations (e.g., CDB, CIA, CTO, CTRC, World Bank), presents complete and consistent longitudinal data for any of the case studies or the Caribbean as a whole. The problem is compounded by the fact that many statistics provided (e.g., growth rates, rankings) were calculated by the author using data from a large number of sources. On the assumptions that most readers are not concerned with specific sources for each and every statistic and that the provision of all references in the text would unnecessarily overwhelm most readers, only those references that are considered particularly important or unusual are provided. The author will respond to requests for specific references. A single table of longitudinal data for major variables is provided for each case study (e.g., Table 4.1 for Dominica).

[5]Lowenthal (1992, p. 24), however, notes that bananas serve as a deterrent to diversification through alternative commodities, for unless a set minimum of bananas is produced each quarter, the island will be dropped from Geest's tightly scheduled refrigerated ship runs.

[6]The latter is a contention with which a frequent flyer to Dominica might disagree.

[7]As a measure of the density of tourism development, the number of rooms/km^2 does not take into account the tendency for Caribbean hotels to be spatially concentrated along beaches and near ports, with few in the interior of islands. Moreover, development is frequently concentrated on a small number of islands in the case of an archipelago (e.g., New Providence and Grand Bahama in the Bahamas). In that sense, it suffers from the same problem as the number of rooms per 1,000 local population, in that the spatial distribution of the local population may not coincide with that of hotels. Nevertheless, these and other measures have utility as relative and longitudinal measures of change.

[8]Although definitions of *ecotourism* vary greatly (including, when commandeered by big business, "environmental opportunism" or "eco-exploitation" [Wight, 1993]), Hawkins (1994) defines it as "purposeful travel to natural areas to understand the cultural and natural history of the environment, taking care not to alter the integrity of the ecosystem, while producing economic opportunities that make the conservation of natural resources financially beneficial to local citizens" (p. 261). The Island Resources Foundation [IRF] and Anguilla Archaeological and Historical Society [AAHS] (1993) defines ecotourism as "an environmentally-focused visitor experience that has educational benefits for the tourist and economic benefits for the host community. It engenders local participation in *managing*

the resource which should suffer no damage or loss; in fact, the resource should be enhanced by the management process. In this regard, ecotourism is more than a new name for nature tourism (simply an observational focus on nature) and should not be confused with it'' (p. 108).

[9]Bryden (1973, p. 162) suggests a multiplier of 1.195 for Dominica, a figure that is very similar to Archer's (1982) 1.20—the highest figure for 10 island countries that the latter describes worldwide. There is, however, little empirical evidence to support such figures.

[10]The terms physical planning, land-use planning, and town and country planning are used almost interchangeably in the Commonwealth Caribbean (CCA, 1991a, p. 165).

[11]This Act, as in other Eastern Caribbean countries, was formulated in the 1970s as the basis for planning and development control with the assistance of a UNDP-sponsored, region-wide Physical Planning Project (CCA, 1991a, p. 182) and is based on the British act of the same name.

[12]This was followed by an unusual and convoluted caveat: "This is admittedly a rather arbitrary figure, but is not excessively optimist. Long term forecasts of this nature must, in any case, be viewed with caution, particularly in the tourist field'' (Shankland Cox, 1971b, p. 7).

[13]Gilles (1980), however, gives a figure of 13,000 for 1970.

[14]The Northern Forest Reserve is actually larger (88 km^2) and the protection afforded it is similar to that of the Morne Trois Pitons National Park. The Forest Reserve may have a higher diversity and contains richer and better forests (CCA, 1991a, p. 45).

[15]Much of the marketing ideas in this document are based on an earlier study by Tromson Monroe Advertising (1979).

[16]In 1990, The Division of Forestry and Wildlife proposed a third national park, encompassing a 25-km^2 forested area along the western slopes of Morne Diablotin in the Northern Forest Reserve (or 28% of the Reserve's total area), as well as an 82.5-hectare area that has been proposed as a parrot reserve (CCA, 1991a, p. 45). A draft management plan for the park was developed (F. Gregoire, 1991, personal communication), but not implemented.

[17]J. Hepple (1992, personal communication) argues that the lack of information about markets is a common problem in the planning process of all countries in the Caribbean region.

[18]Weaver (1991, 1992), in contrast to Oppermann and Sahr's (1992) argument that conventional mass tourism is inevitable for every destination, including Dominica, argues that the scale of tourism in Dominica is so small that even a policy to double accommodation cannot be seen as a policy toward mass tourism.

Chapter 5

St. Lucia

The global and regional trends indicate that . . . [St. Lucia] will become even more affected by events external to it in the 21st Century. (Venner, 1989, p. 83)

Introduction

Located in a central position in the Windward Islands, St. Lucia has an area of 616 km^2 and maximum dimensions of 42×22 km (see Map 5.1). With a maximum elevation of 950 meters above sea level at Mt. Gimie, it is a mountainous island of volcanic origin; there are thermal springs of confirmed geothermal potential of 10 kW at Soufriere, but exploration of the feasibility of tapping them has been long and costly. There is little flat land: only about 10% of the island has slopes of less than 5%, and only 2.6% of the land is Agricultural Land Capability Class I (M. C. Williams, 1983, p. 110) and only 3.1% is Classes II–IV (Organization of American States [OAS], 1987b, p. 9).[1] The climate is tropical marine, with vegetation ranging from Mediterranean to rain forest, depending on orientation, topography, and the steep precipitation gradient (1500–3500 mm). Deforestation, caused by cutting for firewood and charcoal and by expansion of agricultural land, is a serious problem (Wilkinson, 1987a). The only known mineral resource is a vast untapped source of talc.

St. Lucia was first occupied by the Ciboney in approximately 500 BC, followed by the Arawaks who had become firmly established on the island by about 200 AD. They in turn were invaded by Caribs around 1000 AD; within 200 years, the Arawaks had been totally taken over by the Caribs (CCA, 1991b; Devaux, 1975, 1984, 1987). The Carib name for the island was *Iouanalao* (thought to mean "there where the iguana is found"); the pronunciation has eventually evolved into *Hewanorra* (the present name of St. Lucia's international airport). The first European explorer to see St. Lucia may have been Juan de la Cosa, Columbus' mapmaker, who sailed through the southeastern Caribbean in 1499 and included an island called "The Falcon" on a map a year later; or Columbus' lookout may have seen the island in June 1502 when the Admiral's fleet put into nearby Martinique. It is not known which Spaniard gave the island the name of Santa Lucia; the name was later changed to Ste Lucie by the French and to St. Lucia by the English.

St. Lucia Channel

Pigeon Island National Park

Gros Islet

Atlantic Ocean

Rodney
Bay

Vigie Airport

Castries

O Roseau

Anse la Raye

Canaries

Dennery

Mt. Gimie

Soufriere

Petit Piton

Grand Piton

Micoud

Anse L'Ivrogne

Choiseul

Laborie

Hewannora Airport

Vieux Fort

N

0   5
km

St. Vincent Channel

Map 5.1. St. Lucia.

The first attempt at European settlement occurred in 1605 when 67 Englishmen
bound for Guiana put into the Vieux Fort area because of a food shortage on
board; most were killed by the Caribs. A similar fate awaited a formal attempt at
settlement in 1639 by an English planter from St. Kitts. Later English attempts
were more successful, with the Caribs eventually being defeated in 1663. Mean-
while, the French also laid claim to the island, through a grant of territory to the
newly formed French Company of the Isles of the Americas. The result was 200
years of turbulent history, with the island changing hands between France and England 14 times prior to 1803, when England retained eventual control; St. Lucia
was formally ceded to Britain with the 1814 Treaty of Paris.

In addition to being an important naval base, the island had a plantation industry
focused on indigo, coffee, tobacco, and cassava, using slaves originating in Africa.
Because of the continuing warfare, sugar cane did not emerge as the primary cash

crop until the beginning of the 19th century when it soon came to dominate the economy. With Britain abolishing slavery in 1834 and emancipation being secured in 1838, approximately 13,300 former slaves were freed. Attempts were made to find new cash crops (e.g., coconut plantations were first established in the 1870s). A major form of economic diversification came with the construction of new shipping wharves in Castries' fine natural harbor, which resulted in it becoming a major coaling station for the region. Between 1880 and 1930 (when oil replaced coal as a fuel for ships), more than 1,000 steamships per year called at the coal-bunkering station. Triggered by a strike of coal carriers in 1907, the early part of the century was characterized by labor unrest, as was the Depression when a strike of sugar workers in 1937 led to reformist labor legislation. The first half of the century saw some further agricultural diversification, including sea-island cotton, bananas, and limes, but sugar remained dominant until 1956.

Although English is the official language and the Government follows the Westminster parliamentary tradition, the population is mainly Black and Roman Catholic, with a French-based patois (*Kwéyol*) as an important language (unwritten, until recently) and a land-tenure system based on the Code Napoléon—a result of the fact that the island was primarily occupied by the French prior to 1803, with English occupation being limited to five short interludes totaling less than 12 years. A strong sense of local tradition and culture exists. A British possession until 1967, when it was granted associated statehood, St. Lucia achieved complete independence in 1979. It is governed by a Governor-General appointed by the British Crown, an elected legislative assembly, and an appointed Senate, with a legal and legislative system based on that of Britain.

With a population of approximately 142,000, St. Lucia is extremely densely settled: 230 persons per km^2 in total or 3,944 per km^2 of arable land (Agricultural Land Capability Classes I–IV). The population is almost equally divided between urban and rural areas, with the pattern of distribution being characterized by a drift toward the capital city, Castries (population 40,000) and its environs.

The Economy

Venner (1989) notes that the economic history of St. Lucia is marked by dependence on a series of singular activities, particularly cane sugar, military outpost, the Port of Castries as a coaling station, United States military base in World War II, and bananas: "It is only in very recent times that more than one economic sector has played a significant role in the economy at the same time" (p. 80). Currently, compared to many Windward and Leeward Islands, St. Lucia has a relatively diversified economy: export agriculture (mainly bananas), tourism, and manufacturing for the regional market. Nevertheless, although the GDP per capita (US$3,100 in 1993) is higher than many other developing countries, it is one of the lowest in the Caribbean region.

This diverse economy, and its ongoing strengths and weaknesses, can be related to the argument that St. Lucia has seen four major economic revolutions in the last half-century. First, the British/American Lend-Lease Program in World War II saw the construction of a seaplane base north of Castries and a major air base at what is now Hewanorra Airport near Vieux Fort, the second largest town. The result was new-found—if temporary—prosperity resulting from employment in construction and service industries. There also was significant cultural change (e.g., the war-related decline in sugar exports led to a decrease in the agricultural work force and a shift to the towns). The expanding urban population and the growing cash economy resulted in modest beginnings for locally based manufacturing, particularly for consumer goods. The existence of an airport capable of being relatively easily upgraded to international standards just as jet charters became a factor also provided the opportunity for a very fast entry into the mass tourist market.

Second, the island was just emerging from a postwar economic depression when the world sugar cane market collapsed in 1956. Within a year, St. Lucia's sugar cane was almost totally replaced by bananas—one export monocrop succeeding another. By 1964, bananas accounted for 85% of the value of St. Lucia's exports (Persaud, 1966).[2] The recovery was significant, particularly as British-based Geest Industries developed a virtual monopoly over banana exports in the British Windward Islands and guaranteed entry to a single market, Great Britain. In the long run, however, this left the industry vulnerable to changes in EEC tariff policies after 1993. Also, the altered nature of agricultural production resulted in the need for fewer agricultural workers (although workers had greater access to cash payments for their crops) and increased rural–urban migration.

The third revolution was the tourist "boom," which began in the mid-1960s, a change that was to affect all sectors of St. Lucian society.

Just as tourism was becoming a central feature in the economy, the fourth revolution was initiated by the "energy crisis" in 1973, which resulted in disruption of all sectors of the economy, rapid inflation, and a growing balance of payments problem. Up to that point, largely because of the growth of tourism and the strength of the banana industry, the economy had enjoyed rapid expansion during the 1960s and early 1970s when GDP growth averaged over 7% per annum and inflation was relatively low. Despite the world economic recession that began in the mid-1970s and concomitant declines in national agricultural production, the economy soon began to experience satisfactory growth, in part because of the rebounding of the tourism sector.

In 1979, however, growth was again curtailed by world recession, rapid inflation, rising energy costs, and closing of several industries. Unemployment was officially 20% by 1980 (Dann, 1992), but unofficially much higher. The problem was exacerbated by Hurricane Allen in August 1980, which severely damaged several hotels, some of which were not fully operational for over a year. It also destroyed the banana crop, resulting in no banana exports until February 1981. Despite the serious curtailment of foreign income for nearly a year, the energy import bill continued to rise. There were delays in shipments of gasoline, diesel fuel, and propane, causing gasoline shortages, electricity outages, and cold water in hotels—and increased deforestation resulting from increased local demand for wood and charcoal, as petroleum-based energy prices rose (Wilkinson, 1984).

After several years, banana production began to increase because of relatively high world prices, with receipts of US$65.6 million in 1988 on a production of 136,000 tonnes (an increase of 47% over 1987). The future of the banana industry, however, remains unclear even after the 1993 changes in EEC policy and possible exposure to lower cost competition; therefore, agricultural diversification is important (CDB, 1989c, p. 5). It is not clear, however, what crops can foster diversification on the scale that is needed. Coconut production, for example, was adversely affected by the loss of traditional markets (e.g., Guyana, Trinidad and Tobago). Breadfruit and mangoes are the other main exports, but by 1988 demand for these and other produce exports (e.g., hot peppers, plantain, sweet potato, sour sop, paw paw [papaya]) exceeded volume shipped. The major problems are: insufficient air cargo space and lack of established sea linkages to the United Kingdom, Canada (the two main markets, with 73% and 14% of the agricultural export market, respectively), and the United States; quality and quantity of produce; and shortage of corrugated packaging material (Government of St. Lucia [GOSL], 1988, p. 7).

It is not surprising, particularly given the expansion of tourism, that construction is a growing activity in St. Lucia, with major projects for hotels, commercial projects, housing, capital works, and industrial estates.

Government and private sector attempts to attract more manufacturing have, however, met with little success. Some 230 companies employed approximately 6,000 persons in 1990 (over half were employed in the apparel and textile industry, with electronics also being important), but growth has been very slow since 1984 (GOSL, 1990, p. 25). Manufacturing accounts for only 8% of GDP (World Bank, 1990, p. 90), a figure that has remained roughly constant since 1980 (CDB, 1989c, p. 6; GOSL, 1990, pp. 151–152). Despite some improvement through intraregional trade, growth in manufacturing has been hindered by the relatively high costs of production, limited access to regional and international markets, limited pools of managerial and entrepreneurial skills, difficulties in gaining access to domestic credit, small size of domestic market, high cost of imported inputs, and relatively high wage levels.

Venner (1989) argues that "while there has been growth and modernisation, the all round development of the economy has lagged as it is still structurally unbalanced and not capable of self sustaining growth. To put it in the jargon of the economist it is open, vulnerable and dependent" (p. 81). One of the most serious indicators of these characteristics is the estimated annual balance of payments deficit on visible trade (US$105 million in 1988, US$100.8 million in 1989, and US$144.4 million in 1990 [CDB, 1989c; CTO, 1990; GOSL, 1991]). This deficit is largely related to energy imports and the fact that the Eastern Caribbean currency is tied to the United States dollar, as is the cost of most imports, whereas revenues from bananas are tied to the Pound Sterling (GOSL, 1990). When all trade (including the "invisible" exports related to tourism) is included, the current account balance of payments situation is much more positive; indeed, in this sense St. Lucia is among the better managed economies in the region.

Despite these problems, the national economy had a real growth of 4–5% per annum since the late 1980s, largely because of the strong performances of agriculture, tourism, and construction. However, a growth of 7% is needed to absorb increases in the labor force of 2,000 per annum and to deal with unemployment, which is currently estimated to exceed 20% (CDB, 1989c, p. 5), although the official rate is 5% (see Table 5.1). This level of unemployment is a result of the high rate of population growth (2%), low rate of job creation, and fast turnover of school-leavers. The majority of unemployed are unskilled workers and women whose labor force participation has increased in recent years. Moreover, the unemployment problem could accelerate if agricultural workers are eventually displaced by EEC policy changes.

Other infrastructure problems exist, largely related to the Government's financial problems. For example, the road system (which once could be described as one of the best among the smaller Caribbean islands [Peters, 1980, p. 18]) is in a serious state of disrepair, as a result of the lack of continuing foreign aid support for road maintenance; indeed, Dann (1992) describes road transportation as being the main handicap to St. Lucia's tourism development. In 1990, a program of road improvements began, supported by British aid and CDB loan funds; however, it seems to be a case of "one step forward, two steps backward," with, for example, a severe tropical storm in August 1994 destroying many of these improvements. The decline in the agricultural sector and the high proportion of food that is imported are also serious economic concerns. As Latimer (1985, p. 33) argues, however, the problems in agriculture and food production in developing island nations are related to a complex set of economic and social factors, including falling world prices for export crops (e.g., bananas, sugar, copra) and changing tastes in local food consumption.

Although not free of problems (e.g., difficulties in the airline industry), "Tourism is the fastest growing sector in St. Lucia and the second largest contributor to the economy [after agriculture]" (CDB, 1989c, p. 7). There is even evidence to suggest that tourism is now St. Lucia's prime export earner, with the contribution to GDP of estimated visitor expenditures having risen from 32.1% in 1980 to 52.9% in 1992.

The Government has given highest priority to the expansion of the tourism sector as a strategy for reducing unemployment, a policy that is reflected in its recently increasing encouragement of tourism-related activities. The CDB (1989c, pp. 6–8), however, argues for a more broadly based policy (1) to promote industries with opportunities for self-employment, partly through skills training, and (2) to diversify agriculture, increase efficiency in banana production, stimulate private sector investment, and improve the competitiveness of the manufacturing sector. These concerns seem to be clearly recognized by Government, particularly in light of the fact that 65.2% of the projected capital expenditure budget in 1988–89 was dependent on foreign or overseas sources.

Saint Lucia cannot expect its existence to be subsidized by the international community and to this end a clear focus of its development strategy must be

Table 5.1. St. Lucia: Tourism Statistics

Year	Stay-Over Tourists No. (000s)	% Annual Change	Excursionists No. (000s)	% Annual Change	Cruise Passengers No. (000s)	% Annual Change	Total Tourists No. (000s)	% Annual Change	Visitor Expenditure US$ (M)	% Annual Change	Tourist Rooms No.	Av. LOS (No. Nights)	No. Tourist Nights/Yr (000s)
1980	79.7	-9.3	2.1	0.0	59.0	NA	140.8	NA	32.9	-8.4	1245	10.0	797.0
1981	68.6	-13.9	2.1	0.0	18.9	-68.0	89.6	-36.4	29.4	-10.4	1384	8.5	583.1
1982	71.5	4.2	2.1	0.0	33.8	78.8	107.4	19.9	32.4	10.2	1384	8.5	607.8
1983	77.4	8.3	1.9	9.5	33.3	-1.5	112.6	4.8	39.7	22.5	1442	10.2	789.5
1984	87.3	12.8	2.6	36.8	37.2	11.7	127.1	12.9	68.4[a]	72.3	1705	10.4	907.9
1985	94.5	8.2	2.1	19.3	55.0	65.2	151.6	19.3	90.0	31.6	1735	10.0	845.0
1986	111.7	18.2	3.8	81.0	58.8	6.9	174.3	15.0	118.0	31.1	2003	10.4	1161.7
1987	117.6	5.3	7.8	105.3	83.8	42.5	209.2	20.0	126.2	6.9	1748	12.8	1505.3
1988	133.0	13.1	9.5	21.8	79.5	-5.1	222.0	6.1	134.2	6.3	2149	11.6	1542.8
1989	132.8	-0.2	5.6	41.1	104.3	31.2	242.7	9.3	144.6	7.7	2204	11.6	1540.5
1990	138.4	4.2	7.7	37.5	101.9	-2.3	248.0	2.2	153.8	6.4	2370	10.7	1480.9
1991	159.0	14.9	7.0	-9.1	152.8	50.0	318.8	28.5	173.4	12.7	2464	10.8	1717.2
1992	177.5	11.6	6.5	-7.1	164.9	7.9	248.9	9.4	207.9	19.9	2659	10.7	1899.3
1993	194.1	9.4	6.5	0.0	154.4	-6.4	355.1	1.8	221.0	6.3	2919	10.6	2057.5

NA: not available.
[a]Estimated.

to modernize its economy, to make its economic sectors competitive and productive, to become effective in the management of its affairs and to build an
environment which is conducive to the investment of development capital in
key income and employment generating enterprises. (d'Auvergne, 1989, pp.
17–18)

There is also recognition that the lack of capital and resources within the private
sector means that dramatic economic growth will not come quickly and that
changes are necessary within government, in terms of restructuring and increased
efficiency (Elliott, 1988, p. 14).

The Government's current national economic strategy is contained in its Medium
Term Economic Strategy (1993–1996), which has the following objectives: (i)
broad-based economic growth; (ii) strengthened public finance; (iii) improved standard of living through continued good economic management, with emphasis on
human resource development; (iv) increased productivity and domestic savings;
and (v) environmental protection to safeguard the tourism base (GOSL, 1994, p.
1). This suggests the Government's ongoing commitment to the development of
the tourism sector as the leading force in the economy.

The Tourism Sector

The Government has had a long-standing interest in promoting tourism as a means
of diversifying St. Lucia's economy beyond its agricultural (and, to a much lesser
extent, industrial) base. With some exceptions, its attitude has been a "hands-off"
approach, which has welcomed increased foreign investment in the tourism sector, resulting in its steady growth. As a result, St. Lucia represents a mid-Stage II
(Transition) destination, characterized by rapid change, foreign investment and
control, large-scale hotels (particularly all-inclusives), tax incentives, and significant cruise ship activity.

The Beginnings

St. Lucia offers an attractive tourism product: "good climate and beaches, lush
tropical landscape and arresting mountain and sea views, outstanding yacht cruis-
ing, inexpensive arts and crafts, and warm, welcoming people" (Spinrad, 1982,
pp. 70–71). Interest in tourism had surfaced immediately after World War II, as indicated by the formation of the St. Lucia Tourist Board (SLTB) (now a statutory
arm of the Ministry of Tourism) in 1946. Whereas tourism emerged as "the lead
sector in the postwar restructuring of the St. Lucian economy" (CCA, 1991b, p.
211), the tourist sector did not really take off until the mid-1960s with the advent
of jet charter tours from the United States, Great Britain, Canada, and Western Europe (still the major sources of tourists). St. Lucia was well-poised to enter into
this tourism explosion because of the former American Air Force base at Vieux
Fort, which was easily transformed into an international airport. The presence of
the airport also allowed St. Lucia to become one of the first Eastern Caribbean tourism destinations to tap successfully the European market (Spinrad, 1982).

Related to both tourism and broader national economic development, international aid programs resulted in significant investment in housing and road (Great Britain), airport (Canada), and health services (United States). Encouraged by Government policy on favorable tax concessions for foreign investors, major investments in hotels were made by MNCs, notably Cunard Lines, Court Lines (both British), Holiday Inns International (Canadian), and Steigenberger AG (West German). In cooperation with major international tour operators (e.g., Kuoni, Thomson, Skylark, Paramount), several airlines began to operate regular (e.g., Eastern, British West Indies Airlines, British Airways, Air Canada) and charter (e.g., Wardair) flights into Hewanorra Airport. LIAT and several minor airlines use Castries' smaller Vigie Airport in Castries.

Stay-Over Tourist Arrivals

There were only 5,000 tourists in 1959 (CTA, 1960), a figure that rose to 30,000 in 1970 (Gilles, 1980); this dramatic growth saw annual increases exceeding 20% between 1961 and 1968 (Bryden, 1973). The number of tourists more than doubled between 1969 and 1974 to a peak figure of 51,816, but because of the "energy crisis" of 1973, the number of visitors dropped dramatically in 1975. This was caused mainly by the bankruptcy of the Court Lines in 1974 (then Britain's largest tour operator) as a result of several factors, including rising energy costs; the temporary closing of four hotels in St. Lucia affected more than one quarter of the island's hotel rooms (Britton, 1978, p. 180). These hotels, plus a Holiday Inn, were soon taken over by various combinations of foreign and Government support. Nevertheless, St. Lucia's performance in the 1970s ranked among the top third of 20 comparable destinations in the Eastern Caribbean (McElroy & de Albuquerque, 1989), as the number of tourists rose steadily to 105,500 in 1978 with improvements in marketing and infrastructure.

Tourism growth was again halted when several airlines and tour operators cut back flights as a result of increased fuel costs in 1979 and when several hotels were severely damaged by Hurricane Allen in 1980. The Government was forced to take over the Halcyon Days Hotel at Vieux Fort, the largest (256-room) hotel on the island, and keep it open with foreign management.[3] In the next few years, there were also cutbacks in the construction of new hotels, with several small (locally owned) hotels not proceeding with planned expansions and one major complex completely halting. Steigenberger AG's proposed 1,500-bed complex—which would have increased energy demand on the is land by 30%—was canceled, thus relieving for the moment the Government's need to make a decision to overhaul the electricity system.

At about the same time, a (confidential) report by the OAS suggested a vast increase in the island's tourism infrastructure, including several large, new, first-class hotels, an aquarium complex, and various improvements in existing tourist attractions (e.g., national park, museum). However, no action was taken on this report because of the softening of the tourist market, its energy implications, and the Government's mounting balance of payments problem. This report seems to have suffered from the problem noted by Peters (1980): "Too often in the past, so-called tourism master plans, funded by donor nations, have been drawn up with grandiose disregard for absorptive capacity and for market potential. These studies neglected implementation—which is of crucial importance to development" (p. 16).

Despite some instability among tour operators (e.g., the collapse of Sunflight and Skylark in Canada), a modest recovery began in 1982, with tourist arrivals slowly rising to 1979 levels by 1984. Since then, there has been an almost steady rise, to 194,100 tourist arrivals in 1993, a 143.6% increase since 1980. In the same period, this growth is paralleled by the increase in tourist arrivals per 1,000 local population per year from 644 to 1,387, the tourist penetration ratio from 17.63 to 40.20, and the tourist density ratio from 3.50 to 9.15.

This growth in tourist arrivals, however, represented only the 16th highest rate of increase of 30 countries in the Caribbean region throughout the period; as a result, St. Lucia's position as the 19th most visited destination in the region remained constant. The question arises as to whether this pattern is related to the fact that the SLTB's marketing expenditure per stay-over visitor remains among the lowest of the case studies.

St. Lucia attracts tourists from a variety of markets, a pattern reflected in the distribution of direct scheduled international air connections per week: 11 to the United States, 8 to Europe, and 3 to Canada (Mather & Todd, 1993). Europe was the major market with 78,000 arrivals in 1993; however, the 148.4% increase in this market since 1980 was only the 19th highest rate of increase of European arrivals for 30 countries in the Caribbean region and reflects the trend of St. Lucia decreasing relatively in importance from seventh to 11th as a regional destination for European arrivals in that period. In contrast, American arrivals increased by 300.0% to 56,400—the sixth highest rate of increase as a destination for Americans—raising St. Lucia from 20th to 16th as a destination for Americans. At 12,100, there was a 6.9% decrease in Canadians, making St. Lucia only the 17th fastest growing destination for Canadians in the Caribbean and dropping to Canada's 14th largest regional destination. The United States, the United Kingdom, and the Caribbean region accounted for a market concentration ratio of only 77.8, indicating the importance of the rest of the European market and Canada for St. Lucia.

Accommodations

The growth in the number of tourists is clearly correlated with the expansion of the hotel industry. In 1964, there were only two hotels with a total of 20 rooms; a decade later, there were over 1,000 rooms (World Bank, 1985b, p. 31). The 1974 bankruptcy of Court Lines, however, forced the temporary closure of over one quarter of St. Lucia's hotel beds (Britton, 1978, p. 180). The fact that one MNC can represent such a major force reinforces the fragility of tourism in such a small nation. Expansion soon began again, however, and by 1980 there were 1,245 rooms. Spinrad (1982) describes St. Lucia at that time as having "a rapidly growing tourist industry" characterized by "explosive growth" (p. 88). Only a few years later, it appeared that the explosion had ended and that, at best, tourism had reached a plateau.

A major problem in the early 1980s was the continuing financial instability of Halcyon Days, which was finally closed by the Government in 1984. The impact on tourist arrivals was minimal because the deteriorating condition of the hotel had resulted in lack of interest by tour operators, but the impact on local employment was extremely serious. At least one MNC expressed an interest in the property, but only if it were granted a gambling concession. A vigorous national debate ensued, in which religious interests and other groups concerned with maintaining traditional island culture were strongly involved; eventually, the Government decided against gambling. Finally, an arrangement was made with Club Méditerranée, which reopened the hotel in 1986. The effect of increased employment was generally considered to be more important than any suspicion about the results of what was recognized to be increased "enclave" tourism merely 1 km from the international airport.

By 1987, it was clear that the supply of visitor accommodations was constraining tourism development. Although there had been selective extensions to existing hotels, no new hotels had been constructed in the previous 10 years. The fact that 1988 saw a record average annual occupancy rate of 74.5% spurred construction of hotels and villas (CTO, 1990; World Bank, 1990, p. 64) (e.g., Royal St. Lucian Hotel, the villas of Windjammer Landing Resort). By 1993, considerable expansion resulted in a total of 2,919 rooms (CTO, 1994). Although there has been more than a doubling in the number of tourist rooms per 1,000 local population from 10.1 in 1980 to 20.9 in 1993 and in the number of rooms/km^2 from 2.0 to 4.7, an increase in the average annual occupancy rate from 61.9% to 67.9% in the same period has resulted in a 125.6% increase in the tourist occupancy function (rooms) from 6.3 to 14.2.

A growing trend in St. Lucian tourism is all-inclusive resorts; by 1990, 41.2% of all hotel rooms were in all-inclusive resorts (e.g., Club Méditerranée, Couples) (GOSL, 1990, p. 22). The trend continues, with the former Cunard La Toc Hotel reopening in 1993 by the Jamaican-owned Sandals chain. Whereas Poon (1988) argues that all-inclusives are an innovation that provides a competitive edge to the Caribbean in terms of tapping a growing market segment, concern has been expressed in St. Lucia that there could be an oversupply of this type of vacation product, which would militate against a prudent diversification of the sector. Furthermore, because most of the all-inclusive tourist's expenditure takes place (prepaid in the origin country) within an individual resort, the effective diffusion of such expenditure throughout the economy is severely restricted (World Bank, 1990, p. 64). Mather and Todd (1993, pp. 71–72) provide the arguments for and against all-inclusives in the context of St. Lucia: high environmental standards, longer average length of stay, a more consistent pattern of demand, higher annual occupancy rates, higher profits, linkages with airlines, and considerable marketing clout. They caution, however, that enthusiasm is usually limited to just two to three all-inclusives on a small island. Moreover, with foreign ownership and large quantities of imported foodstuffs, much of the profits is not retained; the segregated environment creates resentment toward visitors among the local population; and very little money filters out into the local community in terms of use of services, restaurants, etc.

This proliferation of all-inclusives is contrary to the Government's policy (see below) to encourage small-scale local hotels; nevertheless, it is understandable why the Government permits all-inclusives when faced with possible closure of otherwise unprofitable large hotels.

The average length of stay (10.6 nights in 1993) has traditionally been relatively high and steady in St. Lucia; when combined with the growing number of tourist arrivals (particularly long-stay Europeans), this has resulted in a 159.0% increase to 2,057,500 in the annual number of tourist nights in the period 1980–1993. St. Lucia has one of the lowest levels of seasonality in the region (CCA, 1991b, p. 213): its index of seasonality dropped from a moderately low 1.146 in 1989 (de Albuquerque & McElroy, 1992, p. 627) to 1.026 or virtually no seasonal variation in 1993. This lack of seasonality is largely a result of inexpensive summer charter tours and higher levels of tourists from within the Caribbean region in the summer. It is also related to very great seasonal differences in average room rates that encourage summer travel: the average winter rate of US$129.50/night in 1987–88 was among the highest in the region (ranking seventh of 31 countries), but the summer decrease to US$69.80 (ranking 18th) of 85.8% was the greatest decrease in the region (Curtin & Poon, 1988).

With the exception of the larger hotel projects, most of the hotels in St. Lucia were originally financed by equity funds generated internally and by very limited funds borrowed on relatively short terms from local commercial banks. Because local bank deposits depend on the state of the banana trade, the banks were quite liquid in 1988 and 1989 and they started to offer mortgages and other long-term finance for apartment hotels, time-sharing units, and condominiums (World Bank, 1990, pp. 65–66), but these sources of funds dried up in the subsequent recession (N. Thomas, 1991, personal communication; D. Theobalds, 1991, personal communication).

Excursionists

Day excursionists represent a stable but very small part of the St. Lucian tourist sector, with 6,500 visiting the island in 1993, a 209.5% increase since 1980. The other measures illustrate the minor nature of this component: in 1993, 47 arrivals per 1,000 local population, a penetration ratio of 0.13, and a density ratio of 0.13—all low compared to the other case studies for which data are available. In 1990, they spent only US$0.2 million or about 0.1% of total estimated visitor expenditure on the island (SLTB, 1991).

Cruise Passengers

Cruise and (to a much lesser extent) yacht passengers are much less important in economic terms, with estimates of their proportion of total visitor expenditures ranging from 2.5% (GOSL, 1990, pp. 20–22) to 3.2% (SLTB, 1991) to 5% (CCA, 1991b, p. 227). It has been estimated, for example, that a cruise passenger spends only about US$44 in *total* during a short stay of only a few hours,[4] compared to a stay-over tourist who spends US$68 per day for an average stay of over 10 days (CCA, 1991b, p. 225).

As a result of the Caribbean cruise industry's use of larger, more fuel-efficient carriers (formerly not as easily accommodated in St. Lucia) and the demand for shorter trips from the main gateway port in Miami, the number of cruise passengers arriving in St. Lucia had been in decline since the peak of 69,084 in 1976 and bottomed in 1981 to 18,934 with rising energy prices and the worldwide recession (CCA, 1991b, p. 211; Caribbean Tourism Research and Development Centre [CTRC], 1988, p. 102). Despite this serious downturn in the early 1980s, St. Lucia has been able to improve slightly its ranking as a cruise destination, rising from 16th to 14th in 1993 of 24 countries in the Caribbean region. The numbers have increased, in part because of the Pointe Seraphine pier and shopping facilities in Castries harbor,[5] which allows for better and easier docking, but there have been wide fluctuations. In 1993, there were 154,400 passengers, a 706.2% increase since the bottom of the trough in 1981 (SLTB, 1991)—the second highest rate of increase in the region since 1980. Nevertheless, St. Lucia remains as having the second lowest number of cruise passengers per 1,000 local population (1,104 in 1993) and penetration ratio (3.02), and second lowest density ratio (0.69) among the case studies.

Yacht passengers are a minor factor, with only 5,595 being recorded for 1989 (CTO, 1990); they spend only an estimated US$12 per day (CCA, 1991b, p. 225) and usually stay for only a very short time period.

Total Tourists

St. Lucia's 152.2% increase between 1980 and 1993 to 355,100 total visitors is indicative of the strong growth expected of a Stage II destination. The other measures show similar growth, placing it in the middle of the Stage II case studies: 2,538 visitors per 1,000 local population, a penetration ratio of 43.44 (both above only Dominica), and a density ratio of 9.87 (above the Bahamas and Dominica).

Tourist Expenditures

Rising from 19th to 16th highest in the region between 1980 and 1993, estimated visitor expenditures were US$221.0 million in 1993, representing as much as 52.9% of GDP in 1992. Three other measures of the growing dependence on tourism are expenditures as 42.2% of total account receipts in 1989, the ratio to merchandise exports at 2.1 in 1993, and the percentage of external debt at 213.5% in 1992. Similarly, visitor expenditure per capita of local population is increasing rapidly, rising 494.0% from US$266 in 1980 to US$1,580 in 1993. Finally, the value-added contribution of the hotel and restaurant sector was 10.4% of GDP in 1993.

However, it is hard to estimate what the net tourist expenditure is after leakages are taken into account. Leakages are important measures because gross expenditure figures mask net local economic impact. For example, the 1988 SLTB/CTO survey indicated that tourists had an average daily rate of expenditure of US$103.40 in summer and US$87.99 in winter, with two thirds of the total being spent on accommodation and 13% on food and drink (Dann, 1992). A large proportion of these amounts, however, does not remain in the local economy. For example, 62% of the tourists surveyed were traveling on prepaid package tours, resulting in much of their expenditure on accommodation being retained by travel agents in their countries of origin and in the accounts of hotel MNCs; even with direct expenditures on food and drink (to say nothing of package or all-inclusive food and drink arrangements), much leaks out as tourists consume steaks from the United States and whisky from Scotland.

The Economist (Anonymous, 1989c, p. 22) suggests that the leakage rate for most small countries is 40–50%, whereas both the CTRC (1987b, p. 10) and Elliott (1988, p. 15) argue a figure of 58% for Caribbean islands. C. Smith and Jenner (1992) state that the leakage rate for St. Lucia was 44.8% in 1978, which is very similar to Spinrad's (1982, p. 85) estimate of 45% in the same year, whereas Laventhal & Horwath (1986a, p. 21) estimate 60.7% for 1986. Although they do not give an exact figure, Poon, Sobers, Williams, and Mitchell (1990) state that direct imports for the tourism sector amounted to US$37.42 million, 28% of the US$134.2 million in total imports in 1989; they argue that the total leakage was considerably higher when all second and subsequent round expenditure is taken into account.

Whatever the actual leakage rate, it is clear that gross expenditure estimates are not good measures of the true economic impact of tourism (GOSL, 1990, pp. 23–24). The potential to decrease leakages through intersectoral linkages with tourism is limited, however; the most obvious possibility is substitution of local foods, but tourists spend only 16% of their expenditures on food and much of that is tied to products that do not lend themselves well to local substitution (e.g., meat, dairy products, brand-name goods) (Laventhal & Horwath, 1986a, p. 22).

Another measure of the economic impact of tourism is the multiplier: Spinrad (1982) estimates it at 0.54 in 1978, very similar to Laventhal & Horwath's (1986b, p. 10) estimate of 0.52 in 1983. However, no detailed studies have been undertaken to verify such estimates.

Finally, employment generated by tourism is another measure of the economic impact of tourism; however, there have been many estimates of tourism-related employment, with very little agreement, let alone the provision of data collection methods to allow for a comparative analysis. It seems reasonable to suggest, however, that tourism provides approximately 3,500–4,000 direct jobs and 4,000–5,000 indirect jobs (CTO, 1992; GOSL, 1990; McHale, 1989; United States Agency for International Development [USAID], 1985; World Bank, 1985b, 1990). For many people employed directly in tourism, their jobs provide a personal income that is undoubtedly higher than that of the average St. Lucian worker, although that figure is not available. For example, Dann's (1992) survey of 70 (nonmanagerial) hotel employees indicates an average total income (salary plus tips) of over

US$4,000. Another sample of 393 residents demonstrated a recognition of the employment and income generation importance of tourism, with most feeling that the economic impacts of tourism were more important than any intangible impact (e.g., culture) (Dann, 1992).

Tourism Policy and Planning

Given the growing importance of tourism in St. Lucia's economy and the Government's stated intention to use tourism to increase employment, a policy and planning framework has evolved to carry out this goal of increased dependence on tourism.

The Policy and Planning Context

Responsibility for tourism policy appears to be formally vested in the (current) Ministry of Tourism, Public Utilities, Civil Aviation, and National Mobilization, but actually controlled at the Cabinet level. Urban and land-use planning became a formal part of the administrative fabric of government in 1946, with the passage of the Town and Country Planning Ordinance; although focused on human settlements and public health concerns, the law established the basis for planning through the preparation of "regional schemes" and the regulation of building construction and general development control. Clearly, tourism has been only one concern within the planning process, but it has received considerable attention over the years.

The Beginnings

As the postwar worldwide tourism boom began to affect the Caribbean, the Government recognized the need to encourage expansion of the very small accommodation sector. Under the Hotel Aids Ordinance of 1959, hotels and other guest accommodations could obtain an income tax holiday for 7 years and import duty-free the materials and equipment required for construction. The ordinance had little immediate effect, but clearly provided incentive to hotel developers (particularly MNCs, e.g., Cunard, Holiday Inns) beginning in the mid-1960s when the jet charter boom began.

Private sector investment, however, did not increase as fast as the Government had hoped, forcing it to become an active player. Its first major direct involvement occurred in 1970 with the formation of Rodney Bay Ltd., 90% of the equity being held jointly by the Government and the British Commonwealth Development Corporation (CDC) (Towle, 1985). The company was formed to develop the tourist potential of Rodney Bay in the north of the island, following major infrastructural works to create marina lagoons and over 160 hectares of development land, including 1 km of new beach, reclaimed in the creation of a link between the mainland and Pigeon Island (GOSL, 1977, p. 31). The peak construction boom in 1970–1973 resulted in several MNC-owned major hotels, followed by a slow process of further hotel and marina construction that goes on to the present; however, the proposed development at Rodney Bay has still not been fully implemented. Most important, the causeway to Pigeon Island—first the site for the proposed Steigenberger hotel complex and more recently the focus for several MNC proposals for a casino–convention center complex—remains undeveloped, despite the fact that it was created specifically to be a major hotel development site.

After a virtual halt in the expansion of the accommodation stock for several years in the early 1980s because of the worldwide recession, St. Lucia continues to attract major hotel investments, largely because of the favorable taxation and incentives climate initiated with the 1959 Ordinance. In July 1991, a Tourism Incentives Act was tabled. Going beyond the 1959 Ordinance, it deals with a wide range of tourism projects: construction of new or renovation of existing hotels (of at least six rooms), furnishing and equipment of hotels, recreation facilities, historic attractions, restaurants, information and interpretation centers, and museums. Projects approved by Government are eligible for certain tax benefits: income tax holidays for up to 15 years (including changes in ownership) for new construction and 10 years for renovations; exemption from customs and excise duties on building materials and equipment. Tourism investment subsidies currently available in St. Lucia include: assistance with project financing, tax holidays, investment and other tax credits, accelerated depreciation, double tax relief, leasing of property, marketing support, and training support (Arthur Young, 1988).

Plans and Planning—Formulated But Not Approved

As infrastructure expansion and suburbanization grew in the late 1960s and early 1970s in the Castries area caused by economic growth related to tourism development and construction, there were increasing demands for improved management of urban areas and for long-term planning. In 1971, the Land Development (Interim Control) Act (amended 1984) was implemented; its purpose was to extend planning control to the entire island without the requirement of a physical plan. It was to be an interim measure while full planning legislation was considered; however, a Land Planning and Development Act, although circulating in draft for several years, was not approved.

In 1977, as a result of administrative problems associated with the dispersal of "planning and development" functions throughout the Government, coupled with external donor pressure for improved project management, a Central Planning Unit (CPU) was formed as the core of the (now) Ministry of Planning, Personnel, Establishment, and Training. The CPU developed a St. Lucia National Plan (GOSL, 1977); it was never formally accepted by Government, but its Physical Development Strategy and Technical Supplement remains the most comprehensive attempt at national physical planning in St. Lucia. The Plan noted that, as tourism began to take off, several problems had become apparent: socioeconomic imbalances, seasonality, boom and recession cycles, and limited air access (GOSL, 1977, p. 31). Nevertheless, the Government decided to make tourism a key focus of the Plan:

> Government is committed to promoting the growth of tourism to fully utilize
> the natural resources of climate and scenic beauty with which the island is
> richly endowed. These qualities, coupled with the warmth and traditional
> friendliness of the people, offer every prospect for St. Lucia to keep ahead of
> its competitors in this field. (GOSL, 1977, p. 33)

Eight specific objectives are stated to guide policy decisions over the following decade: effective marketing and improved airline services; controlled and balanced
growth of the tourist sector; full and stable employment in the hotel industry; establishment of links with the agricultural and manufacturing sectors; concentration of tourist activity in selected areas; identification, development, and protection of environmental attractions; the development of local support services; and
harmonization of the growth of tourism with regional development thrusts
(GOSL, 1977, p. 34).

Despite later approvals of major proposals, the Government, however, seems to
have been somewhat wary of large-scale development:

> Government will not generally encourage the development of luxury hotels
> until there is evidence of substantially improved occupancy and minimal sea-
> sonal fluctuations in the existing units. Government has already found it nec-
> essary to legislate to protect jobs through financial and other direct interven-
> tion in the hotel industry in the wake of the problems created by the [1973]
> energy crisis. (GOSL, 1977, p. 34)

The Plan goes on to state that the policy would be to promote the development of
smaller hotels and guest houses with development concentrated in the Rodney
Bay area where efforts were to be made to attract investment to develop a "series
of flexible-unit low rise holiday villages" (GOSL, 1977, p. 35) (which, however,
did not occur).

With a target by the year 2000 of 6,000 new beds being added to the existing
2,000 tourist beds, the Plan calls for tourism development to be focused on the
northwest coast (4,000 beds), including the Rodney Bay area, with secondary concentrations around Vieux Fort (1,500 beds) and Soufriere (500 beds). This ceiling
of 8,000 beds reflects the view that further expansion could result in the over-
weighting of tourism in the socioeconomic structure because tourism, by creating
2,500–3,000 new jobs, would then employ approximately one third of the labor
force. Although the targets will not be reached by the year 2000, development has
largely maintained the spatial pattern set out in this (unapproved) Plan.

The Government recognized that a major problem in international tourism was seasonality (a problem that eventually was overcome); therefore, one of the aims of
the Plan is to develop facilities (most of which were never built) that would attract
Caribbean tourists to St. Lucia to help bridge the gap created by the off-peak season of the traditional tourist sector. Similarly, programs for the conservation and
enhancement of the island's natural and human-made attractions were to be insti-
gated; some development took place at Pigeon Island and Soufriere, but lack of
capital and operating funds were constant problems. Also, there was to be regional

cooperation on interisland air transport; despite the fact that the Government is a
minor shareholder in LIAT, this remains a problem area. Similarly, other overall elements of the plan did not materialize. The creation of horizontal links with the agricultural sector by gearing production and marketing to the hotels of local produce as a substitute for imported foodstuffs, although laudable, was not realized:
only 10–15% of food consumed in hotels is locally produced (mainly fruit) for a
variety of reasons, including volume, tradition, quality control, and tourist preferences (T. Louis, A. Satney, 1989, personal communication). A cooperative craft
market, to be established with Government support, did not develop.

Finally, one overall goal that was at least partially achieved was the development
of training programs for hotel management and catering skills. A Hotel Trades
School (now part of the Sir Arthur Lewis Community College) was instituted, but
there have been many calls for the expansion of its program and/or more private
sector initiatives to meet the demand for skilled labor.

The tourism section of the Plan ends on a positive note: "If, as many expect, the
growth of tourism experiences another boom matching that of the early seventies,
Government aims to be in a position to respond swiftly in rapidly changing circumstances" (GOSL, 1977, p. 35).

As a follow-up to the 1977 Plan, a consulting firm (Economic Consultants, 1979)
was hired to identify and assess the market potential of tourism to St. Lucia, to
identify current deficiencies in the tourism sector, and to propose appropriate re-
medial actions. The resulting Tourism Development Study, however, has some suspect figures. For example, the number of stay-over tourists in 1978 is presented as
69,000 (Economic Consultants, 1979, p. 4), whereas the actual figure appears to
be less than 33,000 (CTO, 1990). The report does predict relatively accurately a total of 129,000 stay-over visitors by 1990 (the actual figure being 138,400), but the
validity of this figure is spurious given that the base was incorrect and the result
was a function of selecting a modest growth rate of 4%. Moreover, it predicts that
this number of visitors will require about 2,900 rooms (Economic Consultants,
1979, p. 16), far above the 2,370 rooms that in 1990 well-served a similar number
of tourists at an annual occupancy rate of only 70.4%. The report is slightly more
accurate—probably by luck rather than skill—in predicting the number of cruise
ship passengers, suggesting an increase from 76,000 in 1978 to a (very broad)
range of 109,000–150,000 in 1990 (Economic Consultants, 1979, p. 8).

Despite the growing economic importance of tourism into the 1980s, the Government devoted little formal attention to either tourism policy or planning. Tourism,
however, was not alone, as the only official development policy activity occurred
in the early 1980s, when the CPU produced an unpublished series of issue papers
on 13 major physical development topics. The result was a new (draft) Physical Development Strategy for the years 1986–1991; however, this document was neither
officially endorsed nor released by Government. Even if it had been accepted, the
impact on tourism would have been minimal as very little of the document was devoted to tourism.

The Greening of Tourism

It could be argued, however, that the Government did indeed have a tourism policy because the SLTB, a government-funded statutory agency, has a marketing plan that has positioned the country as an upmarket destination because of several factors: high air travel costs from the major markets; a focus on high-income tourists to maximize economic benefits and to minimize environmental impacts; and the high demand for the island's natural beauty making price less important in the buyer's decision-making process (A. Francis, 1993, pp. 72–73). As a result, the SLTB worked with the Government's Development Control Authority to promote new accommodation and facilities that would be acceptable to an upmarket clientele. The feeling was that the economic impact of mass tourists, although positive, is limited, whereas the sociocultural and environmental impacts are mainly negative (A. Francis, 1993, p. 76).

As a result, in 1990 the SLTB developed a new "Green Tourism" marketing theme, as proposed several times previously (e.g., Canford Associates, 1990; GOSL, 1989). A "green" market positioning—defined in terms of ecotourism—was agreed on, with the target market being environmentally conscious tourists. The goal was not to constrain the existing market, but to augment the volume of tourist traffic, while at the same time having minimum negative impacts on the environment.

The SLTB's green theme was being developed at approximately the same time as a (then) Ministry of Industry, Trade, and Tourism's national tourism policy, which includes a similar approach, so it appears that this will be a major marketing strategy for St. Lucia in the future.

The development context is described in a series of national development goals and objectives: sustainable economic growth, expansion of employment opportunities and reduction in unemployment, a diversified production base and a continuous expansion of production and exports, and improved general welfare of the population (GOSL, 1989, pp. 1–2). Arguing that the economic, physical, and social infrastructure has greatly improved in recent years, the Policy calls for this foundation to be more firmly established by broadening its base through economic diversification—one route to which is tourism. Specifically, tourism is seen as having the potential for providing:

- increased national income, employment, foreign exchange earnings, and linkages with agriculture, manufacturing, and services (thus decreasing leakages);

- increased social and economic benefits;

- financial justification for the preservation of historical attractions and for the expansion of artistic expression.

Conversely, it is recognized that the effects of an improperly managed tourism sector on the physical, cultural, and social environment can be catastrophic (GOSL, 1989, pp. 3–4).

Because of the important role that tourism plays in the economic development of the country, the Policy states that the sector cannot be permitted to develop in an ad hoc manner; rather, a policy framework is required that establishes the parameters within which the development and expansion of the sector will be encouraged. Fundamental for the orderly growth of the sector are the following principles:

- tourism can and must play a vital role in economic development;

- although a continuing need exists for attracting foreign investment and technology transfer, the sector must be open to full participation by all segments of St. Lucian society and its benefits as widely distributed as possible;

- over time, the sector must be characterized by increasing levels of local ownership and management;

- linkages with agriculture, manufacturing, and services must be exploited;

- the people's right to enjoyment of scenic and other natural resources should be safeguarded in the development of the sector;

- protection of the physical and social environment must be of paramount concern in the planning and development of tourism (GOSL, 1989, p. 5).

These principles form the following policy measures, which constitute a "tourism development strategy":

- encouragement of investment, including provision of incentives;

- increased local participation in accommodation development and in support services;

- increased public support for the tourism through education;

- consultation among public and private sector agencies to protect the physical environment, including strengthening existing legislation;

- monitoring market segmentation and all-inclusive packages to avoid over-concentration in any one area;

- diversification of the tourism plant and of markets, by directly seeking to develop new markets and working with other Caribbean countries in the development of multidestination arrangements;

- promotion of St. Lucia's competitiveness and uniqueness;

- development and maintenance of a reputation for good quality and value;

- establishment of a Consultative Group on Tourism Development with membership from a wide cross section of the community (GOSL, 1989, pp. 6–10).

In essence, the Policy calls for a "hands-off" attitude toward public sector entrepreneurship and ownership of tourism-related business and, instead, "an active and leading role in the provision of the infrastructure, fiscal and other incentives together with promotional support for tourism" (McHale, 1989, p. 35). This Policy responds directly to concerns expressed by external agencies about the direction of tourism development in St. Lucia. The World Bank (1985b, 1986c, 1988b), for example, emphasizes the need to increase local involvement in tourism to increase employment opportunities and points out particular areas of concern: promotion, facilities, foreign exchange leakage, seasonality, occupancy rates, training, costs, marketing, and weak linkages between agriculture and tourism. The World Bank (1988b, p. iii) also warns about a likely softness in demand in the future due to slower growth projected in the main tourist markets, a relatively slow growth in Caribbean tourism, and the emergence of cheaper destinations (e.g., Mexico, Venezuela, Dominican Republic).

Nevertheless, the Government continues to encourage the expansion of hotel facilities in general and of large, international-scale hotels in particular. Developments include the 115-villa Canadian-owned Windjammer Landing Villa Resorts north of Castries and the 100-villa Jalousie Resort between the Pitons near Soufriere; there are also proposals for the New Vigie Beach Hotel next to Vigie Airport to be replaced by a 60-room five-star hotel, a 300-room Venezuelan-owned hotel to be built near the Club Méditerranée at Vieux Fort, and Carnival Cruise Lines' 300-room hotel for the Pigeon Island Causeway near Gros Islet, the latter to be tied into "fly and cruise" packages. These developments seem to contradict the Government's stated policy of encouraging small-scale local hotels. The creation of immediate jobs appears to be taking precedence over the creation of a sector geared to maximizing local participation; moreover, the lack of policy and action regarding training on a national level for the tourism sector appears to be symptomatic of emphasis being placed upon the development of the physical plant without the development of human resources to service the plant (D. Coathup, 1992, personal communication).

This is not to say the Government is receptive to all development proposals. The Jalousie project, located in a saddle between the two volcanic-plug Pitons, was extremely controversial for archaeological, historical, and ecological reasons, to say nothing of the public outcry at development on a site of national pride: the Pitons are symbolized on the St. Lucian Flag. That project was permitted, but a later proposal by a German company for a resort at Anse L'Ivrogne just to the south, which would have included a cable car to a revolving restaurant on top of the Gros Piton, was denounced publicly by the Prime Minister. Also, the Government became a signatory to the World Heritage Conservation Treaty of UNESCO in 1992; the St. Lucia National Trust (SLNT) has proposed that the Soufriere-Pitons area be nominated as a world heritage site (G. Romulus, 1992, personal communication).

With respect to market diversification, although the Policy does not specify which nontraditional markets are of interest, there are at least three obvious ones that are well-suited to St. Lucia and that have already received some degree of study and interest (including the SLTB's "green" theme described above): ecotourism or nature tourism, focused on St. Lucia's rain forest, birds, and other wildlife (P. Butler, 1985; Canford Associates, 1990; Romulus, 1990); underwater tourism, particularly scuba diving (Jackson, 1986; Renard, 1985, 1989); and historical tourism (Arthur Young, 1989a).

The potential for an increased marketing focus on nontraditional tourist segments is strongly related to long-standing efforts to develop a national parks and protected areas plan (Romulus, 1989, 1990, 1992). In 1991, there was a proposal by the Prime Minister to vest the Pitons and other lands in the Soufriere area to the SLNT for management as a "nature conservation reserve," which the SLNT (1992) then proposed be designated as the Qualibou[6] National Park.

This specific suggestion is related to the SLNT's proposal, with the support of the Government, for a system of 22 protected marine and terrestrial areas (L. Hudson, Renard, & Romulus, 1992). The proposal calls for the active participation of the SLTB in the establishment and management of the system in such areas as the promotion of sites as attractions for visitors, integration of protected areas in the overall policy and program framework for tourism development, training of guides and other professionals in the hospitality sector, educational campaigns for visitors and nationals, and conducting market surveys, evaluations, and other studies to enhance the contribution of protected areas to tourism as well as the contribution of tourism to host communities. Implementation of the proposal awaits approval by the Government.

Toward the Future

In 1992, the Government accorded the tourism portfolio a higher national priority by transferring it from the Ministry of Trade, Industry, and Tourism, where it was not a major focus, to the Ministry of Tourism, Public Utilities, Civil Aviation, and National Mobilization, in which tourism is the main area of responsibility. This was a result of both a strong lobby from the private sector and the Prime Minister's view of the importance of the sector (Mather & Todd, 1993, pp. 104–105). Claiming a commitment to environmentally sound tourism, the Government placed a temporary moratorium on new hotel development until a full-scale economic impact study of the tourism sector has been carried out. Importance has also been accorded to establishing linkages with other sectors such as agriculture and manufacturing, increasing tourism awareness, and greater participation by the local population in, for example, the running of guest houses or small-scale businesses supplying the tourism sector. Mather and Todd (1993) suggest that

> With the creation of a new ministry and the increased tourism budget, tourism has been placed at the forefront in St Lucia. In this the government appears to be recognising that tourism is going to be the main engine of growth for the country's economy and dynamism that is clearly apparent in the new team reflects this commitment. (p. 105)

There has also been an expansion of the SLTB's role, previously concerned mainly with the promotion of St. Lucia, to include a technical advisory capacity focused on the future direction of the sector and the task of making recommendations to the minister to take to cabinet. The SLTB was reorganized so that the sales and the administrative functions are separated and staff additions include the areas of product development (including public awareness), marketing, finance, and education. More cooperative work with the private sector is planned, partly through a plan for a tourism fund, with hoteliers contributing EC\$1 per occupied room and businesses 3% of gross profits, which would be utilized for marketing, but also for other aspects such as an education awareness program; a marketing development committee (with hotel industry, Chamber of Commerce, and GOSL members) would manage the fund. The goal is to focus on upmarket and green images, previously described as being concerns of the Board.

Despite this apparent increase in Government interest in tourism policy and planning, the future of St. Lucia's tourist sector remains unclear. Given the current positive economic climate backed by strong public support for tourism, particularly because of foreign exchange and employment benefits (Dann, 1992)—buoyed by a recent upswing in tourist arrivals, the construction of several small and large hotels and of a major five-star villa complex, and the expansion of an existing major hotel—future expansion of the hotel plant in the form an international-class, large-scale casino and convention center and several other hotels is being considered. The Government has set a target of doubling the country's hotel capacity by 2000 (Anonymous, 1989d). Volatility in the world airline industry, however, remains a question mark. There are positive trends: BWIA has increased its flights and routes in recent years, American Eagle has started a new route from Puerto Rico that is the regional hub for its parent American Airlines, and Club Méditerranée has increased the charter traffic. On the other hand, service has been discontinued by the bankrupt Eastern Airlines, a major international airline, and Air Antilles, a St. Lucia-based charter firm. Both airports have been upgraded: Vigie Airport was extended so that it can handle jets up to the size of a Boeing 727; another terminal, a taxi strip, and extra parking were constructed at Hewanorra Airport.

In general, however, increased tourist arrivals will depend on stability in the airline and tour operator industries and on improved marketing. Traditionally, St. Lucia marketed itself largely as a mass tourism destination, with a heavy reliance on package-tour visitors coming primarily on charter flights (Spinrad, 1982, p. 71). More recently, however, an upmarket approach has been adopted with promotion efforts focusing on the country's distinctive Créole culture and history, the volcanic sulphur springs and history of Soufriere, scuba diving, and charter sailboating (CCA, 1991b, p. 211).

The CCA (1991b) argues that a number of definable qualities makes St. Lucia distinctive among its major small-island competitors in the region: long average length-of-stay; large percentage of Europeans in the visitor mix; evenly balanced market shares among North American, European, and Caribbean tourists; more even distribution of rooms between large hotels and smaller types of establishments; and low level of seasonality. A fundamental tension exists, however, on St. Lucia's position on a continuum of low- to high-density tourism:

> It would appear that, along a continuum of tourism styles, St. Lucia represents an intermediate position between the low-density ''European'' type and the high-density ''American'' type. This intermediary stage has policy im-

plications because historically it has represented a transitional phase toward high-density mass tourism. If the experiences of other more mature destinations are any guide, and in the absence of strong regulatory controls such as in Bermuda, completing this transition is invariably associated with increasing environmental stresses. (CCA, 1991b, p. 222)

Such stresses include destruction of coastal vegetation and of reefs and mangroves; beach erosion; decreased water quality; and increased sewage, solid waste, traffic, and noise (Blommestein, 1985; Hunte, 1985).

There are clear indications that St. Lucia is already facing these stresses (Environmental Commission of St. Lucia, 1987). For example, M. C. Williams (1983, p. 112) long ago notes that the St. Lucian tourist sector did not demonstrate much interest in environmental quality; he describes alteration of coastal configurations and beach profiles, discharge of untreated sewage wastes, removal of beach sand for construction or other purposes, destruction of wetlands and mangroves, construction of large hotels in areas of high scenic value, and restrictions placed on the island citizens' freedom of access to beaches. These negative impacts have a direct relationship to the choice of the type of tourism development:

> Such amenity losses threaten the comparative advantage provided by the tropical island environment and mark the transition away from natural attractions toward high-volume, man-made attractions such as duty-free shopping and gambling.

> The policy dilemma now facing St. Lucia is whether to devise strategies to compete more fully in the riskier, high-density, mass tourism market or to resist that transition in favour of the low-density tourism style that has succeeded in the past. While this is a policy issue open to debate, the latter approach has demonstrated comparative advantages elsewhere, including improvement of the rate of domestic return, diminishment of import leakages, and enhancement of the long-term viability of cultural and environmental amenities. (CCA, 1991b, pp. 222–223)

Four factors argue for taking the low-density option: the fastest growing, most lucrative Caribbean tourism markets reflect this style; it is less vulnerable to political pressures and more socially acceptable; it is less stressful to both human and natural environments; and it tends to require resource management policies that preserve options for future development.

The CCA (1991b, pp. 223–224) goes on to argue that if St. Lucia is to preserve and enhance its distinctive tourism style, specific environmental, economic, and infrastructural needs have to be addressed:

- **environmental:** a coastal zone management policy and related legislation;

- **economic:** long-term tourism planning that emphasizes increasing the tourism multiplier, rather than more short-term policies that are usually directed at raising the volume of visitors;

- **infrastructural:** review of large-scale projects because of their potential to alter the country's low-density tourism style and to place stress on the natural environment and overload available infrastructure; and consideration of requirements for energy and potable water self-sufficiency, self-contained sewage treatment plants, tippage fees for solid waste, yardage fees for construction sand, and maintenance of a dispersed pattern of distribution of infrastructure and large-scale facilities.

The CCA (1991b) concludes that ongoing expansion of tourism facility construction and increasing international recognition of the island as a prime Caribbean destination suggest that

> . . . market momentum may be carrying St. Lucia forward along the continuum from low-density to high-density tourism. If this movement is sustained over the near-term, it will alter the country's present tourism style and leave open to question the long-term economic viability and environmental sustainability of this key economic sector. (p. 224)

There are many government and quasi-government agencies in St. Lucia with potential linkages to tourism planning. The CCA (1991b, p. 272) concludes that St. Lucia's sector-specific approach to resource management has prevented serious attempts at integrated resource management or protection strategies. On the other hand, the technical expertise of personnel in several of the Government's resource management units is highly regarded both in the country and in the Eastern Caribbean. The lack of strong cross-sectoral coordination between agencies weakens the ability of any single unit to share information and mitigates against country-level assessments of cumulative environmental impacts.

Although the CCA's (1991b, pp. 286–290) concerns cover environmental issues in general, it does make seven recommendations that are directly relevant to tourism planning. These procedural changes, some requiring legislative action, would allow the Government to integrate environmental considerations into the decision-making process and to facilitate the resource management responsibilities of Government:

- provide legislation for and require standardization of Environmental Impact Assessments for development projects;
- prepare and approve a National Land Use Plan, augmented by local development and land-use plans where appropriate;
- formalize procedures for environmental input at all phases of project planning, implementation, and assessment;
- harmonize and rationalize environmental laws and avoidance of overlaps in institutional responsibilities;
- provide public consultation and participation in national and local planning;
- create a public information and documentation center;
- establish monitoring programs as an integral part of resource management activities.

The CCA (1991b, p. 291) concludes that effective implementation of resource management programs in St. Lucia will require public sector consensus on general resource management objectives, sufficient political will to support those objectives, and sharing of program goals and development objectives between central government agencies, interest groups, and local communities. This conclusion echoes a long-standing complaint about small countries in general and St. Lucia in particular:

> Most small countries adopt no explicit natural resource conservation policies. In the medium to long term, however, such inaction may jeopardize their development prospects. Among the reasons for this absence of resource conservation activities from current government planning are the perception of conservation activities as a burden, the paucity of accurate quantitative data, institutional weaknesses, and the myopic nature of the development process itself. . . .

> To break the vicious circle caused by inadequate information and weak institutions, strong political commitment from involved governments is required. (Rojas, Wirtshafter, Radke, & Hosier, 1988, p. 282)

The problem is compounded by a planning philosophy that tends to deal with each new development proposal in an isolated, nonintegrated manner. Although referring specifically to coastal zone management, the CCA (1991b, pp. 143–144) describes the state of planning as a whole in St. Lucia as focusing on each new project as an isolated activity. Such "compartmentalized" development suggests that a conceptual, structural planning problem exists, thus increasing the risk of user conflicts and adverse impacts, and that a more comprehensive approach to coastal resource planning and management is required, including the adoption of formal environmental impact assessment (EIA) procedures as a requirement for all coastal and marine development projects.

It is to be hoped that the implementation of a Land Conservation and Improvement Act (1992) will result in these and other issues being addressed effectively.

Conclusion

> The tourist industry will be one of the major foundations of the St Lucian economy in the 21st Century. (Venner, 1989, p. 92)

With four important exceptions, the history of tourism policy and planning in St. Lucia has been characterized by a "hands-off" philosophy in which the Government has focused on dealing with specific private sector (usually foreign) development proposals on a project-by-project incremental basis. In effect, the approach has basically been characterized by site-specific land-use planning. The results have been mixed. On the one hand, the number of tourists and the level of expenditures have slowly but continuously risen over the past decade and new developments and development proposals have steadily come on line. The consequence is what the CCA (1991b) describes as an intermediate position between low- and

high-density tourism. On the other hand, a transition to high-density tourism—
which potentially could cause severe environmental stress—seems almost inevitable unless the Government takes a more proactive role in tourism policy and planning. Such an emphasis on high-density tourism could cause local dissatisfaction,
because there is strong evidence that the St. Lucian people want more local
involvement in the sector; for example, Dann (1992) finds that three quarters of
his sample of residents want local people to have more say in tourism decision
making.

The four exceptions indicate the Government's willingness to consider alternative
forms of involvement in the tourism sector. The first two exceptions concerned direct government participation in tourism development and operation. In the Rodney Bay Development, the Government was an active partner in a scheme to develop a major tourism zone (which was only partially completed). The second
instance was reactive, in which the Government became involved in the operation
of several financially troubled hotels in the mid-1970s. Most notably, it took over
the bankrupt Halcyon Days Hotel and ran it while searching for an international
hotel chain to take it over. The ensuing debate on gambling led to a major policy
stance based on strong cultural convictions of the public—which may be reversed
in the future on pragmatic grounds related to major employment opportunities represented by casino development.[7] Given the fiscal position of the Government,
however, future direct participation in the tourism sector seems unlikely, a policy
position stated in the 1991 National Tourism Policy.

The third exception was the 1976 National Development Plan, which was never
adopted officially, but set the framework for tourism zoning that remains today. A
new national planning agenda is, however, needed to avoid the current and potential environmental problems related to tourism.

Finally, the 1991 National Tourism Policy seems to provide a strong direction to
guide the future style, form, and location of tourism development. The question remains, however, as to how and whether such a policy can be integrated with a
land-use planning process that is focused on particular development proposals,
rather than the overall structure of the tourism sector. For example, although the
Policy calls for an emphasis on small hotels with a high degree of local participation, there seem to be few resources available to foster such development and, indeed, innovation in general in the tourism sector.[8] Conversely, the Government
continues to approve large-scale hotels owned by MNCs.

The danger is clear: mass tourism characterized by large numbers of tourists, but
tourist expenditures with high leakage rates and low multipliers—and increased environmental stress. Clearly, a reconciliation of policy and practice is in order; otherwise, serious environmental degradation is likely.

Notes

[1]Class I land capability is defined as "level soils suitable for cultivation with almost
no limitations on use," whereas Class IV is "level to undulating soils suitable for

cultivation with very severe limitations that restrict the choice of plants and/or require very careful management" (OAS, 1987b, p. 7).

[2]This percentage is much higher than in the so-called "banana republics" of Latin America (Thomson, 1987).

[3]Such arrangements have long been common. Dunning and MacQueen (1982) state that, between 1975 and 1982, over 90% of new associations with MNCs in developing countries were by management contracts or franchising, not partnerships or leasing. They contend that the energy situation changed the nature of the international tourist business more than that of the tourists themselves.

[4]Mather and Todd (1993, p. 68) provide a lower figure of US$34 for 1991.

[5]The Pointe Seraphine facility was later discovered to have serious environmental impacts on other harbor installations resulting from altered wave patterns (Organization of Eastern Caribbean States [OECS], 1988).

[6]*Qualibou* is probably derived from Amerindian words referring to the solfatara or collapsed caldera that is now the Sulphur Springs as "the place of death" (Devaux, 1992).

[7]A. Francis (1993, p. 74) states that the GOSL intends to legalize casino gambling as a way of diversifying the tourism product.

[8]Coathup (1992, personal communication) relates this to the fact that "Planners within a developing tourism sector are often restricted due to lack of exposure to global tourism. This often results in policies that are historical rather than innovative being implemented. An analysis of the success of these historical policies is often not carried out or they are not adapted to the local conditions."

Chapter 6

The Cayman Islands

The natural environment of the three Cayman Islands is characterised by a number of common factors: the land area of each island is small, the offshore shallow shelf is unusually narrow, arable land and fresh water are in short supply and the marine and terrestrial ecosystem are heavily interrelated. (Government of the Cayman Islands [GOCI], 1987, p. 114)

Introduction

The most isolated islands in the Caribbean in the sense of being the farthest from other islands, the Cayman Islands consists of three islands covering 260 km²: Grand Cayman, 240 km south of Cuba and 460 km west of Jamaica; Little Cayman, 100 km to the east-northeast; and Cayman Brac, 6 km farther on (Map 6.1). Grand Cayman (35 × 13 km) is low-lying and flat, covering 199 km², plus the North Sound, a large reef-protected area of shallow sea (11 × 10 km). Cayman Brac (19 × 2 km) covers 36 km²; marked by a high bluff that rises to a 450-m vertical cliff at the eastern tip, it has the highest elevation in the three islands. Little Cayman (16 × 3 km) is the flattest at less than 12 m above sea level and covers 25 km². May to October is the hot–wet season (20–30°C) and November to April is the cool–dry season (15–25°C); rainfall averages 1,500 mm, but varies spatially with the eastern end of Grand Cayman and the two smaller islands tending to have less. Although the islands are in the hurricane belt, there has not been a major hurricane since 1932; however, the edge of Hurricane Gilbert in September 1988 caused US$16 million in property damage.

The islands are the outcroppings of the Cayman Ridge, a range of submarine mountains extending southwest from the Sierra Maestra range of Cuba to the Misteriosa Bank in the direction of Belize (Rigby & Roberts, 1976). They consist of calcareous rocks divided into two distinct formations: an older limestone layer forms the central portion of each island, whereas the low coastal terrace, known as ironshore, is a formation of consolidated coral-sand, marl, and limestone (R. C. Smith, 1984). Fertile soil is found sporadically in pockets of the limestone, the largest area being on top of Cayman Brac's bluff; such soil can produce good root and other crops, although irrigation is a problem. There are mangroves along coastlines in several areas, notably North Sound, and remnants of mahogany and other native trees, many of which were used in the wooden ship-building industry. Tall thatch palms

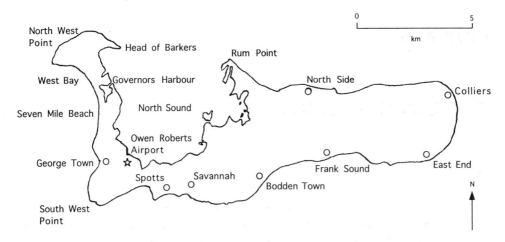

Map 6.1. Grand Cayman.

dot the landscape—a reminder of an industry that died, rope-making. There are 21 species of endemic flora, including several orchids, but there are few terrestrial fauna, with eight species of bat being the only native mammals. There are 45 species of breeding birds; although many are migrants or transients, there are 16 endemic subspecies, including parrots.

Between the islands and Jamaica lies the Cayman Trough, at 6,100 m the deepest part of the Caribbean (Raymont, Lockwood, Hull, & Swain, 1976). Although reefs almost surround Grand Cayman and Little Cayman, Cayman Brac has reefs only to a limited extent on its southwest coast. These reefs and the immediate deep waters represent some of the best scuba diving areas in the world, partly because the absence of rivers and runoff from the islands results in high water clarity. Except for Cayman Bank, a 14-km^2 shoal area between 30 and 40 m deep located 16 km west of Grand Cayman, there is no continental shelf and therefore no possibility of a major fishing industry (Winker, 1992, pp. 225–228).

Cayman Brac and Little Cayman were sighted by Columbus on his fourth and final voyage on May 10, 1503. Ferdinand Columbus, in his *Life* of his father, states that "We were in sight of two very small and low islands, full of tortoises [turtles], as was all the sea about, insomuch that they looked like little rocks, for which reason these islands were called Tortugas" (N. Williams, 1992, p. 1). Although it is not known which other Europeans explored the islands, the Turin map of 1523 is the first to show all three islands placed in reasonably correct positions and names them as *Lagartos* (alligators or large lizards). By the time of the Wolfenühttel map (1527–1530), the name *Caymanas* was used. It is derived from the Carib word for the crocodile family as a whole and for the marine crocodile in particular; later naturalists, such as William Dampier, noted that such creatures once abounded on Little Cayman, where an example of the species was reported in the early 20th century. It is reasonable to assume that the crocodiles of Little Cayman, the island most often visited in early times, gave their name to the whole group, supplanting the earlier *Las Tortugas*, a name with which the islands' development was to be so closely linked. N. Williams (1992, p. 2) believes that this is a more plausible explanation than the one that earlier visitors to Grand Cayman mistook the iguanas or edible lizards for alligators.

N. Williams (1992) notes that "Once discovered and charted the islands remained unexplored, unsettled and almost forgotten" (p. 2). They served only as temporary ports for pirates and privateers looking for water, provisions, and wood, and careening the hulls of ships, until the mid-1660s when deserters from Oliver Cromwell's disbanded army in Jamaica (following conquest of that island by Spain in 1655) established small settlements. When Jamaica was re-conquered by the British, the Cayman Islands came to be considered part of the territory of Jamaica. With the end of piracy in the 1730s came a period of continuous settlement, the first royal grant of land in Grand Cayman coming in 1734 (N. Williams, 1992, pp. 7–17). By 1774, the population was only 176, but this had risen to 922 (of whom 544 were slaves) in 1802 when the first official census was taken (Laventhol & Horwath, 1981, p. II-10).

With the exception of returns to piracy during such periods as the American Revolution, the Islands' economy was based on the trade in turtles, which started in the late 17th century. By the 1830s, with the local turtle population having been exhausted, Caymanian fishermen were forced to go to Honduras to hunt turtles; thus began the Islands' long history of out-migration, both permanent and temporary. It was also the start of a century of isolation, particularly as the introduction of steampower meant that ships could take direct routes from Jamaica to Britain without having to follow safer routes that included stopovers in the Cayman Islands.

Although there was a gradual and slow development of roads, schools, government, etc., the Cayman Islands was slow to prosper (England, 1928). A display at the Jamaica Exhibition of 1891 resulted in an increased production of rope and articles made from thatch palm, whereas 1901 saw the sale of first local postage stamps—the beginning of a new export industry that continues to the present. Between 1900 and 1912, many Caymanians worked on construction of the Florida East Coast Railway; in turn, many Caymanians settled permanently in the United States. By 1906, 1,500 men out of a total population of 5,000 were sailing on merchant vessels of the United States, Honduras, and Panama. This seafaring tradition continued for many years, with, for example, over 2,000 Caymanian men sailing on foreign ships in 1970 and providing a major source of Island income with the sailors' remittance income totaling US$1.5 million per annum. This employment, however, died as ship technology changed and as flags-of-convenience ships switched to crews mainly from developing countries in Asia and Africa.

In 1960, there was a population of 7,500 and in 1970 it was 10,600 (N. Williams, 1992, p. 88). Largely as a result of the need for expatriate labor, the 1992 Caymanian population has grown to 26,800; it is concentrated on Grand Cayman (25,326), with Cayman Brac having a population of 1,441 and Little Cayman only 33.

The GDP has grown dramatically and regularly since the early 1980s, increasing from US$207.8 million in 1983 to US$670.0 million in 1993. With a GDP per capita of US$22,700 and a median household income of US$47,400, it is now the most prosperous state in the Caribbean (GOCI, 1992c). The Cayman Islands has the highest wage rates in the region, despite the absence of labor unions; there is no official legislated minimum wage rate, but it generally equals and sometimes exceeds those of the United States and Canada (Cayman Islands Chamber of Commerce [CICC], 1991, p. 49). Given this situation and a growing economy, there is virtually full employment. One result has been the increasing proportion of the population who do not have Caymanian citizenship, but who are attracted by the shortage of local labor needed to match development pressures, despite a long-standing policy of reserving jobs for nationals (Caulfield, 1978). For example, in 1979, 26.4% of the workforce of 5,966 was non-Caymanian (Laventhol & Horwath, 1981, p. II-16), a figure that rose in 1991 to 35.2% of the workforce of 15,755 (GOCI, 1992c, p. 18). These figures are comparable to the proportion of the total population who were non-Caymanian: 23% in 1980 and 34% in 1990 (GOCI, 1992d, p. 5).

There is no income tax, company or corporation tax, inheritance tax, capital gains or gift tax, property tax or rates, or controls on the foreign ownership of property and lands (GOCI, 1991b, p. 10). Until 1975, capital projects were financed by grants from Britain; from then until 1980, there were interest-free loans from Britain on generous repayment terms. Since 1980, the Government has always been able to finance its recurrent expenditure from local revenue and to have a surplus in most years, without the need to look to Britain for grant-in-aid funds to balance the annual budget. Government revenues are based on import duties (37%); license fees for banks, trust companies, and company registration (15%); stamp duty on real estate transactions (13%); and work permit fees, tourist accommodation and travel taxes, and sales of commemorative stamps and numismatic coin issues (GOCI, 1990b, pp. 2–3). Although consistently running a relatively large visible trade deficit (US$259.6 million in 1993), the balance of payments is greatly offset by the invisible exports resulting from the large visitor expenditures (US$258.5 million in 1993).

Until 1952 when the Cayman Islands became a separate Crown Colony, government authority was vested through Jamaica, although formal annexation had not occurred until 1863. Half of the eight-member Legislative Assembly was appointed by the Governor of Jamaica and the rest elected by Caymanians; the chief administrator was the *Custos* (chief magistrate) appointed from Jamaica and, after 1898, a Commissioner. The Islands' first constitution in 1952 (revised when the Cayman Islands became a British Dependent Territory on August 22, 1972) created a Legislative Assembly of 12 elected members (with elections every 4 years) and three official members appointed by the Governor. Day-to-day government is a function of the Executive Council (ExCo), which consists of four elected and three official members, and is presided over by the Governor. Unlike other Commonwealth states (even other dependent territories, e.g., Anguilla), there is no ''prime'' or ''chief'' minister. Indeed, there are no ministers with portfolios per se; rather, there are "members responsible" for particular areas (e.g., tourism). All governmental matters including the formulation of policies and the drafting of laws for approval by the Legislative Assembly are their responsibility, although the Governor (appointed by the British Crown) presides over all governmental affairs and has the power to reverse decisions by the Assembly after approval by the British Government (GOCI, 1971).

The Economy

Over the years, the Cayman Islands has been the home to a number of forms of economic activity that have died out with changing times (GOCI, 1987, pp. 7–8). Local turtle fishing ended as the stocks were depleted, forcing the fishermen to travel to the cays and banks off Central America, where turtling remained a key activity into the 20th century. Because of the fishing industry, there was a long tradition of ship building using local hardwoods; the industry peaked with the construction of two minesweepers for the United States Navy in World War II and finally ended with two barges for the Turks and Caicos salt trade in the late 1950s. Thatch palms provided the base for a rope industry, which produced 2.2 million meters of rope in 1921 and 3.7 million meters in 1950, but ended in the 1960s with competition from human-made fibers produced in Jamaica. Coconuts were important for many years, especially on Cayman Brac, but a hurricane in 1915 and subsequent disease ended that industry.

Despite the limited area of agricultural land, high soil fertility and climate can support livestock, fruits, vegetables, and tubers (Benjamin, Joseph, & Taffe, 1992, pp. 286–287). Once self-sufficient in agriculture, the Cayman Islands exported at various times cotton to England, beef cattle to Jamaica, and wood, oranges, avocados, guavas, and coconuts to Central America and the southern United States. Until the early 1900s, Grand Cayman had prosperous farms with limes, avocados, pineapples, bananas, and tomatoes. Again self-sufficient in food in the two World Wars, as late as 1953 two thirds of the food was local. By the 1960s, however, production had declined to the point where agriculture was no longer profitable. With Government encouragement, however, agriculture has doubled since the mid-1980s; in 1990, there were 10 farms totaling over 40 hectares on Grand Cayman, growing tomatoes, bananas, lettuce, honey, mangoes, citrus fruits, cassava, yam, watermelon, pineapples, cabbage, corn, beans, pumpkin, green peppers, cucumbers, and coconut. Nevertheless, food imports were valued at US$25.0 million in 1985, rising to US$35.3 million in 1990 (GOCI, 1991b, p. 2).

In 1990, a 5-year Agricultural Development Plan was implemented as part of a "Buy Caymanian" campaign, taking a nontariff approach by providing US$18 million over 5 years in technical and financial assistance to farmers (CICC, 1991, p. 37). Designed to facilitate expansion of the sector so that farmers can take advantage of rapidly increasing marketing opportunities, its aims are: research and development to improve productivity, introduction of new crops and livestock, training and technical assistance, development of agricultural infrastructure, improved marketing, purchase by Government of arable lands for long-term lease to farmers (Benjamin et al., 1992, p. 288).

There is an oil trans-shipment base off Cayman Brac/Little Cayman where super-tanker mother ships anchor and transfer oil to smaller ships, which then proceed to shallow ports of the United States, Mexico, and South America. The operation results in full employment on Cayman Brac and Little Cayman and in several million dollars per annum in royalty fees.

Despite many efforts to encourage economic diversification (e.g., Pioneer Industries [Encouragement] Act of 1950, Trade and Industry Advisory Committee of 1977, Agricultural and Industrial Development Board of 1979), the economy is based almost completely on tourism and offshore companies. It has been argued that there were three economic milestones that led to a modern economy: the completion of the Grand Cayman airport in 1954 (which opened up the tourist sector), the decision to become a Crown Colony in 1962 (which led to political stability compared to Jamaica), and the Banks and Trust Companies Regulation Law of 1965 (which, although not the first piece of legislation related to offshore companies, was to become the cornerstone of that sector) (GOCI, 1987, p. 10).

The Companies Law of 1960 was the first formalized piece of legislation introducing a tax exemption status for offshore companies. The Cayman Islands has since become the second largest host of offshore companies in the Western Hemisphere after Bermuda, with the main attractive forces being secrecy, accessibility, and political stability (Dommen & Hein, 1985, pp. 167–168), plus the flight of capital from Hong Kong prior to the return of that colony to China in 1997 and increasing costs of doing business in Bermuda (Kersell, 1987, p. 104).

By 1966, when a set of exempting legislation was in place, there were three offshore banks registered in the Cayman Islands—a number that grew to 200 in 1975 (Giglioli, 1976, p. A3), 324 in 1980 (Laventhol & Horwath, 1981, p. II-28), and over 535 in 1989 (GOCI, 1990b, p. 5). Even more spectacular was the growth in offshore corporations established by individuals and corporations for preserving capital and income that may otherwise have been absorbed through taxation in other countries: 132 in 1966 (Giglioli, 1976, p. A3), 1,362 in 1973, 2,311 in 1980 (Laventhol & Horwath, 1981, p. II-28), and 20,000 in 1989, including 400 insurance companies (second in the latter only to Bermuda) (GOCI, 1990b, p. 5). They provide substantial revenues to government in terms of license fees rising from US$1.2 million in 1975 (Laventhol & Horwath, 1981, p. II-28) to US$21.4 million in 1991 (GOCI, 1992c, p. 35). Over time, they have come to be significant employers. Whereas Laventhol & Horwath (1981, p. II-28) argue that employment in 1981 generated by these offshore companies was limited, the Government (GOCI, 1992d, p. i) describes them as being first in 1991 in providing direct jobs (although the tourism sector probably has a larger impact when indirect jobs are included); for example, in 1991, there were 1,350 people employed in banking and 215 in insurance (GOCI, 1992c, p. 18), most of whom presumably work for offshore companies.

The Tourism Sector

> It is hoped also that tourists in search of peace and quiet will be induced to
> visit the island, which, though possessing few attractions to offer, is yet en-
> tirely free of dust, with good sea-bathing in parts and wild duck shooting.
> (Cayman Islands 1914, in Weaver, 1990, p. 11)

Although the Cayman Islands have only a very short history of tourism, it has proceeded rapidly to having the characteristics of a late-Stage II (Transition) destination: rapid change, high levels of foreign investment and control, rising international visibility, large-scale hotels, aggressive visitor promotion, a focus on diving
as a market niche, and major cruise ship activity.

Stay-Over Tourist Arrivals

Noting that tourism data for the Cayman Islands prior to 1964 are speculative,
Weaver (1990, p. 11) estimates that there were 1,000–1,500 tourists annually between 1950 and 1960, whereas Blume (1968) gives a figure of 2,000 in 1962. Dramatic growth began to occur in the early 1960s, with only 3 years between 1962
and 1991 showing negative growth. The first two minor declines, in the early
1980s, were related to the worldwide recession. The third occurred in 1991: the
Gulf War, rising fuel costs, fear of terrorism, a major American recession, and the
demise of Pan American Airways led to a 6% decrease in air arrivals (and consequently the commissioning of the 10-year tourism development plan described below) (GOCI, 1992b, p. 165).

A total of 277,300 stay-over tourists in 1993, combined with the relatively small
population, results in the Cayman Islands having the second highest ratio between
stay-over tourist arrivals and local population in the Caribbean (after St Martin/St.
Maarten): in 1993, 9,577 arrivals per 1,000 local population. The tourist penetration ratio (128.56) was the highest among the case studies and the tourist density
ratio of 14.83 second only to Barbados (see Table 6.1).

Given the proximity of the islands to the United States, it is not surprising that
Americans have long been the dominant market. Absolute numbers continue to
grow, a trend for many years, with an average annual growth of 2.7% since 1980;
in relative terms, the Cayman Islands has stayed as the ninth most popular market
in the Caribbean for Americans since 1980. (All 112 direct scheduled international
air connections outside the Caribbean region during the 1992 high season were to
the United States [Mather & Todd, 1993].) The Caribbean is the second largest market, with nearly all of it being accounted for by Jamaicans. The United Kingdom
has recently replaced Canada as the third largest market. These three markets account for most tourists, with a very high concentration ratio of 90.9.

Accommodations

The first tourist hotel was the 40-room Galleon Beach Club on Seven Mile Beach in
1950; this was followed soon after by three small hotels on the George Town wa-

Table 6.1. Cayman Islands: Tourism Statistics

Year	Stay-Over Tourist No. (000s)	% Annual Change	Cruise Passengers No. (000s)	% Annual Change	Total Tourists[a] No. (000s)	% Annual Change	Visitor Expenditure US$ (M)	% Annual Change	Tourist Rooms No.	Aver. LOS (No. Nights)	No. Tourist Nights/Yr (000s)
1980	120.2	19.5	60.7	2.9	180.9	13.4	44.6	23.2	1418	4.5	540.9
1981	124.6	3.7	78.0	28.5	202.6	20.0	52.7	18.2	1792	4.7	585.6
1982	121.2	-2.7	158.3	102.9	279.5	54.5	56.2	6.6	1968	4.3	521.2
1983	130.8	7.9	177.2	11.9	308.0	10.2	61.6	9.6	1992	4.2	549.4
1984	148.5	13.5	203.6	14.9	352.1	14.3	70.9	15.1	2015	4.2	623.7
1985	145.1	-2.4	258.7	27.1	403.8	14.7	85.5	20.6	2061	4.3	633.9
1986	166.1	4.5	270.9	4.7	437.0	8.2	93.5	9.4	2026	4.0	664.4
1987	209.0	25.8	271.7	0.3	480.7	10.0	146.3[b]	56.5	2519	4.5[c]	940.5[c]
1988	218.7	4.6	315.6	16.2	534.3	11.2	176.2	20.2	2579	4.9[c]	071.6[c]
1989	209.7	4.1	403.9	28.0	613.6	14.8	177.4	0.7	2589	4.7[c]	985.6[c]
1990	253.2	20.7	361.7	-24.1	614.9	0.2	235.7	32.9	3064	4.9[b]	1240.7[c]
1991	237.4	-6.2	474.7	31.2	712.1	15.8	223.3	-5.3	3275	4.9[c]	1163.3[c]
1992	241.8	1.9	613.5	29.2	855.3	20.1	229.6	2.8	3428	4.9[b]	1184.8[c]
1993	287.3	18.8	605.7	-1.3	892.3	4.3	258.5	12.6	3453	4.9[c]	1407.8[c]

[a]Number of excursionists not available.
[b]Based on new exchange rate.
[c]Hotels only (i.e., excluding apartments).

terfront (Sea View Lodge, Pageant Beach, and Bay View) and the Rum Point Club on the northeast corner of North Sound (Colonial Office, 1953, 1955; Stocken, 1956; Weaver, 1990, p. 11). Contrary to a posited pattern of initial local ownership of small-scale accommodations when the tourist cycle begins (Butler, 1980), all of these facilities were apparently financed and operated by non-Caymanian interests (Weaver, 1990, p. 13). By 1961, there were 300 rooms in eight hotels, patronized mainly in winter months; there was some fishing and diving and the beginning of vacation houses (Jacobs, 1962).

The growth in the number of hotel rooms was regular but slow throughout the 1960s, but the total stock did not really take off until the 250-room Holiday Inn, the first international-class hotel in the Cayman Islands, opened in 1971, bringing the total number of rooms to about 700. The amount of sandy shoreline was limited, so further growth would have been impossible without large-scale land reclamation. The first swamp reclamation project began in 1966 using draglines and later hydraulic dredges; six major projects had been completed by 1975 (Giglioli, 1976)—resulting in major alterations to the terrestrial and marine environment. There has been some reclamation since then, but many of the developments (particularly those aimed at the vacation residence market) remain half empty with unsold lots. Although the first condominium units were built in 1974, the condominium boom did not really begin until 1977 (GOCI, 1979, p. 3); in 1980, there were about 580 units (in a total accommodation stock of 1,418 rooms). A construction boom really took off, with 26 hotel–apartment complexes beginning construction (GOCI, 1980). By 1993, there were 3,453 rooms. Unlike most other Caribbean islands, this development occurred without the need for many specific investment incentives. For example, whereas the GOCI does give tax and duty concessions to foreign investors in the tourism sector, tax holidays per se are not needed as there is no direct taxation (CICC, 1991, p. 51).

This level of accommodation development means that the Cayman Islands has one of the highest densities of hotel rooms per km[2] in the Caribbean and the highest among the case studies at 13.3 in 1993. In terms of the ratio between the number of hotel rooms and 1,000 local population, however, it was first at 115.1. It is the tourism occupancy function, however, where the impact of tourism is most apparent: the figure of 81.8 in 1993 surpasses the other case studies.

The domination of the accommodation scene by small hotels and condominiums is shown by the facts that fewer than a third of the hotel rooms are in establishments of 100+ rooms, that there are only three hotels of 200+ rooms and none between 100-199 rooms, and that the average hotel size in 1992 was 72 rooms. There is, however, a wide range of types of accommodation, with 63% of stayover arrivals staying in hotels, 23% in apartments and guest houses, and 14% in private or unregistered accommodations (mostly condominiums) in 1993. Given the domination of the nearby American market, however, average lengths of stay are quite low compared to other destinations, consistently being under five nights since the early 1980s; as a result, there was a 160.3% increase in the annual number of tourist nights between 1980 and 1993, parallel to the 143.5% increase in the total number of stay-over arrivals.

Excursionists

No data are available on excursionists to the Cayman Islands.

Cruise Passengers

Cruise passenger arrivals were very low until 1975 when dramatic growth began as Norwegian Caribbean Lines selected the Cayman Islands as port of call for M/S *Southward*, resulting in 22,500 cruise passengers arrivals that year. Although it soon backed down in the face of ever-growing demand and the creation of many new services aimed at cruise passengers, the Government (GOCI, 1975a) adopted a short-lived (and today largely forgotten) policy to limit cruise ship arrivals to no more than one in port on any given day: "This is a healthy approach to a difficult problem. The size and number of facilities would be so overtaxed with any more cruise business as to be completely impossible to deal with" (p. 5). Not until 1993 was a similar policy reinstated, with a limit of no more than three cruise ships or 5,500 passengers per day.

One impact of these numbers is that the small town that is George Town is altered significantly nearly every day of the year by the rapid infusion of large numbers of cruise passengers arriving via lighters from the ships anchored offshore:

> It's early on a flawless spring morning and five cruise ships swing at anchor at the edge of the spectacular coral reefs off George Town, capital city of the Cayman Islands. The invasion is about to begin.
>
> By 10, the waterfront and business districts of this tiny port city are already bulging as the parade of open boats continues to ferry the ships' passengers ashore. Quickly through the neat dockside terminal they troop, past the ever-present calypso-reggae group and out into the bright heat of Church Street. . . .
>
> Despite the crush of numbers, an air of orderliness prevails. One is struck by the calm efficiency and the quiet patience of the waiting van and cab drivers.
>
> Something's missing! There are no hawkers, no pushers, no beggars, no urchins, no pamphlets, no smelly garbage in the streets. Hey, this IS the Caribbean, isn't it? (MacFarlane, 1992)[1]

With the exceptions of a large decrease in arrivals in 1990 related to the Gulf War and a minor decrease in 1993 related to the American recession, cruise passenger numbers have grown almost steadily to 605,700 in 1993, largely because of the visit every 2 weeks by the mega-ship *The Ecstasy*, with over 2,600 passengers. Like the Bahamas, the Cayman Islands is unusual in that it receives more cruise passengers than stay-over tourists. Three other measures indicate the phenomenal presence of cruise passengers in the Cayman Islands: in 1993, there were 20,190 arrivals per 1,000 local population, a penetration ratio of 55.328, and a density ratio of 6.38—figures that are much higher than those for the Bahamas, the largest cruise destination among the case studies. Presumably, the number of ships will drop somewhat in the future with the Government's new restrictive policy, but the construction of ever-larger ships (such as *The Ecstasy* and its sister ship, *The Fantasy*) might still result in growing number of cruise passenger visits even with the 5,500/day limit as one large ship can carry more passengers than three small ones.

The environmental impact of cruise ships has long been a concern in the Cayman Islands, first for the reason noted above of possible overtaxing of facilities and later for the ecological impacts of waste discharge and reef damage (S. H. Smith, 1988). The latter problem has been the source of many unsuccessful calls (e.g., GOCI, 1987, p. 46) for permanent mooring buoys (because there are no berthing facilities for large ships, they anchor offshore, thus presenting the danger of coral damage by anchors), whereas the former has been the subject of successful court action. In 1992, a cruise ship was found guilty of discharging sewage into the harbor; the company agreed to plead guilty and pay the US$4,200 fine as long as the company and not the captain was charged. The same ship was charged again following a second incident a few weeks after the first one (D. Vousden, 1993, personal communication). In 1993, the maximum fine was raised from US$6,000 to US$600,000 for marine dumping or destruction by ships of any kind—the stiffest fine in the Caribbean (Showker, 1993, p. 38). Cruise ships are now monitored by aerial photography several times each stay to check for dumping (W. Whitaker, 1993, personal communication).

Questions have also been raised as to how significant is the economic impact of cruise passengers, despite their large numbers, in comparison with stay-over visitors (B. Boxhill, 1993, personal communication). One estimate (Pratt, 1993, p. 262) is that cruise passengers account for only 6% of tourist-related revenues for the Islands.

Total Visitors

The Cayman Islands' position as a late Stage II destination is reinforced by the aggregated statistics for stay-over and cruise visitors, for whom, between 1980 and 1993, there was a 393.3% increase—highest among the case studies—to 892,300 total arrivals. This was matched by the other measures: 29,767 visitors per 1,000 local population, a penetration ratio of 183.88 (both first), and a density ratio of 21.21 (second to Barbados).

Expenditures

Even as early as 1967, tourism was a major economic activity in the Cayman Islands, with hotels and guest houses contributing 6.2% of the GDP and tourist receipts being 28.5% of national incomes (Bryden, 1973, p. 27). By 1970, the growth in tourism and offshore companies had led to virtual full employment for Caymanians, resulting in pressure to increase the number of work permits for non-Caymanians (Colonial Office, 1972, pp. 3–4). Although figures are not available before then, tourist expenditures were still quite modest at that time, with an estimate US$10.0 million in 1973. Since the late 1970s, there has been a continual and remarkable growth in every year but 1989 (apparently related to disruptions in the American airline industry through bankruptcies caused by airline deregulation). In 1993, estimated expenditures totalled US$258.8 million.

One of the major reasons for such large expenditures is very high room rates. In 1987–1988, the Cayman Islands had the second highest winter rates (US$140.40) and third highest summer rates (US$102.00) in the Caribbean (Curtin & Poon, 1988). The 37.6% difference between the winter and summer rates is modest, probably because of relatively high demands during the summer by scuba divers, one of the Islands' major markets,[2] resulting in a low and stable index of seasonality of 1.177 in 1989 (de Albuquerque & McElroy, 1992, p. 627) and 1.151 in 1993.

Although the offshore company industry is a major economic factor, the importance both absolutely and relatively of tourism in the Caymanian economy is immense—and growing. Tourism expenditures were US$8,617 per capita of local population in 1993—an unrivalled figure in the Caribbean. This represented 34.8% of GDP in 1993 (with the hotel and restaurant sector alone accounting for 7.8% of GDP) and 489.6% of external debt in 1992. The lack of alternative visible exports resulted in visitor expenditures having a ratio of 51.0:1 to merchandise exports in 1992. However, no recent figures are available to compare with Bryden's (1973, p. 162) estimate of 0.65 as the tourism multiplier in 1963.

There have been many estimates of tourism-related employment, but there are inconsistencies and discrepancies in the numbers. In some cases, it is not clear whether the numbers presented represent direct or total employment (e.g., GOCI, 1992e). In other cases, there are inexplicable decreases for the late 1980s (e.g., GOCI, 1992c). It would appear that about 1,200–1,300 people were directly employed in the sector by 1993 (CTO, 1994; GOCI, 1992e; Mather & Todd, 1993). Another inconsistency is the Government's figure of 1,530 people being employed in the hotel and condominium sector alone in 1991 (GOCI, 1992c, p. 18).

As with most other sectors of the economy, a high proportion of non-Caymanians have long been employed in tourism-related jobs. For example, Bryden (1973, p. 130) states that, in 1970, nearly 65% of employees in managerial and administrative occupations in the tourism sector were expatriates, whereas overall, 32.1% of the labor force in hotels and guest houses were expatriates; however, 42.7% of the total wage and salary bill of that sector accrued to expatriate labor. A recent figure that is only partly comparable (as it does not represent the entire tourism sector) is that 26.7% of the 1,530 hotel and condominium employees in 1991 were non-Caymanians (GOCI, 1992c, p. 18). Personal conversations with several people involved in the tourism sector, however, indicate the increasing difficulty of attracting Caymanians into tourism jobs, at all levels, in the face of competing employment opportunities in other sectors such as government and offshore companies, with higher pay, more prestige, and better working conditions, including regular 9–5 work schedules. Further expansion of the tourism sector will clearly exacerbate this situation.

Given the economic importance of tourism, it is not surprising that the Government spends more on marketing per stay-over visitor than any other destination, rising from US$26.00 in 1986 to US$57.59 in 1993. The 42.9% increase in the number of stay-over tourist arrivals during this period was also one of the largest among the case studies, but it came at a high price: a 216.6% increase in the budget from US$4.3 to US$13.7 million. Given the increased visitor expenditures noted above, however, this seems to have been a successful investment.

Tourism Policy and Planning

Weaver (1990) quotes a former Caymanian politician responsible for tourism: "This remarkable surge of visitors to our shores is not a sudden or random happening. Our consistent and dependable growth has been the direct result of extensive marketing planning and intensive implementation of those programmes, both at home and abroad" (p. 3).

The Policy and Planning Context

With little pressure for development, planning controls in the Cayman Islands did not receive much attention until the late 1960s when the dramatic rise in tourism and the formation of the offshore financial industry resulted in an unprecedented construction boom. It became clear that the Government should exercise better control over physical development to minimize the public costs and ensure that irreparable damage was not done to the environment. Although a Regional Planning Law was in existence, it was considered antiquated and inadequate as it permitted uncontrolled building and development in the vast majority of areas (GOCI, 1987, p. 83). The Land Development (Interim Control) Law of 1969 and the subsequent Regulations of 1970 were designed "to produce ordered and sensible development of the Islands and not to allow indiscriminate building and development which may be against the public interests" (GOCI, 1987, p. 83). Two development control boards were created by this law: the Grand Cayman Development Board and the Cayman Brac and Little Cayman Development Board. It also introduced a procedure for planning permission for any building development or change in land use and regulations for the preservation of amenities and control of advertisements.

In 1971, the interim law was replaced by the Development and Planning Law (and subsequent Regulations in 1972), which created a Central Planning Authority in overall control of planning, appointed a Director of Planning and a planning staff, and required a development plan and update every 5 years. A Draft Concept Plan (GOCI, 1973b) was produced in 1973 with the aid of a United Nations Regional Planning Team. In 1975, the Government (GOCI, 1975b) proposed a Development Plan that emphasized the importance of environmental management. It discussed in detail the effects of overdevelopment through dredging, marl removal, limestone mining, sewage impacts, and destruction of mangroves; as a result, it suggested stringent limits on any further development. The proposal, however, was soon withdrawn as being too controversial. A second Development Plan (GOCI, 1977) and Regulations were approved in 1977, which established that the Planning Department is to process planning applications, but the Central Planning

Authority (established under the Development and Planning Law of 1977 [Pratt, 1993, p. 263]) makes planning decisions.

Most land in the Cayman Islands is privately owned and, following a survey in the 1970s, every piece of land is registered (Colonial Office, 1973, p. 3). There is no restriction on foreign ownership of land and, although there is no property tax on developed or undeveloped land, there is a stamp duty on the purchase of land (7.5% on all land and property valued up to $250,000 and 10% above that figure) (GOCI, 1990a, pp. 1–2).

The 1977 Development Plan recognized many environmental problems and began a path of environmental legislation that continues to the present (e.g., Endangered Species Propagation and Protection Act of 1978, Marine Conservation Law of 1978). By 1986, there were marine parks on all three islands, with well-defined replenishment, park, and environmental zones (GOCI, n.d). Partly in response to an incident of serious reef damage resulting from a cruise ship dragging its anchor (S. H. Smith, 1988), cooperation between the Government and the Cayman Islands Watersport Operators Association (CIWOA) has resulted in the placement of 206 permanent mooring buoys at dive sites on the three islands (Showker, 1993, p. 40).

In April 1993, the Government founded a Department of the Environment, which combined the Environmental Health Section, Natural Resources Unit, and Mosquito Research and Control Unit, under the Portfolio of Tourism, Environment, and Planning; its overall mission is the protection and conservation of the natural environment (W. Whitaker, 1993, personal communication). There is also a very active National Trust for the Cayman Islands that operates a captive breeding program of the endemic Blue Iguana, reserves (e.g., 250-hectare Salina Reserve on Grand Cayman, 40-hectare Brac Parrot Reserve on Cayman Brac), heritage sites, and public awareness programs (A. Pedley, 1993, personal communication).

The Government (GOCI, 1987, p. 87) recognizes that the ability of the Planning Department to implement effective environmental protection is constrained by a shortage of qualified staff, lack of an effective mechanism for obtaining wider public support for national planning proposals, overcomplex and confusing procedures for obtaining planning permission, lack of effective control over building developments, and lack of modern aids for more efficient operations. There have been at least two government proposals recently to provide a means to fund improvements in these areas. First, the initiation of "development impact fees" has been proposed to cover the costs of constructing new infrastructure (e.g., roads, sewers, water) related to the development. Second, there has been a call for the development of a "capital improvement plan" emphasizing infrastructure development in areas the Government would like development: "Government first needs to identify where they would like to be through a proactive plan as opposed to waiting for development to direct the growth of the country through reactive planning" (GOCI, 1992a, p. 8). As described below, a long-term review of the 1987 development plan underway, which could address many of these problems, began in 1992.

The Early Days of Tourism

There had been at least one early instance of interest in promoting tourism, when in 1908 an advertisement appeared in *The Caymanian* (a short-lived newspaper that ceased publication in 1910) for the Cayman Hotels Company, Ltd., announcing a share offering worth £1000: "The objects of the Company are to purchase land suitable for Hotel premises, and to erect thereon a small Hotel, to encourage tourists to visit Grand Cayman" (Anonymous, 1908, p. 4). There is no evidence, however, that the share offering was purchased, let alone a hotel built (P. Pedley, 1993, personal communication).

The beginning of the modern age came with the appointment in 1934 of Allen W. Cardinall as Commissioner; responsible for supporting wireless radio connections (1935), telephones (1937), roads, and public buildings,

> Cardinall made good use of his journalistic skill to tell the world about the Caymans in radio broadcasts in which he invited his listeners to pay the dependency a visit. He foresaw the great possibilities of a tourist trade and never ceased telling people that "Grand Cayman has what is probably the most perfect bathing-beach in the West Indies." He successfully inaugurated the January Regatta in 1935, which attracted craft from all over the Caribbean. (N. Williams, 1992, p. 76)

A remarkable (undated, but actually 1937) advertising pamphlet extolling the potential of the Cayman Islands as a tourist destination was printed anonymously; even more extraordinary is that the anonymous author was Commissioner Cardinall, who personally arranged for it to be printed and distributed (P. Pedley, 1993, personal communication). Although the pamphlet is more than somewhat at odds with the official reports (e.g., Colonial Office, 1939) in which he himself wrote of the lack of paved roads, the limited electricity, and the infrequency of supply boats, it nevertheless presents a fascinating perception of the islands:

> The capital of the Island is Georgetown [sic] and has a population of merely some 1400 people, but the shops are surprisingly well stocked and the writer has often wondered where the market can be. You can buy anything you want from photo-films to sandals, from saucepans to suites of furniture, motor tyres to saddlery. There are tailors and barbers; there are garages and filling stations, ice cream, electric light, telephone. There is very little indeed that one cannot obtain in Georgetown, and prices are extremely moderate as well they must be in a community dependent on the sea. (Cardinall, 1937, p. 11)

Noting that growing numbers of people are seeking a place in the sun each year, Cardinall (1937) recommends the Cayman Islands as "a tranquil place within reasonable reach of the busy world, but away from all its blare and noise" (p. 1)—but fails to define what form of transportation can cover that "reach." His description of Grand Cayman is accurate, if flowery:

Grand Cayman offers a variety of joys which Providence seems to have heaped in one small spot. Foremost, perhaps, are the bathing beaches. That these rival those of any other place is certain—we of the Islands claim that they are nowhere surpassed, not even equalled. (Cardinall, 1937, pp. 1–2)

Nevertheless, he does downplay somewhat the island's major environmental hazard:

. . . there are beaches everywhere, small and large, completely hidden and completely open, beaches fringed with the sea grape and the almond, beneath the shade of which one can picnic and rest and just laze away one's holiday, undisturbed, with nothing to worry about, nothing to fear, either from heat of sun or bite of insect.

The last expression would not be true for the summer months because mosquitos in Cayman as in most parts of the Caribbean are at that time occasionally very numerous. (Cardinall, 1937, p. 5)

Whether the Commissioner's advertising efforts were actually responsible for any tourists visiting the islands is not known, but the onset of World War II ended for some time the chance of a tourist boom.

In a wartime study for the British government on the postwar development potential of the West Indies, Thompson (1943) predicts the potential for tourism in the Cayman Islands:

As a tourist resort, the Islands appear to offer some attraction. There are good bathing beaches and moderate sports fishing. In many ways they offer the same peaceful charm which attracted tourists to Bermuda. But accommodation for tourists is very inadequate and the poorness of the utilities would be a great disadvantage in competing for the North American trade. Suggestions have been made for the establishment of a rather simple type of accommodation, rather in the nature of a tourist camp. Whether the extensive mosquito crop would allow such a scheme to operate should be considered. (p. 8)

Other than some commercial fishing potential, Thompson (1943) feels that tourism is the only potential form of economic development, but suggests that it must be low-key:

Though the possibilities of attracting tourists are limited, it should be borne in mind that a relatively small income from this source could have a profound effect on this small economy. If a tourist trade is to be developed, reliance will have to be placed upon the peaceful calm rather than of offering excitement in either living or sport; no grandiose scheme would be warranted. (p. 31)

An even more enthusiastic view of tourism—but with a very different conception of the type of appropriate development—appears to have been the first local expression of modern interest in investment in tourism. In a letter to the Government, O. C. Webster and H. J. Ashwell (1946) proposed to purchase Crown land on West Bay Beach (now called Seven Mile Beach) on Grand Cayman and to drain a swamp area: "The intention is to develope [sic] Grand Cayman on very exclusive lines as there is a demand for a resort of this type today. Grand Cayman lends itself admirably to a high class Tourist trade on account of its small size and the natural courtesy and friendliness of the population." Their proposal includes a hotel, golf course, yacht club, marina, electric power plant, ice factory, and passenger air shuttle service between Montego Bay and Grand Cayman. They conclude that "There is no single Industry which so benefits all classes of a Community than Tourism and with Caymans [sic] natural resources and climate and sea bathing facilities there is no reason why this business should not bring in millions of dollars annually and in this way make a valuable contribution to the Empire's economy." For unknown reasons, Webster and Ashwell did not proceed with their plans (P. Pedley, 1993, personal communication).

Prosperity was slow to come after the war and the Cayman Islands remained largely unknown to the rest of the world, their only claim to fame being the turtle industry (cf. D. D. Duncan, 1948; Maloney, 1950). Sea transport to the Cayman Islands was "sketchy" and regular service from Kingston, Jamaica was frequently canceled (Anglo-American Caribbean Commission, 1945). Although there had been the occasional cruise passenger before World War II, the real tourist trade started in 1946 with the first seaplane service from Miami to North Cape on Grand Cayman (GOCI, 1987, p. 8). In 1946, weekly seaplane service began between Grand Cayman and Jamaica, "but this service came to an end in June 1947 because of the poor condition of the 'planes [sic] of the Jamaica Air Transport Company" and was not resumed until 1948 (N. Williams, 1992, p. 80). Interest, however, had begun to revive in the tourism sector:

> The possibility of the establishment of a small tourist industry has also been pursued during the year. The potentialities of the excellent five-mile-long beach on the west coast of Grand Cayman[3] and the south coast of Little Cayman have attracted a number of capitalists from outside the Dependency and it is hoped that with the improvement of transportation between the Cayman Islands and the United States and Jamaica some action will be taken in this connection in the near future. (Colonial Office, 1948, p. 3)

The first hotel, Galleon Beach at the west end of George Town, opened in 1950; airstrips were inaugurated in Grand Cayman in 1953 and Cayman Brac in 1954; and by 1956, there were adequate electricity, banks, hospital, and a newspaper. Once again, it took leadership from a Commissioner, A. M. Gerrard, to open the door to the future by inviting a delegation of people from the Jamaican tourism sector to consider investment (N. Williams, 1992, p. 82). Tourism soon began to grow by leaps and bounds, bringing unimagined prosperity, with an expanding economy and population—and major changes to the environment.

Growing Government Involvement

Weaver (1990) notes that in the early days of tourism in the Cayman Islands in the 1950s, there was little government effort to promote tourism:

A nondescript mimeographed fact sheet produced for tourists by the Government in 1956 refers nonchalantly to "indifferent roads" and a cable office which was usually closed. Potential tourists were reminded, "You must console yourself with the thought that life anywhere is impossible without a little healthy frustration" (Gerrard, 1956). (p. 13)

A Hotel Aid Law had been passed in 1955 (and amended in 1960) to encourage the building of hotels (Colonial Office, 1957, 1961), but little if any use was made of it. Promotion really began with the formation of a Tourist Board in 1961, but it was not particularly influential until a Tourist Board Law was passed in 1965 and instituted in 1966, the same year when a Tourist Board Office was opened in Miami (Weaver, 1990, p. 13). In addition to training for the sector, the Board had the principal function "to develop the tourism of the Cayman Islands without destroying the fragile island environment or placing undue stress upon the island infrastructure and the local labor force" (GOCI, 1973a, pp. 1–2). In 1970, the Board began to use American advertising agencies and public relations counsels to publicize the Cayman Islands to travel agencies and the mass media and also established tourism offices in New York, Chicago, Houston, Dallas, Seattle, and Los Angeles.

Through the Tourism Law of 1974, the Board was changed into a Department of Tourism at the recommendation of a study under assignment of the British ODA (Transport and Tourism Technicians Ltd., 1972). The Law had three further significant changes:

- funding tourism activities that greatly increased the ability to promote the Islands' vacation experience to prospective visitors and the sector (e.g., in 1977, the Pirates Week Festival, a promotional event to stimulate October off-season arrivals; successful from the beginning, it continues to the present);

- the Hotels Licensing Board, with the power to inspect premises and grant licenses;

- data collection to track tourism activity and its impact on the economy (Pratt, 1993, p. 263).

It was becoming clear that continued growth of tourism was dependent on reliable air transportation—a sector that seemed to require increasing Government involvement. Privately owned Cayman Islands Airways Ltd., founded in 1946, was soon bankrupt. It was followed by Cayman International Airways Ltd. in 1948, which was wound up soon after an airplane crash in 1953; its routes were taken over by BWIA, but the Government soon entered into a lease arrangement with Lineas Aereas Costarricenses, SA (LACSA) (GOCI, 1987, p. 55). The Government established Cayman Airways, Ltd. (CAL)[4] following the termination of a lease agreement with LACSA in December 1977. The following were seen as the benefits:

Economic problems experienced by other countries would not jeopardize service to the Cayman Islands and labour disputes could be domestically controlled and/or directed. Most importantly, the Caymanian government would set policy, manage, administer and coordinate the primary means of access to the Islands. (Laventhol & Horwath, 1981, p. III-3).

Government involvement in the airline industry, however, has not been without serious problems. In the 1981 Tourism Development Plan (see below), Laventhal & Horwath (1981, p. VI-8) contend that projected growth in tourist arrivals means that (a) CAL would have to increase its fleet size or (b) get bigger planes or (c) an open-sky policy would be needed to meet the demand. The first two contentions did eventually come to pass in 1989 when CAL sold its two Boeing 727s that it had bought in 1981 and entered into an expensive lease for five Boeing 737-400s (R. Wilson, 1993, personal communication). (The third contention was always unlikely because, as the Cayman Islands is a Crown Colony, air agreements are a responsibility of the British government.) CAL was soon criticized for major losses: of its US$42 million accumulated loss between 1983 and 1991, fully US$26 million was incurred between 1988 and 1991. After the election of 1992, the new Government expressed a policy of either making CAL profitable or closing it down; however, recognizing the prestige of a national airline and the marginal benefit of at least some control over air transport, the Government agreed to continue to provide a subsidy of nearly US$5 million per annum for the short term. If the financial picture does not turn around, the Government intends to hold a national referendum on CAL's possible closure. In the meantime, CAL has canceled the lease on three of its planes and reoriented its mission to providing a least-cost airline (with its annual operating loss of US$15.4 million in 1991 being reduced to US$7.0 million in 1992) and a backup in case other airlines pull out of the island in the face of the volatile international airline industry. Much of CAL's problem seems to be the battle for regional control by American Airlines (which has 55% of the region's market share) and United Airlines, resulting in a price squeeze that CAL simply cannot match (DeLuca, 1993, p. 18).

CAL appears to be an example of the classic case described by Jenkins and Henry (1982, pp. 517–518) of the conflicting pressures faced by a small state considering the establishment of a national airline. There are potential advantages: reduction in dependency on foreign airlines; the opportunity to develop new air services and perhaps new markets; foreign exchange earnings accruing from air fares; and a source of pride and a means of supplementing the creation of an international image. However, there are reasons to suggest that it will be an expensive and difficult undertaking: large investments requiring foreign exchange spending; type of aircraft affecting the nature and quality of services offered; operating margins affected by high unit operating costs as a result of the small scale of operations; time required to establish a reputation for quality of service and for safety; and rising fuel costs. The results of all of these pressures have been intensified price competition, major changes in route networks, and demands for government protection against "unfair" competition. The Government appears to have recognized these problems and decided that the only viable solution is a minimal service operation designed to plug the gaps in the route offerings of international carriers, yet maintaining a presence in the industry for reasons of national image. As a result, the

Government is handling a US$20 million recapitalization loan provided by a consortium of banks, which will help the airline to manage its debt (DeLuca, 1993, p. 19).

A Series of Plans

The 1977 Development Plan (GOCI, 1977) applies only to Grand Cayman (but includes specific guidelines as appendices for Cayman Brac and Little Cayman rather than a full-scale development plan):

> The primary objective of the Development Plan is to maintain and enhance the environmental character of the Cayman Islands and the well-being and prosperity of its people. It is intended to define and develop a planning strategy for the Islands which is however flexible enough in concept and implication to accommodate individual requirements, special circumstances and changing conditions. (p. 1)

It (GOCI, 1977, pp. 1–2) sets out specific policies, including: further development of the tourist and banking industries; development of manufacturing, service, and food industries with a goal of self-sufficiency; and environmental preservation and protection, particularly freshwater conservation. While setting out categories of zones (e.g., hotel and tourist-related development, scenic shoreline, public access, public open space), the Plan notes that "The designated land use of each zone is not in any way inflexible. . . . [T]he zoning is intended to indicate the primary land use of each zone. Thus, other development may be permitted providing that it can be demonstrated that it will not adversely affect the primary use of the zone" (GOCI, 1977, p. 2).

A great deal of the Plan focuses on the protection of the natural environment, as an asset for both local people and tourists. Emphasis is placed on preservation of mangrove swamps (for ecological, biological, and storm protection functions, but there remains a considerable area of land available for reclamation and development), coral reefs, beaches, freshwater, sewerage, and national parks. Arguing that hotel and tourist-related development requires a high standard of design and construction, the Plan calls for maximum use of high-quality landscaping and compliance with the recommended standards laid down for density, lot size, site coverage, set-backs, and provision for vehicle parking.

To meet the tourism policy goals of the 1977 Development Plan, the Government commissioned a Ten-Year Tourism Development Plan in 1981. On the whole, the consultants (Laventhol & Horwath, 1981, p. VI-1) foresee a positive picture for the sector, largely because of the apparent political commitment to the future of tourism by the Government. While noting that the Cayman Islands has managed to avoid many of the economic and social problems plaguing other Caribbean states (e.g., high population, unemployment, and illiteracy, and unsatisfactory income distribution), Laventhol & Horwath (1981, p. VI-2) describe other existing problems: escalating land prices; negative impacts of immigration on the Caymanian population; incomplete national and ecological planning; lack of hotel management expertise; increasing social tension; and a rapidly changing social environment.

Leventhol & Horwath (1981, pp. VI-3–4) argue that "proper planning and control" are required to balance the growth of tourism through three primary elements: development closely aligned to population growth, labor force, key industries such as banking, and the Islands' infrastructure capacities; the number of foreign visitors controlled to permit the local population to render adequate service; all tourism plans, policies, and legislation conforming to and complementing the local culture and the ongoing needs of the population. Stating that recent and projected growth patterns could disrupt the elements of a balanced tourist product, they point to the dangers arising from the rapidly expanding construction activity, the capacity constraints of the infrastructure, the limited skilled labor pool, and lack of evidence of profit reinvestment in products and services.

A series of objectives is proposed as future development criteria: controlled and planned growth of tourism; educational programs on all facets of the travel sector; decreased dependency on expatriate labor and temporary work permits; maximized land use to better accommodate and service foreign visitors; and quality superstructure and infrastructure with the fewest negative implications (Laventhol & Horwath, 1981, p. V-4). Rather than expansion of the accommodation sector, they suggest that these objectives are best met through the enhancement and/or adaptive reuse of existing establishments, along with upgrading of the airports, ground transportation, road system, and cruise-related shuttle and ground transport. They warn that further large-scale development of Grand Cayman could destroy its attractiveness and that Little Cayman and Cayman Brac should be kept small scale in order to protect their natural environments and their up-scale market niche (Laventhol & Horwath, 1981, pp. VI-32–VI-35).

Maintenance of high standards of environmental quality is emphasized, both because such factors as water and sewerage needs place limits on the scale of development and because of the demands of the type of tourists attracted to the Cayman Islands (Laventhol & Horwath, 1981, p. V-40). A number of methods of controlling development are suggested: a moratorium on new lodging facilities, phasing of construction approval, and restrictions on imported labor for construction. The types of tourists are also seen as being critical to controlling growth; therefore, they argue for resisting pressure by private investors to shift from "class" to "mass" tourists in marketing and for exploring new markets (e.g., Europe) with long average lengths of stay and high expenditures (Laventhol & Horwath, 1981, pp. VI-53–VI-55).

Despite recognizing that the economy should be diversified because of the linkages of both tourism and offshore companies to the fragility of the international economy, the Government (GOCI, 1987) defines its primary development goal for 1988–1992 in its second Development Plan as "steady development in established directions and not one of radical change" (p. 27) through continued reliance on tourism and the offshore financial industry. Environmental protection receives a great deal of emphasis, with proposals to support the Marine Parks System, protection areas for various marine species, and the provision of public open space (GOCI, 1987, p. 116). The fragile environment and culture of Little Cayman and Cayman Brac are recognized and, although the desire is stated to provide them with a degree of prosperity comparable with that of Grand Cayman, it is recognized that the scale and type of development have to be carefully controlled.

The Government (GOCI, 1987, p. 132) clearly reiterates its view that tourism development is to be a private sector concern, although it will be carefully controlled by government policy and planning.

Despite major constraints to industrial development (e.g., labor, raw materials, small internal market, shortage and high cost of land, absence of building material, limited water supply, sewage system, high costs of air services, high cost of living, preference for imported items), the Plan calls for economic diversification, particularly where there are possible linkages with the tourism sector (e.g., crafts, agriculture, aquaculture).

The Government seems to have been too successful in promoting economic growth. With rates of growth of 13% in 1987 and 12% in 1988, concerns began to be raised about an overheated economy: "Calls have made by the Chamber [of Commerce] for growth management strategies and policies. A petition presented to us and signed by over 1,000 Caymanians asked for controlled growth, even if at a cost of personal financial sacrifice" (CICC, 1991, p. 35). As a result, the Government formed a National Planning Committee in 1989 and accepted its recommendation of a 3-year moratorium on new hotel construction on Seven Mile Beach; however, condominiums, apartments, cottage colonies, guest houses, and extensions to existing hotels were exempted and hotel construction that had received prior approval was not affected. The Cayman Islands Chamber of Commerce (CICC, 1991, p. 36) wanted the Government to be even more conservative, preferring the moratorium to be applied throughout Grand Cayman and extensions to hotels also being subject to the order, on the grounds of shortage of labor resources and infrastructure. In 1993, however, the Government decided not to reimpose the moratorium on new construction on Seven Mile Beach under pressure from a construction industry suffering from a downturn in business. As a result, a new condominium complex and a shopping center were built in 1994 on Seven Mile Beach and another condominium project and a five-star hotel are planned for 1995 (Hurlston, 1995, pp. 47–48).

The overall objective of the Government's (GOCI, 1992d) Ten-Year Tourism Development Plan, the first tourism plan for the Cayman Islands, is

> . . . to provide a clear set of policies, strategies and implementation guidelines to chart the way forward for tourism. At the launching of the study in February 1992, it was stressed that, while tourism should continue to stimulate the economy for the benefit of the Caymanian people, it was imperative that this be achieved in the context of the preservation of the heritage, culture and environment of the Islands. (GOCI, 1992b, pp. 165, 167)

Recognizing an average annual increase of 8% in tourist arrivals from 1980 to 1990, the Plan credits the growth of global tourism, government marketing and policy initiatives, and private sector investment, but warns that

> Historically it has been shown that uncontrolled growth typically results in a degeneration of product and service. The resources which motivate tourists to come to the Cayman Islands must be maintained at a high level of quality. The current "breathing time" [i.e., a period of slower growth in the global tourism industry] is essential for the Cayman Islands to further build management and planning control strength, institutionally, in the private sector and in the non-profit sector. (GOCI, 1992d, p. i)

It sees the tourism and the offshore financial sectors as the long-term bases for the economic development of the Cayman Islands.

Described as a strategic management plan (see Chapter 9) rather than a master plan for physical development, the document specifies the management needs, growth guidelines, and specific growth initiatives required for effective management of the sector focused on three major strategic changes:

- the price–value relationship must be enhanced, in terms of both affordability and value;

- a managed entrepreneurial spirit is required to ensure that tourism is managed for the long-term benefit of all Caymanians;

- expatriates should be seen as a resource, not as a problem, because the high employment and low birth rates for Caymanians could result in a local labor shortage if tourism growth continues (GOCI, 1992d, pp. ii–iii).

Arguing that visitor numbers alone do not measure growth accurately, it is suggested that various "trigger mechanisms" be monitored: government revenue, jobs, pressure on/costs of social services, occupancy rates, property transactions, pressure on/costs of infrastructure, attractions, recreation services, crowding/social impact, environment (i.e., carrying capacity), retail sales, and economic impact (GOCI, 1992d, p. iii).

Without an appropriate legislative base and organizational structure, however, tourism development cannot be managed. Legislation (e.g., Planning Act, Tourism Act, natural resources legislation), therefore, needs to be revised to reflect the objectives of the Plan. Then an organizational structure should be put in place: a National Tourism Committee (coordination and focus); a Tourism Quality Council (standards, training, recruitment, awareness, education); enhancement of the Historic Sites Committee (including the establishment of a Foundation to support fund-raising); and concentration of Department of Tourism functions (marketing, program development, accommodation development and inspection, and research) (GOCI, 1992d, p. iii).

Describing a basic choice that must be made between continued rapid growth in tourism (yielding supposed economic benefits, but increasing social and environmental problems) and no growth (with the opposite effects) (GOCI, 1992d, p. 16), the Plan (GOCI, 1992d) argues for "progressive but not overheated growth" (pp. v–vi) through meeting specific guidelines:

- 5% per annum growth for the next 5 years and 6.5% per annum growth over 10 years;

- increase air arrivals from 240,000 in 1992 to 306,000 in 1997;

- increase average occupancy rates to about 80% before allowing or encouraging additional development;

- no new development until 1998–1999;

- maintain current number of air seats per week at 7,000 (364,000 per annum);

- adapt departure schedules to customer demand;

- increase the average length of stay through increases in attractions and product development;

- increase visitor and resident satisfaction;

- limit cruise passengers to 4,500–5,000/day, target premium-to-luxury ships only, develop deep-sea permanent moorings, and increase the head tax;

- increase linkages with other industries and reduce leakage by 10% by 1997 by increased use of Island products;

- increase Caymanian participation in tourism employment, particularly at higher management levels;

- extend the runway at the Grand Cayman airport to allow jumbo jets;

- maintain current balance of one third of all accommodation units as condominiums or apartments (excluding private homes).

Essential to the achieving of such objectives is environmental protection and enhancement, which is critical for a quality tourism experience; therefore, the plan recommends (GOCI, 1992d, p. viii):

- an environmental protection and enhancement leadership role as it relates to tourism management;

- comprehensive environmental legislation;

- environmental policies;

- environmental assessments;

- carrying capacity guidelines;

- institutional awareness; and

- ecotourism.

Two types of ecotourism are defined: "One is non-specialized and is an adaptation of rubber-tired touring with an emphasis on natural history. The other is more specialized and would include bird watching, photography, and perhaps even sampling" (GOCI, 1992d, p. 31).

Particular concern is expressed about the overdevelopment of the Seven Mile Beach area of Grand Cayman (and the danger that it might spread throughout the rest of that island and to the sister islands):

> It is pertinent to note that, without building style guidelines and without local knowledge regarding climate and appropriate materials, many of the structures along Seven Mile Beach tend to have been executed in a style inappropriate to the Tropics.

> Coupled with franchise architecture, the Seven Mile Beach Strip, as it has become known, has developed a character which is not Caymanian, and in fact has been compared with Miami and other coastal U.S. resorts. (GOCI, 1992d, p. 35)

A zoning scheme is presented for the islands, along with detailed guidelines on such matters as themes, aesthetics, landscaping, interpretation, heritage, setbacks and height restrictions, environmental assessments, coordination, and planning authorities. Grand Cayman is and should remain the primary tourist destination of the three islands, with Cayman Brac having a focus on marine and terrestrial resources[5] and Little Cayman being low-key and nature oriented (GOCI, 1992d, pp. 38–52).

The Plan's basic conclusion is that

> . . . the "willed future" for the Cayman Islands will be one whereby quality, price-value and a moderate level of growth will be achieved. It will be characterized by environmental and cultural protection and enhancement and a thorough understanding of the industry by the public and the government. It will also be characterized by a unified tourism industry for the three Islands and, finally, it will be a managed industry. (GOCI, 1992d, p. 23)

The adoption of the Plan has led to a longer term process. Recognizing that numerous changes (e.g., population growing at an annual rate of 4.2%, traffic jams, concern over water quality and reef damage) are affecting Grand Cayman, the GOCI (1992e) initiated a long-term review of the development plan to examine a wide range of questions:

Q. Where should new roads be constructed?
Q. How is the water supplied?
Q. Is there adequate public access to beaches and other coastal areas?
Q. How many people are going to live there in the future?
Q. Are the Cayman Islands growing too fast? Too slow?
Q. How do we deal with issues arising from the impact of development on culture?
Q. What do people feel about the impact of growth on the environment? (pp. 5, 7)

A Development Plan Review Committee was set up by the Central Planning Authority, along with District Subcommittees in every district on Grand Cayman and district meetings to encourage public participation. A later exercise will deal with similar issues for Little Cayman and Cayman Brac.

There are signs that the Review Committee is taking at least some steps toward environmental protection. For example, although not officially recognizing them as ecologically important areas, the Committee successfully recommended that a number of environmentally sensitive areas on Grand Cayman (e.g., Central Mangrove, Barkers Wetlands, Salt Creek Mangroves, Meagre Bay Pond, Salina Reserve) be designated "public open access"; however, much of the land surrounding these areas is zoned as "hotel/tourism" or "beach resort residential" (Hurlston, 1995, p. 47).

The Third Caribbean Conference on Ecotourism (1993)

The Third Caribbean Conference on Ecotourism, held in George Town on May 4–7, 1993, used the International Eco-tourism Education Foundation's definition of ecotourism: "A tourism ethic that believes well-planned, economically and environmentally sound tourism practices produce travel experiences that leave the traveler and the environment nurtured and protected" (CTO, 1993, p. 5). The Hon. Thomas Jefferson, then ExCo Member for Tourism, Environment, and Planning, told the conference about proposed changes in Cayman's cruise tourism policy and the plan to amend the Marine Conservation Law to raise the fines for illegal dumping of sewage or any kind of waste by ships in its waters to international standards. He also stated that there would be a limit of three ships or 5,500 passengers per day in George Town Harbour and that measures would be taken to ensure local participation in tour operations, shopping, etc. (Anonymous, 1993b, pp. 1–3).

The 1994 Tourism Management Policy

In a document designed to provide a tourism management policy for the years 1995–1999, the Government (GOCI, 1994) continues the concern for the impact of cruise ships, entrenching as policy the limits on the numbers of ships and passengers announced in 1993 and finally deciding against a cruise ship dock at George Town Harbour in favor of permanent mooring buoys. A later report (Madigan Pratt & Associates, 1995) supports the buoys being placed in deep water far offshore (Catlin, 1994, 1995).

The policy continues the emphasis on seeking to attract "upmarket" stay-over tourists, calling for continued discouragement of charter and other low-priced markets; however, charter flights (e.g., Canadian Holidays, Caledonia Airways) continue, particularly in the summer slow season. There is also a major emphasis on promoting ecotourism through ecotourism "programs" and "themes" on all three islands, but little concrete information is given on details of such programs/themes or the institutional frameworks (e.g., education and training) needed to support them (Hurlston, 1995, p. 55), despite providing a list of marine and terrestrial sites of both ecological and cultural importance that are given "priority" as attractions for tourism development. Moreover, the policy provides much less detail than the 1992 plan (GOCI, 1992d), including little detail on Cayman Brac and Little Cayman or how an ecotourism program on those islands relates to their overall development (Hurlston, 1995, pp. 101, 107). Nor does it explain how "sustainable tourism" is possible while still pursuing tourism statistic growth rates of 5–10% per annum (Hurlston, 1995, p. 106).

Conclusion

Weaver (1990, p. 15) concludes that the Cayman Islands has developed a secure tourism sector, given the encouragement of a high degree of local control and participation and strong environmental controls. Pratt (1993, p. 264) argues that the best explanation for the success of Caymanian tourism can be expressed in a single word: consistency. Focusing on the more upscale and sophisticated traveler, marketing programs have been aggressive, positioning the Islands as "quiet, safe, and friendly"—characteristics that these primary target vacationers want. In turn, the emphasis has been on providing a "high-quality" experience in a relatively expensive destination (because of such factors as high labor costs, the need to import most goods, and the Caymanian dollar being pegged at US$1.20). This upscale market is prepared to pay a high price for a quality product. Research has shown, for example, that there is an inverse relationship between household income and perception of personal travel being a luxury: as incomes rise, the perception of personal travel as a luxury declines (Louis Harris and Associates, Inc., 1989). The fact that Caymanian tourism seems to have hit the mark in matching visitors and their vacation expectations is demonstrated by the fact that, on exiting the Islands, 63% of stay-over visitors rate their experience as having been "excellent," whereas another 33% rate it "good"; less than 1% say the experience was "poor" (GOCI, 1991a). Similarly, past vacationers were found to perceive the Cayman Islands to exceed their "ideal" warm weather destination on 10 criteria (warm and friendly, safe and secure, relaxing atmosphere, confident of good vacation, warm and sunny, friendly people, good hotel and restaurant service, beautiful beaches, and places to explore); only was the scenery seen as being less than ideal (Bernard Englehard & Associates, 1989).

The picture, however, is not entirely rosey. The CICC (1991), for example, is very concerned that tourism development—the main driving force of the economy along with the offshore banking industry—should be managed so that it is "sustainable":

> A planned and managed approach to tourism development will work in the best interest of everyone. The tourists will enjoy maximum benefits of existing facilities; the local community will see increased economic activity without straining the existing infrastructure, ecology, or compr[om]ising social or cultural values which are essential for future generations. In short, tourism growth should be managed so that the potential economic benefits of increased employment (or the disadvantages of overemployment) and foreign

exchange earnings are realized without degradation of the natural and cultural environment. (CICC, 1991, p. 75)

The CICC argues that a careful assessment of the tourism sector needs to be undertaken to determine if it is on a sustainable path:

> For many countries, tourism generates significant prosperity in the form of employment, foreign exchange, government revenue, etc. There can also be some drawbacks such as cultural decay, social erosion, environmental degradation, flight of foreign exchange to buy necessary touristic commodities, capital flight, etc.

> Tourism is also very sensitive to social and political disturbances.

> To ensure that tourism is developed in a sustainable fashion, we must ensure that education at all levels is aggressively carried out, culture (history, museums, crafts, music, dance, art, etc.) and social values are enhanced, the infrastructure is maintained in an equitable fashion, and the environment is carefully protected and managed.

> There comes a time when a developing, or developed tourist destination needs to undergo a comprehensive internal audit to ascertain where they are and where they wish to go.

> This audit should highlight the nature of the tourist promotion, their needs, cultural and social values, awareness, service, costs, benefits, varied impacts, etc. (CICC, 1991, p. 75)

Whether the Development Plan Review process will result in steps that heed such warnings remains to be seen.

Finally, the recent tourism management policy (GOCI, 1994) appears to provide little concrete direction on how tourism can actually be "managed" in a sustainable manner in the light of government's continuing goals that appear to be more than somewhat contradictory: an upmarket image, ecotourism, and continued growth.

Notes

[1]The Director of the Environment has the authority—and uses it—to ban such activities as street vendors (W. Whitaker, 1993, personal communication).

[2]Dixon and Sherman (1990) estimate that diving brought direct expenditures of US$52.3 million to the Cayman Islands in 1985, a figure that had risen to US$90 million by 1994 (Anonymous, 1994). Approximately 40% of stay-over visitors to the Cayman Islands are either already divers or intend to learn once there (Catlin, 1995). Moreover, it is estimated that approximately 55% of divers are repeat visitors (Martins, 1994).

[3]Exactly when and by whom this five-mile beach was given the name Seven Mile Beach is unclear.

[4]By that time, the acronym "CIA" described another organization.

[5]Despite this statement, in July 1992, the GOCI's Cayman Brac and Little Cayman Development Board granted approval in principle to Island Resort Development Ltd. for a 125-room hotel and 50-room condominium near West End Point on Cayman Brac (Anonymous, 1993a).

Chapter 7

Barbados

The nicest thing about not planning is that failure comes as a complete surprise and is not preceded by a period of worry and depression. (B. Taylor, 1986)

Introduction

Lying 160 km to the east of the curve of the volcanic Windward Islands, Barbados is geologically very different from the other islands in the Eastern Caribbean. A roughly pear-shaped island of 430 km^2 with maximum dimensions of 34 × 23 km and 92 km of coastline, it is a sea-mount lying on a foundation of Tertiary rock approximately 60 million years old, 86% of which is covered by younger capping rock of coral limestone (averaging 70 m in thickness) laid down in the form of a reef. The basic topography is gently undulating, with deep gullies and a series of nearly vertical cliffs, which are old coral reefs, rising to 340 m above sea level. Most of the soils in the coral region are fertile clays (Government of Barbados [GOB], 1988c). Unlike its neighbor islands, Barbados does have petroleum resources, its resources meeting about one half of domestic requirements (C. Y. Thomas, 1988, p. 106).

Marine life is not abundant in the waters around Barbados (Wilson, 1983). There are, however, 111 beach sites, but only 48 are "safe" for swimmers, most of which are on the west and south coasts rather than the more rugged east coast (GOB, 1988c, p. 59).

The island has a relatively uniform tropical climate strongly influenced by the Northeast Tradewinds. Temperatures range from 22 to 28°C and are rarely below 20°C or above 31°C; rainfall ranges from 1250 to 1650 mm, although it varies considerably annually, seasonally, and spatially. Most of the rivers are dry due to the permeable coral rock. Through gullies and sink-holes, water finds its way into underground water reservoirs, which are the only source of potable water. The natural vegetation is drought-tolerant forest and shrubs, developing into tropical forest in the moister, sheltered regions; sea cliff, sand, and swamp conditions support specially adapted plants. With most of the original forest cover having been removed by 1665 (D. Watts, 1987, p. 219)—a period in Barbados and the English Leeward islands described as "The Great Clearing" (Bridenbaugh & Bridenbaugh,

1972, p. 268)—relict forest is now restricted to gullies and undercliff areas, whereas swamp conditions are also greatly depleted.

Although archaeological remains indicate that villages had been established by about 400 BC, the Barrancoids (who originated in South America) left the island around 600 AD. They were replaced about 200 years later by the Arawaks, but their population drastically declined around 1200 AD, probably as a result of domination by the aggressive Caribs, who controlled the island for the next 300 years. Although there are Spanish and Portuguese[1] accounts of Caribs on the island in the 16th century, they had disappeared by the time the English arrived in 1625; enslavement by the Spaniards, disease, and famine have all been suggested as causes, but there is no generally accepted explanation. It has even been proposed that Barbados was not permanently settled at all (Knight, 1990, p. 7), so perhaps European pressure simply pushed the Caribs to abandon the island. Soon after the English arrived, they brought 40 Arawaks from Guyana to teach them how to grow Caribbean crops. Other than archaeological sites, crops, and remnants of Carib and Arawak language (e.g., *huracan, canaua, tobaco*), little trace of indigenous culture remains.

Originally, the English intended to create a settler colony on Barbados beginning in 1627 at Holetown on the west coast. Because the entire island had been granted by the Crown first to a London merchant, Sir William Courteen, and later to the Earl of Carlisle, the first settlers did not own land or stock, but acted as freeholders or tenants. They worked small plots of land, planting tobacco, cotton, ginger, and indigo (R. S. Dunn, 1972, pp. 53–54), with the labor of two or three European indentured servants or perhaps African slaves. The predominance of the settler concept in these early years is demonstrated by the fact that African slaves were a small minority: "According to historian Hilary Beckles, the number of blacks on Barbados didn't exceed 800 through the 1630s. Even a decade later, in 1643, the population numbered roughly 37,000 whites to only 6,000 blacks" (Wilder, 1986, p. 24). Political infighting, drought, and a decrease in food production led to changes in land ownership and the establishment of a House of Assembly in 1639.[2]

The introduction of sugar cane in 1637—not by the Spanish via the Greater Antilles, but by the Dutch via northeastern Brazil (Galloway, 1989, pp. 77–83)—resulted in first rum production and then by 1642 a profitable sugar industry. Because land values rose dramatically, the idea of the settler colony had been abandoned by 1650 in order to pursue sugar plantation agriculture in an exploitation slave economy; by 1680, 350 estates on Barbados produced 8,000 tonnes of sugar (Knight, 1990, p. 112). The plantation estates still serve as the basic agricultural, industrial, residential, and transportation pattern framework for the island (GOB, 1988c, p. 6).

The white population declined as small planters were bought out by rich planation owners, who imported large numbers of slaves. Wilder (1986, p. 29) estimates that, by 1684, there were 20,000 whites and 60,000 slaves. Knight (1990, pp. 114–115) is more conservative in estimating the number of slaves, but shows the correlation between sugar and slavery: in 1712, Barbados produced 6,343 tonnes of sugar and had a slave population of 42,000; in 1800, production reached 19,000 tonnes and the slave population stood at 82,000. This rapid population growth and intensive agricultural development quickly resulted in massive environmental change: there was

> [T]he virtually total removal of the ecologically intricate, stable tropical seasonal- and rain-forest, along with the associated coastal scrub, which had been present on the island. . . . The speed with which this was effected must be almost without parallel in an agricultural area. By 1655, only very small pockets of forest remained within the gullies of isolated districts, so that most potential refuges of the native flora and fauna had been eliminated; and in most localities a simplified, totally exploitative and potentially unstable agricultural system had taken its place. (D. Watts, 1987, p. 219)

Richardson (1992, p. 30), in describing the abruptness of these environmental changes as being unprecedented, notes that local reports of soil erosion and similar environmental stress occurred almost simultaneously with the clearing. Caribbean environmental decisions, however, were no longer being made in the Caribbean itself, because Barbados and the other sugar islands had been absorbed into an expanding European-centered commodity exchange, which demanded increased sugar productivity schedules that accelerated soil erosion rates or heightened drought susceptibility as a result of deforestation.

The plantation structure persisted largely unchanged until the emancipation of the slaves in 1834, when the tenantries system came into being to provide dormitories for estate workers. In parallel was the gradual development of small free-holds, leading after the 1920s to the emergence of a growing number of free-hold villages. This process was aided by remittance income when, for example, by the end of the 19th century, substantial remittances from migration to Panama to work on the construction of the Canal (Richardson, 1986), coinciding with a slump in the sugar industry, led to new house and shop construction and the purchase of small lots of land from marginal plantations (Connell, 1988, p. 28; Marshall, 1982, p. 459).

As a consequence of such fluctuations in the sugar industry, there was a slow drift of the population to Bridgetown from inland agricultural areas. Starting in the 1950s and accelerating in the 1960s and 1970s, urbanization in the southwestern part of the island intensified as the economic base diversified and grew; secondary activities, especially manufacturing and tourism, developed and led to the growth of service activities, most of which were located in or around Bridgetown (see Map 7.1). Traditional fishing villages on the southern and western coasts became attractions for residential and tourism development. By 1980, the Greater Bridgetown area contained 43% of the population of 247,129, whereas the urban continuum from Speightstown in the north through Bridgetown to Oistins in the south and St. Philip parish in the southeast contained 62% of the population; the remainder of the population lives in numerous villages and tenantries scattered all over the country and ranging in size from a few hundred to over 3,000 persons (GOB, 1988c, pp. 6–7). In total, settlement land use (including urban settlements, rural

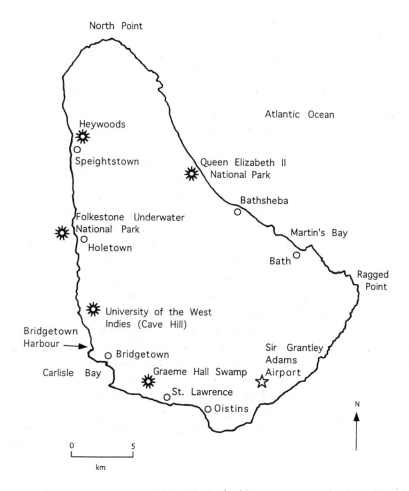

North Point

Atlantic Ocean

Heywoods

Speightstown

Queen Elizabeth II
National Park

Bathsheba

Martin's Bay

Folkestone Underwater
National Park

Holetown

Bath

Ragged
Point

University of the West
Indies (Cave Hill)

Bridgetown
Harbour

Bridgetown

Sir Grantley
Adams
Airport

Carlisle Bay

Graeme Hall Swamp

St. Lawrence

Oistins

N

0   5
km

Map 7.1. Barbados.

villages and tenantries, and urban and rural infrastructure) covers approximately 22% of the total land area of the country (GOB, 1988c, p. 15).

With a population of approximately 263,500 in 1994—96% of whom are descendants of African slaves (Thomas, 1988, p. 277)—Barbados is one of the most densely settled countries in the world, with 635 persons/km^2. Similarly, the island has one of the most dense road networks in the world: 1370 km of paved and asphalted roads and 320 km of all-weather private roads, for a density of 3.9 km roads/km^2 (GOB, 1988c, p. 70).

Barbados, which became an independent state in 1966, is governed by a Governor-General appointed by the British Crown and an elected legislative assembly, with a legal and legislative system based on that of Britain.

The Economy

Sugar remains a major economic force, albeit with a decline in number of workers and share of the economy.[3] In 1946, Barbados had 52 sugar factories, producing nearly 100,000 tonnes of sugar and employing more than 25,000 persons during crop time; by 1980, although production had increased, there were only eight factories and the number of employees was slightly less than 9,000 (Knight, 1990, p. 278). By 1991, there were only four factories operating, a goal set out in the first Physical Development Plan (GOB, 1970) as an efficiency measure.

Although not all agricultural laborers are engaged in sugar production, the percentage of the labor force in agriculture dropped from 16.7% in 1980 to 8.4% in 1984; similarly, the percentage contribution of agriculture to GDP at factor cost dropped: 26% in 1956, 12.0% in 1974, and 4.5% in 1989 (GOB, 1988c; Inter-American Development Bank [IDB], 1987; Mather & Todd, 1993; UNECLAC, 1984; World Bank, 1988a, 1986b). The area under sugar cultivation decreased from 19,058 hectares in 1960 to 15,841 hectares in 1981 as a result of expanding urban development, low yields, high production costs, and the substitution of alternative crops (GOB, 1988c, p. 18). The sugar industry continues to fail to achieve its planned output of 85,000 tonnes: 80,246 tonnes in 1987 (with a value of US$35.6 million), 67,900 tonnes in 1988 (US$33.6 million), and 65,670 tonnes in 1990—the lowest since the 1940s (Anonymous, 1991b; CDB, 1989a). Production has been adversely affected by a number of factors, including high production costs, labor shortages, and cane fires, but the fundamental problems are the extremely low price for sugar on the world market and the measures adopted by foreign governments to protect their own beet-sugar industry. Sugar also faces an uncertain future because of trade liberalization within the EEC in 1993 and the possible loss of the guaranteed United Kingdom market. No increase in output is planned in the sugar industry. There is, however, some increase in other forms of agriculture, such as vegetable production, using modern techniques of chemical fertilizers and spray irrigation, and specialized chicken farms (Aspinall & Momsen, 1987).

Barbados had been widely proclaimed as the region's success story because it largely escaped the economic crises that have gripped other West Indian countries since the 1970s (Thomas, 1988, p. 268). For example, the World Bank (1986b) notes that

> The economy of Barbados performed impressively during the 1960s and 1970s, despite its limited natural resources and high population density. Economic growth averaged 5% per year, living standards rose and low growth of . . . population . . . permitted per capita income to advance to US$4,680 in that year. Meanwhile, the economic base diversified away from a sugar-dependent agriculture to one featuring strong tourism and manufacturing sectors. These developments are largely attributable to the country's outward-looking strategy, reliance on regional markets, a judicious balance between the roles of Government and private enterprise and the country's social and political stability. (p. 1)

Other writers provide an even more glowing picture. For example, Jainarain (1976, pp. 205–229) estimates annual growth rates of 9.5% between 1956 and 1971 and 11.5% between 1964 and 1971, giving Barbados the highest per capita income growth rate in the West Indies. The growing prosperity was marked in part by the growing value of land, with the price of land in some parts of Barbados increasing by almost 50% per year in the early 1970s (Crandall, 1987). Indeed, Barbados' economic success was so highly regarded that other Caribbean islands were urged to look to this successful model of development (Cazes, 1983). As a result, Haynes and Holder (1989) note that

> The Barbadian public entered the 1970s with great expectations. The 1960s had been a period of exceptional growth and relatively low inflation. The international economy was experiencing a boom and, as a result, Barbados benefited from substantial foreign investment in the private sector. The manufacturing and tourism sectors responded positively to government's fiscal incentives schemes and the economy appeared to have gained in resilience even though there was some contraction of the manufacturing sector between 1967 and 1969. The fiscal deficit was kept within acceptable limits and foreign borrowing was extremely modest. (p. 91)

Underlying this apparent growth were significant changes in industrial structure. Industrialization, especially import-substitution manufacturing, began to be a major economic force by the mid-1950s as government policy shifted away from agriculture and toward light manufacturing, particularly textiles and electronics (Levy & Lerch, 1991, p. 68). Foreign manufacturers were attracted both by government incentives and low wage rates, particularly for women who made up about 70% of the Barbadian manufacturing labor force (Safa, 1986; Stoffle, 1977).

In the mid-1960s, manufacturing replaced sugar as the prime source of domestic exports: sugar exports dropped from 69% of domestic exports in 1965 to 10% in 1985, whereas manufacturing exports (including rum) rose from 15% to 88% in the same period (Thomas, 1988, p. 272). Economic growth was reflected in growing GDP per capita, which rose (in constant dollars) from US$400 in 1957 to US$1571 in 1980 (Knight, 1990, p. 318). By 1985, manufacturing accounted for about 10% of GDP and 13% of employment (World Bank, 1986b, p. 11), with 90% of export earnings originating in export-processing zones (EPZs), especially in electronics.[4] Such high-technology "screwdriver" industries were attracted to Barbados by access, political stability, low wages, and weak unions (Sunshine, 1985, p. 141); the latter two points were particularly important as 94% of all workers in enclave industries were female and minimum wages in the EPZ were lower than in any other sector of the economy (Long, 1987, p. 69). These factors, plus levels of productivity said to be as high as in the United States (Long, 1987, p. 65), also attracted data-processing industries (Dommen & Lebalé, 1986, p. 19); their main clients are airlines, hotels, car rental agencies, and credit card companies.

Evidence began to mount, however, that the economy as a whole was not as strong as often suggested. For example, despite general growth in the economy, the unemployment rate remained high: 15% in 1965, 18% in 1985, 18% in 1987, and 17% in 1989 (CDB, 1989a, p. 1; Thomas, 1988, p. 272). In addition, by 1986 GDP per capita was US$5,140 (in current dollars) (World Bank, 1988a, p. 9), but given the effect of inflation, the IDB argues that this represented little real improvement since 1980 (Anonymous, 1989b). By 1989, the GDP per capita had risen to only US$5,700, again suggesting little if any real improvement, particularly because it had dropped to US$5,300 by 1994. It also appears that the real GDP in 1987 was less than 5% above that of 1980 (World Bank, 1988a, p. 9), a situation that appears to be getting worse. Indeed, the IDB (1989a, p. 3) argues that in May 1989, using 1987 as a base year for calculation, the declines in per capita GDP were such that Barbados had fallen to 1979 levels in real terms.

In effect, Barbados was riding the roller coaster of the global economy. Haynes and Holder (1989, pp. 90–92) argue that the impetus for this changing economic structure began with a fiscal incentives program in the early 1960s (Cox, 1982), which enabled the economy to make the transition from heavy dependence on export agriculture to a more diversified base of agriculture, manufacturing, and tourism, along with a rapid growth of service industries in response to the increased level of local activity. The rosey picture of the late 1960s began to pale early in the 1970s as spiraling prices underlined the vulnerability of open economies however diversified, such as that of Barbados. Oil price increases adversely affected output, employment, and prices, although deterioration in the balance of payments was averted by a sharp but temporary increase in sugar prices; however, sluggish economic activity and inflationary pressures led to a serious fiscal deficit.

Following a degree of recovery in the late 1970s, the second oil shock resulted in higher inflation, but adequate reserve levels were sustained by the export sectors and increased borrowing by the public and private sectors. Attempts by the industrial countries to curb inflation through adjustment measures slowed global economic expansion, resulting in a balance of payments problem in Barbados throughout the first half of the 1980s. Inflation decreased, but the weakness of the export sector forced the Government to impose stringent measures to reduce import demand and correct fiscal imbalance. Having driven the economy throughout this period, the entire export sector—sugar, manufacturing, and tourism—faltered. Sugar became less important as world sugar prices dropped. The manufacturing sector tottered as the rapidly expanding regional export market shrunk, dropping from 11.3% of GDP in 1980 to 7.5% in 1989 (Mather & Todd, 1993). Finally, tourism rose and fell with the economies of the industrialized countries, but excess capacity impaired the sector's financial viability.

Public finances began to deteriorate in fiscal year 1987–1988, when a current account deficit equal to nearly 1% of GDP was realized, the first such deficit in at least 11 years. Similarly, the overall deficit widened to a record US$110 million, reflecting heavy investment in infrastructure, particularly road rehabilitation and construction (CDB, 1989a, pp. 1–2). Since then, the accumulated deficit has continued to grow, for example, by US$46.8 million in 1989. Similarly, the trade deficit was rapidly growing, reaching US$441.0 million in 1989. By late 1991, the Government was experiencing severe fiscal problems.

The tourism sector accounts for about 12% of GDP and is the biggest employer and prime generator of foreign exchange (World Bank, 1986b), although it too is not without its problems:

The major growth sector in 1987 was tourism, followed by wholesale and retail trade and construction. . . . [However], the sector has tended to stagnate
in recent years and real value added in 1987 was still 4.8% below that of
1980.

. . . Tourism is the leading growth sector in the economy. Since 1982, its contribution to GDP has averaged around 11.6%, and it affects a wide range of
activities. Real output growth in this sector was 3.5% in 1986 and an estimated 12.7% in 1987. (World Bank, 1988a, pp. 9–10)

The Tourism Sector

Barbados has developed the characteristics of a mid-Stage III (Maturity) destination: mass tourism, growth stagnation, high densities, host–guest friction, significant cruise ship activity, and growing emphasis on all-inclusive resorts.

Stay-Over Tourist Arrivals: The Dilemma

In addition to its pleasant climate, coastal resources, and historical resources (e.g.,
Arthur Young, 1989c, 1989d), Barbados is well-suited to tourism because its infrastructure (including roads, water, electricity, international airport, hospitals, and
education system) is among the best in the Commonwealth Caribbean (Thomas,
1988, p. 271). All postindependence governments in Barbados have continually upgraded the infrastructure and basic services:

> The quality of the island's roads, air and sea ports, housing stock, tourism
> plant, communication, education and health facilities, industry and its elec-
> tronic sub-sector, non-sugar agriculture, the media and forms of entertain-
> ment have all undergone such transformation as to have placed Barbados
> high among the better-off countries of the Third World. (CDB, 1985, p. 4)

There has also been significant development of a wide range of tourism attractions: bus and helicopter tours of the island, submarine tours of a coral reef, day
cruises, fishing, scuba diving and snorkeling, caves, plantation tours, shopping, restaurants, night clubs, etc.

Because of its central location in the Eastern Caribbean, its proximity to major shipping lanes, and the availability of flat land for an international airport (Sir Grantley
Adams International Airport), Barbados has a long history of tourism. By 1959,
there were 30,000 stay-over arrivals (CTA, 1960), a figure that rose to 156,000 in
1970 (Gilles, 1980) just as the jet charter business started to boom. The prospects
were bright, although problems loomed on the horizon:

> The prospects seemed good for tourism in 1970, so long as the economies of
> the US and Canada continued to expand. The industry was still enjoying a sus-
> tained period of robust growth. The demand for holidays in Barbados
> showed a healthy response to growing national incomes in North America.
> There was spare capacity in the Barbados hotel sector, allowing room for
> quick expansion in visitor arrivals. However, low hotel occupancy during

the summer months continued to depress overall occupancy rates. . . . Barbados' tourism continued to suffer from haphazard promotion, poor quality controls, amateurish management and casual attitudes to service. In addition, there were some imponderables that could alter the prospects. The real cost of air fares might change (in the event they rose sharply and then declined) and competing tropical resorts were being developed elsewhere in the Caribbean. Overall, though, tourism seemed promising, though the going was bound to be tougher. (Worrell, 1987, p. 53)

Growth was rapid, reaching a peak of 370,900 in 1979, only to be followed by a severe downturn for several years. As a consequence, some hotels were closed and others sold, retail sales fell, and unemployment rose. Real GDP had increased by an average of 4.3% in 1961–1980, but it fell by 3.1% in 1981 and by 4.6% in 1982 (Economist Intelligence Unit, 1985).

Although the simplest explanations for this situation were related to the worldwide recession and energy situation, several writers provide more complex reasons. Romsa and Blenman (1987) describe the situation as the "Prime Minister's dilemma." On the one hand, the effects of the economy were so great that then Prime Minister Tom Adams wrote to the Director of the Barbados Board of Tourism suggesting that "Barbados' failure had been catastrophic and in a less well-structured society would have been destructive of the very cement that held the society together" and taking the view that "Barbados had somehow become a bad product . . . and that no matter how much you advertised a bad product, it remained difficult to sell" (Anonymous, 1983). On the other hand, the Board of Tourism seemed to be saying that changes in the economies of the tourist-generating countries were the main causes and that increased advertising would be needed. Romsa and Blenman (1987) describe the confusion:

> Other countries in the Caribbean were subject to the same sources of tourists, and the same world conditions. Indeed, St. Lucia (a less developed island) seemed to be gaining at the expense of Barbados. Likewise, the major increases in arrivals to Barbados had occurred when advertising expenditures were less than those by Jamaica, Bahamas, and Bermuda. It was indeed a perplexing situation. Seen in a regional perspective, it was difficult to understand how the changes in the system, whether external (as in the Tourist Board's view) or internal (as the Prime Minister saw it) could have produced such disastrous results in an island with so lengthy and successful tourist development. Small wonder the Prime Minister considered that more damage had occurred than "a serious hurricane would have done" [Anonymous 1983]. (p. 241)

Building on the Prime Minister's hurricane analogy, Romsa and Blenman (1987, p. 241) liken the situation to a *catastrophe* (i.e., a sudden and unexpected discontinuous change in a system [Thom, 1975]), arguing that a constellation of regional forces came together suddenly that served to undermine the best-laid plans for Caribbean development (Blenman, 1983). These forces included bankruptcies of major charter companies (e.g., Laker Airways, Suntours) in the late 1970s, rising energy costs resulting in higher aviation costs, natural hazards (e.g., Hurricane David in August 1979 that devastated Dominica, volcanic eruptions in St. Vincent), and social disruption (e.g., Jamaica, Trinidad, Dominica, Grenada). All of these events were beyond Barbados' control and in some cases (e.g., hurricanes) did not affect Barbados at all, but nevertheless made the region generally less attractive in tourists' eyes. Some destinations (e.g., St. Lucia) seemed to weather the catastrophe better than Barbados, but that is because they were much less well-known destinations and still had a high level of "curiosity" attractiveness.

Second, C. Hall (1989) argues that Romsa and Blenman (1987) ignore the exchange rate as a key factor in the decline, because exchange rates affect all of the costs of a vacation and not just airline fares. In the 1980s, Barbados maintained its currency pegged to the United States dollar, which rose strongly against most other world currencies in this period (e.g., from 1979 to 1982, approximately 24% against the British Pound Sterling, 59% against the French Franc, and 10% against the Canadian dollar). This had two effects (Rosenweig, 1986): Barbados became more expensive for European and Canadian tourists (who accounted for nearly two thirds of stay-over arrivals in Barbados in 1980) and other destinations that had lower exchange rates became more attractive to American tourists.

A third argument is presented by Palmer (1993), who demonstrates that 84% of the variation in tourist arrivals from the United States to Barbados from 1977–1987 was explained by variation in real disposable income in the United States. Given the recession in the early 1980s in the United States, therefore, this relationship more than offset the favorable exchange rate between Barbados and the United States and resulted in fewer American tourists during the crisis period.

Finally, Worrell (1987, p. 59) argues that the situation was exacerbated in 1981 and 1982 when tourist arrivals dropped off because of a misalignment of local hotel rates too far above those for the competition.

Clearly, the situation was complex; the best explanation is probably that all of the above factors were important. The 1979 level of stay-over arrivals was not regained until 1986; then there was significant growth (largely related to summer air charters) to 461,300 in 1989, which for a while strengthened the view of tourism's position as the most dynamic sector of the economy, despite its major problems. Since then, however, tourist arrivals have decreased significantly again, falling to 394,000 in 1993 (Table 7.1).

Barbadian tourist arrivals seem to have suffered more than most other Caribbean countries, with growth in the period 1980–1993 of only 6.7%, a small fraction of the 71.5% growth experienced by the region as a whole and ranking 26th in growth out of 30 countries in the region. Another measure of this curtailed growth is that the number of tourist arrivals per 1,000 local population rose only 1.3% from 1485 in 1980 to 1,503 in 1993. Nevertheless, in the same period, there have been greater increases in the tourist density ratio (highest at 28.19) and the tourist penetration ratio (in the middle among the case studies at 46.11). This low level of increased tourist arrivals has occurred despite the fact that the public sector has increased its tourism marketing expenditure considerably (e.g., between

Table 7.1. Barbados: Tourism Statistics

Year	Stay-Over Tourists No. (000s)	% Annual Change	Cruise Passengers No. (000s)	% Annual Change	Total Tourists No. (000s)	% Annual Change	Visitor Expenditure US$ (M)	% Annual Change	Tourist Rooms No.	Aver. LOS (No. Nights)	No. Tourist Nights/Yr (000s)
1980	370.0	−0.2	156.5	NA	526.5	NA	251.0	24.6	6680	9.6	3552.0
1981	352.6	−4.7	138.8	−11.3	491.4	−6.7	261.9	4.3	6680	9.8	345 5.5
1982	303.8	−15.8	110.8	−20.2	414.6	−15.6	251.6	−4.1	6547	9.1	2764.6
1983	328.3	8.1	102.5	−7.5	430.8	3.9	251.6	0.2	6627	8.8	2889.0
1984	367.7	12.0	99.2	−3.2	466.9	8.4	284.2	13.0	6548	9.6	3529.0
1985	359.1	−8.3	112.2	13.1	471.3	−1.0	309.2	8.8	6852	9.7	3483.3
1986	369.8	3.0	145.3	29.5	515.1	9.3	326.9	5.7	6799	9.8	3624.0
1987	421.9	14.1	228.8	58.2	650.7	26.3	378.7	15.8	6672	10.0	4219.0
1988	451.5	7.0	290.3	26.6	741.8	14.0	460.0	21.5	6654	11.1	5011.7
1989	461.3	2.2	337.1	16.1	798.4	7.6	527.8	9.8	6653	11.5	5305.0
1990	432.1	−6.3	362.6	7.6	794.7	−0.5	493.5	−6.5	6709	10.6	458 0.3
1991	394.2	−8.8	372.1	2.6	766.3	−3.6	459.7	−6.8	5387	10.9	429 6.8
1992	385.5	−2.2	399.7	7.4	784.5	2.4	462.5	0.6	5902	10.6	4086.3
1993	396.0	2.7	428.6	7.2	824.6	5.1	528.0	14.2	5580	11.2	4435.2

1986 and 1993, the public sector marketing expenditures rose 110.5%, but the number of stay-over visitors rose only 7.1%) (Mather & Todd, 1993).

Between 1980 and 1993, Barbados' rank in the number of tourist arrivals among 30 countries in the Caribbean region dropped from seventh to eleventh, largely because the mix of tourists has also changed: a large decrease in Canadian tourists has been offset by increased European visitors. The decline in Canadians is particularly notable as Canada was actually the largest market until 1979, but by 1987 had dropped to third behind the United States and the United Kingdom. Many other destinations are growing much faster for these and other markets, with growth in the number of American, Canadian, and European tourists to Barbados since 1980 ranking 21st, 27th, and 21st, respectively, among 29 countries in the region. Despite this pattern, Barbados has one of the most balanced distributions of direct scheduled international air connections per week of the case studies: in the 1992 high season, there were 49 flights to the United States, 8 to Canada, and 11 to Europe—the latter figure representing 57.9% of all direct scheduled flights to Europe among the case studies (Mather & Todd, 1993). This balanced distribution is reflected in the relatively low market concentration ratio of 66.2, the second lowest (next to Dominica) among the case studies.

Accommodations

Up until 1970, the hotel sector consisted of a small number of very high-quality, luxury hotels catering primarily to long-stay visitors, mostly from North America and Europe. In the 1970s, the growth in tourist accommodations was dramatic; for example, the number of tourist *beds* rose from 2,750 to 13,375 between 1964 and 1983—an average annual increase of 11.2%. Growth was greater in this period in relatively lower cost facilities such as apartments, apartment hotels, and cottages (11.8%) than for hotels (7.3%); however, over half of the accommodation stock was hotel oriented (55% in 1983) (GOB, 1988c, p. 34).

During the 1970s, expansion in apartment accommodations occurred mainly on the south coast, compared to higher class hotels being built on the west coast (and, to a lesser extent, the southeast coast). This resulted in a spatial differentiation by type and quality as encouraged first in the 1970 Physical Development Plan (GOB, 1970) and later in other plans. In 1981, the mean density of tourist accommodation was 158 beds/hectare on the west coast and 210 on the south coast. By 1983, of the total of 13,375 tourist beds, 7,557 (56.5%) were on the south coast, 4,507 (37.7%) on the west coast, and the remainder (776 or 5.8%) elsewhere (mainly the southeast coast). In total, tourism and ancillary facilities occupy only 426 hectares (0.1% of the country's area) (GOB, 1988c, pp. 36–37).

Any increases in the accommodation stock in the 1980s were offset by closures of other establishments; therefore, the number of tourist *rooms* decreased from 6,680 in 1980 to 5,580 in 1993. In contrast, the mean number of rooms per hotel dropped from 86 in 1983 to 70 in 1988, where it has remained stable. Exact data on the number of hotels per annum are not available, but these trends suggest that the closure of numerous small hotels was not offset by the construction of a small number of larger establishments (e.g., Heywoods, as noted below).

Occupancy rates have also fluctuated widely, from a high of 68.6% in 1980 to a low of 40.9% in 1985 to 53.7% in 1993, resulting in the tourist occupancy function (rooms) falling overall from 18.4 to 11.4 in that period. Current data are not available on occupancy rates by type of accommodation, although in 1987, when the average *room* occupancy rate was 57.5%, the average *bed* occupancy rate was a similar 55.4%.

There is a high degree of Barbadian ownership of accommodation, with 67 hotels (73%) having 2,899 rooms (61% of hotel rooms) being locally owned (OAS, 1987a). Although Barbadian ownership dominates in the small hotel category, a significant share of the large hotels is also locally owned, including the 308-room Heywoods hotel complex and the 185-room Hilton Hotel, which are both Government owned, but operated by MNCs (Wyndham and Hilton, respectively). Most of the rest of the large hotels, however, are foreign owned.

Despite a recent change in how place of stay is recorded, which appears to confuse patterns, approximately one quarter of tourist arrivals stay in hotels, with about one half staying in private or unregistered accommodations or in apartments or guest houses. The high rate of local ownership in the latter categories suggests great potential for direct economic impacts; however, many of these establishments are in lower price categories, are in need of considerable refurbishment and upgrading, and have low occupancy rates for much of the year.

With the bell-shaped curve in the number of tourist arrivals since 1980 (for an overall increase of only 6.7% in that period) and the modest 16.7% increase in average length of stay from 9.6 to 11.2 nights, the annual number of tourist nights increased 25.0% in the period 1980–1993 from 3,552,000 to 4,435,200.

The very modest gains, moreover, have been somewhat offset by three factors. First, there was a relative collapse of the Trinidad and Tobago market (which had traditionally been a major off-season market) because of the devaluation of the TT dollar (CDB, 1989a, pp. 2–3): in 1985, there were 32,526 tourists from Trinidad and Tobago (9.1% of all tourist arrivals to Barbados), a figure that had fallen to 16,002 (4.0%) in 1993 (CTO, 1994).

Second, there has been a great loss of North American business; for example, Canadian tourists dropped from 90,990 (28.7% of arrivals) in 1978 to 49,200 (12.4%) in 1993 (CTO, 1994; CTRC, 1986). Much of this loss is a result of cheaper competition from Cuba, Mexico, and the Dominican Republic.

Third, deterioration in the quality of the sector's assets occurred as hotel and apartment owners suffered from high interest rates and lower revenue. The buyers' market of the 1980s showed that lowering room rates to improve occupancy rates (especially in the summer) did not increase revenue, particularly as labor costs were rising; the result was an erosion of both working capital and equity (World Bank, 1986b, p. 10). In 1987–1988, for example, the average winter rate in Barbados was the same as the average for 31 countries in the Caribbean region at US$117.50/night, ranking 13th highest, whereas the summer rate of US$69.00 was 19th and much below the regional average of US$85.20. Most significant, however, was the fact that the difference of 70.3% between winter and summer rates was the third greatest in the region (Curtin & Poon, 1988). Perhaps because of these low summer rates, Barbados has a very low index of seasonality: 1.115 in 1989 (de Albuquerque & McElroy, 1992, p. 627) and 1.094 in 1993.

As so often happens in the tourism sector, views of the future change quickly and the opinions of various actors are widely divergent. There appeared to be consensus that there were no significant development plans for the near future aimed at seriously increasing the stock of hotel accommodations on Barbados; indeed, there seemed to be common acceptance of the view that consolidation and upgrading are the two major needs, backed by improved marketing (L. Nurse, 1991, personal communication). More recently, however, a major development plan has been proposed by a Canadian company, Thornbrook International Inc., to build five golf courses (golf being an activity aimed at upscale tourists), two luxury resort hotels, and 2,200 residential units covering 2.3% of the island's total area. There is concern, however, that the golf courses not only would remove prime agricultural land, but would also require large amounts of water for irrigation and could be at odds with the very sophisticated zoning system in the 1988 Physical Development Plan (GOB, 1988c) related to groundwater protection. Part of the proposal, for example, calls for development of Graeme Hall Swamp on the south coast for hotel and golf course purposes, despite that fact that the Plan (GOB, 1988c, p. 176) suggests that this area be designated as a Nature Reserve (L. Nurse, 1991, personal communication). As a result, there has been a great deal of opposition from groups with environmental interests on various grounds, including loss of agricultural land, water demand, and pesticide use (Marotte, 1992). Presumably, the economic rationale for such proposals is based on the trend of golf being the fastest growing outdoor recreational activity for middle-aged North Americans (particularly for women) (Wilkinson, 1993). Only time will tell if the proposals go further; however, it is difficult to imagine the economic viability of such a proposal.

Excursionists

No data are available on excursionists to Barbados.

Cruise Passengers

In 1993, Barbados attracted 428,600 cruise passengers, a 174.3% increase over 1980, thus maintaining its rank as the region's eighth largest cruise destination. The pattern over the decade has, however, been very uneven, with large decreases in the early 1980s, followed by rapid growth in the late 1980s and then modest growth in the early 1990s. Nevertheless, Barbados ranks only third among the case studies in terms of arrivals per 1,000 local population (1,627 in 1993) and penetration ratio (4.46), but second in density ratio (2.72).

The decline in the mid-1980s is related to the worldwide cruise slump caused by high energy costs and recession; however, the later dramatic increase is probably as much a function of the provision of improved cruise ship and cruise ship passenger facilities at Bridgetown Harbour as it is of improvements in the global economic situation. Also, the deep-water harbor is capable of handing large ships. This suggests that Barbados has a continuing future as a cruise destination, given the recent construction of "superships" capable of holding up to 2,700 passengers. Of course, the question arises as to whether the rest of the cruise infrastructure (e.g., taxis, tour buses, stores, restaurants) is capable of sustaining such demand and whether the lower per capita spending of cruise passengers can offset declining stay-over tourist expenditures.

Total Visitors

Second to the Bahamas among the case studies at 824,600 total arrivals in 1993, Barbados is clearly a Stage III destination as this figure represents only a 56.7% increase since 1980—the lowest among the case studies. Just as the overall number of arrivals has virtually plateaued since 1990, so too have the number of arrivals per 1,000 local population (3,130 in 1993), penetration ratio (50.57), and density ratio (30.91). The latter figure is still the highest among the case studies, however, and suggests the hypothesis that Barbados has surpassed the point of tourist saturation.

Expenditures

In terms of estimated visitor expenditures, Barbados remains one of the major destinations in the Caribbean region, with its US$528.0 million ranking seventh in 1993; however, it has slipped in importance, dropping from fourth in 1980, and the figures have fluctuated dramatically year by year. Assuming even a modest rate of inflation, the 80.4% increase in expenditures in the period of 1980–1991 probably represents an actual decline.[5] This is also suggested by the fact that the estimated visitor expenditure per capita of local population increased only from US$1,008 in 1980 to US$2,004 in 1993. Similarly, although average stay-over visitor expenditure rose from US$615.30 in 1980 to US$1,093.80 in 1989 in current terms, it fell in real terms from US$615.30 in 1980 to US$564.55 in 1987 when inflation was taken into account (Barbados Board of Tourism [BBT], 1991; Palmer, 1993).

There are various measures of the importance of tourism in the Barbadian economy. For example, the Government (GOB, 1988c) states that the contribution of tourism to GDP in 1971 was US$13.5 million or 9.3% of the total GDP of US$144.6 million; by 1981, it was US$97.2 million or 11.8% of the total GDP of US$823.4 million. The latter figures are quite close to CTO (1990, 1989) data, which state that the value-added contribution of the hotel and restaurants sector to GDP was US$88.4 million in 1980 or 11.7% of GDP; by 1993, the contribution had reached US$181.5 million, but was a similar 13.1% of GDP, again suggesting that inflation accounted for most of the increase. A very dated estimate of the leakage rate of tourist expenditures is 42% (B. H. Archer, 1981, p. v-9; Chernick, 1978).

Although different from the contribution of tourism to the GDP, the measure of estimated visitor expenditure as a percentage of GDP also indicates the lack of growth in both visitor expenditure and the economy as a whole, hovering around 27–38% throughout the 1980–1993 period. Given the lack of real growth in visitor expenditure, the modest increase in such expenditure as a ratio to merchandise exports from 1.0 in 1982 to 2.9 in 1993 indicates the weakness in other export sectors. Similarly, the increase from 75.9% in 1982 to 99.9% in 1993 in estimated visitor expenditure expressed as a percentage of external debt suggests the weakness of the overall economy.

Recent data on tourism-related employment are not available. Although one estimate states that only 2% of the labor force was employed in tourism in 1970 (Gill, 1984, p. 28), other figures are higher. For example, the Government (GOB, 1988c) estimates total direct employment in hotels and guest houses rising from 4,069 or 4.9% of the work force in 1970 to 7,215 or 7% by 1981. Indirect employment is estimated to have accounted for a similar number, so that tourism accounted for approximately 14,230 persons or 14% of the work force,[6] in comparison with 9,500 (9.5%) in agriculture and 15,300 (15%) in manufacturing (GOB, 1988c). Other estimates for the 1970s are that tourism employment ranged from 10% to 20% of the work force (Marshall, 1978, p. 5; Phillips, 1982, p. 108).

Tourism Policy and Planning

Although the history of tourism in Barbados has been marked by a general lack of Government involvement in tourism policy and planning, various Government activities have directly and indirectly affected tourism.

The Policy and Planning Context

Rather than having a tourism policy or a tourism plan per se, the Government deals with tourism primarily through two mechanisms: national development plans and physical development plans. The former deal predominately with social and economic policies, whereas the latter translate these into land-use policies. Both are guided by the ongoing development of government policy as presented in Throne Speeches and in the party manifesto of the governing party (E. Layne, 1991, personal communication) It has been argued, therefore, that the Barbados Government is really only involved in tourism land-use planning (and marketing planning, as discussed below) and not tourism development policy or planning (C. Squires, 1991, personal communication).

Thomas (1988, pp. 269–272) argues that such an approach to tourism is consistent with overall economic policies pursued in Barbados since independence, describing such policies as having five major elements:

- wholly nonideological, purely technocratic, pragmatic, and rational;

- outward oriented and reliant on imported capital;

- promoting political and social stability as a vital economic necessity;

- facilitating the inflow of foreign capital;

- continually upgrading infrastructure and basic services.

These elements have resulted in a tourism policy and planning context that: promotes foreign investment and MNCs, while still encouraging local participation; seeks to diversify its tourist markets; and provides an educational, social, and physical infrastructure that makes the island an attractive destination for tourists.

One of the major results is a highly fragmented approach to tourism policy and planning with several major players (e.g., Board of Tourism, Barbados Hotel Association, Government) managing the tourism economy with, at least until recently, little evidence of coordination or cooperation (J. Hepple, 1992, personal communication).

This policy environment has been operationalized through a series of policies, plans, and pieces of legislation dating from the mid-1950s.

Tourism Legislation and Government Structure

The only piece of legislation dealing directly with tourism development, the Hotel Aids Act (passed originally in 1956) is a mechanism that can be used in tourism planning only in a growth period because its benefits apply solely to new developments in specific geographic areas slated as tourism zones (which were articulated in the 1970 Physical Development Plan [GOB, 1970]). Specifically, the Act provides for duty-free importation of materials for the construction and expansion of approved hotel (but not condominium) plant and related infrastructure; the cost of such materials can be deducted as an expense in arriving at the income of the hotel that would otherwise be subject to corporate tax. It appears, however, that this latter provision is rarely used because few hotels have recorded a profit from which they could deduct such expenses.

The Act also led to the establishment of the Barbados Board of Tourism (BBT) (a statutory board of the Government constituted through the separate Tourist Board Act of 1958), the duties of which included advertising, ensuring adequate shipping and airline facilities, providing training, classifying and grading facilities and services, and conducting surveys and monitoring services (Thomas, 1988, pp. 145–146). Through these duties, the BBT (1991, p. 1) has several objectives: improving the utilization of all sectors of the accommodation plant, further reducing seasonality, increasing stay-over and cruise ship arrivals, increasing overall occupancy and length of stay, and developing a national awareness of the importance of the sector. Although very successful in the early years following the passage of the Act, a number of factors currently constrain the meeting of these objectives: reduced air-seat capacity (e.g., the 1989 bankruptcy of Eastern Airlines, the 1990 decision of American Airlines to use Puerto Rico as a hub and to discontinue direct flights from New York to Barbados, the 1992 bankruptcy of Pan American Airways), decreased disposable incomes in most source markets, intensified competition of Caribbean destinations, and social factors that have a negative impact on the sector (especially crime and harassment of visitors).

In 1984, the Act was extended to permit hotels to import free of duty materials required for refurbishment of facilities. Although several hotels have taken advantage of this incentive, others urgently in need of refurbishment and upgrading have not done so, due to lack of access to the necessary finances or inability to service the additional debt burden. Tourism investment subsidies currently in place include assistance with project financing, tax holidays, double tax relief, leasing of property, marketing support, amenities aid, and training aid (Arthur Young, 1988). Because most are not in a taxable position, few hotels can take advantage of a 1986 extension permitting hotels to deduct 150% of costs incurred in developing non-CARICOM markets outside from income otherwise liable to corporate tax (OAS, 1987a, p. C46).

Plans . . . and More Plans

The first Physical Development Plan (GOB, 1970) (which, in fact, did not come into effect until 1976) allocated lands for tourism development on the east, south, southeast, west, and northwest coasts. A subsequent policy revision that focused on preservation of the scenic but rugged east coast for a potential national park resulted in no appreciable development there, but tourism development occurred in virtually all of the other areas indicated. The level of development was not as high as foreseen, however, because the growth in numbers of tourists did not reach predicted levels. Overall, the Plan was relatively successful in concentrating tourist development in particular zones and protecting some of the more environmentally sensitive areas and agricultural zones. This tourism development, however, led to the substantial destruction of coral reefs, extensive beach sand loss, and coastal water contamination as a result of insufficient regulatory foresight (E. D. Archer, 1985; Cambers, 1985).

The Physical Development Plan was followed by the 1979 National Development Plan. It (GOB, 1979, pp. 70–80) recognizes the importance of tourism, not just for its direct and indirect economic impacts, but also for stimulating infrastructure development (e.g., airport, harbor). It expresses concern, however, that unplanned and unrestrained growth could weaken efforts to strengthen indigenous culture and adversely affect environmental quality of the country. As a result, four short- and medium-term objectives are stated:

- increase the level and annual growth rate of tourist expenditures;
- increase levels of local ownership and management;
- establish better linkages with agriculture and other sectors to decrease leakages;
- control the quantitative and qualitative growth of the sector to maintain an acceptable balance between numbers of visitors and the indigenous population, to optimize employment opportunities, and to minimize adverse social and environmental impacts.

Although recognizing the adequacy of the land and infrastructure for the anticipated expansion of the sector, the Plan notes several constraints: limited availability of local capital investment resources, inadequacy of local management capability and training, insufficient linkages with other sectors, foreign dominance of the external market, and concerns about the maintenance of quality and of price competitiveness—concerns that appear to remain valid today.

A goal of an annual increase of 8% in the number of visitors is set, which would have resulted in an increase from 371,000 in 1979 to 466,000 in 1983. (In fact, there was an actual decrease to 328,000 in 1983.) The goal was to be achieved through a mix of strategies, some of which were achieved:

- general zones to guide the form and location of tourism development (reinforcing and elaborating on the zoning policy in the 1970 Plan);

- upgraded and expanded training;

- increased range and number of tourist attractions.

Other strategies, however, were not successful, mainly because of the lack of funds and personnel:

- enforcement of maximum densities and other building controls to avoid coastal and environmental erosion, provision of coastal conservation works, maintenance and expansion of beach access, and provision of national parks and public beach facilities;

- encouragement of locally owned hotels and increased standards;

- increased marketing to expand the mid- to upper-income segments of the market, diversify the geographic and ethnic sources of visitors, and maintain and enhance the tourism image;

- encouragement of low and incentive air fares;

- increased linkages with local agriculture and manufacturing.

The Plan gives potential negative social impacts of tourism a great deal of attention—but provides few solutions. Specifically, it calls for the need to avoid congestion and displacement of Barbadians by visitors, to preserve and enhance Barbadian rights, to define acceptable standards of conduct and behavior by visitors, and to strengthen the social and cultural fabric of the country.

With the number of tourists having peaked in 1979 and the economy beginning to show symptoms of weakness, the 1979 Plan was replaced in 1983 by a second National Development Plan. It (GOB, 1983, pp. 78–92) recognizes that the tourism sector performed below the expectation of the 1979 Plan for a number of reasons: weak demand for travel due to the worldwide recession; increased competition from other Caribbean destinations; and image problems for Barbados in terms of price, standards, and service. The Plan recommends a shift in emphasis to quality rather than quantity; whereas it argues that the physical carrying capacity of the country is about 1 million visitors per year,[8] a medium-term goal of 600,000 is set and a short-term goal of 380,000 by 1987 (the latter eventually being exceeded at 421,900). No new major hotel developments led by the Government are foreseen for the duration of the Plan. (In fact, with the exception of the Heywoods hotel complex, there have been very few new hotels of any size built in Barbados since the late 1970s and many hotels have closed.)

The emphasis on the enhancement of quality leads to a number of recommendations, some of which were successful: registration and classification of hotels, more training programs, increased access by Barbadians to tourism facilities, improved maintenance of beaches, parks, and historic monuments,[9] and upgrading of the airport and Bridgetown Harbour. Others were partially successful: greater community education and awareness of the economic role of tourism; greater efficiency and effectiveness in marketing and promotion; continued cooperation with charter and tour operators; encouragement of the development of full-service hotels and the restriction of apartments; and implementation of a sewage system for the south and west coasts.[10] Still others were not successful: broadening into new markets; increased regulation and control to secure maximum Barbadian participation in the tourism sector; increased multiplier effects through creation of more productive linkages with agriculture, fishing, and manufacturing; and greater private sector participation in planning and implementation of programs.

The mixed success of the 1983 Plan is related to several factors that, although apparent at the time, were only publicly acknowledged the following year by a joint public–private sector committee. Faced with slow growth in the number of tourists and rising costs of goods and services, a Joint Committee of major institutional creditors, related government departments, and representatives of the Barbados Hotel Association was formed (GOB, 1984). It adopted a more critical stance than the 1983 Plan, concluding that the boom years of the late 1970s masked many problems in the Barbados tourism sector, including deficiencies in management, lack of planning, little or no emphasis on productivity, and insufficient attention to market research and marketing. Over the years, Barbados moved from being mainly an upmarket destination toward a reputation as a vacation spot for budget-minded tourists on package tours. As a result, there was increased reliance on MNC tour operators and airlines; many of these went out of business in the early 1980s (e.g., Laker Airways), with each bankruptcy sending shock waves through the sector. With a rapid increase in the number of hotel rooms and a growing number of competing destinations (e.g., Mexico), Barbados became even more dependent on foreign tour operators and was often exploited by the operators when there was a downturn in travel. The Committee suggested that the goal should be to regain the upper-class market, thus necessitating both public and private sector action.

In addition to improvements in such matters as marketing, tax assessments, water rates, and a beautification program, the committee made three major recommendations to Government:

- a 2-year moratorium on incentives and support for the addition of new hotel rooms (a recommendation that, given the weakness of the economy, required little action to implement);

- the provision of long-term funding for upgrading and renovation of hotels (which led to the 1984 Hotel Aids Act);

- the need for long-term planning (which apparently had little impact until the 1988 National Development and Physical Development Plans).

Several Committee recommendations targetted the private sector, including upgrading management standards, reevaluating marketing policies, urging lending institutions to consider rescheduling capital loans, reviewing room rates, improving food service and entertainment, paying more attention to maintenance, using more energy-saving devices in hotels, and instituting an educational and public relations program to create a better image for the sector. The upgrading and renovation program appears to have been somewhat effective; for example, by 1988, many properties had been repaired and two existing hotels reopened after major renovation programs (GOB, 1988a). On the other hand, a large proportion of local operators receiving assistance from a mortgage assistance program failed, resulting in the closing of many small establishments (J. Hepple, 1992, personal communication).

On the whole, little Government action seems to have resulted from the Committee's report. Not until the 1988 National Development Plan did the Government even begin to address the problems of the tourism sector. Having recognized the impending economic problems, the Government chose the path of outward-looking, export-led growth, as set out in the 5-year Public Sector Investment Programme (PSIP) contained in the 1988 Plan (GOB, 1988b). Tourism, nonsugar agriculture, and manufacturing were expected to continue to be the leading growth sectors, with projected average annual growth rates of 3%, 2%, and 2.5%, respectively.

In tourism, the Government gave priority to marketing and product development, especially prevention of beach erosion. It projected that tourism growth would continue (although the analysis presented above paints a less optimistic picture); however, the Government recognized that it is unlikely that this sector will be able to improve the employment situation in the near future (GOB, 1988b).

The Plan calls for strengthening other economic sectors in order to expand the Government's revenue base, stimulate exports, and create greater employment opportunities. It notes that manufacturing continues to experience difficulties because of production (e.g., high labor costs, entrepreneurial response) and marketing (e.g., international price competitiveness, the international trade policy of the Government, devaluation of the currencies of major CARICOM trading partners) problems. A program of factory shell construction was to be continued with a loan from the CDB to facilitate a shift of industrial strategy towards more skill-intensive industries in electronics, garments, and information technology (CDB, 1989a, p. 3).

Although the agricultural sector is still dominated by sugar, diversification out of sugar is seen as being essential. Attempts at agricultural diversification, however, have been only moderately successful because of disease, inadequate rainfall, and labor shortages. The shortage of labor—in a labor-surplus economy—gives a clear indication that agricultural activity is not the chosen form of employment for the young unemployed.

Noting that, although tourism accounts for 10% of GDP and the targeted number of visitors had been exceeded, the performance during the previous 5 years was mixed, the 1988 National Development Plan (GOB, 1988b, pp. 97–103) calls for a long-term strategy with two basic features. The first is to make Barbados a more attractive destination by giving better value—a theme repeated from the 1983 National Development Plan. This requires stronger links with other sectors, improved education and training, improving and upgrading hotels, providing new beach facilities, providing more on-shore facilities for cruise passengers, and assisting small and medium hotels (most of which are locally owned) with marketing, financial, and organizational management, and physical upgrading. The second element of the strategy is to diversify into new markets and to strengthen existing ones. For example, sports tourism (e.g., golf, tennis, equestrian events, swimming, marathons) and conventions are to be encouraged.

Given that the number of tourist arrivals has stayed virtually the same since 1989, it seems fair to suggest that the 1988 National Development Plan has had little impact in terms of invigorating the tourism sector.

An amendment to the first 1970 Plan, the 1988 Physical Development Plan's (GOB, 1988c) main objective is "to indicate a national settlement development strategy and policy for the country . . . to the year 2000" (p. 2). It also incorporates physical development policies for land use, economic activities, housing, services, transportation, utilities, recreation, and conservation. Consistent with the earlier National Development Plans, which discourage new hotel development on the already heavily developed south and west coasts and forbid it on a large part of the east coast, the 1988 Plan directs hotel expansion (projected at an additional 3,780 tourist beds requiring a total additional land area of 28 hectares by the year 2000) at the west, south, and southeast coasts, with a gradual implementation of a program of rationalization in land uses (GOB, 1988c, pp. 126, 136). The Plan (GOB, 1988c, pp. 38, 154–155) argues that, before deciding on further decentralization of tourism development, other possibilities should be analyzed (e.g., infilling in existing tourist zones, areal renewal, conservation and enhancement of prime beaches, relocation of nontourist activities to accommodate expansion, and improvement of infrastructure—particularly sewers). It also suggests that many of the current accommodation facilities are too small in size to be economically viable and should therefore be replaced by larger units or that smaller units be consolidated. This option would be particularly relevant should future strategy call for an increase in luxury hotel developments, which would preferably be located close to the beaches of the west and south coasts.

The Plan notes that beach erosion has been a serious problem in many areas. Much of the problem is caused by long-term and unregulated waste discharge into the sea from domestic, commercial, industrial, and agricultural sources, which has resulted in the slow destruction of many parts of the coastal coral reefs, thus reducing their effectiveness as a barrier to coastal erosion from wave action (Resource Systems Management International, Inc. [RSMI], 1988, pp. 2–23). The negative effect of sewage on marine ecosystems has been partly overcome by the sewerage project in Carlisle Bay to deal with the capital of Bridgetown (A. B. Archer, 1988). Nevertheless, environmental degradation has reached a point where, in the opinion of B. J. Hudson (1986), Barbados may be losing potential visitors who perceive the island as being spoiled.

Unfortunately, the optimism expressed in the National Development Plan was not justified: "The Barbados economy, after years of being the most buoyant in the Caribbean, collapsed in 1991. . . ." (Anonymous, 1992). Palmer (1993, p. 66) contends that the problem was directly related to the United States recession, which quickly reduced foreign exchange and tax revenues, creating budgetary and balance-of-payments deficits and forcing a realignment of the exchange rate. This position had been supported earlier by the World Bank (1988b, p. 36), which noted that the competitive structure of the Barbados hotel industry, an overvalued exchange rate, and tariff-protected local producers had contributed to keeping the price of goods and services artificially high; the recommendation was that "prices should be lowered" to stimulate recovery. Similarly, the CDB (1989a, p. 7) had concluded that diversification would not be successful and that economic growth in Barbados would come mainly from an increase in visitor arrivals because the CARICOM market for manufactured goods shows little sign of recovery as regional demand remains depressed, whereas nonregional demand for garments and electronic components is likely to grow slowly in view of forecasts of slower growth in the United States. The future of the fledgling captive insurance sector is uncertain.

Given its recent implementation, the lack of concrete proposals for new tourism development, and the country's current fiscal situation, it remains to be seen what effect this Plan will have on future development, although its strengthening of land-use plans seems to have the potential to be a positive factor. On the other hand, there seems to be little evidence to support the projected growth in hotel accommodation.

External Criticism . . . and Reaction

By the late 1980s, trends in tourist arrivals and expenditures appear to have spurred the CDB and the World Bank to criticize both the private sector and the Barbados Government for not taking a strong hand in the marketing and upgrading of the tourism sector, thereby leaving the most dynamic—but still troubled—sector of the economy to stagnate.

The CDB (1989a, pp. 1–7) argues that, to maintain the level of arrivals in the peak season at current levels—let alone to exceed those levels—many establishments in Barbados must upgrade their facilities; such action is necessary if Barbados is to maintain its competitiveness in terms of quality of its product with other Caribbean destinations. Similarly, the World Bank (1986) focuses on the interconnections between marketing and product quality. It proposes closer cooperation in marketing, flexible targeting to those markets where an exchange rate advantage is perceived, pressuring airlines to organize favorable fare deals, and supporting and encouraging the Board of Tourism in marketing Barbados as an upmarket or high-class destination with exclusive resorts as well as more downmarket special interest tourism and special affinity groups: "More importantly, reaching the upmarket segment of tourism calls for an upgraded tourist product and highlights the importance of hotel refurbishing and renovation" (World Bank, 1986, p. 10). The World Bank (1988a), emphasising growing competition in the region, further states that "The problems besetting the industry in Barbados are many and need to be approached on a broad front. The complacency that has crept into the industry should be recognized and a greater effort made to improve the quality of the product being offered" (p. 11). It goes on to make several further points: more imaginative marketing is needed, particularly for smaller hotels with low occupancy rates; whereas accommodations at middle and lower ends appear adequate for the moment,[11] the occupancy rate in the luxury sector suggests the need for additional rooms; facilities for large conventions are limited; refurbishing and renovation of existing accommodations are needed; the problems of smaller establishments are related to poor management, lack of training, and complacency.

Such criticisms seem to have had results, as demonstrated by marketing actions taken by the Barbados Hotel Association (BHA) and policy positions by the Government. The BHA, the trade association of large hotels, works through a Joint Committee with the Board of Tourism to coordinate marketing; the division of responsibilities is that the former deals with marketing and promotion of hotels and the island's attractions, and the latter deals with developmental marketing (H. Husbands, 1991, personal communication). Their collective efforts include joint publications (e.g., "Barbados: Relax the Bajan Way," 1991) and the introduction of a toll-free reservation number in North America, offering a service for a wide range of hotels at nearly all scales. The BHA is also involved in working with the National Conservation Commission (e.g., antilitter and signage campaigns), lobbying government (e.g., to extend the sewerage project to the south coast), training, information, cooperative advertising, and encouraging air carriers to develop innovative programs (e.g., Lada Air's "comfort tourism" charters, which emphasize quality on charter flights).

In the summer of 1991, the Association prepared a confidential marketing plan for the island as a whole focusing on hotels and services rather than the island as a destination (H. Husbands, 1991, personal communication). One aspect of the plan is an attempt to market an innovative variation on the all-inclusive concept that focuses on the island as a whole; that is, tourists can purchase at point of sale a package at a wide range of price levels, which can include accommodations, trips, car rentals, etc.

The Government clearly recognizes that the Barbadian tourist sector is largely ruled by exogenous variables over which it has little or no control, a primary example of which is that of international airlines (E. Layne, 1991, personal communication). As noted above, the bankruptcy of Eastern Airlines and changes in routing by American Airlines have seriously affected Barbados. Another example stems from the Government's efforts to diversify its markets: even though British Airways was unwilling to include Manchester in its routes to Barbados, it objected successfully to Air Holland adding a flight from Manchester in addition to its current weekly charter from Amsterdam (Anonymous, 1991a). In contrast, however, the Government would like to encourage the incentive travel and convention markets, a direction that requires a large five-star hotel—which, inevitably, means the involvement of an MNC hotel (E. Layne, 1991, personal communication).

The Government intends to continue its policy not to permit gambling establishments in any hotels. It also wants to improve the quality of service through increased support for training, service awards, etc. Because it sees cruise ships as not being central to the economy, but instead useful in spreading the positive economic effects throughout the island, the Government aims to encourage increased numbers of cruise ships. Finally, based on OAS support for small hotels in terms of marketing, design, and accounting, the Government intends to help small hotels overcome their problems in getting loans for improvements (E. Layne, 1991, personal communication).

The Government supports the Tourism Development Corporation (TDC) in an attempt to bring the ideas, expertise, and finance of private enterprise to bear on major marketing issues. Working in close cooperation with government tourism authorities and the BHA, the TDC is unique in that it is solely funded by the private sector supported by a generous fiscal benefit (member companies contribute 2% of their taxable income to the TDC fund, which can them be claimed at a rate of 150% for tax purposes). The initial focus has been on marketing, but product development is becoming increasingly more important, including plans to launch a program to raise awareness on solid waste and water and a greener environment program (Blommestein, 1993).

In late 1992, the Government agreed to undertake an IMF program leading to structural adjustment. The program is related to a UNDP assistance package of US$579,000, part of which is to be aimed at technical assistance to upgrade environmental management. Noting that tourism is Barbados' main foreign exchange earner, Jan Wahlberg, UNDP representative, described the sector's impact on the island's environment, particularly water pollution and inadequate sewerage:

> From a tourism point of view that is what you are marketing, the beauty of the islands and if that's endangered in any way the country becomes less and less attractive. . . . I think that there is an urgent need to have a firm action plan to deal with these issues. (Anonymous, 1992)

Conclusion

> Barbados is frequently cited as a country that began its tourism life as a quality destination and subsequently flirted with mass tourism in order to increase occupancy levels outside the traditional winter peak period. It is now at the crossroads with an uncertain image. (Mather & Todd, 1993, p. 130)

This analysis demonstrates the Government's long-standing interest in promoting tourism as a major sector of the Barbadian economy. With exceptions, however, the Government seems to have adopted a laissez-faire attitude, preferring to encourage such policies as first growth, then quality control, and more recently market diversification, rather than becoming an active agent in planning for tourism development. The results are a plateauing of tourist numbers and expenditure and an aging accommodation stock, much in need of refurbishing and renovation, some major exceptions notwithstanding.

For many years, up until about 1980, Barbados was often presented as "the success story" of the Commonwealth Caribbean: a diversified economy, the highest standards of public services and facilities, and rising per capita incomes. The fragility of the system, however, seemed to be undermined from all angles at virtually the same time: world recession, rising energy costs, increased regional and global tourism competition, falling sugar prices, downturns in high-technology offshore assembly production, etc. The result is an economy in general that is in serious difficulty; more specifically, the current mainstay of the economy—the tourism sector—may even be on the point of drastic decline:

> Under the gradual decline scenario the underlying reasons may be more obscure and cause and effect relations remain unclear. Indeed in the initial stages there may not be as yet an awareness or consensus that there is a problem since, after all, tourist arrivals are still going up. After this period there will be a slow but profound malaise in the tourism industry, characterized by declining tourist arrivals, deteriorating plant and attractions and a perception—by the tourist—of low value for money ratio. This may be the situation which faces Barbados at the moment. (Blommestein, 1993, p. 8)

Analysis of the Government's tourism policy and planning history and of the major characteristics of the tourism sector shows that a major factor in this situation is that the Government is not really involved in tourism development policy or planning, but rather only in tourism land use and marketing planning. As Thomas (1988) argues, this approach is not unique in Barbados to tourism; rather, it is consistent with overall economic policies pursued since independence.

Mings (1978, pp. 1–3) suggests that governments have three possible options related to tourism:

1. the "no change" option: ignore the problems and protests; this is hazardous for both government and tourism because the sector depends on local support and no elected government can disregard unpopular and unsuccessful activities for long;

2. withdraw public support for tourism and even attempt to curb private promotion of tourism; this involves the danger of premature government reaction and of "jumping off the band-wagon" too soon;

3. pursue rationalization of the sector to make it more beneficial; this involves an assessment of the problems and prospects, and a plan of action to remedy weaknesses and to direct the sector toward long-term goals.

The first option has been reflected in the history of tourism in Barbados; the results are obvious.

The third option seems the most reasonable in general, and in particular for Barbados, but it raises two major issues (Wilkinson, 1989b). First, can the various problems related to tourism be remedied satisfactorily? There is evidence to suggest that the answer might be negative, for reasons related both to Caribbean tourism in general and to Barbados in particular, notably the high operating costs and low profits of Caribbean hotels. Hepple (1992, personal communication) argues that the operating performance profile of hotels in Barbados is very similar to that for the Bahamas (see Chapter 8). This means that the only way to answer the first question positively is for the Government to change its support for the tourism sector based solely on the short-term prospect for job creation and replace it with a more reasoned approach, which emphasizes long-term economic, social, and environmental viability (i.e., sustainable development).

Second—if the answer to the first question appears to be positive—will the (economic, social, and environmental) contributions of the surviving sector be of sufficient magnitude to warrant public support? Murphy (1985) contends that the answer will be positive only if the needs of the local community are placed before the goals of the tourism sector:

> The industry possesses great potential for social and economic benefits if planning can be redirected from a pure business and development approach to a more open and community-oriented approach which views tourism as a local resource. The management of this resource for the common good and future generations should become the goal and criterion by which the industry is judged. This will involve focusing on the ecological and human qualities of a destination area in addition to business considerations. (p. 37)

This community approach to tourism has the objective of producing a "Community Tourism Product"—an amalgam of the destination's resources and facilities that the community as a whole wishes to present to the tourism market (Murphy, 1985). This approach is similar to Farrell's (1986) notion of "cooperative tourism," in which "a consortium of active players—local people, sector managers, government, and visitors—share in responsibilities and rewards" (p. 126). To date, the Barbadian tourism sector has not developed in such a way. Given the current state of the tourism sector in Barbados, it would seem prudent for the Government to consider adopting such a stance, although it is not clear whether there would be adequate public support.

Although no formal policy action has yet been taken, the Government appears to have recognized that the Barbadian tourism sector is not healthy, at least partly because of the lack of a formal tourism policy that would give direction and support for a more long-term view of the role of tourism in the economy. Then Prime Minister Erskine Sandiford publicly stated the need for such a policy (G. Dann, 1992, personal communication). In 1994, however, disagreements within the Cabinet over an appointment to the Board of Tourism led to a vote of "no confidence" in the Assembly, which the Government lost. The September 6, 1994 election resulted in the overwhelming defeat of the Government.

Notes

[1]The Portuguese referred to the island as *Los Barbados*, meaning "the bearded ones"; the reference is unclear, having variously been attributed to Barbados' bearded fig trees, bearded Arawak men, or even the pre-European presence of bearded African men (Wilder, 1986, pp. 22–23).

[2]Although only the third elected parliament in the world (after Great Britain and Bermuda), the Barbados House of Assembly could hardly be described as democratic until the country achieved independence from Britain in 1966. For example, as late as 1938, only 3% of the adult population had the vote (Thomas, 1988, p. 56).

[3]The decline in the importance of sugar was not the result of a deliberate choice, but rather of the Caribbean-wide structural weakness of agriculture (Thomas, 1988, p. 276).

[4]Worrell (1987, p. 53), however, argues that the phase of rapid growth in manufacturing ended in 1969, when light industry had nearly exhausted the capacity of the domestic market and the growth rate of 15–20% per annum in the late 1960s fell to less than 10% per annum.

[5]Indeed, Phillips (1982) argues that this trend started even earlier, as mass tourism hit the island and as summer tourism increased. He observes that, between 1961 and 1980, real per visitor expenditure declined by 3.2% per year.

[6]These figures seem to have originated with Boxhill's (1982) estimate of 14,430 direct and indirect jobs, or 14% of the 1980 labor force.

[7]Consistent with this point, the Government formed a corporation with the intention to bring together seven individually operated and Barbadian-owned hotels, totaling 308 rooms, at a new development site at Heywoods on the northwest coast. Unfortunately, before construction was completed, there was a downturn in tourism and the local participants withdrew, forcing the Government to retain ownership of the complex and turn its management over to an MNC (Wyndham Hotels). Hepple (1992, personal communication) notes serious problems with the initial concept (e.g., attempting to create a new destination in a nontraditional part of the island, seven hotels using common facilities and common marketing) and with construction costs, which were twice as much as budgeted. Cambers (1985) also notes the negative environmental impacts of the complex, particularly accelerated coastal erosion.

[8]The method by which this figure was calculated is not provided.

[9]The Plan does not call for a national park on the east coast, despite earlier recommendations (GOB, 1979, 1970; Pennington, 1983).

[10]The south coast project (with its focus on Bridgetown) is complete, but no plans are in place to extend it to the west and southeast coasts (A. Archer, 1990, personal communication).

[11]The CDB (1989a) presents the opposite view about middle and lower end accommodations.

Chapter 8

The Bahamas

I am optimistic because I think the problems we face [in tourism] can be solved with good organization, advanced technology and a bit of luck. Why am I also pessimistic? Because I'm not sure there's any real base for my optimism. (Nanus, 1979)

Introduction

Not located in the Caribbean Sea but in the Atlantic Ocean to the east of Florida, the Bahamas is an archipelago consisting of 29 islands, 661 cays, and about 2,387 rocks covering 13,940 km^2 of land in an ocean area of approximately 260,000 km^2 and having a coastline of 3,542 km. The Bahamas begin at the Manzanilla Bank about 80 km east of south-central Florida and extend 1,200 km southeast to within 80 km of Haiti and Cuba (Map 8.1). At its widest, it stretches 600 km from the Cay Sal Bank off Cuba to San Salvador, at the edge of the Atlantic (Craton, 1986, p. 11). The climate is tropical marine, with winter temperatures (16–23°C) being insulated from North American weather by the Florida Channel and summers (25–33°C) cooled by the Northeast Tradewinds. Rainfall varies greatly, with Nassau receiving 1,400 mm annually; the hurricane season is June to November (Government of the Commonwealth of the Bahamas [GOCB], 1988a).

The islands are generally low and flat, with the highest point being 60 m on Cat Island:

> The islands are of low relief, usually long and narrow, each rising from the shore line to a low ridge. They are composed mainly of calcareous sand, originally derived from marine shells, which were piled up into low ridges and rounded hills by wind action at a time when the whole shelf stood above the sea. Some rocks are still loose and sandy, but others have been consolidated by age and weathered in upland areas into typical karst scenery. Lying beyond these ridges are mainly lagoons and swamps. The islands stand together with many coral reefs, on two shallow submarine banks in which passages deep enough for shipping are hard to find. The only deep water between the islands, [sic] lies outside the barrier reef off the east coast of Andros, and is known as the Tongue of the Ocean [which is over 2000 m deep]. (GOCB, 1988a, p. 5)

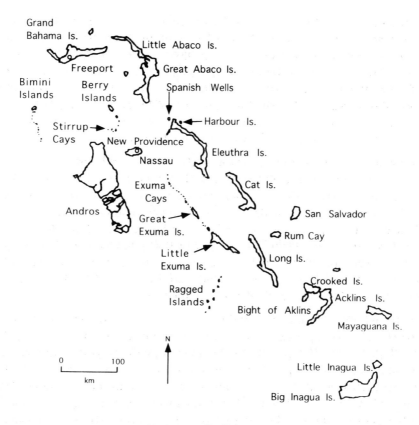

Map. 8.1. The Bahamas.

All three types of coral reef formation occur: fringe reef (nearly all islands on the ocean side), barrier reef (less common, but including parts of Bahama Bank, Great Bahama Bank, and Bight of Acklins), and coral atolls (two: Hogsty Reef and Cay Sal Bank) (Craton, 1986, p. 11).

Because of the flatness of the islands and the porous rock, there are no rivers or streams. Campbell (1974) describes the vegetation:

> The Bahamian forests are lean. Only those species adapted to the stresses of salt, wind, incessant sun and consistently sparse and porous soil have persevered since the rising sea obliterated most of the once vast Pleistocene habitats. . . . [M]uch [of the land] is salina or waterless cays with slight floral diversity. Yet 1,371 species, varieties and hybrids of flowering plants, a small number by subtropical standards, compete for tenuous foothold on this inhospitable space. (p. 37)

Much of the rich vegetation on some of the islands has been introduced, with only 56 plants being indigenous. Although there are 204 species and subspecies of birds (100 of which nest on the islands) and a variety of reptiles and snakes, the only native mammal left is the jutia, a rat-like rodent on Atwood Cay. There is, however, a rich marine and reef life; in fact, the barrier reef off Andros is the third largest in the world (after Australia's Great Barrier Reef and the Belize Barrier Reef). Minerals are scarce, with no petroleum resources having been found. Only two minerals are mined: aragonite—an extremely pure (95%) calcium carbonate used in the manufacture of cement, concrete, glass, and fertilizer—is taken from the 100 billion tons of reserves found in shallow underwater dunes stretching 35 km between Bimini and Andros; and salt is mined on Ragged Island and Inagua, the latter's 1.2 million tonne capacity being one of the largest in the world.

It is probable that the first inhabitants were the Ciboney, who migrated to the Greater Antilles more than 2,000 years ago; they appear to have fled later Amerindian migrants and were either conquered or enslaved, leaving very few signs of their habitation.[1] Columbus made first landfall on an island called *Guanahani*, which he renamed San Salvador (and which was later named Watling's Island before being renamed once again San Salvador in 1926) on October 12, 1492. Spending 15 days exploring the archipelago, he visited what are now called San Salvador, Rum Cay, Long Island, Crooked Island, and the Ragged Islands before proceeding on to Cuba in search of gold and the Orient.

The people whom Columbus met in the Central Bahamas called themselves *Lukkucairi* (or "island people"), which later was corrupted into *Lucayans* (Barratt, 1989, p. 29). Practicing a culture comparable to the early neolithic cultures of Europe (Moya Pons, 1984, p. 20), which anthropologists call *Tainan* ("good" or "noble") (Richardson, 1992, p. 22), they were a branch of the Neo-Indian Arawaks found in Cuba, Haiti, Puerto Rico, and Jamaica. Originating on the mainland of South America, but pushed north by fiercer Caribs, they arrived in Jamaica around 400 AD and in southern and central Bahamas between 500 and 600 AD.

> But for the advent of the Europeans, the Caribs might have pursued the Arawaks right into the Bahamas archipelago and finally destroyed them there. As it is, it was merely a matter of timing that decreed that it is the Lucayan Arawaks not the Caribs whom we have to regard as the first certain Bahamians— with the Spaniards not the Caribs as their destroyers. (Craton, 1986, p. 18)

There is no evidence that the Spaniards ever had a permanent settlement in the Bahamas. Basically, the only thing that the Spaniards wanted out of the Lucayan Islands were the Lucayans: between 1500 and 1520, virtually the entire population of about 20,000 was enslaved and shipped to other islands where they soon all died. The Spanish did, however, give the Bahamas its current name. In 1513, Ponce de León described what is now called Little Bahama Bank as *baja mar* ("underwater" or "shallow water"). By the time of the publication of the Turin map in 1523, the name "Bahama" was applied to the area around what is now called Grand Bahama, even though that island is not discernible on the map. The name "Bahamas" was later applied to the entire archipelago (Barratt, 1989, p. 33).

England's King Charles I granted the Bahamas to Sir Robert Heath, his Attorney-General, in 1629 as part of vast land grant covering the Carolinas and the Bahamas, but no permanent settlement resulted. Then a marginally more effective charter was given to six of the eight Proprietors of the Carolinas in 1670; the

Proprietors, as tenants-in-chief of the King, could grant acreages as large as they wished to any individuals, provided that the holders paid an annual quit rent (usually less than a penny an acre). The first unofficial settlements had occurred in the interval between the two grants while there was a republican interregnum in England when, in 1648, settlers from Bermuda were drawn by the possibility of political and religious freedom (after which their main refuge was named Eleuthera for the Greek word for "freedom," *eleutheria*) or the promise of unencumbered land. By 1670, there were settlers in New Providence, northern Eleuthera, Harbour Island, and Spanish Wells. With their new charter, the Proprietors attempted to augment their revenue by asserting their rights to quit rents from established settlers and by attracting new colonists with generous grants of quit-rent land. Craton (1987) notes that "These moves, however, were doomed to failure by the immigration of pirates, who condemned New Providence to anarchy, isolated the settlements of northern Eleuthera, and made the rest of the Bahamas Islands an extremely insecure prospect for potential settlers" (p. 91). Many settlers fled to Jamaica and Massachusetts and it was not until 1686 that New Providence was resettled and the village of Charles Town laid out again and renamed Nassau. By 1718, order, if not prosperity, was restored with the Crown's assumption of political control in the person of Woodes Rogers, Captain-General and Governor-in-Chief of the Crown Colony of the Bahamas. By 1729, there was sufficient settlement to warrant the creation of an elected Assembly of 24 members.

There was slow progress in promoting sugar and cotton planting, ship-building, and salt production, with the most prosperous times occurring when Nassau was intermittently a privateering base during the wars with Spain (and again later with the United States in the War of 1812). On the whole, "however interesting their history, the Bahamas were insignificant in the grand panorama of the eighteenth century" (Craton, 1986, p. 136). The population (a total of 2,303, including 964 slaves in 1740) exploded in the 1780s as 1,600 white American Loyalists, along with 6,000 slaves, fled to the islands at the end of the American Revolution and took up several hundred land grants totaling perhaps 40,000 hectres. Most of the larger islands were settled for the first time, with the intention of developing cotton plantations or salinas, producing solar salt. Cotton and sea island cotton boomed for a while, but died off slowly as the thin soils lost their fertility through overuse and destructive land clearing (de Albuquerque & McElroy, 1986).

Although never strong, the plantation system effectively ended with emancipation of the slaves in 1838 and the colony sank deeper into obscurity. Only with the beginning of the Civil War in the United States did prosperity, however temporary, return as New Providence became a major port for blockade runners. In turn, however,

> . . . the ending of the blockade-running deflated the economy with the speed of a punctured balloon. So severe and prolonged was the depression that most Bahamians came to wish that they had never enjoyed the brief interlude of garish prosperity during the war. . . .

The sudden development of Nassau had been over-optimistic. Once emptied
of cotton and war supplies, the new warehouses lay empty for fifty years.
Emptied of its wartime profiteers, the Royal Victoria Hotel was offered for
sale, but not a single tender was received. In Bay Street the thirty-four new
street lamps usually went unlit. (Craton, 1986, p. 225)

Later industrial booms—pineapples, sponge, sisal—were short-lived and poverty
was endemic throughout the islands from 1865 onwards.

In the 20th century, the two World Wars and Prohibition in the United States
brought temporary prosperity of another sort. For example, in 1921, because of
Prohibition, more than 20 giant liquor concerns sprang up in Nassau almost overnight; reexports of liquor averaged over £500,000/year from 1922 to 1932 and customs receipts skyrocketed. Not surprisingly, official figures represented only a proportion of the trade as much was smuggled into the United States. There was a
close correlation between the liquor magnates and the exploitation of real estate,
thus buttressing the land boom of the 1920s that was linked with that of Florida.
Although money continued to flow in until the end of Prohibition, the Depression
and then the beginning of World War II led to a period of "savage depression" in
the Bahamas (Craton, 1986, p. 255), which did not end until the United States entered the war in late 1941. The war had important economic impacts from the construction of airports, operation of an air training base, staging-post on the trans-
Atlantic airplane ferry service, and lend-lease American navy base. After the war,
5,000 Bahamian laborers were temporarily engaged in agricultural work in the
United States; continuing for 20 years, this source of remittance income had important socioeconomic impacts.

For the first time, the traditional slump did not set in when a war ended. The next
25 years saw unparalleled expansion of the economy and growing prosperity because of tourism and offshore financial services.

Of the 29 major islands, 22 are inhabited. Although only 210 km^2, New Providence—with Nassau as the country's government, financial, tourism, and business
center—contains 172,000 people, about 65% of the population of 259,000. Grand
Bahama (1,400 km^2) has 41,000 people or approximately 16% of the population
and Freeport, the second largest city with its tourism, oil refinery, and port. The
other islands with the largest populations are Abaco (10,000 inhabitants), Eleuthera (8,000), and Exuma (3,600), which are agricultural and tourism islands, and
Andros (8,200), which is the largest island (6,000 km^2) and is an agricultural and
fishing island. The other 16 inhabited islands total about 15,000 people, with economies based on agriculture, salt, fish, shrimp farming, and tourism (GOCB, 1988a,
1991).

With a relatively small population spread out over 22 inhabited islands anchored
in a vast area of sea, the Bahamas has to deal with serious political and economic
realities:

All archipelago states must suffer, at least potentially, from a lack of cohesion and one would assume that the more fragmented the state—that is, the larger the number of islands—the greater the centrifugal force. Even where political cohesion is not a problem it is reasonable to expect

1. the emergence or intensification of a center/periphery dichotomy within the nation (Wallerstein, 1987; Alexander, 1980; Clavel, 1980) and

2. that there will be economic costs attendant upon fragmentation. (Fish, 1989, pp. 241–242)

First, there has been some discontent in the Family Islands—called, perhaps portently, the Out Islands until 1972—that New Providence (and to a lesser extent, Grand Bahama) ignores them; one expression of that feeling was an abortive Abaco separation movement in the 1970s (Dodge, 1983). Second, the provision of services (e.g., comprehensive education, air connections throughout all of the islands) would be extremely expensive, thus reinforcing the central domination of the two largest islands.

Having achieved independence from Great Britain on July 10, 1973, the Commonwealth of the Bahamas is an independent nation within the Commonwealth. Its government is headed by a Governor-General appointed by the British Crown and consists of a bicameral legislature (a 16-seat appointed Senate and a 49-seat elected House of Assembly), with a legal and legislative system based on that of Britain.

The Economy

Although the 1960s was a period of economic growth with an average annual growth rate of 9%, the 1970s was a time of slowdown as the construction boom ended and the recession in the United States cut visitors (World Bank, 1980, p. i). Unemployment was very high in the 1970s, at 21.2% in 1975 and 20.0% in 1978 (Archer, 1981, pp. 41–42); although dropping to 11.0% in 1988 (GOCB, 1988a, p. 115), it rose to 16% in the early 1990s.[2] After a real decline in GDP of 5% from 1969 to 1970 (Ramsaran, 1979, p. 82) and a further real decline between 1973 and 1975, there was an upswing beginning in 1978–1979. Nevertheless, the World Bank (1980) foresaw serious problems ahead:

> The principal development challenges facing the Bahamas are to maintain growth in tourism, to broaden the country's economic base through expansion of agricultural and industrial activities, with linkages to the tourism sector and to accelerate development of the outlying, less advanced islands.[3] (p. ii)

The economy limped into the 1990s with a 1% real growth in GDP. Nevertheless, the GDP per capita remains one of the highest in the Caribbean, at US$11,400.

In 1970, manufacturing represented 9% of GDP and 6% of the labor force; however, it lost momentum in the mid-1970s (because of the approach of political independence, introduction of Bahamianization policies, and international economic recession). This created uncertainty and reduced profitability and the incentive to invest: manufacturing represented only 4% of the labor force in 1977 (World Bank, 1980, p. 19) and 6–7% of GDP in 1979 (World Bank, 1980, pp. 1, 3). More recently, the situation has improved somewhat: with a 3% growth rate in 1990, industrial production represents about 15% of the GDP and is focused on cement, oil refining and trans-shipment, salt, rum, aragonite, pharmaceuticals, and spiral-welded steel pipe.

According to the Bahamas Land Resources Survey (Eneas, 1993, p. 9), there are an estimated 96,000 hectares of land with "excellent agricultural potential," 90% of which is on Grand Bahama, Andros, and Abaco. Agriculture, which represented about 4.5% of the labor force in 1986 and 5% of the GDP in 1990 (down from 6% in 1980 [World Bank, 1980, p. 15]), is dominated by small-scale production of citrus fruit, vegetables, and poultry, although there are some large citrus and vegetable farms on Andros and Abaco aimed at the American market. Agricultural production reached a value of US$69 million in 1991, of which US$51 million was corn production (Eneas, 1993, p. 11). Over 80% of the country's food requirements are imported, the only notable exception being poultry, which is supplied by operations on New Providence, Eleuthera, and Grand Bahama (GOCB, 1988a).

In addition to high wage levels, scarcity of agricultural labor, and the need for irrigation (World Bank, 1980, p. iii), increased domestic and export agricultural production is faced with serious barriers: high transportation costs, proximity of Florida as a competitor and supplier, local consumer preferences fueled by advertising for North American products, and tourist preferences. There appears to be no short-term solution to the immense balance-of-payments problems caused by this situation. Although the Ministry of Agriculture seems to have seen only a very limited role for local agricultural production in the 1980s, there has been, however, more interest in increasing agricultural production in the 1990s.

Fishing remains significant, with US$31 million in exports from offshore fishing and shrimp farming in 1987 (GOCB, 1988a).

A major source of income in the Bahamas in the 1970s came from illegal involvement in the United States-oriented drug trade (McKee & Tisdall, 1990, p. 94). Much of the income derived by Bahamians from the drug trade was indeed invested back into the country, but the social costs of drug addiction and crime remain as significant problems.

Finally, the Bahamas—the oldest offshore banking center in the Western Hemisphere (Ramsaran, 1989, p. 96)—is a major location for offshore financial services. In the late 1950s, there were only about a dozen commercial banks in the country (Ramsaran, 1989, p. 98), but by 1988 there were 385 institutions licensed under the Banks and Trust Companies Regulation Act. Of these, 105 are nonactive or of restricted operation and 280 deal with the general public, but only 29 of the latter actually operate in the Bahamas (GOCB, 1988a, p. 206). There is also a major offshore insurance industry (Francis, 1985). Ramsaran (1989, however, notes that it is very difficult to quantify the costs and benefits of off-shore companies to the host country; in fact, he states that there is often "a highly exaggerated level of importance . . . [of] offshore activities in the domestic economy" (pp. 102–103). McKee and Tisdell (1990, p. 35) are even more doubtful that the Bahamian economy has experienced quite the benefits that planners had anticipated. It appears that offshore industries will remain a major feature of the Bahamian economy for some time. Prime Minister Hubert Ingraham (whose newly formed Free National Movement Party defeated the 25-year-old United Bahamian Party Government of Sir Lynden Pindling on August 19, 1992) has accelerated the regulatory process so that International Business Companies (IBCs) can now be incorporated within 24 hours of obtaining proper documentation; 15,000 IBCs now exist (Newman, 1994).

By the end of the 1980s, it was clear that the economy of the Bahamas was in recession as tourist arrivals flattened out after 5 years of uninterrupted growth:

> This downturn has no doubt hurt the service sector and other sectors directly dependent on tourist activity. Liquidity is tight as the success of the joint U.S.–Bahamian crackdown on drugs has drained the financial system of an important source of foreign exchange. This environment has caused a sharp slowdown in construction activity. As a result, unemployment remains high. (WEFA, 1988, p. 2)

Although not suffering from external debt in the same degree as other countries because tourism revenues have resulted in manageable fiscal and balance-of-payments deficits, the balance-of-payments deficit on visible trade is considerable. For example, in 1991 there were US$306 million in exports (pharmaceuticals, cement, rum, crawfish) and US$1.14 billion in imports (foodstuffs, manufactured goods, mineral fuels), for a trade deficit of US$839 million. When tourism is included, however, the picture is less dark, but there has been a continuous and growing overall deficit in nearly every year since 1968 (GOCB, 1988a, p. 141), including a US$179 million deficit in 1991. Perhaps the most telling statistic is the IDB (1989b, p. 3) calculation that, in May 1989, using 1987 as a base year, the real GDP per capita had fallen to that of 1968.

Clearly, there are serious economic hurdles in the path of future prosperity:

> (1) unemployment, particularly youth unemployment, remains a problem; (2) . . . the labor force is expanding at an estimated annual rate of 4% to 6%; (3) economic development . . . is extremely uneven; (4) the Government crackdown on drug traffickers and on the laundering of "narcodollars" has decreased liquidity . . .; and (5) . . . the tourist sector appears to have reached an advanced stage of maturity and currently faces stiff competition from others in the region just now expanding their tourism sectors. The challenge to policymakers now is can their pragmatism, which has been so vital in the past, still yield rewards. (WEFA, 1988, p. 2)

The problem is compounded by the Government's dependence on indirect taxation revenue that is largely related to the tourism sector. The Bahamas' absence of direct taxation has been criticized by the World Bank (1986b): "The Government's policy of no personal or corporate income taxes, does limit the overall flexibility of the tax system and reduces the government's fiscal flexibility'' (p. 12). As a result, ''The Bahamas' tax structure is inelastic with respect to both money income and to increases in real national income,'' the heavy reliance upon import duties makes the tax structure strongly regressive, and ''ad hoc measures that have been adopted over the past decade have both complicated administration and compliance and increased the possibilities and success of evasion'' (World Bank, 1986b, p. 14).

The Tourism Sector

A late-Stage III (Maturity) destination, the Bahamas is characterized by mass-market tourism, growth stagnation, short-stay visitors, MNCs, high visitor densities, an emphasis on artificial attractions (e.g., gambling, duty-free shopping, golf), loss of local identity, intensive advertising for high-volume visitors, growing cruise ship activity, and packaged charters.

Stay-Over Tourist Arrivals

The numbers of stay-over tourist arrivals (and cruise passengers) expanded rapidly in the 1960s, only to fall off dramatically in the early 1970s. On the surface, there appeared to be a recovery in all visitor categories beginning in the late 1970s. Other measures, however, indicate otherwise. With declining average length of stay and occupancy rates, the number of tourist arrivals per 1,000 local population per year, the tourist penetration ratio, and the tourist density ratio[1] all declined or stayed relatively constant despite absolute growth in the number of arrivals. (In fact, with 1,488,700 stay-over tourist in 1993, the Bahamas was third in the region, behind only Puerto Rico and the Dominican Republic) (Table 8.1). One important feature, however, is a low index of seasonality (1.088 in 1989 and 1.145 in 1993), indicating a very even distribution of tourists throughout the year (de Albuquerque & McElroy, 1992, p. 627).

Similar to the problem noted by C. Hall (1989) for Barbados, the Bahamas seems to have recognized that declines in tourist arrivals from particular sectors were related partly to its dollar being pegged at par with the American dollar, yet it has done nothing about the problem: ''Any recovery in Canadian and European traffic is tied inexorably to currency exchange rates'' (GOCB, 1988a, p. 169). The United States remains the major market source for the Bahamas (at 81.2% of stay-over arrivals in 1993), with the number of American tourists growing steadily; however, the overall rank and growth rate between 1980 and 1993 was very low compared to the rest of the Caribbean. Canadian and European tourists have also declined in both absolute numbers and growth rates, with the Bahamas ranking at the bottom of Caribbean destinations in market performance. Overall, the United States, Europe, and Canada dominate, accounting for a very high market concentration ratio of 96.6.

A major problem has been the instability of the international airline industry, largely as a result of industry deregulation in the United States. A Government comment in 1988 was somewhat premature: ''The Bahamas is well served by ma-

Table 8.1. Bahamas: Tourism Statistics

Year	Stay-Over Tourists No. (000s)	% Annual Change	Excursionists No. (000s)	% Annual Change	Cruise Passengers No. (000s)	% Annual Change	Total Tourists No. (000s)	% Annual Change	Visitor Expenditure US$ (M)	% Annual Change	Tourist Rooms No.	Av. LOS (No. Nights)	No. Tourist Nights/Yr (000s)
1980	1181.3	4.6	113.7	7.3	577.6	21.3	1872.6	NA	595.5	6.0	11429	7.1	8347.2
1981	1030.6	−12.8	117.2	3.1	596.9	3.3	1744.7	−6.8	639.1	7.3	11733	7.3	7523.4
1982	1101.1	6.8	120.9	3.2	719.6	20.6	1941.6	11.3	654.5	2.4	11786	6.8	7487.5
1983	1239.8	12.6	121.5	0.5	854.1	18.7	2215.4	14.1	770.2	17.7	13025	6.6	8142.7
1984	1278.5	3.1	132.2	8.8	907.8	6.3	2318.5	4.7	801.5	4.1	13120	6.4	8182.4
1985	1368.3	0.7	119.8	−9.4	1136.5	25.2	2624.6	13.2	995.0	24.1	13166	6.1	8346.6
1986	1375.2	0.5	131.1	9.4	1495.6	31.6	3001.9	14.4	1105.0	11.1	12877	6.1	8388.7
1987	1479.9	7.6	164.0	25.1	1434.2	−4.1	3078.1	2.5	1145.8	3.7	13184	5.9	8731.4
1988	1475.0	−0.3	177.9	8.5	1505.1	4.9	3158.0	2.6	1149.5	0.3	12480	5.9	8702.5
1989	1575.1	6.8	178.6	0.4	1644.6	9.3	3398.3	7.6	1310.0	14.0	13861	5.7	8978.1
1990	1561.6	−0.9	212.9	19.2	1853.9	12.7	3628.4	6.8	1332.9	1.7	13475	5.7	8901.1
1991	1427.0	−8.6	174.9	−17.8	2020.0	9.0	3621.9	−0.2	1192.7	−10.5	13165	6.1	8704.7
1992	1398.9	−2.0	150.4	−14.0	2139.4	5.9	3688.7	1.8	1243.5	4.3	13541	5.8	8113.6
1993	1488.7	6.4	146.2	−2.8	2047.0	−4.3	3681.9	−0.2	1304.0	4.9	13521	5.8	8634.5

jor U.S. scheduled carriers—Delta, Eastern, Pan American, T.W.A., Piedmont, Midway and Braniff" (GOCB, 1988a, p. 169). Most of those airlines went bankrupt, whereas some of the others that are not bankrupt no longer service the Bahamas. The air transport situation was made even more difficult in 1991 when British Airways withdrew from regular service to the Bahamas, thus creating problems for the Government's desire to increase their market share of European visitors. With the exception of six flights by Air Canada, 569 flights—99.0% of all direct scheduled flights per week in the high season—connected in 1992 with the United States; there were no other direct scheduled flights to any other country outside of the region (Mather & Todd, 1993).

The Government-owned Bahamasair has also had serious economic problems, cutting its labor force from 840 to 550 in March 1991 as part of a restructuring program intended to keep the airline solvent (Wagenheim, 1991). The airline is undergoing further major changes, particularly in routing, after having lost US$11 million on US$38 million in revenue in 1992 (B. McInnis, 1993, personal communication). There are, however, doubts in the industry about Bahamasair's viability (Mather & Todd, 1993, p. 59).

Accommodations

By the mid-1970s, growth in the accommodation sector had halted and the industry appeared to be in serious trouble:

> The hotel industry in the Bahamas . . . may be characterized by huge investments, profitless turnover of money, accumulating losses, a thin and restive labor market aggravated by "rotation" of staff to avoid higher layoffs, a determined effort to Bahamianize the industry, and a substantial number of visitors less than satisfied with service, attention, atmosphere, food and entertainment. Occupancy rates in 1972 were relatively static, but declining average room rates lowered revenues. (Dayton-Keenan, 1973, p. 4)

Dayton-Keenan (1973, p. 4) paints a bleak outlook for the short-term future of Bahamian hotels: increasing competition; competitive pressures to hold prices level; increased labor, utility, and social benefits costs; increased commission rates to wholesalers; rising costs of food, fuel, and hotel supplies; possible water shortages in some areas in high season; small if any increase in volume of tourists. The situation seems to have borne out most of these fears in the next decade. Overall, the number of hotel rooms remained static (11,612 hotel rooms in 1974 and 11,411 in 1984,) but the situation was worse in Grand Bahama where the number of rooms dropped (from 4,304 in 1974 to 3,880 in 1979) (B. H. Archer, 1981, pp. 5, 19). Clearly, the private sector was aware of Dayton-Keenan's (1973, p. 7) warning that a survey of eight hotels on New Providence indicated gross operating profits only half of what could be expected from such properties; net losses after taxes, insurance, interest, and depreciation; negative cash flows; and accumulated losses. Pannell Kerr Forster's (1991) more recent analysis confirms that the picture has not changed.

Although growing slightly since 1980 to 13,521 rooms in 1993, the number of tourist rooms has fluctuated a great deal. Various measures point to a weakening of the accommodation sector, a factor that is particularly important as tourism is the major source of employment opportunities. The number of rooms/km² remained virtually constant between 1980 (0.8) and 1993 (1.0), whereas the number of rooms/1,000 local population actually decreased (from 54.5 to 50.3) because of the growing population. The dropping occupancy rate (from 69.1% to 56.3%) has resulted in significant reduction in the tourist occupancy function from 37.7 in 1980 to 28.5 in 1993. Similarly, despite the growth in the number of stay-over arrivals, the decreasing average length of stay (from 7.1 nights to 5.8) has resulted in only 3.5% growth in the annual number of tourist nights (from 8,437,200 to 8,634,500) in the same period. Average room rates are quite high, ranking 10th in the Caribbean in winter and 7th in summer in 1987–1988 (Curtin & Poon, 1988). Despite these high rates, however, there have been many studies that describe visitor dissatisfaction with the price-for-quality situation.

The World Bank (1986a) notes that 80% of all Bahamian tourist accommodations are foreign owned. A large proportion of the rooms (63.5% in 1989) is accounted for by hotels of 100+ rooms, but several large hotels have closed in recent years; for example, in 1987, there were 15 hotels of 200+ rooms, compared to nine in 1989. Some were old and too costly to refurbish, whereas others were built at the peak of the tourist arrival boom that soon passed. Nevertheless, the accommodation picture is still dominated by large hotels (including the largest hotel, the Crystal Palace at 1,550 rooms), with the mean hotel size of 125 rooms in 1992 being among the highest in the region and the highest among these case studies. The closing of large hotels has also meant that the percentage of stay-over arrivals who stay in hotels, previously one of the highest percentages in the Caribbean (e.g., 84% in 1989), has fallen dramatically (64% in 1993).

Paradise Island—a cay off Nassau harbor, originally named Hog Island—provides an interesting example of the history of tourist accommodation development in the Bahamas. The tourist sector on Paradise Island began in the 1890s when several bathing houses and amusement centers were developed as domestic recreational facilities (Albury, 1990). Debbage (1990, 1991) notes that, by the early 1960s, there was only some small-scale development, with a minimal impact on the economy until the first major development was completed; however, this 52-room hotel and 65-craft yacht basin was unable to attract the mass market as it had no unique attractions nor a bridge connecting it to the main island. In 1966, the property was sold to the United States-based Resorts International (headed by American entertainer, Merv Griffin), which, through delicate negotiations, was able to obtain a casino gaming license. By the end of 1967, the 500-room Paradise Towers Hotel, a 2,000-m² casino, and a connecting toll bridge had been built. In the 1980s, the company, having purchased all the land on the island except part of the western peninsula, owned 42% of the 3,000 hotel rooms on Paradise Island; by 1985, the island had over 25% of the 13,166 hotels rooms in the Bahamas. This high level of development caused water supply shortages, escalating investment costs, regional income inequalities, traffic congestion, destruction of traditional landscapes, and excess hotel capacity at other destinations; as a result, the Government (GOCB, 1987) created a policy of decentralization by emphasizing tourism development in the Family Islands. In 1988, there was a leveraged buyout of Resorts International through "junk bonds"; this led to financial difficulties and a large debt burden and, eventually, in 1989, a Chapter 11 bankruptcy petition in American courts and a reorganization plan to forestall creditors. In May 1994, the property was purchased by South African investor, Sol Kerzner, for US$125 million; refurbished for another US$125 million, including US$60 million spent on a water theme park, the new Atlantis Paradise Island development opened with 1,150 rooms, 12 restaurants, a golf course, and a casino in late 1994 (Clarke, 1995; G. Hall, 1995).

Excursionists

For many years, the number of excursionists visiting the Bahamas has been large—indeed, much larger than the total number of visitors to many Caribbean islands—but it has been in decline since 1990, reaching 146,200 in 1993. Nevertheless, the Bahamas remains the largest excursionist destination among the case studies for which data are available and is highest among the case studies in terms of arrivals per 1,000 local population (543 in 1993) and penetration ratio (1.49). Their average expenditure has, however, declined in real terms for many years (GOCB, 1992a, 1992b, 1993).

Cruise Passengers

The Bahamas has a tradition of receiving cruise passengers that dates from the mid-19th century. The growth that began after World War II has been dramatic, reaching some 2,047,000 cruise arrivals[5] in 1993 and maintaining its position as the largest cruise destination in the region; much of this growth has been caused by the preeminence of Miami as the central hub of Caribbean cruise tourism. The Bahamas, unlike most Caribbean destinations, now receives many more cruise passengers than it does stay-over arrivals. Among the case studies, it is second to the Cayman Islands in terms of cruise passenger arrivals per 1,000 local population (7,610 in 1993) and cruise passenger penetration ratio (20.85). The major problems, however, are that cruise passengers do not spend very much money per capita and that the average expenditure per passenger has been declining in the Bahamas in real terms for many years (GOCB, 1992a, 1992b, 1993). Mather and Todd (1993, p. 68) illustrate another problem for the Bahamas; that is, that the expenditure is unevenly distributed by port, with the Family Islands in particular receiving very limited positive economic benefit from cruise passengers: with an average daily expenditure of US$65, the figure was US$74 in Nassau, US$54 in Freeport, and only US$19 in the Family Islands. On the surface, one could argue that the Family Islands do not provide much other than basic souvenirs and handicrafts for sale, but the problem might be more deep-rooted: perhaps Nassau and Freeport have much higher figures because they have shops that sell such items as expensive imported watches and other jewellery—but that in turn provide little economic benefit to the country once the import cost of such items is included in the equation. Moreover, cruise passenger arrivals do not create as many employment opportunities as stay-over arrivals. For example, B. H. Archer (1981) estimates that one full-time job was created by 30 stay-over visitors compared to one job for 350 cruise passengers.

There is another trend, which suggests that the economic benefit of cruise ships is unlikely to increase for the Family Islands: the phenomenon of the ultimate enclave, the "private island." Some cruise lines have purchased or leased small cays or merely property on larger islands and set up instant "tropical paradise destinations" available only for short visits by their own ships; activities and facilities include private beaches, restaurants, water sports, and shopping. For example, a Norwegian Cruise Line's advertisement for an October 1994 cruise of the *SS Norway* lists the following ports for a 7-day Caribbean cruise: Miami, St. Maarten, St. Thomas, St. John, and "NCL's Private Island, Bahamas" (also called "Pleasure Island" by NCL, but in reality Great Stirrup Cay, an atoll 120 km northwest of Nassau in the Berry Islands).

NCL is credited with pioneering the private island beach experience, with its vessels beginning in 1977 to call on Great Stirrup Cay (Blum, 1992), which it leased from the Bahamian government (Kerr, 1985). NCL purchased the island in 1986, renamed it "Pleasure Island," and upgraded the facilities at a cost of over US$1 million. Other private islands in the Bahamas include Princess Lines' "Princess Keys" (a development on 2.4 km of coast on Eleuthera's southern tip and four minor adjoining cays), Royal Caribbean Line's "Coco Cay" (also in the Stirrup Cays), and Salt Cay. The latter is in some ways the most unusual: located a short distance from Paradise Island and Nassau, it has been subleased on different days of the week by competing companies, with Premier Cruise Lines calling it "Salt Cay," Dolphin Cruise Lines calling it first "Dolphin Cove" and later "Blue Lagoon," and Majesty Cruise Lines dubbing it "Royale Isle." Premier recently changed destinations to a private beach near Port Lucaya on Grand Bahama to add greater variety to its package. Majestic also formerly called on Great Guana Cay in the Exuma Cays (Showalter, 1994), but the difficulty of getting ships in and out of the harbor prompted the change to Salt Cay in 1993 (Clarke, 1994).[6]

The *Norway*'s 2,370 passengers will be included in cruise arrival statistics for the Bahamas, but one has to wonder what—if any—will be the benefits to the country, other than the arrival tax revenue (OAS/CTO, 1988). One also has to wonder about the inauthenticity of this island experience and its impact on the cruise passengers. For example, Clarke (1994) notes that

> Snorkelers in particular like CocoCay, because Royal has developed three snorkeling areas. For one, the line built a concrete replica of Blackbeard's 16th century pirate vessel, broke it in two and sank the pieces 30 feet apart to provide a habitat for tropical fish and other sea life.

> To make another snorkeling area, the line bought a seized drug runner's airplane and sank it offshore. The third area is a natural reef.

Passengers arriving by launch at CocoCay enter a harbor that is guarded by a nine-foot bronze statue of a mermaid—one of only two harbor mermaids in the world, Royal boasts. (The other is the famed Little Mermaid at the Copenhagen harbor.)[7] (p. J5)

The topic of inauthenticity merits research.

Concern has also been expressed about the environmental impacts of such developments on potential reef damage both from berth and turning-basin dredging and from water sports, ocean water quality from oil seepage and wastes, and island water quality from septic tank system seepage, given the necessity to dock large ships on small islands and the landing of large numbers of visitors for very short periods of time. Norwegian Cruise Line, for example, is reported to have "renovated the island [Salt Cay] recently, dredging the beach to make it larger and improving its facilities" (Clarke, 1994).

Total Visitors

The Bahamas' position as a mature Stage III destination is illustrated by statistics on aggregate visitors. Although there was a 93.7% increase between 1980 and 1993 to 3,681,900, most of the increase was caused by cruise passengers. This pattern is reinforced by the contrast between arrivals per 1,000 local population (13,687 in 1993) and penetration ratio (110.28): the former increased by 57.9% in that period, whereas the latter decreased by 7.1%. In other words, there are more arrivals, but they are staying for shorter periods on average, notably the few hours spent by cruise passengers.

Expenditures

Although not exactly a one-industry country, the Bahamas is clearly dominated economically by tourism. The range of statistics that is presented is quite wide. Bounds (1972) states that tourism, as an invisible export, accounted for 90% of GNP in 1963, but that the figure dropped to 70% in 1971 because of the "industrial boom" that occurred in Freeport. Bryden (1973, p. 91) describes tourism receipts as accounting for 10.0% of national incomes and 316.3% of visible exports in 1965. Dependence on tourism is estimated by Checchi (1969, p. ix) as 71% of GNP, two thirds of the labor force, and 55% of Government revenue in the late 1960s. Similar credit is given to tourism by the World Bank (1980) for the 1970s:

> The Bahamas economy is structured around its vast tourism potential and its attractiveness as an international financial center. . . . Directly and indirectly tourism accounts for about 60% of GDP and about 70% of GNP. The absence of most forms of direct taxation, a minimum of regulation on offshore financial business, and the location of the Bahamas in the same time zone as New York, gave the country an advantage over other Euro-currency centers for offshore banking. Chiefly as a result of these two activities, a historically open attitude toward foreign private investment and political stability, the country has a high per capita income relative to the rest of the Caribbean. However, the vast geographic dispersion of the Bahama [sic] islands and of

the country's population, the rapid population growth, in part the result of a steady influx of illegal immigrants and overcrowding on New Providence, the main island of population concentration, create a challenging set of development problems for the authorities. (p. i)

Such high levels of contribution to the GDP seem to have peaked in 1977 when tourism represented 60% of GDP. The most likely figures are that tourism accounted for about half of the GDP, three quarters of the tax base, and over half of the employment directly and indirectly by the late 1980s (GOCB, 1988a, p. 167; O'Reilly, 1993, p. 34; WEFA, 1988, pp. 3–8). By 1979, tourism was responsible for 56% of all government revenue, generated 38,700 jobs (8,800 directly and 29,900 indirectly), and affected two thirds of all employment (B. H. Archer, 1981).

Tourist expenditures are clearly very important to the Bahamian economy, both absolutely and relatively, with US$4848 of expenditures per capita of local population in 1993, a figure much higher than most other Caribbean destinations, but lower even in current terms than in the late-1980s. A similar pattern occurs for tourist expenditures as a percentage of GDP and as a percentage of total current account receipts. In contrast, there has been an increase in visitor expenditures as a ratio to merchandise exports and a decrease as a percentage of external debt. It appears that Bahamian tourism is becoming an even shakier pillar of the national economy.

Estimates of tourism employment have varied greatly over the years. For example, the Government's 1992 figure of 20,520 direct jobs (GOCB, 1992a) is in contrast to the CTO (1994) estimate of 12,263. Even if these estimates are not exactly accurate, it is clear that a very large proportion of the Bahamian labor force depends directly or indirectly on tourism.

Stay-over visitors have always accounted for by far the largest proportion of total visitor expenditures (e.g., 91.0% in 1992 compared to 8.3% for cruise passengers and 0.7% for excursionists) (GOCB, 1993). It is not clear, however, whether these figures are accurate or merely represent guesstimates. For example, the per capita expenditure for cruise passengers in 1992 was US$48—a figure suspiciously close to the US$50 quoted by several studies over the years (e.g., Dames & Moore, 1981, p. 3-36; WEFA, 1988, p. 4).

There is clearly a serious problem related to the leakage of tourist expenditures, but Wharton Econometric Forecasting Associates (WEFA, 1988, p. 3) argue that the picture has improved greatly, with the leakage rate decreasing from 90% to 52% between 1973 and 1987, probably because of lower energy import bills and increased local content in the tourism sector. In contrast, Checchi (1969, p. 18) provides a much lower leakage rate of 43% for 1968.

Tourism Policy and Planning

Unlike most other Caribbean islands, the Bahamas has a history of tourism and of government involvement—or perhaps, noninvolvement—in tourism policy and

planning that dates back to the mid-19th century. The documentation is too volu-
minous to describe here in detail; instead, only the highlights are presented. This
is also true of research reports and planning documents; for example, the Grand
Bahama Island Marketing Board is required by its charter to produce an annual
marketing plan, but only the first one done by an outside consultant and the most
extensive (Madigan Pratt & Associates, 1992) is discussed below.

The Policy and Planning Context

In describing the policy and planning context in the Bahamas as it existed up until
the 1970s, Ramsaran (1979, p. 80) argues that the idea that there might be limits to
the kind of development being pursued appeared to have completely eluded the
Bahamian authorities. They were fascinated by the short-term benefits flowing
from the expansion of tourism that began in the 1950s, which, in the context of
the Bahamas' history of poverty, no doubt had an irresistible attraction. He describes the Government until 1967 as a part-time government run by a group of private businessmen (the so-called "Bay Street Boys") who were too busy looking
after their own interests to be concerned with the broader and longer term implications of their policies. The result was a complete lack of planning on either a sectoral or a comprehensive basis, with resource utilization being determined within
a laissez-faire framework devoid of any direction from a carefully thought-out
strategy or an articulated set of objectives. The implications of this policy—or lack
of policy—have been many and serious: the lopsided nature of the development
with tourism, physical infrastructure, and services mainly concentrated in New
Providence and Grand Bahama; the absence of a land policy, resulting in the alien-
ation of a substantial proportion of the country's land resources and land use that
does not conform to the principles of an optimal pattern from a long-term perspective; and lack of attention to the social implications of such practices as the granting of private beach rights and the encouragement of exclusive residential developments that were an integral part of the country's early development strategy.
Ramsaran's (1979) comment that "The consequences of these policies are still
very much in evidence today"(p. 80) seems to continue as an appropriate description of the situation at the present time.

The Early Days

The earliest recorded point in the history of Bahamian tourism is an 1844 advertisement concerning accommodations for visitors by a Mrs. French, owner of a
boarding house in Nassau called "Graycliff" (GOCB, 1988c). Villard (1976) an-
swers an interesting question as to the early interest in tourism:

> Whatever prompted the creation of a Utopian resort in mid-nineteenth cen-
> tury in such an out-of-the-way spot as Nassau? Actually, it was a quest for
> health, rather than tourist excursions or the imperatives of war, which pro-
> duced enough visitors to warrant the ambitious undertaking. . . . Mark
> Catesby, the British naturalist, in 1725 [said] "The Bahamas Islands are
> blessed with a most serene air and are more healthy than most other coun-

tries in the same latitude, [which] induces many of the sickly inhabitants of
Carolina to retire to them for the recovery of their health." (p. 10)

Recognizing the potential to tap this growing health tourism market of the United
States and Europe (Albury, 1975), the Colonial Legislature passed the first Tourism
Encouragement Act in 1851 in an attempt to encourage ship travel to the Bahamas.
That act and a subsequent one in 1854 had little effect, however, because of the
lack of both regular passenger service and suitable accommodations in Nassau. A
third Tourism Act in 1857 authorized the Government to purchase a site for a
"grand hotel" for winter visitors. The first real tourists, however, did not arrive
until Samuel Cunard signed a contract with the Government to provide the first
regular (monthly) service between New York and Nassau in 1859 for an annual subsidy of £3,000 (Bounds, 1978, p. 171). Erected at a cost of £25,000 (Bounds, 1978,
p. 171), the Government-owned Royal Victoria Hotel opened in 1861. With the beginning of the American Civil War, the hotel was soon filled with blockade runners and the Bahamas prospered for the first time:

> So prosperous were these times that it can accurately be said that the Ameri-
> can Civil War was one of the highest profit making times in Bahamian history
> for government and businessmen alike. Import and export duties on the cot-
> ton and war goods were enough to pay off the debt on the hotel—provi-
> dence from God for a poor colony. (Moseley, 1926, p. 33)

After the war ended, a depression set in and tourism stalled; not until 1873 did the
Bahamas receive the then massive number of 500 tourists—although all were "not
necessarily invalids" (Villard, 1976, p. 14).

Such a low number does not seem impressive now given modern tourism statistics, but the impact of these visitors on the local economy was significant: "The
marked improvement in local conditions may . . . be mainly ascribed to . . . the recent establishment of a winter mail service with Florida, which has resulted in
bringing a vastly increased number of American tourists and visitors to Nassau. . . ."
(Colonial Reports, 1898, p. 14). Revenues of £300 in 1897 and £400 in 1898 from
the Royal Victoria Hotel were the major sources of Government income (Colonial
Reports, 1899, p. 8). Tourism at this time was still oriented toward health; indeed,
Stark (1891, pp. 223–227) describes the Bahamas as the "Sanitarium of the Western World" because its climate and environment are so healing for the invalid and
sickly.

The Government decided in 1898 to try to take advantage of the land speculation
and tourism booms in Florida. New Providence was joined to Jupiter, FL by a tele-
graph cable (which came ashore at Cable Beach) (to be replaced by wireless in
1913) and a Hotel and Steamship Act was passed to attract both hotel construction
and ships. A 10-year contract was signed with Henry M. Flagler, founding father of
Miami, who leased the Royal Victoria Hotel from the government and proceeded
to fill it with tourists from Florida (Villard, 1976, p. 16). Purchasing the site of
Fort Nassau, Flagler opened the Hotel Colonial in 1900, "the first beachfront hotel
in Bahamian tourism history, an indication of the end of puritanism and a beginning of a new type of advertising designed to attract the rich rather than the inval-

ids'' (Bounds, 1978, p. 172). To ensure the success of his hotel, Flagler started his own steamship line to convey ''winter refugees'' from Miami to Nassau (Lawton & Butler, 1987, p. 331; Sutton, 1980, p. 79).

Continuing to recognize the importance of tourism for the local economy, the Government remained active in tourism promotion and transportation subsidies (Colonial Reports, 1910, pp. 28–29). Following further discussion of possible incorporation of the Bahamas into the Dominion of Canada (Colonial Reports, 1911, p. 28), which had begun as early as 1880 (Craton, 1986, p. 246), the Government broadened its advertising efforts, beginning to have a display at the Toronto Exhibition in 1911 (Colonial Reports, 1912, p. 25). With the number of tourists rising to 2,600 (of whom 1,231 were visitors from ships who spent only a few hours in Nassau) in 1913, the House of Assembly followed the example of Bermuda and set up a Tourist Development Board in 1914 with the power to advertise, appoint agents, and negotiate contracts for steamship communication and an annual budget of £3,000 (Colonial Reports, 1914, p. 27). The Board increased advertising in the United States and Canada and approached Thomas Cook & Son to operate tours, but these plans were cut off by war. Because American involvement in World War I did not begin until 1917, the decline in tourism related to war-time disruption of shipping was gradual: 2,680 tourists in the 1915–1916 winter season, 1,286 in 1916–1917, and then a collapse to 125 in 1917–1918 (Colonial Reports, 1917, 1918).

The Hotel Colonial was destroyed by fire in 1922 (which probably saved Flagler from bankruptcy as the Florida boom was crashing[8] [Craton, 1986, p. 245]), leading the Government—rich on Prohibition income—to repurchase the site and sign a 10-year contract with the Bahamas Hotel Company, a subsidiary of the Munson Steamship Line, which in turn built the New Colonial Hotel in 1923 (with a loan of £430,000 from the Government) (Colonial Reports, 1926, p. 6). There was also

> . . . a new golf course, to provide which the Government has advanced large sums of money. The result has been that more tourists than ever have flocked to the Islands from Canada and the United States, and the money spent by these tourists, who belong chiefly to the wealthiest classes, has been of great benefit to the people. The value of house property in Nassau has risen considerably owing to the high prices paid by tourists during the winter months. (Colonial Reports, 1924, p. 4)

The first air service to the Bahamas from Florida had begun in 1919 when Chalk's Airline (which continues to operate today) started a seaplane service. With air service came the beginnings of tourism in the Out Islands; for example, the Bimini Rod and Gun Club—where the main sports seem to have been fishing and rum-running—opened in about 1924 (Albury, 1975, p. 180). In 1925, contracts with the Munson Co. and the Royal Mail Line, and a treaty with Canada, provided steamship service from New York, Britain, and Canada; the result was a land investment boom and a related surge in tourism. To handle this growth, the Government continued its pattern of providing incentives to the private sector by loaning another

£220,000 to a local company to build the Hotel Fort Montagu, which opened in 1926 (Colonial Reports, 1927, p. 5).

Soon after Pan American Airlines instituted a daily 2.5-hour flight by seaplane from Miami in 1929, the Depression arrived and ended the tourism boom for several years. A resurgence was created in the mid-1930s by Sir Harry Oakes, a wealthy Canadian businessman, who had moved to Nassau for tax reasons (and whose later dramatic murder remains unsolved). Oakes and realtor-developer Sir Harold Christie built the first airport at Oakes Field and founded Bahamas Airlines Ltd. for interisland service. Oakes also purchased the New Colonial and renamed it the British Colonial Hotel—the name and the building remaining today as the oldest-surviving hotel in the Bahamas. By 1937, 39,000 tourists flocked to Nassau by plane and boat for the winter season (GOCB, 1988c). Encouraged by the Tourist Development Board's setting up representatives in New York, London, and Montreal, this figure rose to 57,394 in 1938, of whom approximately 10,000 were stay-over visitors (Colonial Reports, 1939, p. 18). Perhaps these figures gave rise to the almost mythical beliefs in the strength of tourism to weather any economic conditions: "Here in the face of a major world depression was an economic activity that did not weather before the onslaught. It was a fact that no British Colonialist could forget" (Bounds, 1978, p. 174).

The coming of World War II slowed but did not end tourism, as many Europeans fleeing the war immigrated to the Bahamas and caused another land investment boom. In 1941, Pan American instituted its first non-seaplane service, which it maintained throughout the war. Soon after the war ended, the speculative land boom in Florida spilled over to Nassau and fueled the rebirth of tourism. By 1950, the Bahamas was seemingly on the road to recovery: 51,975 tourists in 1950, 76,758 in 1951, 99,867 in 1953, and 142,689 in 1954 (Colonial Reports, 1952, 1957).[9] Growth continued unabated through the 1950s and 1960s, with the exception of 1958 when a strike by taxi drivers protesting competition from large transportation interests escalated to a 19-day general strike and caused many tourists to cancel their trips.

By the mid-1950s, hotel and resort expansion was occurring on both New Providence and the Out Islands, all encouraged by the Government's laissez-faire attitude (Ramsaran, 1979, p. 80), large-scale advertising, and investment incentives legislation. This growth was supported the Tourist Development Board, founded originally in 1914 (Colonial Reports, 1914, p. 27). Inactive over the years, it was revived in 1950 under the direction of Sir Stafford Sands, with primary objectives of dramatically increasing tourist traffic and creating a year-round tourist business (GOCB, 1988a, p. 167). With a budget of US$0.5 million, tourist promotion was aimed at the United States, where tourism offices were established in five cities (Clapp & Mayne, 1969, p. 90).

Tourism in the Bahamas is regulated by many pieces of legislation (GOCB, 1988c), only a few of which will be noted. The first and most significant is The Hotels Encouragement Act of 1949 (with subsequent amendments, the most important in 1954), which was designed to "encourage the construction of hotels . . . by providing for the refund of customs duties and emergency taxes and certain other concessions, and for the exemption of such hotels from certain taxation." (The eventual result was various investment incentives: tax holidays, various tax exemptions, subsidized interest rates [OAS/CTO, 1990].)

The Promotion of Tourism Act, enacted in 1963, provided for increasing and developing facilities for tourism and promoting measures for attracting tourists. It also replaced the Tourist Development Board with a Ministry of Tourism operating in a more flexible manner and not subject to the rigid procedures and bureaucratic controls found in the Public Service; its staff are not Civil Servants and all authority concerning appointments, terminations, discipline, and other personnel matters rests with the Minister responsible for tourism. The Ministry now has one of the largest budgets of any such agency in the Caribbean (US$38.6 million in 1990), but the growth of its budget is among the smallest in recent years and it has one of the highest expenditures per stay-over visitor in the region. Finally, The Hotels Act of 1970 made provision for the licensing of hotels, the regulation and improvement of standards in hotels, and the imposition of a hotel guest tax.

On New Providence, the multimillion dollar, American-owned Coral Harbour development, was begun on the south side of the island, with a hotel, yacht club, marina, and residential development focused on artificial canals. (Never completed, today it lies uncompleted and abandoned.) Hotels were built on Eleuthera, Bimini, and Andros—and the boom was underway. Huge vacation subdivisions were planned, many of which led to shattered dreams for both islanders and prospective part-time residents. For example, one developer sold 20,000 lots on Exuma as a "place away from it all," but eventually only a few dozen houses were erected (Craton, 1986, p. 267). Other developments, however, such as Canadian E. P. Taylor's luxurious Lyford Key on New Providence, were successful.

The boom, however, occurred in a virtual planning vacuum: "It was perhaps typical of the 'wheeler-dealing' that went on behind the scenes that hotel concessions and building lots were spoken for before plans were made public and the enabling Bill went before the House of Assembly" (Craton, 1986, p. 268). This expansion had its price. Economic growth led to high inflation, but salaries and wages barely kept pace; in addition, because most investments, tourists, and imports originated in the United States, the entire economy became tied to that of the United States and suffered when recession hit there. Because there was no direct taxation, most government revenue was derived from import duties that, although growing steadily (from £840,000 in 1946 to £18,400,000 in 1967), did not match the pace of growth in either tourism or foreign investment. The result was a general deficiency of service provision ranging from roads to low-cost housing (Craton, 1986, p. 271).

The Hawksbill Creek Agreement and the Grand Bahama Port Authority[10]

The saga of the development of Grand Bahama is of a nature and of a scale unique in the Caribbean. The history and form of its exploitation epitomizes to a large extent the nature of external control over an island system.

Called *Guanahatebey* by the Lucayans, Grand Bahama is among the most northerly of the Bahamas and lies just off the coast of Florida. Inhabited by only about 2,000 people at the end World War II, it was a poor fishing island, with little contact with Nassau, let alone the outside world.

In 1944, the Abaco Lumber Co. moved to Grand Bahama, having temporarily exhausted the pine supply of Abaco. The company was purchased in 1946 by an American, Wallace Groves, who expanded the operation. Groves sold the lumber rights in 1954 to the National Container Corp. (NatCon) of the United States, which later became a subsidiary of the Owens (Illinois) Co. Groves then formed the Grand Bahama Port Authority Ltd., with himself as President; it was a private company, the majority of the shares being owned by Abaco Lumber Co. in the person of his wife. Groves' goal was to turn Grand Bahama into a major port and industrial center.

On August 4, 1955, Grove and the Government signed the Hawksbill Creek Agreement under which the Port Authority was covenanted to create a harbor and develop an industrial community on Grand Bahama and was granted title over 20,000 hectares of Crown Land (Ramsaran, 1979, p. 83). The Government guaranteed to the Port Authority and its licensees that nonconsumable items could be imported into the Port Area free of customs duties and that there would be no excise, export, or stamp taxes for the continuance of the Agreement (99 years); they also guaranteed that for 30 years (later extended by 5 years to 1990) there would be no real estate taxes, personal property taxes, or taxes levied against the Port Authority or its licensees on earnings in the colony. The Agreement vested the Port Authority with the right to administer the Port Area, to exclude undesirables, to plan the Port Area, and to license persons or businesses; this was in effect "government by contract," which allowed the Port Authority to operate almost without any reference to the Government (Barratt, 1989, p. 77).

American billionaire industrialist Daniel K. Ludwig had a deep-water harbor dredged at Freeport in exchange for 2,000 acres of industrial land and announced that he was going to build a ship-building yard. This, however, was really a ploy to pressure a Japanese yard to meet his conditions; then, he sold his land to a subsidiary of the United States Steel Co. (Ludwig retained an interest in the island and came back later as a major real estate developer.) Despite the harbor, the early industrial development of Freeport was slow. A ship-bunkering oil depot was built near the harbor in 1958 and work started on "downtown" Freeport in 1959. In 1963, construction began of a cement plant owned by the Bahama Cement Co., a subsidiary of US Steel; the limestone was to be obtained by further dredging of the harbor, which eventually became the world's largest artificial harbor.

On July 22, 1960, a Supplemental Agreement was signed, acknowledging that the Port Authority had met all the obligations of the Principal Agreement; additional land was granted to the Authority at a nominal price and, in return, the Authority was to build a 200-room luxury hotel by December 31, 1963.

This was not the first plan for an international hotel on Grand Bahama. In 1948, a British entertainment entrepreneur, Billy (later Sir Billy) Butlin, bought a large tract of land at West End (and had an option to purchase 20,000 acres of Crown Land) and began in 1949 to build the Butlin Vacation Village, with a view to providing complete vacations for middle-income American families at a very moderate rate ($99/week). The resort was to have a capacity of 500 rooms for 1,000 people; only half built, the resort lost money for a variety of reasons (e.g., American recession, marketing, transportation, access) and was closed 10 months later. The creditors formed the Grand Bahamas Properties Ltd. (GBPL) and tried to sell the property. A group from Chicago was to buy the property, but the *New York Herald Tribune* stated that the group was supposedly connected with the American gangster group known as Murder Incorporated and that they wanted to introduce gambling; the bid vanished. GBPL, in order to keep the land option alive, reopened the hotel in 1955 after extensive alterations and repairs and ran it as a luxury fishing resort; Turner and Ash (1975, p. 103) suggest that their unattained goal was to obtain a casino license. In 1959, the Jack Tar Hotel chain took over the property, renovated and extended it, and called it the Grand Bahama Hotel. The operation lasted only a few years and the site now stands derelict.

To meet the 1963 deadline for the hotel, Groves joined with Louis Chesler in 1961 to form the Grand Bahama Development Co., which soon began to develop the residential and resort complex of Lucaya, which was focused on a vast system of artificial canals that cut across the island.[11] When the Lucayan Beach Hotel (which included a casino[12]) opened in 1963, it proved insufficient to meet the demand from the growing wave of tourists. As a result, the cruise liner *SS Italia* was converted to accommodate 1,400 persons and permanently berthed for 2 years in the harbor to meet tourist demand until the 500-room Holiday Inn and the 800-room Kings Inn (later renamed the Bahamas Princess) were completed. Further construction followed, with total accommodation in hotels and condominiums reaching 4,304 rooms in 1974; however, the boom was soon over and bankruptcies resulted in this figure falling to 3,850 rooms in 1979.

Bounds (1978) first paints a very glowing picture of Freeport as a resort, but then goes on to describe some of its problems:

> The Freeport resort, while it is set amidst an area which is the most heavily industrialized in the Bahamas, is a complete resort offering all the amenities necessary for a full spectrum resort. Every sport imaginable in a tropical, seaside resort is available and the hotels range from very moderate to ultraplush. All the amenities of the Bahamas are present except the long history and charming architecture as is found in Nassau. . . . Freeport is even more youthful and robust than Miami. . . . [A] problem in Freeport is its new harbour and metal wharf buildings which are not too attractive to cruise ship tourists. There is simply no "ancient charm" nor memories of one-eyed pirates to delight the visitors. An additional problem of the port is that it is a long distance from hotels, downtown Freeport, and from the shopping areas. (p. 178)

This lack of character plagued the island from the beginning; one must wonder what effect it had on the bursting of the bubble of success.

Resentment against the power of the Port Authority was growing throughout the Bahamas, not the least because employment opportunities were few for Bahamians and the control of the Port Authority over the granting of work permits to foreign personnel and the control of immigration in the Freeport area—creating what was, in effect, "a state within a state" (Ramsaran, 1979, p. 84).

> After less than a dozen years of frenetic free enterprise, . . . the almost un-populated bush of Grand Bahama had been transformed into a tourist industrial complex totally unlike the rest of the Bahamas, largely populated and run by non-Bahamians. It also operated almost beyond Bahamian Government control and brought little revenue to the Bahamian treasury because of the overgenerous concessions granted by the UBP [United Bahamian Party]. (Craton, 1986, p. 282)

Political pressure began to grow. In 1966, a further amendment called for the Port Authority to build low- and middle-income houses in Freeport, schools, a clinic, and a water supply system. In 1967, however, the ruling party was defeated in the election. Craton (1987, p. 107) describes the reaction of the new Progressive Liberal Party (PLP) government, which made plans to revise or even cancel the leases of the Grand Bahama Port Authority and Owens-Illinois, to review the terms by which bases had been leased to the United States by the British government, and to draft a comprehensive national Land Act. An unwillingness to jeopardize foreign investment or to antagonize the American government, however, led the government to proceed with very great caution, for reasons related to respect for the rule of law and innate conservatism. No foreign leases were cancelled or shortened without compensation and the American bases were either renegotiated or quietly allowed to lapse by mutual consent.

In 1969, the Port Authority—in "an arcane transaction that itself reflected a lack of confidence in the political and economic future by the original developers" (Craton, 1986, p. 283)—went into partnership with Benguet Consolidated Ltd., a Manila-based mining company, meaning that Port Authority shares were now public. In becoming a minor shareholder (7.5%), the Government agreed to the merger, with the provision that the Authority would consult with the Government before exercising its rights to exclude persons or vehicles from the Port area, planning and laying out of the Port Area, before changing rates and charges for utility services, and before licensing new businesses.

The 1969 agreement began a rapid Bahamianization of Freeport, with increased numbers of government officials and Bahamian businesses. A virtual mutiny over the immigration issue by the Freeport licensees, however, provoked a famous speech by Prime Minister Pindling in September 1969 in which he threatened that, if the regime at Freeport refused to bend, it would be broken. Despite the immigration problem being officially resolved by the Hawksbill Creek Amendment (Immigration) Act in March 1970, the general situation in Freeport was far from eased. New investment dried up; existing capital fled; land sales and tourism slumped; and unemployment soared.[13] The only major subsequent industrial development was in 1970 when a US$100 million American-owned oil refinery was built; since then, several other new but small industries have opened. This was the end of the golden days:

> Though Freeport was hardest hit, 1970 was in fact, a year of economic and political crisis for the Bahamas as a whole, the prelude to a very difficult five year phase. After a record year, tourist arrivals declined, and tourist expenditures fell by a greater degree. Despite an ever-increasing advertising budget, tourism figures [i.e., growth in numbers of arrivals, not real increases in expenditures] did not make a substantial further surge until 1978—being sustained, moreover, by an increase in cruise passenger traffic rather than the more lucrative "stop-over" business. (Craton, 1986, p. 284)

Bounds (1978) provides a rather narrow view of the importance of the Government's attempt to assert its control over its own nation:

> Freeport had a chance to be a great, viable resort and to provide the Bahamas with the economic boost that it needed. Instead the new government picked an inopportune time to dictate economic mobility for Bahamians. It was a good idea but put to work, too hastily, and at the wrong time. The government learned that evolution is sometimes better than revolution when dealing with economics. (p. 180)

A Note of Caution Ignored

In a report that represents one of the few times that an alternative approach is suggested to tourism development rather than the more common preference for increased numbers of tourists and size of the tourism plant, Clapp and Mayne (1969), while dealing with the economy in general rather than tourism specifically, clearly state the importance of tourism for the Bahamas: "The economy is virtually a single-industry economy: tourism, and to a lesser extent, construction and banking. There is very little production for local consumption. Almost all needs are imported and paid for out of foreign exchange earned from exports" (p. 4). Describing tourism as "virtually an off-shore activity" that imports most of its purchases, sells those imports to foreign tourists, and exports the profits to external owners, Clapp and Mayne (1969, pp. 7–8) argue that the only contribution to the Bahamas beyond initial payment for land purchase is limited to wages and salaries to Bahamian staff. Therefore, the "objective of the development program should be the enlargement of the multiplier effect of tourist expenditures" (which is estimated at about one) by greater Bahamian participation in economic activity with backward and forward linkages to the tourism sector, while at the same time maintaining an adequate growth rate in the industry: "the emphasis should not be on the number of visitors, but on the benefits accruing to the Bahamas economy" (Clapp & Mayne, 1969, pp. 99–100).

Although not attempting to create a tourism "plan," the report details a number of restrictions on further tourist development: competition; inadequacy of infrastructure; rising cost of living; limited scope of amenities and differentiating features; minor irritants to tourists (poor service, trash, electrical and water failures, etc.); rising cost of land due to speculation; Nassau airport being inadequate for jumbo jets; Out Island airports not being equipped for night flying; the need for better quality of service and broader spectrum of entertainment and attractions; in order to become a year-round destination, the need to draw more on middle- and lower-income tourists, including young people who will demand a wider choice of activities; and more training so that hotel staff and management can be drawn more from domestic population (Clapp & Mayne, 1969, pp. 99–100).

Similar problems to those noted by Clapp and Mayne (1969) are discussed in the Checchi (1969, pp. ix–x) tourism plan, but the solution is the more common one: growth, but on a decidedly uncommon scale. Arguing that between 1969 and 1974 the Bahamas would need US$315 million in improved infrastructure and services, the plan sees tourism as being able to provide US$200 million of this figure in government revenue as long as the number of tourists is increased from the 1969 figure of 1.1 million to 2.9 million in 1974—an incredible increase of 163.6% in just 5 years. There seems to be an underlying assumption that the Government is in total control of the situation (i.e., that increasing the supply can automatically increase the demand):

> In the Realpolitik of the Bahamas . . . neither the market forecast nor the difficulty in financing the costs of tourist infrastructure is likely to be the critical factor in determining the number of tourists per year on which to base a Ten-Year Plan. Instead, in our opinion, it is the benefits of tourism related to the needs of the government which will determine the optimum number of tourists for the Bahamas.
>
> Tourism should, therefore, be programmed to grow as fast as Government Revenues are required to fund social overhead projects, such as new schools, hospitals and recreational facilities for the Bahamian people. If this optimum growth rate is faster than the market will tolerate, the government's revenue requirements may have to be reduced. If the optimum rate is less than the potential market forecast, the growth of tourism should be limited accordingly. (Checchi, 1969, p. 29)

Then, through a rather unusual jump in logic—to say nothing of a lapse in sound planning principles—the report argues that revenues would be sufficient to require no further increase in the number of tourists until 1979 as long, of course, as average length of stay and expenditures per tourist do not decrease.

This proposed growth would require government investment of US$230 million in infrastructure (water, electricity, airports, etc.) and private capital of US$550 million for 17,000–20,000 new hotel rooms and US$200 million for supporting facilities such as restaurants, shops, and transport equipment. Another rather unusual recommendation was that the Government should develop "an attractive Bahamian U-Drive vehicle" to provide tourists with better mobility to see more of the islands (Checchi, 1969, p. xii). Finally, the plan predicts that cruise passenger arrivals will rise to 561,000 in 1975 and 943,000 in 1980 (Checchi, 1969, p. 5)—levels that were not reached until about 5 years later for each figure.

More sensible suggestions included the creation of a land-use plan, beautifying Nassau's waterfront, preserving historic buildings, and emphasizing Out Island development in order to diversify the product and increase the average length of stay. (These ideas are repeated often in later documents, but were never implemented.)

Just as the Government was beginning to think about implementing such a massive-scale expansion of the tourism plant, the thread began to unravel, heralded by the problems in Grand Bahama. The GDP declined by 5% from 1969 to 1970 (Ramsaran, 1979, p. 82). In October 1970, Bahamas Airways collapsed with the loss of 800 jobs; it was replaced by Bahamas World Airways in December 1970, but this one-aircraft charter operation went into liquidation in 2 years. Travel from Florida was disrupted and travel within the islands themselves was decimated until Bahamasair was created in 1973. Tourist arrivals started to decline.

The dependence of the economy on tourism forced the Government to enter the tourism business for itself in 1974. The Government-owned Hotel Corporation of the Bahamas (HCB) purchased three ailing New Providence hotels to save them from collapse (Holder, 1993). The HCB eventually owned hotels with a total of 1,400 rooms in New Providence (20% of the island's stock) and a 50% interest in the 250-room Lucayan Beach Hotel in Grand Bahama. Despite ongoing weakness in the tourism sector, the Government seemed determined to implement the Checchi theory that increased supply would lead to increased demand. Thus, the Government went on to develop the Cable Beach Hotel and Casino in New Providence, which opened in 1984 at a cost of over US$100 million (GOCB, 1988a, p. 174). There were early warnings of the financial insecurity of the Cable Beach complex (World Bank, 1980, pp. 13–14). Despite such concerns, the HCB still owns 16% of the total accommodation in the Bahamas (O'Reilly, 1993, p. 37)—largely because the private sector is sceptical about the profitability of Bahamian tourism.

Plans in the 1980s

Despite tourism's problems and its domination of the economy, the Government was without a real tourism plan until 1981. Funded by the IDB, a 10-year Tourism Development Plan was developed by Dames and Moore (1981) with the recognition that "Tourism is the Bahamas' principal industry. Like any industrial activity it must be constantly improved if it is to survive and prosper. Its activities must be planned and its facilities maintained and expanded" (p. i-1). With an overall goal "to maximise the country's competitive potential in the world tourism market while minimising the risks of economic loss" (Dames & Moore, 1981, p. i-2), the Plan's objectives were to develop a comprehensive strategic plan, identify improvements required in tourism infrastructure and define a set of priority projects for consideration by international lending agencies, perform prefeasibility studies of a number of the priority projects, and specify terms of reference for detailed feasibility studies to support funding applications.

The Plan was based on demand forecasts that proved to be totally unrealistic.[14] Three forecasts (low, medium, and high—based on increasing compound interest rates) were calculated for 1985 and 1990. The "best" estimate centered on values slightly below the "medium" projections, based on two assumptions: anticipated developments in the economies of origin countries plus competition development; and "the demand for the Bahamas as a vacation destination will not diminish and the country's ability to attract the additional tourists will at least match growth in total regional warm-weather tourism from all tourist-originating countries, with a slightly increased share from Canada" (Dames & Moore, 1981, p. 1-4). Neither of these assumptions proved true. The "medium" forecasts for the number of visitor arrivals for 1985 and 1990 were in fact exceeded by the actual figures, but this is a function of cruise passenger numbers exploding while stay-over visitor numbers grew only slowly. Not even the low forecasts for hotel visitor nights were met, because of both the lower than anticipated numbers of stay-over visitors and the decreasing average length of stay; in fact, the actual number of 1985 hotel visitor nights is less than the 1980 level, whereas the 1990 figure is only marginally higher than the 1980 level. Similarly, the number of hotel rooms stayed virtually static after the construction boom of the early 1980s, despite the plan's recommendation that "7,000 new hotel and hotel-type rooms be constructed in various parts of the Bahamas during the period 1981–1990" (Dames & Moore, 1981, p. 1-5).

The Plan proposes a number of objectives: match development with growth in the number of tourists; diversify development to the Family Islands; encourage a mixture of Bahamian and non-Bahamian private ownership of hotels by planning for a range of hotel sizes in each location; and optimize the number of rooms in each location, in terms of maximizing the resort size while minimizing the total infrastructure costs (e.g., water, power) (Dames & Moore, 1981, pp. 1-5–1-6). It also highlighted a number of serious social and economic problems that it felt would be solved by this proposed expansion and spatial dispersion of the hotel stock: unequal distribution of tourism benefits among the islands; high unemployment and underemployment; and eroded living conditions in Nassau (caused by rural-to-urban migration) (Dames & Moore, 1981, pp. 2-1–2-2)—problems that unfortunately remain to the present.

Despite its argument that the proposed growth is economically viable, the Plan ends on an unusual note, which implies that the Bahamian financial climate must be made even more conducive in order to attract tourism investment (Dames & Moore, 1981, p. 6-12). It points out that the Bahamas levies no income taxes, that most Government income is derived from import duties, and that the Hotels Encouragement Act already provides relief from property tax and import duties for items used in hotel construction. In the absence of any other important taxes, therefore, the Bahamas is unable to employ many of the forms of direct or indirect tax relief used by other governments as incentives. It then suggests other additional incentives: below-market loans, reduction of operating costs (service costs), and the waiving of the modest Business Licence Fee. Even a virtually tax-free environment, therefore, is not sufficient to attract investment to the Bahamas! One has to wonder how this was factored into the consultants' financial analysis, which "demonstrated that all the developments proposed should be viable" (Dames & Moore, 1981, p. 1-24).

Despite these concerns about the financial climate, the early 1980s was a time of expansion of the accommodation stock, particularly on New Providence: the Britannia Beach added 350 rooms in 1981; the Grand Hotel opened in 1982; and the Cable Beach Hotel and Casino opened in 1984. (In addition, the 130-room Cape Eleuthera Resort in Eleuthera and the 100-room Treasure Cay in Abaco opened in 1983.) This expansion on New Providence had been the subject of a report (GOCB, 1983) on the potential impact of proposed hotel development of 2,770 new hotel rooms on New Providence from 1983 to 1987 at a time when the length of stay was dropping, resulting in an absolute decrease in the annual number of tourist nights despite generally increasing numbers of stay-over tourists. The Plan concludes that, unless the average length of stay is increased, there is the danger that the increased accommodation stock will decrease the occupancy rate (63.3% in 1983 and lower in earlier years) below the 60–62% rate that is generally accepted in the sector as the break-even point for large hotels.

Contrary to the claim made in movie *The Field of Dreams* that "Build it and they shall come," the new hotels did not fill up with tourists. Because virtually all growth in tourism since 1979 had come in cruise passenger arrivals (with an average annual growth of 16%), the Ministry of Tourism developed in 1984 a Tourism Marketing Strategy and Development Plan, the main objective of which was to attract higher levels of stay-over arrivals (GOCB, 1984, p. 3.1). On the whole, however, this Plan is basically a "state of the problem" report and provides little concrete direction for either a marketing strategy or a development plan.

The Plan recognizes, however, several problems for the sector: declining share of arrivals, real declines in visitor spending, shorter average length of stay, high prices, loss of regional market share, unreliable air connections, and hotels with closed rooms. This latter concern was somewhat offset by the opening or expansion of the properties noted above.

The overall argument in the 1984 Plan seems to be that, despite these new hotels, the Bahamas was not keeping up with change in the sector as a whole: "By and large these developments can be categorised as additions to an existing product line, rather than new variants. They offer all the amenities of a large, four-star property catering to a traditional market looking for sun, sea, and sand" (GOCB, 1984, p. 6.21). The Plan argues that the Bahamas has to keep up with trends in the market: a return to vertical integration is likely (e.g., Carnival Lines in Cable Beach); the sector is introducing more products to meet the needs of different segments (e.g., Holiday Inns has three different types of hotels); the distribution system may change (fewer but larger travel agencies, consumers have a better idea of what they want); resorts too have to be specialized (convention, health, singles); and timeshare has lost some of its glamour.

The Early 1990s: Plans and Reports—But No Action

By the 1990s, a sense of desperation seems to have set in. Rather than take action, the result was the commissioning of a series of plans and reports, all of which clearly outlined the seriousness of the tourism sector's problems—but which were shelved because of both the private sector and the Government's inability or unwillingness to act on their recommendations. On the other hand, some documents indicate a broadening of scope in terms of issues and/or geography.

For example, the Grand Bahama Island Marketing Board is charged by its charter to develop an annual marketing plan designed to maximize hotel visitors and expenditures. Historically, these plans have been somewhat limited in scope, but in 1992 the Board retained a consultant to develop the plan. Madigan Pratt & Associates (1992, pp. 1–10) begin with a rather mixed summary of the tourism situation in Grand Bahama: air arrivals not keeping pace with the competition; a trend toward shorter vacations which works to Grand Bahama's advantage; a "middle market" destination reputation; poor value for money; and improving friendliness of local people.

In spite of these problems, a number of opportunities are described for Grand Bahama: the underdeveloped Northeastern United States market, diving, golf, and most of the market coming from a relatively small geographic area (thus reducing marketing costs) (Madigan Pratt & Associates, 1992, p. 116). Assuming that there will be little change in the status quo of either the economy in general or the structure of the sector, the plan argues for a "value for money" positioning for Grand Bahama with objectives of increasing visitor numbers, upgrading the visitors' experience, attracting more affluent visitors, and improving the friendliness of local people. This is to be done through several strategies: maintaining an average length of stay of four nights, continuing to attract more repeat visitors, concentrating marketing efforts on the eastern and southern United States, promoting the new positioning of Grand Bahama internally and externally, strengthening coordination with Ministry of Tourism, improving the effectiveness of the "Grand Bahama Smiles" campaign, launching a consumer advertising campaign, and improving air service, particularly jet service to Grand Bahama (Madigan Pratt & Associates, 1992, pp. 117–120).

A positive change in other documents appears to be an increased geographic scope of concern, with more attention being paid to Grand Bahama and the Family Islands. For example, in a report commissioned by the IDB to determine the possibilities of stimulating private investment in the hotel sector and ancillary services in the Family Islands, Poon (1992) argues that, whereas the downturn in Bahamian tourism may be temporary and caused by the United States recession, it signals more deep-rooted causes demanding substantial change. Poon (1992, pp. 12–28) describes signs of structural decline in the Bahamian tourism sector since the mid-1980s: increased share of visitors arriving by cruise ship, reduced air service, heavy reliance on the North American market, reduced length of stay, reduced levels of expenditures, growing importance of time-share accommodations, minimal local involvement in the sector, and dissatisfaction with the product. Although she does not explain whether or not the Bahamian tourism sector attempted to respond to these trends and if they did not, why not, she believes that the Bahamas missed several key trends in international tourism marketing: new geographic markets, market segmentation, all-inclusives, ecotourism, and boating.

Describing the "old" tourism as being based on mass, standardized, packaged vacation, Poon (1992, pp. 29–35) believes that the future of the Family Islands depends on the "new" tourism: flexible, segmented, environmentally sound, diagonally integrated—driven by changing world conditions, sophisticated consumers, and new management techniques. The basis for this change is already present, at least in terms of the characteristics of the typical Family Islands visitor: longer stays, more affluent, better educated, more independent, more spending per visit, feeling they get better value for money, higher levels of satisfaction, more likely to return, more interested in sports, and more likely to be male, older, and from a nontraditional market (Poon, 1992, pp. 36–46). A strategy for the development of the Family Islands is proposed that has five key ingredients (Poon, 1992, pp. 47–66): focusing on the environment; building human resources; Bahamianizing the sector; repositioning Nassau; building Freeport as a vital industrial link. Her overall recommendations call for: a national tourism policy statement, with particular reference to the Family Islands; development being considered as an integrated process involving the entire country; further development of the services sector of the economy; an environmental focus for tourism; and a shift for the Ministry of Tourism away from marketing to product development (Poon, 1992, pp. 72–73).

In a report analyzing the tourism infrastructure of the Bahamas and its potential for future development, Berger (1992, pp. 11–18) argues that, whereas tourism has been and will continue to be the dominant sector of the Bahamian economy, it is faced with real problems: very high costs of doing business, inadequately maintained hotels, lack of value for money, spotty service, dissatisfied customers, lack of willingness to accept responsibility for problems, and the inability or unwillingness to acknowledge change in the sector. He feels, however, that there is potential for further growth, particularly in environmentally sensitive tourism, but there are several general trends in tourism that must be considered: market segmentation, experiential tourism, all-inclusive vacations, the evolution of "new" geographic source markets for tourism, ecotourism, the value of "upscale" tourists, the importance of developing repeat business, and the importance of controlled and restricted development.

Beginning his detailed recommendations with New Providence and Grand Bahama (although he states many of the same concerns apply equally well to the Family Islands), Berger (1992, pp. 31–62, 63–79) believes that hotels are caught in the trap of too little revenue and too high costs, resulting in a lack of investment, low room rates, high food and beverage prices, poor service, and bad maintenance. He recommends: waiving duties payable for refurbishment; extending the 10-year exemption on real property taxes; replace net rate pricing by rack rate or all-inclusive pricing; converting cruise passengers into long-stay visitors; improved air service through increased capital to Bahamasair for equipment; a Development

Authority to run airport and ground transportation; Bahamianization; making loans available to small businesses; and supporting the hiring of local musicians and the promotion of local music and dance.

Building on Poon's (1992) report, Berger (1992, pp. 80–112) then analyzes the Family Islands in detail, noting in particular the lack of infrastructure on many of the islands that contrasts with their great potential for a diversified tourism product (e.g., environmental tourism for Andros, diving and bone-fishing for Bimini, sport fishing and bird watching for Inagua, and diving on San Salvador).

The final section is a series of suggested change strategies (Berger, 1992, pp. 113–125). In a recommendation that is reminiscent of Jamaica's recently established Tourism Action Plan (Wilkinson, 1997), he calls for a more effective structure for the Ministry of Tourism along the lines of a private corporation to coordinate and implement changes; it should also have a special department to stress Bahamian culture. Separate development authorities should be created for New Providence and the Family Islands (Grand Bahama already having such an authority). The Government should restrict approval of any large hotels on New Providence or Grand Bahama as they are not needed in the near future, although hotels of 100 rooms or less aimed at upscale, experience-oriented visitors should be encouraged; most hotel development on the Family Islands should be small scale, but the development of a master plan might indicate the potential for larger units. A much broader environmental policy is required, including an expanded national park system, diving and fishing licenses, a country-wide clean-up program, and an expanded environmental education program. He recommends that, in terms of marketing, there should be a plan to promote each island separately, market the diversity of experiences, reach out to new geographic markets, target special interest markets, and reward frequent visitors and loyal travel agencies. His final suggestion is that a long-range development plan is needed with both short- and long-term goals.

Conclusion

There is a temptation to end this analysis with a glib and probably overly dramatic conclusion: the Bahamian tourism sector is a house of cards that has been built by an incredible cast of legendary players—including Samuel Cunard, Henry Flagler, Sir Harry Oakes, Sir Billy Butlin, Sir Stafford Sands, E. P. Taylor, the Bay Street Boys, Wallace Groves, Daniel K. Ludwig, Louis Chesler, Sir Lynden Pindling, Merv Griffin, and a host of foreign consultants—operating in a turbulent historical environment bombarded by wars, Prohibition, MNC machinations, narcotics, and worldwide recessions.

In some ways, this is the least satisfying of the stories represented by the case studies. The Bahamas has the longest and most complex history of tourism with layers and nuances that may be hidden forever from view to all but a few, but definitely to the outsider. The stakes in this card game were high and it is not clear who won what and who continues to win. And it is not even clear who lost. "Average" Bahamians are better off (in such simplistic terms as per capita income) than their parents and grandparents. Their ancestors saw economic booms (e.g., Civil War,

World Wars, Prohibition), but when the bubbles burst, they were able to turn back to the land and the sea and to eke out a living—an option that will not be available to present and future generations if the tourism house of cards comes tumbling down. Nor will the moribund manufacturing sector be an alternative. Nor will the offshore financial sector—an ephemeral mosaic built on financial legislation in dozens of countries and the ability to store and transfer electronic "money"—employ the former hotel clerks and maids, bartenders, taxi drivers, and dive masters.

Without a major rethinking and redirection driven by knowledgeable and committed leadership in both the public and private sector, the Bahamian tourism sector seems destined to continue to decline—a decline that in effect began before 1970, but that was masked by the smoke and mirrors of seemingly growing numbers of tourists spending dollars that were actually both fewer and devaluing in real terms. In retrospect, it is difficult for the outsider to understand why Grand Bahama's problems were not a clear signal that all was not well with the entire country's tourism sector, yet almost without exception the prevailing preference by both Government and the private sector was for continued expansion.

The Bahamas is the case that most clearly demonstrates the danger of using such simplistic statistics as numbers of visitors and current expenditures as measures of the vitality and strength of the tourism sector.

That having been said, it is not obvious what path one could suggest that the Bahamas should take to rejuvenate tourism. Several conclusions are obviously easy to suggest and undoubtedly difficult to correct:

- ever-increasing cruise passenger arrival statistics are an illusory measure of development success;

- New Providence and Grand Bahama have gained a downscale, short-stay, poor value-for-money image that will be difficult to reverse;

- however numerous, visitors with short average lengths of stay (and not just cruise passengers) have a minimal economic impact;

- the hit advertising slogan of the 1970s, "It is better in the Bahamas," is not true today for most potential visitors in the face of fierce competition from newer mass tourism destinations such as the Dominican Republic and Mexico (which, admittedly, have their own problems that do not auger well for the medium term, let alone the long term) on the one hand, and upscale niche destinations such as the South Pacific on the other hand;

- there are other potential mass tourism competitors on the regional horizon, notably Cuba, for as Sir Lynden Pindling has said, "as the Bahamas got its tourism boost when Cuba went out of business, the Bahamas can get its tourism drop when Cuba gets back in business. One has to face these things head on" (Anonymous, 1993c).

Only a major redirection of thinking about tourism in the Bahamas will result in the possibility of rejuvenation of the Bahamian tourism sector. One potential route may be the adoption of the strategic planning approach suggested in the concluding chapter.

Whatever route is taken, there are four key areas where critical issues need to be addressed:

- **product:** refurbishment of hotels; development of new attractions; an effective tourism awareness campaign; strengthening and enforcement of legislation and regulations relating to tourism-related services;

- **taxation and investment:** review of all taxes, duties, licenses, loans, incentives, and approvals procedures related to tourism;

- **labor and human resources:** review of employment legislation, including work permit policies; improved education and training;

- **operations:** improved property operation and maintenance; more efficient and cheaper water and energy services; review of all gaming legislation, regulations, and restrictions; a joint industry/government tourist board to create and monitor a marketing and product development strategic plan; marketing New Providence, Grand Bahama, and the Family Islands separately; more realistic use of tourism statistics; and improved airline service.

All of these issues must be addressed to avoid the collapse of the Bahamian tourism sector.

Notes

[1]Much of the following brief history is based on Craton (1986, 1987).

[2]As with so many other national statistics in the Bahamas, there is great variation in such measures among the islands.

[3]In light of such comments, it is hard to imagine the source of Bounds' (1978) optimism that "Overall, the diversification of the economy away from tourism has been a success. The only problem of a serious nature that remains is excessive unemployment problems [*sic*]" (p. 184).

[4]Density ratios for the Bahamas, however, do not reflect the fact that most arrivals are for New Providence and Grand Bahama, which together represent only 11.4% of the total land area of the country.

[5]Cruise passenger figures in the Bahamas count only first landings in the country (i.e., a passenger who is on a ship that calls on both Nassau and Freeport is counted only once in the overall figure).

[6]Other private islands have existed or continue to exist in the Caribbean. In order to attract cruise ships, the Dominican Republic developed Cayo Lenatodo near Samana and renamed it "Fantasy Island," but hustlers and petty thieves contributed to its quick demise (Meyer-Arendt, 1992, p. 89). Royal Caribbean subsequently developed Labadee in an isolated area on the north coast of Haiti; with that country's recent political turmoil, the company shifted to the Bahamas' "Coco Cay." Crown Lines and Commodore Lines have recently undergone drastic changes, including selling most of their fleets, but they used to visit Labadee Shores, a development

near Royal Caribbean's Labadee. Finally, a private beach has been developed on Mayreau in the Grenadines for use by Royal Caribbean's deep Caribbean cruises out of San Juan, Puerto Rico (Showalter, 1994).

[7]Technically, the latter statements are correct because Vancouver's statue, "Girl in a Wetsuit," is not a mermaid.

[8]Turner and Ash (1975, p. 26) note a 1926 proposal to build a casino in the Bahamas dying with the Florida land crash, but provide no details.

[9]Figures on tourist arrivals, however, are contradictory. The GOCB (1988c) records 32,000 tourists in 1950 and 68,502 in 1951.

[10]Much of the following section is based on Barratt (1989) and Craton (1986, 1987).

[11]The environmental impact of this massive development seems to have evoked very little concern in the Bahamas. Sealey (1985, pp. 84–85), for example, estimates that about 50 billion gallons of fresh water from the freshwater lens will be lost as a result of canal construction.

[12]The introduction of casino gambling in Grand Bahama was an attempt to woo American tourists deprived of the Havana facilities that Fidel Castro closed in Cuba in 1959 (Ramsaran, 1979, p. 80).

[13]To counter the growing unemployment, the Government began a fairly tough policy of "Bahamization," which attempted to obtain maximum employment of local personnel over a short period of time, sometimes regardless of training and general vocation aptitudes. With the exception of casinos where croupiers and other floor positions were filled by expatriates, "work permits" were given sparingly (Laventhol & Horwath, 1981, pp. III-68–III-69). The work permit policy continues to the present, with employers having to prove that they have unsuccessfully advertised for a Bahamian to fill a particular position before they can hire a non-Bahamian. Sometimes, the search seems fruitless from the start, as, for example, occurred in a 1993 advertisement supposedly seeking a female Bahamian to star in a floor show at a hotel; the unsuccessful search did not turn up anyone with the required excellent skills with a crossbow. Perhaps the hotel was lucky and there was a non-Bahamian unemployed female archer waiting in the wings for a work permit.

[14]In addition, there were several typographical errors and inconsistent uses of numbers in various parts of the report. For example, the "high" forecast for incremental hotel rooms in 1990 is reported as both 11,810 and 12,114 (Dames & Moore, 1981, pp. 1-3, 3-51). Also, the "actual" figure for 1980 total visitor arrivals is not consistent with official statistics, a discrepancy that could be a result of using preliminary data.

Chapter 9

Conclusion and Recommendations

There is plenty of evidence that almost anything we do on islands makes them worse. (Bill Newman, Professor of Oceanography, Scripps Institute) (Gosnell, 1976)

Tinsley's Contention

As stated in Chapter 1, the focus of this book was to determine whether (a) Tinsley (1979, p. 310) was correct in contending that the state of the Caribbean tourism sector up to that point was "the result of twenty-five years of nonplanning" (and nonpolicy), and (b) whether the situation has changed since then.

In terms of these five case studies, Tinsley's contention does not hold true on the whole for the period before 1979, at least in theory if not in practice. Each of these states had explicit and/or implicit policies in place, even if they were never fully implemented through effective planning (Figure 9.1). For example, each had some form of legislation (variously termed hotel aid or encouragement ordinances or acts in four of the cases) to encourage tourism through investment in hotel development. All but one had some form of national development or structure plan, or physical development plan that addressed issues related to the tourism sector, although in many cases these plans were not formally approved by government; the Bahamas is the exception on a national level, but not so in terms of Grand Bahama. Except for Barbados, all had some form of report, plan, or strategy setting a course of tourism development that in many cases remains very evident today.

Since 1979, the same pattern—explicit and implicit policy, but often ineffective plan implementation—holds true for Dominica, St. Lucia, and the Cayman Islands. Their current tourism sectors are the result of deliberate choices taken by the respective governments. That is not to say, however, that the routes taken are not without internal contradictions and inconsistencies (e.g., St. Lucia's policy of encouraging local involvement in the sector, but continuing pattern of approving up-scale MNC developments; the recognition by the Cayman Islands of the dependence of their tourism sectors on the environment, but lack of control over growth). In contrast, Barbados and the Bahamas have essentially drifted in policy and planning vacuums into situations that could result in the continuing deterioration of virtually every aspect of their tourism sectors. Moreover, the only sign in these latter cases that a new approach to tourism policy and planning is possible is

Year	Dominica	St. Lucia	Cayman Is.	Barbados	Bahamas	Year
1946		Tourist Board				1946
1949					Hotels Encouragement Act	1949
1950					Development Board	1950
					Hotels Encouragement Act	
1955			Hotel Aid Law			1955
1956				Hotel Aids Act		1956
1958	Hotel Aids Ordinance					1958
1959		Hotel Aids Ordinance				1959
1961			Tourist Board			1961
1963					Promotion of Tourism Act	1963
					Ministry of Tourism	
1966			Tourism Board Law			1966
1968						1968
1969					Clapp & Mayne Report	1969
					Checchi Tourism Plan	
1970				Physical Development Plan	Hotels Act	1970
1971	Shankland Cox Report	Land Development Act				1971
1972			Central Planning Authority			1972
1973					Bahamasair	1973
1974			Department of Tourism		Hotel Corp. of Bahamas	1974
			Tourism Law			
1975	National Parks Act		Development Plan*			1975
	Kastarlak Report					
1976	National Structure Plan*					1976
1977		National Development Plan*				1977
1979		Tourism Development Strategy	Cayman Airways	National Development Plan		1979
1981			Laventhol & Horwath Plan		Dames & Moore Report	1981
1982	Tourism Board Recommendations					1982
1983				National Development Plan		1983
1984				Joint Committee	Tourism Plan	1984
				Hotel Aids Act		
1985	National Structure Plan*					1985
1986		Physical Development Strategy*				1986
1987	Tourism Policy		Development Plan			1987
	Glersch Report					
1988	National Development Corp.			National Development Plan		1988
				Physical Development Plan		
1989			National Planning Committee			1989
1990		"Green" Tourism Theme				1990
1991	Tourism Sector Plan	Tourism Incentives Act				1991
		National Tourism Policy				
1992		Protected Area Plan*	Development Plan Review		Pratt Report	1992
		Tourism Ministry Changes	10-Year Tourism Plan		Poon Report	
1993			Ecotourism Conference			1993
			Cruiseship Policy			
1994			Tourism Management Policy			1994

* Not officially approved by government
---- Tinsley's "non-planning" time line

Figure 9.1. Significant recent tourism policy and planning developments.

the fact that the problems in tourism are becoming very clear to virtually everyone and that new governments have been elected.

Government Involvement in the Tourism Sector

Not even those case studies that do have some form of tourism policy and planning mechanism, however, are fully involved in all aspects of such policy and planning. The reasons are different in each case, but include a combination of factors (e.g., limited financial and human resources, institutional constraints, political will, and economic imperatives) that have resulted in widely varying and incomplete patterns of involvement in tourism policy and planning.

The level of active involvement by governments in attempting to shape their tourism sectors was raised in Chapter 2, with Jenkins and Henry's (1982) hypothesis that "For each developing country, the degree of active involvement by government in the tourist sector will reflect the importance of tourism in the economy." In terms of Jenkins and Henry's measures of tourism's economic importance (contribution to GDP and national income, foreign exchange earnings, employment and income generated, and contribution to government revenues), the tourism sector in each of the case studies is clearly of major economic significance. There is, however, a great deal of variation in its importance among the case studies, both absolutely (e.g., US$3.22 million in 1993 visitor expenditures in Dominica compared to US$1304.0 million in the Bahamas) and relatively (e.g., visitor expenditures as a percentage of GDP in 1993 ranging from 22.6% in Dominica to 52.9% in St. Lucia).

Nevertheless, if Jenkins and Henry's (1982) hypothesis holds, "one would expect government to intervene actively in the tourist sector " (p. 506). Is this true for each of the case studies? If the question were approached from a simplistic yes–no stance, the answer would be "yes" for each of the case studies, except perhaps for Barbados. Each state has a tourism history that includes a variety of policies, plans, legislation, research, government-operated and/or government-financed infrastructure, superstructure, etc., which could be described as representing policies reflecting active involvement and also, in most cases, passive involvement (Figure 9.2). Moreover, each state has one or more of the five types of plans delineated by the WTO (1980) as potentially being related to tourism.

If, however, the question were approached from a more complex position that took a more evaluative judgement about the effectiveness of government involvement in creating a tourism sector that met Ascher and Healy's (1990) goals of sustainable development, then the answer varies for each state. In fact, if one sets aside such serious concerns as the obvious incompatibility between ever-growing numbers of visitors and environmental integrity, only the Cayman Islands can be described as approaching all four goals.

Moreover, if the question were approached from the even more demanding argument that "It is probable that most governments would be involved in policy-making in each area [foreign exchange earnings, foreign investment, employment

	Dominica	St. Lucia	Caymen Is.	Barbados	Bahamas
Government Involvement in Tourism Policy					
Active: 1. Managerial	*	*	*	*	*
2. Developmental		*	*	*	*
Passive: 1. Mandatory	*		*	*	*
2. Supportive	*	*	*	*	*
Government Involvement in Tourism Planning					
General national	na	na	*	*	
National infrastructure				*	
National tourism development	*	*	*		*
Tourism infrastructure					
National promotion and marketing	*	*	*	*	
The Goals of Sustainable Development					
High per capita consumption, sustainable over an indefinite period	-	-	+	+	+/-
Distributional equity	-	-	+	+/-	-
Environmental protection	+/-	+/-	+/-	-	-
Participation of all sectors of society in decision making	-	-	+	+/-	-
Detailed Government Involvement in Tourism Planning					
Foreign investment earnings:					
Active: 1. Managerial	*	*	*		
2. Developmental					
Passive: 1. Mandatory					
2. Supportive					
Foreign investment:					
Active: 1. Managerial		*	*	*	*
2. Developmental				*	*
Passive: 1. Mandatory					
2. Supportive					
Employment in tourism:					
Active: 1. Managerial					
2. Developmental		*			
Passive: 1. Mandatory	*		*	*	*
2. Supportive					
Land use policies:					
Active: 1. Managerial					
2. Developmental				*	*
Passive: 1. Mandatory	*				
2. Supportive					
Air transport:					
Active: 1. Managerial			*		*
2. Developmental					
Passive: 1. Mandatory					
2. Supportive	*	*		*	

*Denotes involvement; + meets the goal; - does not meet the goal; +/- partly meets the goal. na, not approved.

Figure 9.2. Summary.

in tourism, land use policies, and air transport], if only in a passive role" (Jenkins & Henry, 1982, p. 506), then the answer is negative in all cases.

Alternative Models of Tourism Development

The question was also raised in Chapter 2 whether any of these case studies provide examples of governments that have adopted models of tourism development (as articulated in tourism policy and planning) other than traditional mass tourism in order to avoid many of the negative impacts and to increase the positive impacts.

The simple answer is "no." Among the case studies, there is no evidence of the implementation of alternative development models that could assist governments in the formation of policies and plans aimed at more effective routes to sustainable national development. For example, St. Lucia, a mid-Stage II destination, seems to be headed on a path towards late Stage II with its acceptance of growth based on mass tourism, all-inclusives, and MNC investment, in contradiction to a stated policy of small-scale, local investment. Barbados and the Bahamas, in fact, represent examples of what could almost be described as classic cases of the problems inherent in late Stage III as a result of actions (or lack of them) that have encouraged mass tourism, and they appear to heading into serious decline.

A more equivocal answer is "perhaps" in terms of Dominica, which has developed policies and plans focused on nature tourism that have to date avoided mass tourism; however, it could be argued that this is so because Dominica has no other choice. It is still a minor Stage I destination, even after nearly a quarter of a century of interest in tourism, but it has serious environmental constraints and access (i.e., lack of an international airport) problems that might keep it at the Stage I phase for a long time. One gets the sense, however, that if an international airport could be built, the doors would be happily opened by many people to mass tourism.

An even more equivocal answer is "nearly" in the case of the Cayman Islands, which has adopted a clear policy path from the beginning of the destination cycle. It has chosen a form of tourism development that follows a policy of upscale tourism and niche marketing, backed by a strategic management (see below) approach to tourism. Its major constraints, however, are also environmental limits; as a late Stage II destination, it needs to control growth and to avoid a shift with mass tourism into Stage III, a fact that its most recent tourism management policy (GOCI, 1994) does not deal with adequately.

Finally, Chapter 2 noted Edgell's (1987, p. 28) argument that most tourism policy focuses on only two goals: maximization of tourist arrivals and improvement in the balance of payments through international tourism receipts. This argument certainly seems to hold for all of the case studies except the Cayman Islands, which has a tourism policy with multiple purposes (see below).

From Unique Case Studies to Generalization

Clearly, each case study represents a unique story that is not directly comparable to other Commonwealth Caribbean states, let alone to other states in the Caribbean or elsewhere. Moreover, because each case study represents a different policy context in terms of its location on the destination life cycle, the problems they face vary by the stage of development of their tourism sectors. As a result, they face policy and planning challenges that are specific to that stage and thus require approaches that reject the traditional mass tourism model and that reflect their own stage and style of tourism development. The case studies do, however, suggest conclusions that have the potential for generalized applicability.

The interpretive stories told here clearly show the varying but always complex context in which tourism is involved. Moreover, they strongly suggest that tourism policy makers and planners are indeed faced with situations described so well by Ackoff (1979) as messes: "dynamic situations that consist of complex systems of changing problems that interact with each other" (pp. 99–100). (Yet, only rarely have they adequately defined the context and conceptualized the problem, the first steps to managing messes [Steed, 1988, p. 7].) Nor have they met the necessary conditions for any subsequent technical problem solving: recognizing a problem setting, making sense of an uncertain situation, and developing perspectives (Schon, 1983). Moreover, it seems that, however difficult policy making may be, its implementation—planning—is even more problematic, for too often policy is made without instruments being in place for its management (de Kadt, 1992, p. 65). Also, even when tourism plans do exist, the WTO's (1980) general observations about them seem to hold: many were not implemented, few integrated tourism with socioeconomic objectives, plans giving priority to social aspects over profitability were rarer, few made firm and specific provision for environmental protection, and most were not supported by specific legislation. And finally, at least one case—Barbados—and perhaps a second—the Bahamas—seem to contradict the WTO's (1980) conclusion that "[a desire to plan] exists in the tourism sector" (p. 22).

A major reason for these tourism messes is that government policy makers and planners are in control over only a small portion of their particular mess. No state has complete power over all the forces and actors that are in play in the global tourism system—a fact that applies to small and large states. They are all affected by global and regional politics and economics, hotel and airline MNCs, changing tastes and interests of potential tourists, regional and extra-regional competition, and their own changing social environments.

Even though their social and economic contexts vary greatly, all of the case study states appear to have tourism sectors that have not been shaped totally by external forces, but rather have used tourism policy and planning to a greater or lesser degree to shape their own presents and futures. Despite the fact that each case study is at a different stage of development and that their stories are still being played out, the essential lesson that seems to arise from these case studies is as follows. In the absence of (a) a deliberate, chosen policy that presents a vision of a tourism future that is appropriate to a destination's unique context and (b) the ability and will to implement that policy through effective planning, an island destination bowing to the almost inevitability of tourism as a development path is likely to see initial "success" evolve into a mess replete with social, economic, and biophysical problems.

The case studies, however, do not provide evidence that effective policy and planning guarantee avoidance of these problems if adopted early in the development process because the potential "success story" here in that sense, the Cayman Islands, is still in the middle stage of development. Nor is there evidence that, despite the absence or weakness of policy and planning in the earlier stages of development, the adoption of effective policy and planning even after all of the problems are evident can result in rescuing a destination from apparent decline. That is, the question remains unanswered as to whether Barbados and the Bahamas are too late to avoid disaster through immediate adoption of effective policy and planning.

Normative Proposals

These conclusions suggest several normative recommendations that Caribbean governments should consider. Ritchie (1987, p. 20) delineates three types of policy research output as forms of normative analysis:

- the identification of *policy options*: key dimensions that underlie future organizational priorities;

- the provision of recommendations concerning the *priorities* required to implement the different policy options;

- the nature of the *action* required to implement the selection of options: given the situation described in these case studies, a new approach to tourism policy and planning is required.

Policy Options

Limits to Growth

Given the fact that much of the success of tourism depends on high levels of environmental quality, "One of the pivotal issues in this [tourism] planning process will be environmental management" (Bell, 1993, p. 22). One of the key factors in environmental management should be the recognition that there are limits to growth that are determined by a complex blend of environmental factors: social (e.g., the Caymanian domestic labour force), economic (e.g., the decreasing level of real expenditures by the growing number of cruise passengers in the Bahamas), and biophysical (e.g., the fragile rainforests of Dominica).

The problem is that there are no simple mechanisms or tools that can be used to predict when the limits will be reached. Unfortunately, it is probably easier to recognize subjectively when they have already been exceeded. For example, Mather and Todd (1993) conclude that

> Industry observers in some [Caribbean] countries are now of the opinion that, with developments in the pipeline included, limits have been reached and that before further expansion takes place they must turn their attention to the quality of the product and the supply of infrastructure, and generally assess the overall carrying capacity. . . . (p. 80)

Because tropical islands are among the most fragile environments and because they are relatively small, an attempt should be made to set limits. Initially, it is better to set conservative limits, thus allowing movement upwards at some later time as the situation is monitored, rather than being only able to recognize the limits have been exceeded when disaster strikes. The limits must be developed through research and in the context of politically debated policy, backed by planning that includes monitoring and enforcement. Unfortunately, it is not easy to decide what measures to use to determine the limits. The case studies clearly demonstrate that such measures as total number of visitors and visitor expenditures are dangerously simplistic and must be augmented by a range of other measures, both objective (e.g., density ratio, penetration ratio, tourism occupancy function) and subjective (e.g., perceptions of both hosts and guests).

Increased Professionalism
Commonwealth Caribbean islands are minor players in the world tourism system and they suffer from growing competition, both regionally and globally. The competition is both real (e.g., Dominican Republic, Mexico, South Pacific) and potential (e.g., Cuba) and it is influenced by a variety of characteristics, including price, value for quality, innovation, marketing, and government intervention. Bell (1993) concludes that

> Those destinations that will flourish over the next decade will be those that are able to identify consumer trends in travel correctly, and succeed in marrying them to the national interest in a comprehensive yet flexible plan. Such destinations must also find a way to bring together the multiple public and private sector tourism components to implement that plan effectively. (p. 220)

The case studies support Bell's (1993) prediction that by 2000

> Tourism development across the region will have been far from uniform. Those countries with carefully integrated, professionally managed, tourism plans, coupled to a realistic regulatory and tax climate, will have surged ahead. Those where the public and private sectors remain fragmented and tourism has been asked to subsidize the rest of the economy will be moribund. (p. 234)

In order for their tourism sectors to survive as major components of their economies, these states should therefore increase their ability to manage tourism professionally. That professionalism will require research, policy, planning, legislation, regulation, enforcement, training, education, and public–private sector cooperation.

Modernization and Upgrading of the Accommodation Sector
A common theme in several case studies is the need to modernize and upgrade the accommodation sector. In some cases, the problem lies with small-scale, locally owned establishments, in others larger-scale apartment complexes, and in still others international-scale establishments. Mather and Todd (1993, p. 92) argue that the Caribbean accommodation sector should face its need for modernization and upgrading if it is going to compete at an international level; moreover, governments must acknowledge the very real difficulties being experienced and play their parts in providing a climate in which the sector is able to move forward.

Part of the problem, as noted below, relates to the lack of incentives available to local entrepreneurs, a subject that should receive attention through a variety of possible mechanisms, including easier access to credit.

Moving From Incentives Policies to the Removal of Constraints

All of the case study states have incentive policies that either directly (e.g., tax holidays) or indirectly (e.g., policies of no income or corporation tax on any activity) encourage investment in the tourism sector. In some cases, the incentives are aimed at foreign investment, whereas in others they are aimed at local investment (although in some cases, e.g., St. Lucia and Barbados, the financial climate is such that local investors are rarely in a positive financial position that would allow them to take advantage of such incentives). The case studies, however, provide little evidence of the utility of such incentives, yet governments continue to make them available. In fact, even in a country such as the Bahamas, which has no corporate taxes and still cannot attract significant foreign investment in the tourism sector, there have been calls for the adoption of other incentives.

This view of the questionable utility of incentives is supported by other sources. For example, Mather and Todd (1993) conclude that "There is evidence . . . that investment incentives do little to influence investment decisions" (p. v). Similarly, Arthur Young (1988, p. 1-1) contends that existing incentives for encouragement of tourism investment in the Caribbean region play a smaller role in attracting new investment than is generally ascribed to them and function differently depending on the stage of development of the tourism sector in the particular country concerned. Rather, the primary concerns of potential investors are political stability, economic stability, labor unrest, training costs, importation costs imposed on essential operating supplies, and seasonality of demand. For these reasons, "To a large extent, future success of the Caribbean region in attracting and maintaining tourism sector investment depends on eliminating or minimising the impact of the constraints" (Arthur Young, 1988, p. 1-1). Constraints include complex administration, discrimination or inconsistency concerning foreigners, bureaucratic delay, petty regulation, restrictive work permit practices, frequent modification of rules, lack of government confidence, excessive or inappropriate forms of taxation, inappropriate import licensing, excessive exchange control regulation, threat of non-convertibility or devaluation, complex customs procedures, inadequate air access, inadequate infrastructure and support services, cost and inefficiency of labor, inadequacy of trained labor and of training facilities, high cost or unreliability of utilities, inventory costs, high cost of construction, high cost of hotel marketing, seasonality, small domestic market size, negative social factors, political risk, limited capital market, and attitudes to foreign investment (Arthur Young, 1988, pp. 3-1–3-10).

If governments decide to provide some form of financial inducement, there are alternatives to the usual tax holidays and exemptions. For example, Wanhill (1986) concludes that "Apart from guaranteed investment security most tourism incentives are unnecessary the primary instrument should be the capital grant, or its equivalent in the provision of facilities" (p. 2). Similarly, Mather and Todd (1993) conclude that "There is evidence [in the Caribbean] . . . that investment incentives do little to influence investment decisions, and there is a case for concluding that incentives in the Caribbean would be better aimed at operating costs, which are high, than at capital investment" (p. v). Thus, there is a strong argument to be made that governments need to reconsider their incentives policies.

Ecotourism

Ecotourism has been the buzz-word of the 1990s, not only in the Caribbean, but also worldwide. Regionally, it has been the subject of annual conferences organized by the CTO since 1992. And virtually every Caribbean state seems to be either actively pursuing the ecotourism market or considering it. Yet, there is little discussion, let alone agreement on what it is:

> [T]here is no clarity what eco-tourism is and what it implies. Indeed on occasion, eco-tourism is perceived as a means to expand the tourism frontier using a slightly toned down version of the current model. This approach is strikingly similar to the incipient tourism efforts of the fifties and sixties, and embodies the danger that eco-tourism will evolve along the same path as mainstream Caribbean tourism. (Blommestein, 1993, p. 9)

Moreover, there is little research on how large the market niche is, how many slices of what size the pie can be cut into, how long term a niche it might be, or how to market it. If Caribbean governments are going to invest their marketing and promotion budgets in ecotourism, then the need for solid market research is clear.

A major failing of those case studies that have chosen a policy of promoting ecotourism is their lack of ability to actually implement such a policy, particularly in light of the apparent conflicts between increased pressure from growing numbers of tourists and fragile island environments. Clear plans backed by solid management and enforcement are needed.

Regional Cooperation

There is a satisfying logic to G. K. Lewis' (1987) comment that "According to the well-known law of international relations, the more friends you have the safer you are. There is safety in numbers" (p. 157). The history of the Commonwealth Caribbean is replete with calls for regional cooperation on a wide range of topics from political union to economics, education, and the legal system. Yet even those efforts that have lasted (e.g., CARICOM) have been of limited real success, simply because even when working together, the sum of Caribbean states in terms of size and power is still relatively small. Moreover, "despite the seemingly obvious advantages of small Caribbean states grouping together, lasting federations have thus far eluded them. Big is not always beautiful in the eyes of Caribbean politicians and Caribbean peoples, and so far the appeal of local sovereighty [sic] has outweighed the theoretical promise of inter-island unification" (Richardson, 1992, p. 192).

There is also the fear of many governments that regional cooperation in tourism planning and marketing will result in the market being unable to differentiate among the islands. One way of overcoming this fear would be to accentuate the heterogeneity of the islands in advertising and to create multi-island vacations.

There are many possible combinations of destinations that would attract both tourists who cross over particular market niches (e.g., combining St. Lucia's luxury hotels for a week with Dominica's nature-oriented tourism for another week) and those who want diversity within one type of experience (e.g., multi-island scuba diving trips).

Priorities

Presumptuous as it is for an outsider to set out a list of policy options, it would be even more audacious to prioritize them; moreover, the circumstances of each state are so different that no specific list of priorities would apply equally to all. Nevertheless, the above ordering of policy options suggests a sequence of priorities that might be considered.

Towards a New Approach to Tourism Policy and Planning: Integrated Development

To be able to choose among these and other policy options, to prioritize them, and ultimately to implement them, a new approach to tourism policy and planning is needed. The approach suggested here builds on the concept of integrated development.

Although tourism—both worldwide and in the Caribbean—has grown nearly continuously for the past several decades, concern has often been expressed that continued expansion at the present rate and in its existing form is neither desirable nor sustainable. Arguing that policy and planning should be directed at restraining and redirecting growth rather than encouraging it, Mathieson and Wall (1982, p. 177) enumerate a number of factors that have contributed to this undesirable situation:

- **inadequate forecasting** has caused many overloading and congestion problems;

- **the resource-oriented emphasis of tourist marketing** has produced spatial and temporal concentrations of tourists in many areas with unique and frequently fragile resources;

- **the inefficiency of planning measures** has resulted in a failure to recognize the many disparate components of the tourism sector and to integrate them into an overall planning framework;

- **a tendency to sacrifice long-term benefits for short-term gains**;

- **inadequate attention to the appropriate scale of development** with too frequent emphasis on large prestigious projects when more modest developments might have been better in terms of costs and benefits;

- **a failure to specify goals adequately** means that it is not always clear who the major beneficiaries of tourism development are expected to be.

Recognizing that tourism is a complex phenomenon that produces diverse and often contradictory effects, Mathieson and Wall (1982) argue that tourism planning is a necessary and multifaceted process involving economic, social, and environmental factors that should begin with the consideration of alternative development policies:

> Tourism, then, is a complex phenomenon which gives rise to diverse and often contradictory effects. It is easy to say that planners of tourism should maximize the benefits from tourism and minimize the costs. However, it is not possible to maximize some effects and minimize others at the same time. Trade-offs will be required and compromise will be necessary. Alternative development policies should be considered prior to the commitment of resources and assessed for their feasibility, limitations, effects and ability to satisfy the requirements of hosts and guests. (p. 178)

Reime and Hawkins (1979) propose a set of criteria for selecting desirable development alternatives: economic viability, social compatibility, physical attractivity, political supportability, complementarity, and marketability, to which D. G. Pearce (1989) adds environmental sustainability.

Unfortunately, however, de Kadt's (1979) comment—that he is aware of no evidence that any government has deliberately set out to assess the overall effects of alternative types of tourism in order to promote those that appear to promise the greatest net social benefits—seems to remain valid in terms of the case studies (with the possible exception of Dominica, as discussed above). He concludes that tourism policies and plans emphasise gross expenditures and numbers of tourism, with little attention to maximizing net returns and improving income distribution.

> Instead, it would appear that tourism projects are often developed without being tested within the framework of a sectoral plan, while their costs and benefits may not even be compared with those of alternative projects in the same sector. Most seriously, although the sectoral plan should establish the place of tourism within the development strategy for the whole economy, in many cases such a plan is nonexistent or not decisively implemented.

> Where tourism planning has been undertaken it has often been remedial, attempting to intervene after much development had already taken place. As in other fields, many countries have exhibited limited ability to learn from mistakes made elsewhere, and much planning may be characterized as "shutting the stable door after the horse has bolted." (de Kadt, 1979, p. 21)

Mathieson and Wall (1982) reach a similar conclusion:

> It is imperative that planners become less preoccupied with the visitor and devote more attention to the welfare of those being visited. Planners should be asking such questions as: how many and what type of tourists does an area want to welcome and how can tourists contribute to the enhancement of the lifestyles of residents of destination areas? (p. 179)

In more recent years, however, there appears to have been a significant evolution in normative approaches to tourism policy and planning, with a move away from a narrow concentration on physical planning or promotional planning aimed at facilitating the growth of tourism and toward a broader, more balanced approach incorporating the needs and views of the local community and not just the tourists (Acerenza, 1985; Baud-Bovy, 1985; Braddon, 1982; Getz, 1986a, 1986b, 1987; Murphy, 1985). In line with the evolution in the changing attitudes to development, tourism policy and planning have come to be more concerned in theoretical terms with the integration of tourism with other forms of social and economic development (D. G. Pearce, 1989, p. 245).

Recognition of the great complexity of policy and planning and the limitations of even the most skilled professionals has led to the concept of *integrated development* (Lang, 1986a).[1] This concept acknowledges that planners, managers, politicians, and developers face difficult problems: interconnectedness, complicatedness, uncertainty, ambiguity, pluralism, and societal constraints (Mason & Mitroff, 1981). As illustrated by the case studies, these are problems that certainly are characteristic of tourism policy and planning contexts.

Mitchell (1986) defines the concept of *integrated development* as "the sharing and coordination of values and inputs of a broad range of agencies, publics and other interests when conceiving, designing and implementing policies, programs or projects" (p. 13) (which can occur at normative, strategic, and operational levels). He (1986, pp. 14–17) describes it in terms of four interrelated components:

- **Multiple purpose, multiple means, and multiple participant strategies:** the ultimate target of developing strategies in which multiple purposes are blended with multiple means and multiple participants requires the diverse values and inputs of various agencies and private interests to be identified, shared, and coordinated.

- **Blending various resource sectors:** attitudes of managers and organizational structure of the public sector must accommodate a need to identify and blend the sometimes complementary but more often conflicting values associated with different resource sectors (e.g., water, forests, agriculture).

- **A mechanism for social change:** rather than an end in itself, it should be seen as a means to enhance positive social and economic change (i.e., to improve the quality of life of the people in the region while maintaining the integrity of the environment).

- **Achieving accommodation and compromise:** in order to incorporate sharing, cooperation, and coordination regarding diverse values of a variety of interests, conflicts and disagreements can be expected to occur and, thus, mechanisms for bargaining and negotiation are required.

Mitchell (1986) concludes that "These are demanding criteria. It is not surprising that few situations have been able to address them all adequately" (p. 22). He suggests three barriers to the successful implementation of integrated development:

- the long time required for such comprehensive policy and planning;

- the failure to implement a plan because it is outdated, has vague recommendations, is not realistic relative to available means, or is more concerned with process than product;

- the sensitivity of line agencies and interests to sharing and coordination that could be seen as their giving up authority or responsibility.

Rather than conventional planning, which implies a static state when a plan has been produced, the achievement of integrated development relies on *strategic planning*, a practical process of implementation that implies action.

> A strategy can be seen as a proposed sequence of mutually reinforcing actions directed toward an interrelated set of objectives. "Strategy" is more dynamic than "plan." A strategy indicates not only what we want and the means for achieving it but also how we intend to proceed step-by-step to get there, and what we will do if things change. Furthermore, strategy conveys the idea of choosing a course of action in the face of opposing forces with different intentions and objectives. [Radford, 1980, p. 143] Strategies, which tend to address inter-organizational situations where the agency has only partial control, differ from policies, which tend to be unilateral statements of intent that guide actions for which the agency has more or less sole responsibility. (Lang, 1986a, p. 32)

Strategic planning, therefore, involves establishing long-term goals (e.g., market), schedules, and resource requirements within a plan of action that allocates and organizes the available resources to achieve the goals and identifies the transitions that confront the organization as it moves in new directions.

As argued by Mitchell's criterion, which includes multiple participants, attempts to integrate require interaction with the stakeholders "in the search for relevant information, shared values, consensus and, ultimately, proposed action that is both feasible and acceptable" (Lang, 1986a, p. 35). Lang (1986a, pp. 36–37) argues that interaction is made necessary by four factors:

- **Dispersed information:** relevant information needed to solve complex problems is distributed among various groups and individuals, not just planners.

- **Shared action space:** plans cannot be implemented completely by one agency's unilateral action, but require interdependence with other agencies and stakeholders.

- **Concern about legitimacy:** for plans to have broad public support and acceptance, the public must view the agency's role as legitimate and have confidence and trust in the agency and its planning process.

- **Need for behavioral change:** because both structural (e.g., a new park) and behavioral (e.g., limits on how people use the park) changes are involved, involvement in planning processes can smooth the way for needed behavioral change, which is often difficult to achieve by coercion.

There is no single best means to achieve interaction; rather, a combination of information–feedback, consultation, collaboration, and negotiation is required, depending on the specific situation. Strategic planning, however, is not without its critics. Mintzberg (1994), for example, provides three criticisms:

- the emphasis on process in strategic planning can strangle an organization;

- hard data are required, but much of the data that are used in the planning process are available only because they are measurable, whereas other potentially more important "soft" information is ignored;

- the emphasis on process can also lead to detachment from the problem and from action.

Moreover, Taketa (1993) notes a danger that the strategic plan can become an end in itself, not a means to an end; in that event, a rigid planning process revises the plan on a regular basis, but does not change it fundamentally. Furthermore, with the rapid pace of change in the world, 5-year plans, for example, are frequently obsolete in 6 months.

Taketa (1993) suggests that strategic planning should be replaced by *strategic thinking*:

> Strategic thinking is a continual processing of external and internal information and adjusting to changing situations. The manager looks out into the future and identifies the changes the future may bring: changes in markets, changes in products, changes in technology, or changes in regulatory or financial environments. The plan becomes a statement of how to deal with these changing conditions. The plan is subject to continuous evolution as the manager attempts to achieve a strategic competitive advantage in a changing environment (M. Porter, 1985). (p. 467)

The argument is that the strategic planner works within a predetermined planning horizon, whereas the strategic thinker operates within a changing environment, adjusting continuously as the situation dictates; strategy is "crafted" out of the raw materials in the environment, not derived from a rigid set of procedures (Mintzberg, 1982).

Such an approach has attraction, particularly given the complex nature of tourism; however, as the case studies demonstrate, the state of the art in tourism policy and planning is so far from integrated development and strategic planning that contemplation of the adoption of strategic thinking is barely possible at this point. It could, however, be argued that, although not going as far as strategic thinking, the Cayman Islands has the potential at least for moving toward integrated development in a manner consistent with Mitchell's (1986) model.

The Cayman Islands' Ten-Year Tourism Development Plan (GOCI, 1992d) is described as a "strategic management plan" (which, in terms of the analysis presented in Chapter 2, appears to be more of a policy than a plan) designed "to provide a clear set of policies, strategies and implementation guidelines to chart the way forward for tourism'' (p. 165). The Plan appears to have at least the potential for matching Mitchell's (1986) four components of integrated development. It is based on a normative goal of a form of development focused on the tourism and offshore financial sectors and then goes on to build a *strategic* framework that is consistent with Mitchell's model.

In terms of the first component, the Plan is *multiple purpose*, having the normative goals of not only stimulating the economy, but also preserving the heritage, culture, and environment of the islands. It intends to do so through focusing on three major changes within the tourism sector: enhanced price–value relationship, a managed long-term entrepreneurial spirit, and a more positive view towards and use of expatriate labor. It employs *multiple means*: the use of "trigger mechanisms" to monitor growth; research; legislation, regulation, and zoning; organizational change; and specific guidelines for the development of the tourism sector. *Multiple participants* are involved: government, private sector, education, NGOs, and individuals (the latter notably through the follow-up Development Plan Review).

Second, the Plan *blends various resource sectors* in the sense of considering tourism, heritage, culture, and environment and promotes the integration of other sectors of the economy with tourism (which will be difficult given the domination of the economy by the service sector, i.e., tourism, offshore financial operation, and government).

Third, it is seen as a *mechanism for social change*, focusing strongly on improving the quality of life in the Cayman Islands through the tourism sector. Mention is made, for example, of education, cultural heritage, environmental quality (particularly through an emphasis on ecotourism), managed growth, increased resident satisfaction, crowd control, employment, better relations with expatriates, etc.

Finally, the subsequent Development Plan Review provides an opportunity for *achieving accommodation and compromise* in the subsequent *operational* phase of development by providing an opportunity for all sectors of the population to become involved in district subcommittees, meetings, and workshops. Whether or not that implementation stage will meet Lang's (1986a) characteristics of strategic planning remain to be seen. The major barriers that are apparent now involve the willingness of Caymanians to accept managed development and to make environmental protection a primary concern—otherwise, there will probably be a drift into mass tourism and environmental destruction. Moreover, there is little evidence in the recent tourism management plan (GOCI, 1994) that the Government is prepared to reconcile the contradiction between goals of continued growth, ecotourism, and maintenance of environmental quality.

A Time for Reflection

The uncertainty about the future growth pattern of tourism leaves tourism policy makers and planners in a quandary: it seems logical that "facilities and amenities for tourists must be gauged to expected flows of visitors" (Bélisle et al., 1982, p.

155), but it is not clear whether such "expected flows" can be predicted accurately, even in the short term (Wilkinson, 1987b, p. 140). In addition, Butler (1986, personal communication) raises the important question of whether decision makers can afford to be reactive and wait for such "expected flows" of tourists to continue forever or whether they should be more proactive and take concrete steps to promote the flow.

Tourism patterns are dynamic and unstable, in both the long and short terms (Wilkinson, 1987b, p. 141), for a variety of reasons: economic recession and inflation, weather, competition, political forces, etc. As English (1986) notes, "relative to most traded goods, tourism is unusually vulnerable to political and other disturbances at the travel destination" (p. 21). The sensitivity of the tourism sector is such that a negative political event need not be a physical disruption such as a revolution or civil strife, but merely an ideological stance. For example, a vote by Mexico in the United Nations equating Zionism with racism (and, thereby, implicitly condemning Israel) in 1975 led to a temporary, but serious, boycott of Mexico by many Americans (Anonymous, 1976). Other factors are related to social forces, such as the negative impact of crime in Honolulu on Hawaiian tourism in the late 1970s and early 1980s, which was curtailed to a great extent when airlines and tour operators provided free travel back to Hawaii for any tourists who had been victims of crimes and had to attend trials. On the other hand, Kjellstrom (1974, p. 367) concludes that tourists generally have a short memory and soon return to popular destinations once a source of disturbance has been eliminated.

Ideally, the policy maker and planner must work on two fronts simultaneously: the rejuvenation of the tourist industry and the search for alternative economic prospects (Wilkinson, 1987b, p. 143). The stories presented here suggest that tourism is simply too fragile and unpredictable an economic sector on which to base total national development. Rejuvenation of a failing tourism sector, however, is not a simple task, for it is dependent upon infusions of capital, which in the case of developing countries usually means foreign investment. Whereas statements about local ownership and management and about "alternative" tourism opportunities ("local" as opposed to "international" experience) are laudable, they still require capital—often a scarce commodity in such situations.

Diversification provides two benefits. First, it provides economic insurance in case of decline in the tourism sector. Tourism is a highly unstable export sector, subject to strong seasonal variations, pronounced and unpredictable influence from external forces, and the heterogeneous nature of tourist motivations and expectations. Tourism is also highly elastic with respect to both price and income (Mathieson & Wall, 1982, p. 38). These factors combine to promote a low level of customer loyalty in terms of destinations, modes of travel, accommodation units, and travel intermediaries. ("Customer loyalty" might in fact not be an appropriate term to use in connection with tourism, as there is evidence to suggest that many tourists deliberately and constantly select different destinations for each vacation in order to experience something different.) Second, diversification provides potentially stronger linkages between local industry and tourism, thus reducing leakages, increasing local employment and the gross domestic product, and providing the possibility of exports. In short, policy makers and planners must recognize that tourism is merely part—albeit often an important part—of an overall economic development process.

Development, however, may be extremely difficult to achieve in small island nations, due to the lack of resources, trained personnel, infrastructure, and local capital. Such small islands have the most difficulty in identifying viable development strategies that do not rely heavily on tourism (de Kadt 1979, pp. 16–17). There is, in addition, Butler's (1986, personal communication) warning that not every—let alone, any—tourist destination may be capable of rejuvenation and that no such rejuvenation can be maintained ad infinitum. For some islands, rejuvenation of the tourism sector may be the only possible route. It might involve a variety of actions: rehabilitation and/or expansion of tourism facilities and services; more aggressive marketing; the provision of new or alternative opportunities that would attract new market segments (e.g., adding new human-made attractions or taking advantage of previously untapped natural resources); the provision of off-peak season incentives; or enhanced infrastructure. The problem, of course, is the lack of local capital; increased dependence on foreign capital will only exacerbate the leakage situation (Wilkinson, 1987b, p. 144). (Larger, more developed nations can also suffer the same fate; the stagnating Canadian tourist industry is a prime example.)

If one were prepared to ignore the many negative economic, social, and biophysical environmental costs of tourism . . . and to concentrate solely on the positive impacts, one might state that "nonpolicy" and "nonplanning" sufficed in a time of seemingly endless growth. With the shattering of that myth, however, must come the recognition of the need for tourism planning at both the national and international levels. To repeat Lundberg's (1980) phrase of a number of years ago, the time for "reflection" is truly now at hand.

Note

[1]This is somewhat different than Jenkins and Henry's (1982, p. 240) use of the term "integrated development" (i.e., integrated tourism development), which they see as tourism development in small states that is characterized by smaller scale, more indigenous capital and management, and lower prices that are geared to a different type of tourist, one who is perhaps more easily assimilated into the host community (although there is little research on this latter point). Unfortunately, there are few, if any, examples of microstates that have successfully implemented such a policy. The most frequently cited example is St. Vincent's short-lived policy of attempting to create an "indigenous and integrated" tourism industry, characterized by spatial zoning, gradual growth, local production, indigenous architecture, joint ventures, and low-cost marketing. The success of the policy was limited, however, largely by factors unrelated to the plan itself, such as the general tourist market, inflation, and high energy costs (Britton, 1977).

Glossary

Cruise passenger: a type of excursionist who is a passenger on a cruise ship who visits a port for less than 24 hours. Cruise passengers may visit more than one port in a country, but are usually counted only once per country. In some cases, cruise passenger arrival figures represent the number of passengers on a ship's manifest, which is not necessarily the number of passengers who actually disembark at a given port. Because each country keeps its own count, a passenger on a multiport trip will therefore be counted for each country visited.

Excursionist: A visitor to a country who stays less than 24 hours (English, 1986, p. 4). (See Cruise Passenger.)

Gross domestic product (GDP): the sum of the value-added contribution of each good and service produced in the economy (CTO, 1990, p. 151).

Gross National Product (GNP): the sum of the value-added contribution of each good and service produced in the economy, plus foreign exchange earnings (e.g., remittances, profits from abroad).

Hotel and restaurant sector: business activities related to hotels and restaurants, but this represents only a part of the tourism sector for which there is, as yet, no commonly accepted definition (CTO, 1990, p. 155).

Index of seasonality: number of stay-overs during winter (December–May) divided by the number of stay-overs during summer (June–November) (de Albuquerque & McElroy, 1992). (This is obviously a Northern Hemisphere definition.)

Invisible export: essentially, a service performed by one nation for another nation, in lieu of a transfer of goods (visible exports). In the case of tourism the service is the resort, hotel, entertainments, restaurants, sports, beaches, swimming pools, etc., for which the visitor pays for the use of while on vacation (Bounds, 1978).

Leakages: the loss of tourism foreign exchange caused, in large part, by the need to import goods and services required by the tourism industry; first-round leakages flow out of the tourist destination almost immediately due in large part to the import of goods such as foods and liquor, whereas second-round leakages are foreign exchange earnings that circulate at least once through the economy of the tourist destination before flowing out (Seward & Spinrad, 1982).

Linkages: the extent to which tourism subsectors use goods and services available in other sectors of the economy; if most goods and services used are produced domestically, tourism is said to have strong linkages with other sectors of the economy and a low level of leakage (Seward & Spinrad, 1982).

Market concentration ratio: the share (percentage) of the market accounted for by the top three origins (D. G. Pearce, 1987).

Multiplier: money spent by tourists goes into the pocketbooks and bank accounts of local businesses. This money, in turn, is spent on salaries, supplies, insurance, and taxes. Each time a tourist makes an expenditure, a ripple of additional spending is sent through the economy. This ripple is called a multiplier. The multiplier describes the additional spending or job creation caused by a given level tourist spending. . . . The multiplier is a difficult, expensive, and unstable statistic to derive. The reason it generates so much interest is that omission of the multiplier means one necessarily misses a substantial portion of the real effects of tourism (S. Smith, 1983, pp. 171–172)

Tourism: "Tourism" is a sum of the . . . elements (travel, destination areas, tourist), resulting from the travel of non-residents (tourist, including excursionist) to destination areas, as long as their sojourn does not become a permanent residence (Murphy, 1985, p. 9). Tourism may be defined as the sum of phenomena and relationships arising from the interaction of tourists, business suppliers, host governments, and host communities in the process of attracting and hosting these tourists and other visitors (McIntosh & Goeldner, 1986, p. 4).

Tourism employment: the number of full- and part-time jobs generated by tourism; direct employment is created by the first round of tourism expenditures within tourism subsectors (e.g., hotels, restaurants, local transport, shops, entertainment), whereas indirect employment is created by the second round of tourism expenditure, particularly in the nontourist sectors of the economy (e.g., government, construction) that, although not directly involved with tourism, partially benefit from it (Seward & Spinrad, 1982).

Tourism multiplier: a measure of the total economic effects which result from tourist expenditure that is not lost through leakages: direct effects result from expenditures on goods and services, including tourism-generated exports and investment; secondary effects include indirect expenditure in which money remaining in the area is respent locally in successive rounds of business transactions (e.g., hoteliers purchase goods from local retailers or wholesalers) and induced expenditure in which additional personal income generates further consumer expenditure (e.g., hotel workers purchase goods and services with their wages) (B. H. Archer, 1982).

Tourist: A (stay-over) tourist is any person visiting, for at least 24 hours, a country other than that in which he or she usually resides, for any reason other than following an occupation remunerated from within the country visited (WTO, 1981, p. 23).

Tourist density ratio (TDR): attempts to show the density of (stay-over) tourists (number per km^2 in any time on average); its value is limited by the fact that tourist flows are seasonal and tourism activity tends to be concentrated in specific geographic areas (tourist zones) (CTO, 1992, p. 159). The TDR is calculated as:

$$\frac{\text{average length of stay} \times \text{number of stay-over tourists}}{365 \times \text{area in km}^2}$$

Because the TDR deals only with stay-over tourists, three further ratios are presented here. The excursionist density ratio (EDR) is calculated as:

$$\frac{\text{number of excursionists}}{365 \times \text{area in km}^2}$$

The cruise passenger density ratio (CPDR) is calculated as:

$$\frac{\text{number of cruise passengers}}{365 \times \text{area in km}^2}$$

Note that both excursionists and cruise passengers will tend to be even more spatially concentrated than stay-over tourists because of their short stays in a country. Finally, the visitor density ratio (VDR), the sum of the other three ratios, represents the average number of stay-over tourists, excursionists, and cruise passengers per km^2 and is calculated as:

$$\text{TDR} + \text{EDR} + \text{CPDR}$$

Tourist occupancy function (rooms) (Tof$_r$): whereas the number of tourist rooms per 1,000 local population is similar to Defert's Tf ("tourist function") (Defert, 1967), it is a crude measure of the importance of tourism within a regional economy in that it is ratio between the number of tourist beds and the resident population: $\text{Tf} = 100(N)/P$, where N is the number of tourist beds and P is the local population. Because it is only a surrogate for the actual importance of tourism in a region, it must be used with caution (S. Smith, 1989, p. 204). Statistics for the Caribbean, however, frequently include only tourist rooms and not tourist beds; therefore, Defert's Tf cannot be calculated for the region—but because in effect it measures the number of tourist beds per 1,000 local population, it is closely related to another common statistic, the number of tourist rooms per 1,000 local population. Both measure only the potential for tourists rather than the actual numbers; therefore, a new measure is presented here as a more accurate reflection of the actual importance of tourism in the regional economy, as related to the occupancy rate: TOf$_r$ ["tourist occupancy function (rooms)"], where TOf$_r$ is calculated as:

$$\frac{\text{number of rooms}}{1{,}000 \text{ local population}} \times \text{average annual tourist room occupancy rate}$$

Tourist occupancy function (beds) (TOf_b) would be used if data were available on beds rather than rooms.

Tourist penetration ratio (TPR): quantifies the average number of stay-over tourists, per 1,000 local inhabitants, in the country on any day on average. The TPR is calculated as:

$$\frac{\text{average length of stay} \times \text{number of stayover tourists}}{365 \times \text{mid-year population ('000s)}}$$

The value of this ratio is constrained by the facts that tourist flows are seasonal and cruise passengers and other excursionists are not included (CTO, 1992, p. 158). Therefore, additional penetration ratios are presented here. The excursionist penetration ration) (EPR) is calculated as:

$$\frac{\text{number of excursionists}}{365 \times \text{mid-year population ('000s)}}$$

The cruise passenger penetration ratio (CPPR) is calculated as:

$$\frac{\text{number of cruise passengers}}{365 \times \text{mid-year population ('000s)}}$$

Finally, the visitor penetration ratio (VPR), the sum of the other three penetration ratios, thus represents the average number of visitors, per 1,000 local inhabitants, in a country on any day on average; it is calculated as:

$$TPR + EPR + CPPR$$

Visitor expenditure: estimates refer to total expenditure by visitors and do not take into account primary leakages (CTO, 1990, p. 151). It is classified in conventional balance of payments accounts as a separate item under "invisibles" and is usually estimated from bank transfers, travel agency records, or tourist expenditure survey, but these are frequently "very rough" estimates (White & Walker, 1982).

Note: where appropriate, all data are presented in metric equivalents or United States dollars for purposes of comparability.

Bibliography

Acerenza, M. A. (1985). Planificación estratégica del turismo: Esquema metodológico. *Estudios Turisticos, 85,* 47–70.

Ackoff, R. (1979). The future of operational research is past. *Operational Research Journal, 30*(1), 93–104.

Albury, P. (1975). *The story of the Bahamas.* London: Macmillan.

Albury, P. (1984). *Paradise island story.* London: Macmillan.

Alexander, L. M. (1980). Centre and periphery: The case of island systems. In J. Gottmann (Ed.), *Centre and periphery: Spatial variations in politics* (pp. 135–149). Beverly Hills and London: Sage.

Amin, S. (1974). *Accumulation on a world scale.* New York: Monthly Review.

Anglo-American Caribbean Commission. (1945). *Caribbean tourist trade: A regional approach.* Washington, DC: Author.

Anonymous. (1908, March 2). Advertisement for the Cayman Hotels Company, Ltd., *The Caymanian, 1*(1), p. 4.

Anonymous. (1976). National report No. 33: Mexico. *International Tourism Quarterly, 3,* 25–38.

Anonymous. (1983, February 13). Troubled tourism. *The Nation.*

Anonymous. (1989a, October 12). Environment tourism. *Koudmen, 5,* 5.

Anonymous. (1989b, July 15). IDB sees little growth. *Barbados Daily Nation.*

Anonymous. (1989c, March 11). Third World tourism: Visitors are good for you. *The Economist,* 19–22.

Anonymous. (1989d, November 11). US mission for St. Lucia. *Barbados Advocate,* p. 2.

Anonymous. (1991a, August 8). Barbados, St. Lucia in common airline pickle. *Barbados Advocate,* p. 2.

Anonymous. (1991b, August 8). Farmers want to slash food bill. *Barbados Advocate,* p. 1.

Anonymous. (1991c, March 23). World travel and tourism survey. *The Economist,* 8.

Anonymous. (1992, December 5). Barbados to get funds for economic management from UNDP. *IPS.*

Anonymous. (1993a, June 23). Major resort for the Brac? *Newstar.*

Anonymous. (1993b, Spring). New Cayman Islands cruise tourism policy proposed. *Cayman Islands Department of Tourism Newsletter,* 1–3.

Anonymous. (1993c, July 10). Pindling to keynote Cuban conference. *Bahama Journal,* p. 2.

Anonymous. (1993d, July 10). CHA seeks to protect hotels, not destroy cruise lines. *Bahama Journal,* p. 2.

Anonymous. (1994, December 15). Tourism policy debated. *Caymanian Compass.*

Anonymous. (1995, January 31). World tourism up 3 per cent. *Globe and Mail.*

Archer, A. B. (1988). The impact of land-based sources of pollution on the marine environment. *International Association for Impact Assessment Proceedings* (pp. 264–279).

Workshop on Impact Assessment for International Development, May 31–June 4, 1987, Barbados.

Archer, B. H. (1981). *The tourist dollar: Its impact on incomes and employment in the Bahamas*. Report for Ministry of Tourism, Government of the Bahams.

Archer, B. H. (1982). The value of multipliers and their policy implications. *Tourism Management, 3*(4), 236–241.

Archer, E. D. (1985). Emerging environmental problems in a tourist zone: The case of Barbados. *Caribbean Geography, 2*(1), 45–55.

Arthur Young Ltd. (1988). *A study of the impact of tourism investment incentives in the Caribbean Region*. Report for the Caribbean Development Bank.

Arthur Young Ltd. (1989a). *Pigeon Island: Pirate stronghold, naval headquarters and whaling station, St. Lucia—final report*. Report for Caribbean Conservation Association.

Arthur Young Ltd. (1989b). *The Cabrits: Guardian of Dominica and Prince Rupert's refuge—final report*. Report for Caribbean Conservation Association.

Arthur Young Ltd. (1989c). *The historic military structures of the Garrison, Barbados—final report*. Report for Caribbean Conservation Association.

Arthur Young Ltd. (1989d). *The historic township of Speightstown, Barbados—final report*. Report for Caribbean Conservation Association.

Ascher, W., & Healy, R. (1990). *Natural resource policymaking in developing countries*. Durham, NC: Duke University Press.

Aspinall, R. J., & Momsen, J. H. (1987). *Small scale agriculture in Barbados* (Seminar Paper No. 52). Newcastle: Department of Geography, University of Newcastle.

Atkinson, M. M., & Chandler, M. A. (Eds.). (1983). *The politics of Canadian public policy*. Toronto: University of Toronto Press.

Barbados Board of Tourism (1991). *Thirty-first annual report 1989/90*. Bridgetown: Author.

Barbados: Relax the Bajan way [Brochure] (1991). *Tour & Travel News*, Special Supplements Division.

Barnett, T. (1988). *Sociology and development*. London: Hutchinson.

Barratt, P. (1989). *Grand Bahama* (2nd ed.). London: Macmillan.

Bassett, T. (1988). The political ecology of peasant-herder conflicts in northern Ivory Coast. *Annals of the Association of American Geographers, 78*(2), 453–472.

Baud-Bovy, M. (1985). *Bilan et avénir de la planification touristique* (Cahiers du Tourisme C-71). Aix-en-Provence: Centre des Hautes Etudes Touristiques, Université d'Aix-Marseille III.

Bauer, R. A., & Gergen, K. J. (1968). *The study of policy formation*. New York: Free Press.

Bell, J. H. (1993). Caribbean tourism in the year 2000. In D. J. Gayle and J. N. Goodrich (Eds.), *Tourism marketing and management in the Caribbean* (pp. 220–235). London: Routledge.

Beller, W. (Ed.). (1987). *Sustainable development and environmental management of small islands*. Springfield, VA: United States Department of Commerce.

Bélisle, F. J., Seward, S. B., & Spinrad, B. K. (1982). Summary and conclusions. In S. B. Seward & B. K. Spinrad (Eds.), *Tourism in the Caribbean: The economic impact* (pp. 151–163). Ottawa: International Development Research Centre.

Benjamin, A., Joseph, G., & Taffe, C. (1992). Agriculture—part of our Caymanian heritage. In C. Winker (Ed.), *Cayman Islands yearbook '92 & business directory* (pp. 286–292). George Town: Cayman Free Press.

Berger, F. (1992). *An analysis of the infrastructure of the Bahamas as it relates to tourism and its potential for future development*. Report by Hill & Knowlton for Goverment of the Commonwealth of the Bahamas.

Bernard Englehard & Associates, Inc. (1989). *Strategic study to assess the Cayman Islands position and potential in the vacation destination marketplace.* Report for Department of Tourism, Government of the Cayman Islands.

Besson, C., & Momsen, J. (Eds.). (1987). *Land and development in the Caribbean.* London: Macmillan.

Black, J. A., & Champion, D. J. (1976). *Methods and issues in social research.* New York: John Wiley & Sons.

Blenman, E. H. M. (1983). *Tourism in Barbados: The malaise at the start of the 80's.* Bordeaux: Les Antilles Aujourd'hui: Economie et géographie.

Blommestein, E. (1985). *Tourism and environment in Caribbean development: An overview of the Eastern Caribbean.* Port-of-Spain: United Nations Economic Commission on Latin America and the Caribbean.

Blommestein, E. (1988). Environment in Caribbean development: A regional view. In F. Edwards (Ed.), *Environmentally sound tourism in the Caribbean* (pp. 57–61). Calgary: Banff Centre School of Management and University of Calgary Press.

Blommestein, E. (1993). *Sustainable tourism in the Caribbean: Proposals for action.* Prepared for United Nations Economic Commission on Latin America and the Caribbean and Caribbean Development and Co-operation Commission, Port-of-Spain.

Blum, E. (1992, March 2). The popular out island experience. *Cruise Trade, Travel Trade, 24,* 26.

Blume, H. (1968). *The Caribbean Islands.* London: Longman.

Boo, E. (1990a). *Ecotourism: The potentials and pitfalls—volume 1.* Washington, DC: World Wildlife Fund.

Boo, E. (1990b). *Ecotourism: The potentials and pitfalls—volume 2—country case studies.* Washington, DC: World Wildlife Fund.

Boromé, J. A. (1972a). Spain and Dominica. In *Government of the Commonwealth of Dominica. 1972. Aspects of Dominican history* (pp. 67–79). Roseau: Government Printing Division.

Boromé, J. A. (1972b). The French and Dominica, 1699–1763. In *Government of the Commonwealth of Dominica. 1972. Aspects of Dominican history* (pp. 80–102). Roseau: Government Printing Division.

Bounds, J. H. (1972). Industrialization of the Bahamas. *Revista Geográfica, 77,* Dic.

Bounds, J. H. (1978). The Bahamas tourism industry: Past, present, and future. *Revista Geográfica,* Dic., pp. 167–211.

Bourguinon, F., & Anderson, C. (1992). *Adjustment and equity in developing countries: A new approach.* Paris: Organization for Economic Cooperation and Development (United Nations).

Bourne, L. (1989). *Institutional analysis in the area of natural resources management: The case of Dominica.* Castries: Organization of American States and Organization of Eastern Caribbean States—Natural Resources Management Project.

Boxhill, B. (1982). *Employment generated by tourism in the Caribbean region.* Christ Church: Caribbean Tourism Research and Development Centre.

Braddon, C. J. H. (1982). *British issues paper: Approaches to tourism planning abroad.* London: British Tourist Authority.

Bridenbaugh, C., & Bridenbaugh, R. (1972). *No peace beyond the line: The English in the Caribbean, 1624–1690.* New York: Oxford University Press.

Britton, R. A. (1977). Making tourism more supportive of small-state development: The case of St. Vincent. *Tourism Research, 4*(5), 268–278.

Britton, R. A. (1978). *International tourism and indigenous development objectives: A study with special reference to the West Indies.* Ann Arbor, MI: University Microfilms.

Britton, R. A. (1980). Tourism and economic vulnerability in small Pacific island states. In R. Shand (Ed.), *The island states of the Pacific and Indian Oceans: Anatomy of development.* Canberra: Development Studies Centre, Australian National University.

Britton, S. G. (1980). A conceptual model of tourism in a peripheral economy. In D. G. Pearce (Ed.), *Tourism in the South Pacific: The contribution of research to development and planning* (New Zealand Man and Biosphere Report No. 6) (pp. 1–12). Christchurch: Department of Geography, University of Canterbury.

Britton, S. G. (1982). The political economy of tourism in the Third World. *Tourism Research, 9*(3), 331–358.

Britton, S. G. (1987). Tourism in small developing countries: Development issues and research needs. In S. G. Britton & W. C. Clarke (Eds.), *Ambiguous alternative: Tourism in small developing countries* (pp. 167–194). Suva, Fiji: University of the South Pacific Press.

Britton, S. G., & Clarke, W. C. (Eds.). (1987). *Ambiguous alternative: Tourism in small developing countries.* Suva, Fiji: University of the South Pacific Press.

Britton, S. G., & Kissling, G. C. (1984). Aviation and development constraints in South Pacific microstates. In C. G. Kissling (Ed.), *Transport and communications for Pacific microstates: Issues in organisation and management* (pp. 79–86). Apia, Western Samoa: Institute of Pacific Studies, University of the South Pacific.

Bromley, R. D. F., & Bromley, R. (1982). *South American development: A geographical introduction.* Cambridge: Cambridge University Press.

Browlett, J. (1980). Development, the diffusionist paradigm and geography. *Progress in Human Geography, 4*(1), 57–80.

Brownlie, D. (1985). Strategic marketing concepts and models. *Journal of Marketing Management, 1*, 157–194.

Bryden, J. M. (1973). *Tourism and development: A case study of the Commonwealth Caribbean.* London: Cambridge University Press.

Butler, P. (1985). Conservation of natural resources in St. Lucia. In A. E. Lugo & S. Brown (Eds.), *Watershed Management in the Caribbean Proceedings* (pp. 111–117). 2nd Workshop of Caribbean Foresters, St. Vincent, March 19–23, 1984. Rio Piedro, San Juan, Puerto Rico: Institute for Tropical Forestry.

Butler, R. W. (1980). The concept of a tourist area cycle of evolution: Implications for management of resources. *Canadian Geographer, 24*(1), 5–12.

Butler, R. W. (1992). Alternative tourism: The thin edge of the wedge. In V. L. Smith & W. R. Eadington (Eds.), *Tourism alternatives: Potentials and problems in the development of tourism* (pp. 31–46). Philadelphia: University of Pennsylvania Press.

Butler, R. W. (1993). Tourism—an evolutionary process. In J. G. Nelson, R. Butler, & G. Wall (Eds.), *Tourism and sustainable development: Monitoring, planning, managing* (pp. 27–43). Publication Series No. 37. Waterloo: Department of Geography, University of Waterloo.

Buttle, F. (1986). *Hotel and food service marketing.* London: Holt.

Cambers, G. (1985). A major tourist development on the west coast of Barbados at Heywoods. In T. Geoghagan (Ed.), *Proceedings of the Caribbean Seminar on Environmental Impact Assessment* (pp. 267–269). St. Michael: Caribbean Conservation Association and Institute for Resource and Environmental Studies, Dalhousie University.

Campbell, D. G. (1974). *The Ephemeral Islands: A natural history of the Bahamas.* London: Macmillan.

Canford Associates Ltd. (1990). *St. Lucia: A market position for the 1990's and beyond accompanied by executional considerations for a competitive identity and promotion.* Report for St. Lucia Tourist Board.

Cardinall, A. W. (Anonymous). (1937) (n.d.). Grand Cayman—C. I. Y. & S. C. [Cayman Island Yachting and Sailing Club]—Cayman Islands, B. W. I. Pamphlet printed by Robert MacLehose and Co. Ltd., Glasgow.

Cardosa, F. H. (1972). Dependency and development in Latin America. *New Left Review,* *74*(4), 83–95.

Caribbean Conservation Association. (1991a). *Dominica: Country environmental profile.* St. Michael: Author.

Caribbean Conservation Association. (1991b). *St. Lucia: Country environmental profile.* St. Michael: Author.

Caribbean Development Bank. (1985, April–June). *Caribbean Development Bank News.*

Caribbean Development Bank. (1989a). *Annual economic report: Barbados 1988.* Bridgetown: Economics and Programming Department, Caribbean Development Bank.

Caribbean Development Bank. (1989c). *Annual economic report: Commonwealth of Dominica 1988.* Bridgetown: Economics and Programming Department, Caribbean Development Bank.

Caribbean Development Bank. (1989d). *Annual economic report: St. Lucia 1988.* Bridgetown: Economics and Programming Department, Caribbean Development Bank.

Caribbean Development Bank. (1992). *Annual economic report: Commonwealth of Dominica.* Bridgetown: Economics and Programming Department, Caribbean Development Bank.

Caribbean Tourism Association. (1960). *Review of members.* New York: Author.

Caribbean Tourism Organization. (1989). *Caribbean tourism statistical report 1988.* Christ Church: Author.

Caribbean Tourism Organization. (1990). *Caribbean tourism statistical report 1989.* Christ Church: Author.

Caribbean Tourism Organization. (1992). *Caribbean tourism statistical report 1991.* Christ Church: Author.

Caribbean Tourism Organization. (1993). Protecting the Caribbean Sea: Our heritage, our future. *Third Caribbean Conference on Ecotourism,* George Town, May 4–7.

Caribbean Tourism Organization. (1994). *Caribbean tourism statistical report 1993.* St. Michael: Author.

Caribbean Tourism Research and Development Centre. (1984). *Caribbean tourism statistical report 1984.* Christ Church: Author.

Caribbean Tourism Research and Development Centre. (1986). *Caribbean statistical report 1985.* Christ Church: Author.

Caribbean Tourism Research and Development Centre. (1987a). *Caribbean tourism statistical report 1986/87.* Christ Church: Author.

Caribbean Tourism Research and Development Centre. (1987b). *The contribution of tourism to economic growth and development in the caribbean.* Christ Church: Author.

Caribbean Tourism Research and Development Centre. (1988). *Caribbean tourism statistical report 1987.* Christ Church: Author.

Catlin, R. (1994, July 1). West Bay cruise moorings discussed at public meeting. *Caymanian Compass.*

Catlin, R. (1995, January 20). Report on dive tourism. *Caymanian Compass.*

Caulfield, M. D. (1978). Taxes, tourists and turtle men: Island dependence and the tax-haven business. In A. Idris-Soven, E. Idris-Soven, & M. K. Vaughan (Eds.), *The world as a company town: Multinational corporations and social change* (pp. 345–374). The Hague and Paris: Mouton.

Cayman Islands. (1914). *Report for 1913–1914.* Report of the Commissioner.

Cayman Islands Chamber of Commerce. (1991). *Chamber of Commerce directory '91.* George Town: Author.

Cazes, G. (1983). *Le tourisme international dans l'archipel Caraïbe*. Bordeaux: Les Antilles Aujourd'hui: Economie et géographie.

Central Intelligence Agency. (1994). *The world fact book 1994*. WorldWideWeb Site http://www.ic.gov/94fact/fb94toc/fb94toc.html.

Chadwick, R. A. (1981). Some notes on the geography of tourism. *Canadian Geographer, 25*(2), 191–197.

Chardon, J.-P. (1983). Bilan de la desserte aerienne des Antilles françaises. *Bulletin d'Information du CENADDOM, 70*(2), 10–20.

Checchi and Co. (1969). *A plan for managing the growth of tourism in the Commonwealth of the Bahamas*. Report for Ministry of Tourism, Government of the Commonwealth of the Bahamas.

Chernick, S. E. (1978). *The Commonwealth Caribbean: The integration experience*. Baltimore: Johns Hopkins University Press.

Christensen, K. (1982). Geography as a human science: A philosophic critique of the positivist-humanist split. In P. Gould & G. Olsson (Eds.), *A search for common ground* (pp. 37–57). London: Pion.

Christian, C. S. (1989). Cabrits National Parks Project, Dominica, W.I. In W. I. Knausenberger & C. B. Fleming (Eds.), *Proceedings of a Workshop on Coastal Protected Areas in the Lesser Antilles* (pp. 23–25). University of the Virgin Islands, St. Thomas, USVI, July 1986.

Clapp and Mayne, Inc. (1969). *A general diagnosis of the economy of the Bahamas Islands*. Report for Ministry of Development, Government of the Commonwealth of the Bahamas.

Clarke, J. (1994, October 15). You can get 'beached' on private islands. *Toronto Star*, p. J5.

Clarke, J. (1995, January 21). South African entrepreneur opens mega-resort in Bahamas. *Toronto Star*, p. H27.

Clavel, P. (1980). Centre/periphery and space: models of political geography. In J. Gottmann (Ed.), *Centre and periphery: Spatial variations in politics* (pp. 63–71). Beverly Hills and London: Sage.

Clawson, M., & Knetsch, J. (1963). *The economics of outdoor recreation*. Baltimore: Johns Hopkins University Press.

Cohen, E. (1972). Towards a sociology of international tourism. *Social Research, 39*, 164–182.

Cohen, E. (1979). Rethinking the sociology of tourism. *Annals of Tourism Research, 6*(1), 18–35.

Colonial Office. (1939). *Annual report on the Cayman Islands (Dependency of Jamaica) for the year 1940*. London: Her/His Majesty's Stationery Office.

Colonial Office. (1948). *Annual report on the Cayman Islands (Dependency of Jamaica) for the year 1947*. London: Her/His Majesty's Stationery Office.

Colonial Office. (1953). *Reports on the Cayman Islands (Dependency of Jamaica) for the years 1951 & 1952*. London: Her/His Majesty's Stationery Office.

Colonial Office. (1955). *Reports on the Cayman Islands (Dependency of Jamaica) for the years 1953 & 1954*. London: Her/His Majesty's Stationery Office.

Colonial Office. (1957). *Reports on the Cayman Islands (Dependency of Jamaica) for the years 1955 & 1956*. London: Her/His Majesty's Stationery Office.

Colonial Office. (1961). *Reports on the Cayman Islands for the years 1959 & 1960*. London: Her/His Majesty's Stationery Office.

Colonial Office. (1972). *Reports on the Cayman Islands for the years 1966 to 1970*. London: Her/His Majesty's Stationery Office.

Colonial Office. (1973). *Report on the Cayman Islands for the year 1971*. London: Her/His Majesty's Stationery Office.

Colonial Reports. (1898). *Bahamas: Annual report for 1897, No. 238.* London: Her/His Majesty's Stationery Office.

Colonial Reports. (1899). *Bahamas: Annual report for 1898, No. 277.* London: Her/His Majesty's Stationery Office.

Colonial Reports. (1910). *Bahamas: Annual report for 1909–10, No. 650.* London: Her/His Majesty's Stationery Office.

Colonial Reports. (1911). *Bahamas: Annual report for 1910–11, No. 684.* London: Her/His Majesty's Stationery Office.

Colonial Reports. (1912). *Bahamas: Annual report for 1911–12, No. 741.* London: Her/His Majesty's Stationery Office.

Colonial Reports. (1914). *Bahamas: Annual report for 1913–14, No. 809.* London: Her/His Majesty's Stationery Office.

Colonial Reports. (1917). *Bahamas: Annual report for 1916–17, No. 932.* London: Her/His Majesty's Stationery Office.

Colonial Reports. (1918). *Bahamas: Annual report for 1917–18, No. 978.* London: Her/His Majesty's Stationery Office.

Colonial Reports. (1924). *Bahamas: Annual report for 1923–24, No. 1202.* London: Her/His Majesty's Stationery Office.

Colonial Reports. (1926). *Bahamas: Annual report for 1925, No. 1285.* London: Her/His Majesty's Stationery Office.

Colonial Reports. (1927). *Bahamas: Annual report for 1926, No.1330.* London: Her/His Majesty's Stationery Office.

Colonial Reports. (1939). *Annual report on the social and economic progress of the people of the Bahamas, 1938, No. 1901.* London: Her/His Majesty's Stationery Office.

Colonial Reports. (1952). *Report on the Bahamas for the years 1950 and 1951.* London: Her/His Majesty's Stationery Office.

Colonial Reports. (1957). *Report on the Bahamas for the years 1954 and 1955.* London: Her/His Majesty's Stationery Office.

Connell, J. (1988). *Sovereignty & survival: Island microstates in the Third World* (Research Monograph No. 3). Sydney: Department of Geography, University of Sydney.

Cooper, C. P. (1993). The life cycle concept and tourism. In P. Johnson & B. Thomas (Eds.), *Choice and demand in tourism* (pp. 145–160). London: Mansell.

Cooper, C. P., & Jackson, S. (1989). Destination life cycle: The Isle of Man case study. *Annals of Tourism Research, 16*(3), 377–398.

Corbridge, S. (1986). *Capitalist world development: A critique of radical development geography.* Totawa, NJ: Rowan & Littlefield.

Corbridge, S. (1989a). Marxism, post-Marxism, and the geography of development. In R. Peet & N. Thrift (Eds.), *New models in geography: The political economy perspective—volume I* (pp. 224–254). London: Unwin Hyman.

Corbridge, S. (1989b). Debt, the nation-state and theories of the world economy. In D. Gregory & R. Walford (Eds.), *Horizons in human geography* (pp. 341–360). London: Macmillan.

Cousty, S.-A. (1984). *Les liaisons aeriennes France-Réunion et leur rôle dans le développement économique de l'île* (Mémoire pour le DESS "Transports Ariens"). Faculté de Droit et de Science Politique, Université d'Aix-Marseille III, Aix-en-Provence.

Cox, W. (1982). The manufacturing sector in the economy of Barbados, 1946–1980. In R. D. Worrell (Ed.), *The economoy of Barbados, 1946–1980.* Oxford: Basil Blackwell.

Crandall, L. (1987). The social impact of tourism on developing regions and its measurement. In J. R. B. Ritchie & R. Goeldner (Eds.), *Travel, tourism, and hospitality research* (pp. 373–383). New York: John Wiley & Sons.

Craton, M. (1986). *A history of the Bahamas* (3rd ed.). Waterloo: San Salvador Press.

Craton, M. (1987). White law and black custom: The evolution of Bahamian land tenures. In C. Besson & J. Momsen (Eds.), *Land and development in the Caribbean* (pp. 88–114). London: Macmillan.

Curtin, V., & Poon, A. (1988). *Tourist accommodation in the Caribbean.* Christ Church: Caribbean Tourism Research and Development Centre.

Daly, H. (1984). *The steady-state economy: Alternative to growthmania.* The Other Economic Summit, London.

Dames & Moore Ltd. (1981). *Tourism development programme final report: Volume I.* Report for Ministry of Tourism, Government of the Commonwealth of the Bahamas.

D'Amore, L. J., & Jafari, J. (Eds). (1988). *Tourism—a vital force for peace.* Montreal: First Global Conference, L. J. D'Amore and Associates Ltd.

Dann, G. (1992). *Socio-cultural impacts of tourism in Saint Lucia* [draft] (Studies in Tourism No. 3). Port-of-Spain, Trinidad: United Nations Economic Commission on Latin America and the Caribbean.

Dann, G., & Cohen, E. (1991). Sociology and tourism. *Annals of Tourism Research, 18*(1), 153–169.

Dann, G., Nash, D., & Pearce, P. (1988). Methodology in tourism research. *Annals of Tourism Research, 15*(1), 1–28.

d'Auvergne, A. (1989). St. Lucia's development strategy. *Saint Lucia: 10th Independence Anniversary Souvenir Magazine*, pp. 17–18.

Davidson, T. L. (1994). What are travel and tourism: Are they really an industry? In W. F. Theobald (Ed.), *Global tourism: The next decade* (pp. 20–26). Oxford: Butterworth-Heinemann.

Day, G. S. (1981). The product life cycle: Analysis and applications issues. *Journal of Marketing, 45*(1), 60–67.

Dayton-Keenan, Inc. (1973). *Study of the hotel industry in the Bahamas.* Report for Ministry of Tourism, Government of the Commonwealth of the Bahamas.

de Albuquerque, K., & McElroy, J. (1986). Bahamian labor migration, 1901–1963. *New West Indian Guide, 60*(3/4), 167–203.

de Albuquerque, K., & McElroy, J. (1992). Caribbean small-island tourism styles and sustainable strategies. *Environmental Management, 16*(5), 619–632.

Debbage, K. G. (1990). Oligopoly and the resort cycle: Tourism evolution on Paradise Island, Bahamas. *Annals of Tourism Research, 17*(4), 513–527.

Debbage, K. G. (1991). Spatial behavior in a Bahamian resort. *Annals of Tourism Research, 18*(2), 251–268.

Defert, P. (1967). *Les taux de fonction touristique: Mise au point et critique* (Cahiers du Tourisme, C-13). Aix-en-Provence: Centre des Hautes Etudes Touristiques, Université d'Aix-Marseille III.

de Kadt, E. (1979). The encounter: Changing values and attitudes. In E. de Kadt (Ed.), *Tourism: Passport to development?* (pp. 50–67). New York: Oxford University Press.

de Kadt, E. (1992). Making the alternative sustainable: Lessons from development for tourism. In V. L. Smith & R. Eadington (Eds.), *Tourism alternatives: Potentials and problems in the development of tourism* (pp. 47–75). Philadelphia: University of Pennsylvania Press.

DeLuca, M. (1993, May/June). Regional airlines brace for more bad times ahead. *Caribbean Tourism Today*, pp. 16–23.

Demas, W. G. (1965). *The economics of development in small countries with special reference to the Caribbean.* Montreal: McGill University.

Dernoi, L. (1981). Alternative tourism—towards a new style in north–south relations. *Tourism Management, 2*(4), 253–264.

Devaux, R. J. (1975). *St. Lucia historic sites.* Castries: St. Lucia National Trust.

Devaux, R. J. (1984, December). Who discovered St. Lucia? *The Voice of St. Lucia,* 6.

Devaux, R. J. (1987). *Conservation of St. Lucia's national and cultural heritage.* Unpublished manuscript, St. Lucia National Trust.

Devaux, R. J. (1992). Why Qualibou? *Qualibou (Newsletter of the Soufriere Regional Development Foundation), 1*, 1–2.

Dhalla, N. K., & Yuspeh, S. (1976). Forget the product life cycle concept. *Harvard Business Review, 54*, 102–110.

Dixon, J., & Sherman, P. (1990). *Economics of protected areas: A new look at benefits and costs.* Washington, DC: Island Press.

Dodge, S. (1983). *Abaco: The history of an out island and its cays* (pp. 110–131). Miami: Tropic Isle.

Doern, G. B., & Aucoin, P. (1971). *The structure of policy-making in Canada.* Toronto: University of Toronto Press.

Dominica Port Authority. (1989). *Plan 2000: Woodbridge Bay—Cabrits.* Report by Novaport Ltd.

Dominica Tourist Board. (1982). *Recommendations for tourism policies.* Roseau: Government of the Commonwealth of Dominica.

Dominica Tourist Board. (1987). *Tourism—a country profile.* Roseau: Government of the Commonwealth of Dominica.

Dommen, E. C., & Hein, P. L. (1985). Foreign trade in goods and services: The dominant activity of small island economies. In E. C. Dommen & P. L. Hein (Eds.), *States, microstates and islands* (pp. 152–184). London: Croom Helm.

Dommen, E. C., & Lebalé, N. (1986). Caractéristiques des exportations de services des pays insulaires. *Interoceanic Workshop on Sustainable Development and Environmental Management of Small Islands,* Nov. 3–7, San Juan, Puerto Rico.

Dos Santos, T. (1972). Dependence and the international system. In J. Cockcroft, A. G. Frank, & D. L. Johnson (Eds.), *Dependence and underdevelopment: Latin America's political economy* (pp. 71–82). New York: Anchor.

Doyle, P. (1976). The realities of the product life cycle. *Quarterly Review of Marketing, 1*(1), 1–6.

Doyle, L., & Gough, I. (1991). *A theory of human need.* London: Macmillan.

Duncan, D. D. (1948, August). Capturing giant turtles in the Caribbean. *National Geographic,* 177–190.

Duncan, J. S. (1985). Individual action and political power: A structuration perspective. In R. J. Johnston (Ed.), *The future of geography* (pp. 174–189). London: Methuen.

Dunn, R. S. (1972). *Sugar and slaves: The rise of the planter class in the English West Indies, 1624–1713.* Chapel Hill: University of North Carolina Press.

Dunn, W. N. (1981). *Public policy analysis: An introduction.* Englewood Cliffs, NJ: Prentice-Hall.

Dunning, J. H., & MacQueen, M. (1982). *Transnational corporations in international tourism.* New York: Centre on Transnational Corporations, United Nations.

Eastern Caribbean Natural Area Management Programme. (1984). *Cabrits 2000 Report.* Report for Caribbean Conservation Association.

Economic Consultants Ltd. (1979). *Saint Lucia: A tourism development study—summary report.* Report for Government of St. Lucia and Commonwealth Fund for Technical Cooperation.

Economist Intelligence Unit. (1985). *Annual supplement: Trinidad and Tobago, Guyana, Barbados, Windward and Leeward Islands.* London: Author.

Edgell, D. L. (1987). The formulation of tourism policy—a managerial framework. In J. R.

B. Ritchie & C. R. Goeldner (Eds.), *Travel, tourism, and hospitality research* (pp. 23–33). New York: John Wiley & Sons.

Edwards, F. (Ed.). (1988). *Environmentally sound tourism in the Caribbean.* Calgary: Banff Centre School of Management and University of Calgary Press.

Elliott, M. (1988, August 6). The Caribbean: Columbus's islands. *The Economist,* 3–18.

Eneas, W. J. G. (1993). The performance of the agricultural sector during the 70's and 80's. In *20 years of independence* (pp. 9–12). Nassau: The Bahama Journal.

England, G. A. (1928, July 21). Grand Cayman. *Saturday Evening Post.*

English, E. P. (1986). *The great escape? An examination of north–south tourism.* Ottawa: North–South Institute.

Environmental Commission of St. Lucia. (1987). *Short run gain—long run pain.* Report of Environmental Retreat held for Community Leaders, Marisule, Oct. 14–15, National Research and Development Foundation.

Erisman, H. M. (1983). Tourism and cultural dependency in the West Indies. *Annals of Tourism Research, 10*(3), 337–361.

European Economic Community. (1990). *The Courier, volume 122* (pp. 50–86). Brussels: Author.

Evans, P. (1986). Dominica multiple land use project. *Ambio, 15*(2), 82–89.

Farrell, B. H. (1986). Cooperative tourism and the coastal zone. *Coastal Zone Management Journal, 14*(1,2), 113–130.

Feldman, E. J. (1978). Comparative public policy: Field or method? *Comparative Politics, 10,* 287–305.

Fish, G. (1989). The Bahamas: The cost of fragmentation. *Caribbean Geography, 2*(4), 241–250.

Francis, A. (1993). Tourism product development and marketing in St. Lucia. In D. J. Gayle & J. N. Goodrich (Eds.), *Tourism marketing and management in the Caribbean* (pp. 69–77). London: Routledge.

Francis, C. Y. (1985). The offshore banking sector in the Bahamas. *Social and Economic Studies, 34,* 91–109.

Frank, A. G. (1972). *Lumpen-bourgeoisie and lumpen-development: Dependence, class and politics in Latin America.* New York: Monthly Review Press.

Frank, A. G. (1981). The development of underdevelopment. In M. Smith, R. Little, & M. Schackleton (Eds.), *Perspectives on world politics* (pp. 291–300). London: Croom Helm.

Franke, R., & Chasin, B. (1980). *Seeds of famine.* Montclair, NJ: Allenheld, Osmun.

Galloway, J. H. (1989). *The sugar-cane industry: An historical geography from its origins to 1914.* Cambridge: Cambridge University Press.

Gayle, D. J., & Goodrich, J. N. (1993). Caribbean tourism marketing, management and development strategies. In D. J. Gayle & J. N. Goodrich (Eds.), *Tourism marketing and management in the Caribbean* (pp. 1–19). London: Routledge.

Geoghagan, T. (Ed.). (1985). *Proceedings of Caribbean Seminar on Environmental Impact Assessment.* St. Michael: Caribbean Conservation Association and Institute for Resource and Environmental Studies, Dalhousie University.

Gerrard, A. (1956). *The Cayman Islands: Information for prospective visitors* [Pamphlet]. George Town: Commissioners Office.

Getz, D. (1986a). Models in tourism planning: Towards integration of theory and practice. *Tourism Management, March,* 21–32.

Getz, D. (1986b). Tourism and population change: Long-term impacts of tourism in the Badenoch and Strathspey district of the Scottish highlands. *Scottish Geographical Magazine, 102*(2), 113–126.

Getz, D. (1987). *Tourism planning and research traditions, models and futures.* Australian Travel Research Workshop, 5–6 November, Bunbury.

Giersch, W. (1987). *Tourism product and marketing concept for the Commonwealth of Dominica.* Report for Government of the Commonwealth of Dominica.

Giglioli, M. E. C. (1976). The boom years, environmental deterioration, planning and administration. In *Cayman Islands natural resources study, part II.* George Town: Cayman Islands Natural Resources Laboratory.

Gill, M. (1984). Women, work and development: Barbados, 1946–1970. In M. Gill & J. Massiah (Eds.), *Women in the Caribbean project volume 6.* Bridgetown: Bureau of Women's Affairs, Ministry of Labour and Community Development, Government of Barbados.

Gilles, E. (Ed.). (1980). *The big picture: World travel trends and markets.* New York: ASTA News.

Girvan, N. P., & Simmons, D. A. (1988). Synthesis of workshop findings. In F. Edwards (Ed.), *Environmentally sound tourism in the Caribbean* (pp. 131–143). Calgary: Banff Centre School of Management and University of Calgary Press.

Girvan, N. P., & Simmons, D. A. (Eds.). (1991). *Caribbean ecology and economics.* St. Michael: Caribbean Conservation Association.

Gleason, B. (1991, December). *Dominica: The diving capital of the Eastern Caribbean. Skin Diver.*

Goodland, R., & Ledec, G. (1987). Neoclassical economies and principles of sustainable development. *Ecological Modelling, 38,* 19–46.

Gosnell, M. (1976). The island dilemma. *International Wildlife, 6*(5), 24–35.

Gould, P. (1985a). *The geographer at work.* London: Routledge and Kegan Paul.

Gould, P. (1985b). Will geographic self-reflection make you blind? In R. J. Johnston (Ed.), *The future of geography* (pp. 276–290). London: Methuen.

Goulet, G. (1968). On the goals of development. *Cross Currents, 18,* 387–405.

Goulet, R. (1993). *Society, policy and policy analysis—review and critique of a theoretical debate?* Unpublished paper, York University, North York.

Government of Barbados. (1970). *Barbados physical development plan.* Bridgetown: Author.

Government of Barbados. (1979). *National development plan 1979–1983.* Bridgetown: Author.

Government of Barbados. (1983). *National development plan 1983–1988.* Bridgetown: Author.

Government of Barbados. (1984). *A report on the problems facing the Barbados tourism industry with proposals for corrective action with special reference to the hotel sector.* Report by Joint Committee of Major Institutional Creditors, Related Government Departments and Institutions, and Representatives of the Barbados Hotel Association.

Government of Barbados. (1988a). *Barbados economic report 1988.* Bridgetown: Economic Affairs Division.

Government of Barbados. (1988b). *Barbados national development plan 1988–1993.* Bridgetown: Author.

Government of Barbados. (1988c). *Barbados physical development plan (amended 1986).* Bridgetown: Town and Country Planning Office, Ministry of Finance.

Government of the Cayman Islands. (n.d.). *Welcome to Cayman!! Things every visitor should know about our conservation laws and our marine parks* [Pamphlet]. Portfolio for Education, Environment, Recreation, and Culture.

Government of the Cayman Islands. (1971). *You and your government.* George Town: Government Information Service.

Government of the Cayman Islands. (1973a). *Annual report.* George Town: Department of Tourism.

Government of the Cayman Islands. (1973b). *Draft concept development plan.* Prepared for Government of the Cayman Islands and United Nations Regional Planning Team.

Government of the Cayman Islands. (1975a). *Annual report.* George Town: Department of Tourism.

Government of the Cayman Islands. (1975b). *Development plan for the Cayman Islands.* George Town: Author.

Government of the Cayman Islands. (1977). *The development plan 1977.* George Town: Central Planning Authority and Department of Planning.

Government of the Cayman Islands. (1979). *Annual report.* George Town: Department of Tourism.

Government of the Cayman Islands. (1980). *Annual report.* George Town: Department of Tourism.

Government of the Cayman Islands. (1987). *The Cayman Islands development plan 1988–1992.* George Town: Economic Development Unit.

Government of the Cayman Islands. (1990a). *Real estate and development in the Cayman Islands* [Pamphlet].

Government of the Cayman Islands. (1990b). *The economic development of the Cayman Islands* [Pamphlet].

Government of the Cayman Islands. (1991a). *Airport exit survey.* Unpublished survey, Department of Tourism.

Government of the Cayman Islands. (1991b). *Living in the Cayman Islands* [Pamphlet].

Government of the Cayman Islands. (1992a). *Annual report 1991.* George Town: Central Planning Authority and Department of Planning.

Government of the Cayman Islands. (1992b). *Cayman Islands annual report 1991.* George Town: Author.

Government of the Cayman Islands. (1992c). *1991 Cayman Islands compendium of statistics.* George Town: Government Statistics Office.

Government of the Cayman Islands. (1992d). *A ten year tourism development plan (1992–2002).* George Town: Portfolio of Tourism, Aviation and Trade (Coopers & Lybrand Consulting, New York).

Government of the Cayman Islands. (1992e). *Islands are special places!!! Cayman Islands development plan review* [Pamphlet]. George Town: Central Planning Authority and Department of Planning.

Government of the Cayman Islands. (1994). *Cayman Islands tourism management policy 1995–1999.* George Town: Department of Tourism.

Government of the Commonwealth of the Bahamas. (1979). *National accounts of the Bahamas.* Nassau: Department of Statistics.

Government of the Commonwealth of the Bahamas. (1983). *Potential impact of proposed hotel developments: New Providence 1983–1987.* Report by Ministry of Tourism.

Government of the Commonwealth of the Bahamas. (1984). *Bahamas tourism marketing strategy and development plan.* Nassau: Ministry of Tourism.

Government of the Commonwealth of the Bahamas. (1987). *Tourism statistics.* Nassau: Ministry of Tourism.

Government of the Commonwealth of the Bahamas. (1988a). *Statistical abstract 1968–1988.* Nassau: Ministry of Finance.

Government of the Commonwealth of the Bahamas. (1988b). *Tourism statistics 1987.* Nassau, Bahamas: Statistics Unit, Ministry of Tourism.

Government of the Commonwealth of the Bahamas. (1988c). *The history of tourism in the Bahamas* [Pamphlet]. Ministry of Tourism.

Government of the Commonwealth of the Bahamas. (1991). *Census 1990: Preliminary results.* Nassau: Census Office.

Government of the Commonwealth of the Bahamas. (1992a). *Selected economic and social indicators*. Nassau: Ministry of Finance.

Government of the Commonwealth of the Bahamas. (1992b). *Tourism statistics 1991*. Nassau: Ministry of Tourism.

Government of the Commonwealth of the Bahamas. (1993). *Tourism in the Bahamas: 1992 in review*. Nassau: Ministry of Tourism.

Government of the Commonwealth of Dominica. (1976). *Dominica national structure plan 1976–1990: Volume 1: Main report*. Roseau: Tropical Printers.

Government of the Commonwealth of Dominica. (1985). *National structure plan*. Roseau: Author.

Government of the Commonwealth of Dominica. (1987). *Tourism policy*. Roseau: Ministry of Agriculture, Trade, Industry and Tourism.

Government of the Commonwealth of Dominica. (1988). *Statistical digest: Ten years of growth, 1978–1988*. Roseau: Ministry of Finance.

Government of the Commonwealth of Dominica. (1992). *Tourism statistics 1991*. Roseau: Ministry of Finance.

Government of St. Lucia. (1977). *St. Lucia national plan—development strategy*. Castries: Author.

Government of St. Lucia. (1988). *Prix produit—review 1988*. Castries: Ministry of Agriculture.

Government of St. Lucia. (1989). *National tourism policy*. Unpublished draft, Ministry of Industry, Trade and Tourism.

Government of St. Lucia. (1990). *Economic and social review 1989*. Castries: Ministry of Finance, Statistics and Negotiating.

Government of St. Lucia. (1991). *Saint Lucia fact sheet*. A profile of the Trade Information Centre, Ministry of Trade, Industry and Tourism.

Government of St. Lucia. (1994). *Medium term economic strategy paper (1993–1996)*. Castries: Central Planning Unit.

Graycar, A. (1979). *Welfare politics in Australia*. Melbourne: Macmillan.

Graefe, A. R., Kuss, R. F., & Vaske, J. J. (1990a). *Visitor impact management: Volume one*. Washington, DC: National Parks and Conservation Association.

Graefe, A. R., Kuss, R. F., & Vaske, J. J. (1990b). *Visitor impact management: Volume two—the planning framework*. Washington, DC: National Parks and Conservation Association.

Great Britain Ministry of Overseas Development. (1966). *Tripartite economic survey*. London: Her/His Majesty's Stationery Office.

Green, R. H. (1987). Toward planning tourism in African countries. In J. R. B. Ritchie & C. R. Goeldner (Eds.), *Travel, tourism and hospitality research* (pp. 79–110). New York: John Wiley & Sons.

Gregoire, C., & Kanem, N. (1989). The Caribs of Dominica: Land rights and ethnic consciousness. *Cultural Survival Quarterly, 13*(2), 52–55.

Grossman, L. S. (1993). The political ecology of banana exports and local food production in St. Vincent, Eastern Caribbean. *Annals of the Association of American Geographers, 83*(2), 347–367.

Gunn, C. A. (1979). *Tourism planning*. New York: Crane Rusak.

Hahn, N., Bellah, R. N., Rabinow, P., & Sullivan, W. M. (1983). *Social science as moral inquiry*. New York: Columbia University Press.

Hakluyt, R. (Ed.). (1904). *Hakluyt's voyages: Volume IX*. Glasgow: Maclehose.

Hall, C. (1989). Rethinking the Prime Minister's dilemma. *Annals of Tourism Research, 16*(3), 399–406.

Hall, G. (1995, April 22). Atlantis rises with a big splash. *Toronto Star*.

Hall, P. (1970). *Theory and practice of regional planning*. London: Pemberton.

Hannan, M. T., & Freeman, J. (1977). The population ecology of organizations. *American Journal of Sociology, 82*(5), 929–964.

Harrigan, N. (1974). The legacy of Caribbean history and tourism. *Annals of Tourism Research, 2*(1), 13–25.

Hawkins, D. E. (1994). Ecotourism: Opportunities for developing countries. In W. F. Theobald (Ed.), *Global tourism: The next decade*. Oxford: Butterworth-Heinmann.

Haynes, C., & Holder, C. (1989). Monetary and fiscal policy in Barbados, 1970–1985. In R. D. Worrell & C. Bourne (Eds.), *Economic adjustment policies for small nations: Theory and experience in the English-speaking Caribbean* (pp. 89–104). New York: Praeger.

Haywood, K. M. (1986). Can the tourist area life cycle be made operational? *Tourism Management, 7*, 154–167.

Haywood, K. M. (1990). *Resort cycles: A commentary*. Association of American Geographers, Toronto, April 20–22.

Healy, R. G. (1992). *The role of tourism in sustainable development*. IVth World Congress on National Parks and Protected Areas, Caracas, February 10–12.

Heintz, H., & Jenkins-Smith, H. (1988). Advocacy coalitions and the practice of policy analysis. *Policy Sciences, 21*(2), 263–277.

Hintjens, H. M., & Newitt, M. D. D. (Eds.). (1992). *The political economy of small tropical islands: The importance of being small*. Exeter: University of Exeter Press.

Hirschman, A. (1976). Policy-making and policy analysis in Latin America: A return journey. *Policy Sciences, 6*, 385–402.

Hoivik, T., & Heiberg, T. (1980). Centre-periphery: Tourism and social reliance. *International Social Science Journal, 32*, 69–98.

Holder, J. S. (1988). The pattern and impact of tourism on the environment of the Caribbean. In F. Edwards (Ed.), *Environmentally sound tourism in the Caribbean* (pp. 7–19). Calgary: Banff Centre School of Management and University of Calgary Press.

Holder, J. S. (1993). The Caribbean Tourism Organization in historical perspective. In D. J. Gayle & J. N. Goodrich (Eds.), *Tourism marketing and management in the Caribbean* (pp. 20–27). London: Routledge.

Honychurch, L. (1984). *The Dominica story: A history of the island*. Roseau: Dominica Institute.

Honychurch, L. (1988). *Our island culture*. Bridgetown: Letchworth.

Honychurch, L. (1991). *Dominica: Isle of adventure*. London: Macmillan.

Hovinen, G. R. (1981). A tourist cycle in Lancaster County. *Canadian Geographer, 25*(2), 283–286.

Hudson, B. J. (1986). Landscape as a resource for national development: A Caribbean view. *Geography*, 116–121.

Hudson, L., Renard, Y., & Romulus, G. (1992). *A system of protected areas for St. Lucia*. Castries: St. Lucia National Trust.

Huetz de Lemps, A. (Ed.). (1989). *Iles et tourisme en milieux tropical et subtropical* (Collection "Iles et Archipels" No. 10). Talence: Société pour l'Etude, la Protection et l'Aménagement de la Nature dans les Régions Inter-Tropicales, Le Centre d'Etudes de Géographie Tropicale du Centre Nationale de Recherches Scientifique de France et Le Centre Nationale de Recherches Scientifique de France et l'Université de Bordeaux III.

Hunte, W. (1985). Marine resources of the Caribbean. In T. Geoghagan (Ed.), *Proceedings of Caribbean Seminar on Environmental Impact Assessment* (pp. 38–41). St. Michael: Caribbean Conservation Association and Institute for Resource and Environmental Studies, Dalhousie University.

Hurlston, L.-A. (1995). *Exploring the viability of ecotourism in the Cayman Islands as a tool for a policy of sustainable development.* Unpublished BES thesis, Faculty of Environmental Studies, York University, North York.

Inskeep, E. (1988). Tourism planning: An emerging specialization. *APA Journal, Summer,* 360–372.

Inter-American Development Bank. (1987). *Annual statistics digest 1987.* Washington, DC: Author.

Inter-American Development Bank. (1989a). *April/May 1989 report.* Washington, DC: Author.

Inter-American Development Bank. (1989b). *Economic and social progress in Latin America: 1989 report.* Washington, DC: Author.

International Union of Official Travel Organizations. (1968). *The economic review of world tourism.* Geneva: Author.

International Union of Official Travel Organizations. (1976). *The impact of international tourism on the economic development of the developing countries.* Geneva: World Trade Organization.

Isaac, S., & Michael, W. B. (1971). *Handbook in research and evaluation.* San Diego: Edits Publishers.

Island Resources Foundation and Anguilla Archaeological and Historical Society. (1993). *Environmental profile—part I: A resource management framework.* Prepared for Government of Anguilla.

Jackson, I. (1986). Annex IV: Soufriere Town: Recommendations for the management of the immediate coastal zone area. In *Soufriere tourism development programme: First phase projects.* Washington, DC: Organization of American States.

Jacobs, H. (1962). What future for the Cayman Islands? *New Commonwealth, 40,* 16.

Jainarain, I. (1976). *Trade and underdevelopment: A study of the small Caribbean countries and large multinational corporations.* Georgetown: Institute of Development Studies, University of Guyana.

James, A. A. (1985). *Flora and fauna of the Cabrits Peninsula.* Roseau: Forestry and Wildlife Division, Ministry of Agriculture, Government of the Commonwealth of Dominica.

James, A. A. (1988). *The Lake District of Dominica.* Roseau: Forestry and Wildlife Division, Ministry of Agriculture, Government of the Commonwealth of Dominica.

Jemiolo, J. J., & Conway, D. (1991). Tourism, air service provision and patterns of Caribbean airline offer. *Social and Economic Studies, 40*(2), 1–43.

Jenkins, C. L., & Henry, B. M. (1982). Government involvement in tourism in developing countries. *Tourism Research, 9*(3), 499–521.

Jennings, B. (1983). Interpretive social science and policy analysis. In. D. Callahan & B. Jennings (Eds.), *Ethics, the social sciences and policy analysis* (pp. 3–35). New York: Plenum.

Johnston, R. J. (Ed.). (1983). *Philosophy and human geography.* London: Edward Arnold.

Johnston, R. J. (Ed.). (1985). *The future of geography.* London: Methuen.

Jones, P., & Lockwood, A. (1990). *Productivity and the product life cycle in hospitality firms.* Contemporary Hospitality Management Conference, Bournemouth.

Kaiser, C., Jr., & Helber, L. E. (1978). *Tourism: Planning and development.* Boston: CBI.

Kastarlak, B. (1975). *Tourism and its development potential in Dominica.* Castries: United Nations Development Program.

Keller, C. P. (1987). Stages of peripheral tourism development—Canada's Northwest Territories. *Tourism Management, 8*(1), 20–32.

Kerr, J. (1985). Bahama's out island beach party. *Cruise Travel,* 53–55.

Kersell, J. E. (1987). Government administration in a small microstate: Developing the Cayman Islands. *Public Administration and Development, 7,* 95–107.

King, J. M. C. (1984). The air traffic market and tourism: Some thoughts on the South Pacific. In C. G. Kissling (Ed.), *Transport and communications for Pacific microstates: Issues in organisation and management* (pp. 113–123). Apia, Western Samoa: Institute of Pacific Studies, University of the South Pacific.

Kissling, C. G. (Ed.). (1984). *Transport and communications for Pacific microstates: Issues in organisation and management.* Apia, Western Samoa: Institute of Pacific Studies, University of the South Pacific.

Kjekshus, H. (1977). *Ecology control and economic development in East Africa: The case of Tanganyika.* Berkeley: University of California Press.

Kjellstrom, S. B. (1974). *The impact of tourism on economic development in Morocco.* Ann Arbor: Michigan University Microfilms.

Knausenberger, W. I., & Fleming, C. B. (Eds.). (1989). *Proceedings of the Workshop on Coastal Protected Areas in the Lesser Antilles,* July 1986, University of the Virgin Islands, St. Thomas, USVI.

Knight, F. W. (1990). *The Caribbean: The genesis of a fragmented nationalism* (2nd ed.). New York: Oxford University Press.

Kotler, P. (1980). *Principles of marketing* (3rd ed.). Englewood Cliffs, NJ: Prentice-Hall.

Krippendorf, J. (1982). Towards new tourism policies—the importance of environmental and sociocultural factors. *Tourism Management, 3*(3), 135–148.

Lang, R. (1986). Achieving integration in resource planning. In R. Lang (Ed.), *Integrated approaches to resource planning and management* (pp. 27–50). Banff: Banff Centre School of Management.

Lasswell, H. D. (1958). *Politics: Who gets what, when, how?* New York: Meridian.

Latimer, H. (1985). Developing island economies—tourism vs. agriculture. *Tourism Management, 6*(1), 32–42.

Lausche, B. (1986). *Dominica: National legislation related to natural resource management (Country Legal Report No. 1).* Castries: Organization of Eastern Caribbean States-Natural Resources Management Project.

Laventhal & Horwath Ltd. (1981). *Cayman Islands tourism industry: A 10 year development plan.* Report for Department of Tourism, Government of the Cayman Islands.

Laventhal & Horwath Ltd. (1986a). *Leeward and Windward Islands tourism sector study: Volume I.* Report for Canadian International Development Agency.

Laventhal & Horwath Ltd. (1986b). *Leeward and Windward Islands tourism sector study: Volume II.* Report for Canadian International Development Agency.

Laventhal & Horwath Ltd. (1986c). *Leeward and Windward Islands tourism sector study: Volume III.* Report for Canadian International Development Agency.

Lawton, L. J., & Butler, R. W. (1987). Cruise ship industry—patterns in the Caribbean, 1880–1986. *Tourism Management, December,* 329–343.

Leone, R. A. (1986). *Who profits: Winners, losers and government regulation.* New York: Basic Books.

Levitt, K., & Gulati, I. (1970). Income effect of tourist spending: Mystification multiplied—a critical comment on the Zinder Report. *Social and Economic Studies, 19*(3), 326–343.

Levy, D. E., & Lerch, P. B. (1991). Tourism as a factor in development: Implications for gender and work in Barbados. *Gender & Society, 5*(1), 67–85.

Lewis, C. A. (1955). *The theory of economic growth.* London: Allen Unwin.

Lewis, G. K. (1987). *Grenada: The jewel despoiled.* Baltimore: Johns Hopkins University Press.

Liew, J. (1980). Tourism and development: A re-examination. In D. G. Pearce (Ed.), *Tour-*

ism in the South Pacific: The contribution of research to development and planning (New Zealand Man and Biosphere Report No. 6) (pp. 13–17). Christchurch: Department of Geography, University of Canterbury.

Likorish, L. J. (1988). Tourism and international understanding. In L. J. D'Amore & J. Jafari (Eds.), *Tourism—a vital force for peace* (p. 151). Montreal: First Global Conference, L. J. D'Amore and Associates.

Lindberg, K. (1991). *Policies for maximizing nature tourism's ecological and economic benefits.* Washington, DC: World Resources Institute.

Long, F. (1987). 'New exports' of the Caribbean to the international economy. *Development Policy Review, 5,* 63–72.

Louis Harris and Associates. (1989). *The travel & leisure study: A survey of traveling Americans.* Report for *Travel and Leisure Magazine.*

Lowenthal, D. (1960). The range and variation of Caribbean societies. *Annals of the New York Academy of Sciences, 83,* 786–795.

Lowenthal, D. (1992). Small tropical islands: A general overview. In H. M. Hintjens & M. D. D. Newitt (Eds), *The political economy of small tropical islands: The importance of being small* (pp. 18–29). Exeter: University of Exeter Press.

Lundberg, D. E. (1980). *The tourist business.* Boston: Cahners Books.

Lundgren, J. O. J. (1982). The development of tourist accommodation in the Montreal Laurentians. In G. Wall & J. Marsh (Eds.), *Recreational land use: Perspectives on its evolution in Canada* (pp. 175–189). Ottawa: Carleton University Press.

Lynn, W. H. (1990). *Dominica tourism awareness program.* Draft report by Organization of American States for Division of Tourism, National Development Corporation, Government of the Commonwealth of Dominica.

MacFarlane, G. (1992, December 12). A day on the Cays means no-hassle sunning or shopping. *Globe and Mail.*

Madigan Pratt & Associates. (1992). *Grand Bahama Island marketing board: 1992 marketing plan.* Report for Grand Bahama Island Marketing Board.

Madigan Pratt & Associates. (1995). *Diving in the Cayman Islands: Economic impact & requirements for maintaining its premier status.* Report for Government of the Cayman Islands Department of Tourism, Cayman Islands Watersports Operators Association, and Cayman Islands Hotel and Condominium Association.

Maloney, J. (1950, April 8). The islands time forgot. *Saturday Evening Post.*

Manning, E. W. (1993). Sustainable tourism development: Meeting the planning challenge. *International Seminar on Planning for Sustainable Tourism Development in South Asian Countries,* World Trade Organization, Maldives, April.

Marden, P. (1992). 'Real' regulation reconsidered. *Environment and Planning A, 24*(4), 751–767.

Marlow, D. (1992). Constitutional change, external assistance and economic development in small islands: The case of Montserrat. In H. M. Hintjens & M. D. D. Newitt (Eds.), *The political economy of small tropical islands: The importance of being small* (pp. 42–50). Exeter: University of Exeter Press

Marotte, B. (1992, September 16). Canadian development plan draws heat from Barbadians. *Toronto Star.*

Marsh, J. (Ed.). (1986). *Canadian studies of parks, recreation and tourism in foreign lands* (Occasional Paper 11). Peterborough: Department of Geography, Trent University.

Marshall, D. (1978). *Tourism and employment in Barbados* (Occasional Papers Series 6). Cave Hill: Institute of Social and Economic Research, University of the West Indies.

Marshall, D. (1982). Migration as an agent of change in Caribbean island ecosystems. *International Social Science Journal, 34,* 451–467.

Martins, D. (1994, August 2). Concern over reef stress. *Caymanian Compass.*

Mason, R., & Mitroff, I. (1981). *Challenging strategic planning assumptions.* New York: John Wiley & Sons.

Mather, S., & Todd, G. (1993). *Tourism in the Caribbean* (Special Report No. 455). London: Economist Intelligence Unit.

Mathieson, A., & Wall, G. (1982). *Tourism: Economic, physical and social impacts.* Harlow: Longman.

May, P. (1981). *A brief chronology of Dominica's forest utilization and management activities.* St. Thomas, USVI: Island Resources Foundation.

McElroy, J. (1975). Tourist economy and island environment: An overview of structural disequilibrium. *Caribbean Educational Bulletin, 2*(1), 40–58.

McElroy, J., & de Albuquerque, K. (1989). Tourism styles and policy response in the open economy-closed environment context. *Conference on Economics and the Environment,* Caribbean Conservation Association, Bridgetown, November 6–8.

McElroy, J., & de Albuquerque, K. (1991). Tourism styles and policy response in the open economy-closed environment context. In N. P. Girvan & D. A. Simmons (Eds.), *Caribbean ecology and economics* (pp. 143–164). St. Michael: Caribbean Conservation Association.

McHale, A. H. (1989). Tourism is our business. *Saint Lucia: 10th Independence Anniversary Souvenir Magazine,* 35–36.

McIntosh, R. W., & Goeldner, C. R. (1986) *Tourism: Principles, practices, philosophies.* New York: John Wiley & Sons.

McKee, D. L., & Tisdell, C. (1990). *Developmental issues in small island economies.* New York: Praeger.

McNeely, J. A., & Thorsell, J. W.. (1988). Jungles, mountains, and islands: How tourism can help conserve the natural heritage. In L. J. D'Amore, & J. Jafari (Eds.), *Tourism—a vital force for peace* (pp. 109–120). Montreal: First Global Conference, L. J. D'Amore and Associates Ltd.

Meyer-Arendt, K. J. (1985). The Grand Isle, Louisiana resort cycle. *Annals of Tourism Research, 12*(3), 449–466.

Meyer-Arendt, K. J. (1992). The northeast coast and Samana Peninsula. In National Council for Geographic Education and Conference of Latin Americanist Geographers, *Field Trip Guide for 1992 Meetings* (pp. 84–92).

Mings, R. C. (1978). Tourist industry development: At the crossroads. *Tourist Review, 33*(3), 2–9.

Mintzberg, H. (1982). Crafting strategy. *Harvard Business Review, July/Aug.,* 26–37.

Mintzberg, H. (1994). *The rise and fall of strategic planning: Re-conceiving roles for planning, plans, planners.* New York: Free Press.

Mitchell, B. (1986). The evolution of integrated resource management. In R. Lang (Ed.), *Integrated approaches to resource planning and management* (pp. 13–26). Banff: Banff Centre School of Management.

Morley, D., & Wilkinson, P. F. (1985, April). The role of action research in addressing critical issues in very small nations. *The Operational Geographer, 6,* 38–41.

Moseley, M. (1926). *The Bahamas handbook.* Nassau: Nassau Guardian.

Moya Pons, F. (1984, Fall). The Tainos of Hispaniola. *Caribbean Review, 12,* 20–23, 47.

Murphy, P. E. (1985). *Tourism: A community approach.* New York: Methuen.

Murray, J. A. (1991). *The islands and the sea: Five centuries of nature writing from the Caribbean.* Oxford: Oxford University Press.

Naipaul, V. S. (1984). Anguilla: The shipwrecked six thousand. In *The overcrowded barraccoon* (pp. 252–266). Harmandsworth: Penguin.

Nanus, B. (1979). *Growth prospect for energy, transportation and tourism in the 80's.* Australian National Travel Association Conference.

Nelson, R., & Wall, G. (1986). Transport and accommodation: Changing interrelationships on Vancouver Island. *Annals of Tourism Research, 13*(2), 239–260.

Newman, P. (1994, March 28). A sunny welcome for Canadian funds. *Maclean's, 48.*

Nunez, T. (1978). Touristic studies in anthropological perspective. In V. L. Smith (Ed.), *Hosts and guests: The anthropology of tourism* (pp. 207–216). Oxford: Basil Blackwell.

Oglethorpe, M. (1984). Tourism in Malta: A crisis of dependence. *Leisure Studies, 3,* 147–162.

Okey, R. (1987, September/October). Trekking in nature's terrarium. *Americas,* 8–13.

Onkvisit, S., & Shaw, J. J. (1986). Competition and product management: Can the product life cycle help? *Business Horizons, 29,* 51–62.

Oppermann, M., & Sahr, W.-D. (1992). Another view on 'Alternative tourism in Dominica.' *Annals of Tourism Research, 19*(3), 784–788.

O'Reilly, A. M. (1993). Tourism in the Bahamas—an appraisal. In D. J. Gayle & J. N. Goodrich (Eds.), *Tourism marketing and management in the Caribbean* (pp. 31–40). London: Routledge.

Organization of American States. (1987a). *The optimum size and nature of new hotel development in the Caribbean.* Washington, DC: Department of Regional Development.

Organization of American States. (1987b). *Saint Lucia development atlas.* Washington, DC: Department of Regional Development,.

Organization of American States and Caribbean Tourism Organization. (1988). *Caribbean cruise ship study.* Washington, DC: Author.

Organization of American States and Caribbean Tourism Organization. (1990). *The impact of tourist investment incentives in the Caribbean region.* Bridgetown: Author.

Organization of Eastern Caribbean States. (1986). *Description of national legislation related to natural resources management.* Castries: Organization of Eastern Caribbean States—Natural Resources Management Project.

Organization of Eastern Caribbean States. (1988). *Coastal dynamics, Castries Harbour.* Castries: Organization of Eastern Caribbean States—Natural Resources Management Project.

Palmer, R. W. (1993). Tourism and taxes: The case of Barbados. In D. J. Gayle & J. N. Goodrich (Eds.), *Tourism marketing and management in the Caribbean* (pp. 58–68). London: Routledge.

Pannell Kerr Forster. (1991). *Trends in the hotel business: International edition.* New York: Author.

Pearce, D. G. (Ed.). (1980). *Tourism in the South Pacific: The contribution of research to development and planning* (New Zealand Man and Biosphere Report No. 6). Christchurch: Department of Geography, University of Canterbury.

Pearce, D. G. (1987). *Tourism today: A geographical analysis.* Harlow: Longman.

Pearce, D. G. (1989). *Tourist development.* Harlow: Longman.

Pearce, D. G. (1992). *Tourist organizations.* New York: John Wiley & Sons.

Pearce, D. G. (1993). Comparative studies in tourism research. In D. G. Pearce & R. W. Butler (Eds.), *Tourism research: Critiques and challenges* (pp. 20–35). London: Routledge.

Pearce, P. (1982). *The social psychology of tourist behaviour.* Oxford: Pergamon.

Pearce, P., & Moscardo, G. (1985). Visitor evaluation: An appraisal of goals and techniques. *Evaluation Review, 9,* 281–306.

Peet, R., & Thrift, N. (1989). Political economy and human geography. In R. Peet & N. Thrift (Eds.), *New models in geography: The political economy perspective—volume II* (pp. 3–29). London: Unwin Hyman.

Pennington, N. C. (1983). *Barbados National Park.* Report for Government of Barbados.

Perez, L. (1974). Aspects of underdevelopment: Tourism in the West Indies. *Science and Society, 37,* 473–480.

Perez, L. (1975). Tourism in the West Indies. *Journal of Communications, 25,* 136–143.

Persaud, B. (1966). *An abstract of West Indian banana statistics (with special reference to the Windward Islands).* Cave Hill: Institute of Economic and Social Research, University of the West Indies.

Peters, M. (1980). The potential of the less-developed Caribbean countries. *Tourism Management, 1*(1), 13–21.

Phillips, E. (1982). The development of the tourist industry in Barbados 1946–1980. In R. D. Worrell (Ed.), *The economy of Barbados* (pp. 107–139). Oxford: Basil Blackwell.

Pigram, J. J. (1992). Alternative tourism: Tourism and sustainable resource management. In V. L. Smith & W. R. Eadington (Eds.), *Tourism alternatives: Potentials and problems in the development of tourism* (pp. 76–87). Philadelphia: University of Pennsylvania Press.

Pigram, J. J., & Cooper, M. J. (1980). Economic impact analysis in tourism planning and development. In D. G. Pearce (Ed.), *Tourism in the South Pacific: The contribution of research to development and planning* (New Zealand Man and Biosphere Report No. 6) (pp. 19–31). Christchurch: Department of Geography, University of Canterbury.

Pizam, A. (1987). Planning a tourism research investigation. In J. R. B. Ritchie & C. R. Goeldner (Eds.), *Travel, tourism, and hospitality research* (pp. 63–76). New York: John Wiley & Sons.

Poon, A. (1988). Innovation and the future of Caribbean tourism. *Tourism Management, 9*(3), 213–220.

Poon, A. (1992). *The Bahamas tourism sector study: Focus on the Family Islands.* Report for Inter-American Development Bank and Government of the Commonwealth of the Bahamas.

Poon, A., Sobers, A. Williams, S., & Mitchell, W. (1990). *The economic impact of tourism in St. Lucia.* Christ Church: Caribbean Tourism Organization.

Porter, M. (1985). *Competitive advantage.* New York: The Free Press.

Porter, P. W. (1979). *Food and development in the semi-arid zone of East Africa.* Syracuse, NY: Syracuse University.

Potter, R. B., & Binns, J. A. (1988). Power, politics and society. In M. Pacione (Ed.), *The geography of the third world: Progress and prospect* (pp. 271–310). London: Routledge.

Pratt, M. (1993). Cayman Islands: Successful tourism yesterday, today and tomorrow. In J. R. B. Ritchie, D. E. Hawkins, F. Go, & D. Frechtling (Eds.), *Special report: Island tourism. World travel and tourism review: Indicators, trends and issues—volume 3, 1993* (pp. 262–269). Wallingford, UK: CAB International.

Prins, P. (1987). Forestry policy and administration, 1987–1997. In *Natural resources and rural development project, Commonwealth of Dominica.* Washington, DC: Department of Regional Development, Organization of American States.

Rabinow, P., & Sullivan, W. M. (Eds.). (1979). *Interpretive social science: A reader.* Berkeley: University of California Press.

Radford, K. J. (1980). *Strategic planning: An analytical approach.* Reston, VA: Reston Publishing.

Ramsaran, R. (1979). Tourism in the economy of the Bahamas. *Caribbean Studies, 19*(1,2), 75–91.

Ramsaran, R. (1989). *The Commonwealth Caribbean in the world economy.* London: Macmillan.

Raymont, J. E. G., Lockwood, A. P. M., Hull, L. E.,& Swain, G. (1976). Results of the investigations into the marine biology. In *Cayman Islands Natural Resources Study, Part IVA.* George Town: Cayman Islands Natural Resources Laboratory.

Reaud-Thomas, G., & Lesourd, M. (1989). L'absence de développement touristique aux Iles du Cap Vert. In A. Huetz de Lemps (Ed.), *Iles et tourisme en milieux tropical et subtropical* (Collection Iles et Archipels No. 10, pp. 163–182). Talence: Société pour l'Etude, la Protection et l'Aménagement de la Nature dan les Régions Inter-Tropicales, Le Centre d'Etudes de Géographie Tropicale du Centre Nationale de Recherches Scientifique de France et Le Centre Nationale de Recherches Scientifique de France et l'Université de Bordeaux III.

Reime, M., & Hawkins, C. (1979). Tourism development: A model for growth. *Cornell Hotel and Restaurant Administration Quarterly, 20*(1), 67–74.

Renard, Y. (1985). *Tourism and the environment—a case study of the Vieux Fort area.* Report for United Nations Economic Commission on Latin America and the Caribbean and United Nations Environment Program.

Renard, Y. (1989). Conservation and development of the Southeast Coast of St. Lucia, W.I. In W. I. Knausenberger & B. Fleming (Eds.), *Proceedings of Workshop on Coastal Protected Areas in the Lesser Antilles.* University of the Virgin Islands, St. Thomas, USVI, July 1986.

Resource Systems Management International Inc. (1988). *Caribbean Environmental Programming Strategy—final report: Volume 3—background information.* Report for Canadian International Development Agency.

Reynolds, L. (1992, February 22). Montserrat to target 'ecotourists.' *Globe and Mail.*

Richardson, B. C. (1986). *Panama money in the Barbados, 1900–1920.* Knoxville: University of Tennessee Press.

Richardson, B. C. (1992). *The Caribbean in the wider world, 1492–1992.* New York: Cambridge University Press.

Richter, L. (1983a). The political implications of Chinese tourism policy. *Annals of Tourism Research, 10*(4), 395–413.

Richter, L. (1983b). Tourism and political science: A case of not so benign neglect. *Annals of Tourism Research, 10*(3), 313–335.

Richter, L. (1984). *The politics of tourism development in the American states.* American Society of Public Administration, Denver, April 8–11.

Richter, L. (1985). *Bureaucracy and the political process: Three case studies of tourism development in Asia.* International Political Science Association, Paris, July 19.

Richter, L. (1987). The political dimensions of tourism. In J. R. B. Ritchie & C. R. Goeldner (Eds.), *Travel, tourism and hospitality research* (pp. 215–227). New York: John Wiley & Sons.

Richter, L. (1989). *The politics of tourism in Asia.* Honolulu: University of Hawaii Press.

Richter, L. K., & Richter, W. L. (1985). Policy choices in South Asian tourism development. *Annals of Tourism Research, 12*(2), 201–218.

Rigby, J. K., & Roberts, H. H. (1976). *Grand Cayman Island: Geology, sediments and marine communities* (Special Publication No. 4). Salt Lake City, UT: Brigham Young University Geology Studies.

Rink, D. R., & Swan, J. E. (1979). Product life cycle research: Literature review. *Journal of Business Research, 78,* 219–242.

Ritchie, J. R. B. (1987). Roles of research in tourism management. In J. R. B. Ritchie & C. R. Goeldner (Eds.), *Travel, tourism, and hospitality research* (pp. 13–21). New York: John Wiley & Sons.

Ritchie, J. R. B., & Goeldner, C. R. (Eds.). (1987). *Travel, tourism, and hospitality research.* New York: John Wiley & Sons.

Rojas, E., Wirtshafter, R. M., Radke, J.; & Hosier, R. (1988). Land conservation in small developing countries: Computer assisted studies in St. Lucia. *Ambio, XVII*(4), 282–288.

Romsa, G. H., & Blenman, E. H. M. (1987). The Prime Minister's dilemma. *Annals of Tourism Research, 14*(2), 240–253.

Romulus, G. (1989, February 18). A system of parks and protected areas for St. Lucia. *Voice of St. Lucia.*

Romulus, G. (1990). *A system of parks and protected areas for St. Lucia.* Castries: St. Lucia National Trust.

Romulus, G. (1992). Soufriere and the National Parks and Protected Areas Plan. *Qualibou, 1,* 4–6.

Rosenow, J. E., & Pulsipher, G. L. (1979). *Tourism: The good, the bad, and the ugly.* Lincoln, NE: Century Three Press.

Rosenweig, J. A. (1986). Exchange rates and competition for tourists. *New England Economic Review, 14,* 240–253.

Rostow, W. W. (1960). *The process of economic growth.* Oxford: Clarendon.

Ruffing, L. (1979). The Navajo Nation: A history of dependence and under-development. *Review of Radical Political Economics, 11*(2), 25–43.

Safa, H. (1986). Runaway shops and female employment: The search for cheap labor. In E. Leacock & H. Safa (Eds.), *Women's work: Development and the division of labor by gender.* South Hadley, MA: Bergin & Garvey.

St. Lucia National Trust. (1992). *Proposal for the establishment of the Pitons Nature Conservation Reserve.* Reply to the Prime Minister made to St. Lucia National Trust at Soufriere, August 27, 1991.

St. Lucia Tourist Board. (1991). *Tourism statistical analysis 1990.* Castries: Author.

Sayer, A. (1982). Explanation in economic geography: Abstraction versus generalization. *Progress in Human Geography, 6,* 68–88.

Schon, D. A. (1983). *The reflective practitioner: How professionals think in action.* New York: Basic Books.

Sealey, N. E. (1985). *Bahamian landscapes: An introduction to the geography of the Bahamas.* London: Collins Caribbean.

Seers, D. (1979). The meaning of development. In D. Lehmann (Ed.), *Development theory: Four critical studies.* London: Cass.

Seward, S. B., & Spinrad, B. K. (Eds.). (1982). *Tourism in the Caribbean: The economic impact.* Ottawa: International Development Research Centre.

Shankland Cox and Associates. (1971a). *Dominica: A tourist development strategy—planning and policy document.* Report for Overseas Development Administration, British Foreign and Commonwealth Office, London.

Shankland Cox and Associates. (1971b). *Dominica: a tourist development strategy—technical report.* Report for Overseas Development Administration, British Foreign and Commonwealth Office, London.

Sharkey, D. A. (1994). *Alternative tourism in Dominica, West Indies: Problems and prospects.* Association of American Geographers, San Francisco, March 29–April 2.

Showalter, G. R. (1994). *Cruise ships and private islands in the Caribbean.* Association of American Geographers, San Francisco, March 29–April 2.

Showker, K. (1993, November/December). Save our sea. *Caribbean Travel and Life,* 38–41.

Smith, C., & Jenner, P. (1992). *Travel & tourism analyst, report No. 3.* London: Economist Intelligence Unit.

Smith, D. M. (1977). *Human geography: A welfare approach.* London: Arnold.

Smith, R. C. (1984). The maritime geography of the Cayman Islands. *Caribbean Geography, 1*(4), 247–255.

Smith, S. H. (1988). Cruise ships: A serious threat to coral reefs and associated organisms. *Ocean & Shoreline Management, 11,* 231–248.

Smith, S. L. J. (1983). *Recreation geography.* London: Longman.

Smith, S. L. J. (1989). *Tourism analysis: A handbook.* New York: John Wiley & Sons.

Smith, T. (1973). The policy implementation process. *Policy Sciences, 4,* 197–209.

Smith, V. L. (Ed.). (1989). *Hosts and guests: The anthropology of tourism* (2nd ed). Philadelphia: University of Pennsylvania Press.

Smith, V. L., & Eadington, W. R. (Eds.). 1992. *Tourism alternatives: Potentials and problems in the development of tourism.* Philadelphia: University of Pennsylvania Press.

Soler, F. (1988). *Development control and physical planning: The case of Dominica.* Washington, DC: Department of Regional Development, Organization of American States.

Spinrad, B. K. (1982). St. Lucia. In S. B. Seward & B. K. Spinrad (Eds.), *Tourism in the Caribbean: The economic impact* (pp. 67–92). Ottawa: International Development Research Centre.

Spinrad, B. K., Seward, S. B., & Bélisle, F. J. (1982). Introduction. In S. B. Seward & B. K. Spinrad (Eds.), *Tourism in the Caribbean: The economic impact* (pp. 7–22). Ottawa: International Development Research Centre.

Stansfield, C. A. (1978). Atlantic city and the resort cycle: Background to the legalization of gambling. *Annals of Tourism Research, 5*(2), 238–351.

Stark, J. H. (1891). *History and guide to the Bahama Islands.* Boston: James H. Stark, Publisher.

Steed, G. P. F. (1988). Geography, social science, and public policy: Regeneration through reinterpretation. *Canadian Geographer, 32*(1), 2–14.

Stocken, T. (1956, November 4). Idyllic Caymans: Three Caribbean isles have remained unspoiled over the centuries. *New York Times,* X, 20, 3.

Stoffle, R. W. (1977). Industrial impact on family formation in Barbados, West Indies. *Ethnology, 16,* 253–266.

Stynes, D. J. (1983). An introduction to recreation forecasting. In S. Lieber & D. Fesenmaier (Eds.), *Recreation planning and management* (pp. 87–95). State College, PA: Venture.

Sunshine, C. A. (1985). *The Caribbean: Survival, struggle and sovereignty.* Boston: EPIC.

Sutton, H. (1980). *Travellers: The American tourist from stagecoach to space shuttle.* New York: William Morrow.

Taketa, R. (1993). Management and the geographer: The relevance of geography in strategic thinking. *Professional Geographer, 45*(4), 465–470.

Taylor, B. (1986). Corporate planning for the 1990's: The new frontiers. *Long Range Planning, 19,* 13–18.

Taylor, J. (Ed.). (1989). *The Caribbean yearbook.* St. John's, Antigua: FT Caribbean.

Thom, R. (1975). *Structural stability and morphogenesis.* Reading, MA: W. A. Benjamin.

Thompson, E. F. (1943). *The fisheries of the Cayman Islands* (Bulletin No. 22). London: Development and Welfare in the West Indies Program.

Thomas, C. Y. (1988). *The poor and the powerless: Economic policy and change in the Caribbean.* New York: Monthly Review Press.

Thomson, R. (1987). *Green gold: Bananas and dependency in the Eastern Caribbean.* London: Latin American Bureau.

Thorsell, J. W. (1984). National parks from the ground up: Experience from Dominica, West Indies. In J. A. McNeely & K. R. Miller (Eds.), *National parks, conservation, and development* (pp. 616–620). Washington, DC: Smithsonian Institution Press.

Thorsell, J. W. (1990). Research in tropical protected areas: Some guidelines for managers. *Environmental Conservation, 17*(1), 14–18.

Thorsell, J. W., & Wood, G. (1976). Dominica's Morne Trois Pitons National Park, *Nature Canada, 5,* 4 (reprint).

Tinsley, J. F. (1979). Tourism in the Virgin Islands. In J. S. Holder (Ed.), *Caribbean tourism: Policies and impacts* (pp. 295–316). Christ Church: Caribbean Tourism Research and Development Centre.

Torgerson, D. (1986). Between knowledge and politics: Three faces of policy analysis. *Policy Sciences, 19*(1), 33–59.

Tourism Planning and Research Associates. (1991). *Dominica tourism sector plan.* Report for the Ministry of Trade, Industry, and Tourism, Government of the Commonwealth of Dominica.

Towle, E. (1985). St. Lucia C Rodney Bay/Gros Islet. In T. Geoghagan (Ed.), *Proceedings of Carribean Seminar on Environmental Impact Assessment* (pp. 228–243). St. Michael: Caribbean Conservation Association and Institute for Resource and Environmental Studies, Dalhousie University.

Towner, J. (1988). Approaches to tourism history. *Annals of Tourism Research, 15*(1), 47–62.

Transport and Tourism Technicians Ltd. (1972). *The Tourist Board of the Cayman Islands.* Report to Overseas Development Administration, British Foreign and Commonwealth Office, London.

Tromson Monroe Advertising, Inc. (1979). *A program of tourism promotion for the Republic of Dominica.* Report for Dominica Tourist Board.

Trouillot, M.-R. (1988). *Peasants and capital: Dominica in the world economy.* Baltimore: Johns Hopkins University Press.

Turner, L. (1976). The international division of leisure: Tourism and the Third World. *World Development, March*, 205–236.

Turner, L., & Ash, J. (1975). *The golden hordes: International tourism and the pleasure periphery.* London: Constable.

United Nations Commission on Trade and Development. (1971). A note on the 'Tourist Sector.' In *Guidelines for tourism statistics: 30.* New York: United Nations.

United Nations Economic Commission on Latin America and the Caribbean. (1984). *Agricultural statistics, volume VI.* Santiago: United Nations.

United Nations Economic Commission on Latin America and the Caribbean. (1988). Report of the Wider Caribbean Expert Meeting on Tourism and Environment in Caribbean Development, Port-of-Spain, Trinidad and Tobago, December 2–4, 1985. In F. Edwards (Ed.), *Environmentally sound tourism in the Caribbean* (pp. 9–115). Calgary: Banff Centre School of Management and University of Calgary.

United States Agency for International Development. (1985). *St. Lucia country supplement to the Caribbean regional CDSS.* Bridgetown: Author.

Uphoff, N., & Ilchman, W. (1972). *The political economy of development.* Princeton, NJ: Princeton University Press.

Venner, K. D. (1989). The Saint Lucian economy in the 21st Century. *Saint Lucia: 10th Independence Anniversary Souvenir Magazine*, 79–95.

Villard, H. S. (1976). *The Royal Victoria Hotel.* Nassau: Nassau Guardian.

Wagenheim, K. (1991, January). *Caribbean Update*, p. 3.

Walker, S. E., & Duffield, B. S. (1984). The impact of tourism on island environments. In C. Ciaccio & L. Pedrini (Eds.), *Le tourisme dans les petites îles* (pp. 301–325). Messina: Commission on the Geography of Tourism and Leisure, International Geographic Union.

Wallerstein, I. (1987). Periphery. In J. Eatwell, M. Milgate, & P. Newman (Eds.), *The new palgrave: A dictionary of economics* (pp. 846–849). New York and London: Macmillan.

Wanhill, S. R. C. (1986). Which investment incentives for tourism? *Tourism Management, 7*(1), 2–7.

Warren, B. (1989). *Decolonization and world peace.* Austin: University of Texas Press.

Warwick, D. P., & Osherson, S. (1973). *Comparative research methods*. Englewood Cliffs, NJ: Prentice-Hall.

Watts, D. (1987). *The West Indies: Patterns of development, culture and environmental change since 1492*. Cambridge: Cambridge University Press.

Watts, M. (1987). Powers of production—geographers among the peasants. *Society and Space, 5*, 215–230.

Weaver, D. B. (1988). The evolution of a 'plantation' tourism landscape on the Caribbean island of Antigua. *Tijdschrift voor Economische en Sociale Geografie, 79*, 319–331.

Weaver, D. B. (1990). Grand Cayman Island and the resort cycle concept. *Journal of Travel Research, 29*(2), 9–15.

Weaver, D. B. (1991). Alternative to mass tourism in Dominica. *Annals of Tourism Research, 18*(3), 414–432.

Weaver, D. B. (1992). Contention for deliberate alternative tourism. *Annals of Tourism Research, 19*(3), 788–791.

Weaver, D. B. (1993). Ecotourism in the small island Caribbean. *GeoJournal, 31*(4), 457–465.

Webster, O. C., & Ashwell, H. J. (1946, May 20). Letter to the Honourable President and Members of the Justices and Vestry of the Cayman Islands.

Welch, B. M. (1991). The survival of the Windwards banana industry: A case for geographical inertia. In D. Lockhart & D. Drakakis-Smith (Eds.), *Environmental and economic issues in small island development* (Monograph No. 6, pp. 48–61). London: Commonwealth Foundation.

Wharton Econometric Forecasting Associates. (1988). *The impact of tourism on the economy of the Bahamas*. Report for Ministry of Tourism, Government of the Commonwealth of the Bahamas.

Wharton Econometric Forecasting Associates. (1991). *Travel and tourism in the world economy*. Study for World Travel and Tourism Council, London.

White, K. J., & Walker, M. B. (1982). Trouble in the travel account. *Annals of Tourism Research, 9*(1), 37–56.

Wight, P. (1993). Ecotourism: Ethics or eco-sell? *Journal of Travel Research, 31*(1), 3–9.

Wilder, R. (Ed.). 1986. *Barbados*. Singapore: APA Productions Ltd.

Wilkinson, P. F. (1984). Energy resources in a Third World microstate: St. Lucia Household Energy Survey. *Resources and Energy, VI*(3), 305–328.

Wilkinson, P. F. (1987a). The environmental impact of energy use in forest resources: St. Lucia. In J. G. Nelson & K. D. Knight (Eds.), *Research, resources and the environment in Third World development* (Publications Series No. 27, pp. 187–192). Waterloo: Department of Geography, Faculty of Environmental Studies, University of Waterloo.

Wilkinson, P. F. (1987b). Tourism in small island nations: A fragile dependency. *Leisure Studies, 6*(2), 127–146.

Wilkinson, P. F. (1989a). Le tourisme dans les petites Antilles anglophones. In A. Huetz de Lemps (Ed.), *Iles et tourisme en milieux tropical et subtropical* (Collection Iles et Archipels No. 10, pp. 105–124). Talence: Société pour l'Etude, la Protection et l'Aménagement de la Nature dan les Régions Inter-Tropicales, Le Centre d'Etudes de Géographie Tropicale du Centre Nationale de Recherches Scientifique de France et Le Centre Nationale de Recherches Scientifique de France et l'Université de Bordeaux III.

Wilkinson, P. F. (1989b). Strategies for tourism development in island microstates. *Annals of Tourism Research, 16*(2), 153–177.

Wilkinson, P. F. (1990). Tourism and integrated national development: The case of the Caribbean. In P. F. Wilkinson & W. C. Found (Eds.), *Resource analysis research in developing countries: The experience of Ontario geographers* (pp. 83–97). Toronto: Faculty of Environmental Studies, York University.

Wilkinson, P. F. (1993). An environmental perspective on recreation: The 'Environment–recreation interaction model.' *Journal of Applied Recreation Research, 17*(2), 178–210.

Wilkinson, P. F. (1997). Jamaican tourism: From dependency theory to a world-economy perspective. In D. G. Lockhart & D. Drakakis-Smith (Eds.), *Island tourism* (pp. 181–204). London and New York: Pinter.

Williams, M. C. (1983). Country summary for St. Lucia. In J. Wood (Ed.), *Proceedings of Workshop on Biosphere Reserves and Other Protected Areas for Sustainable Development on Small Caribbean Islands* (pp. 110–118). Virgin Islands National Park, St. John, USVI, and United States Department of the Interior National Parks Service, Southeast Regional Office, Atlanta, May 10–12.

Williams, N. (1992). *A history of the Cayman Islands* (2nd ed.). George Town: Government of the Cayman Islands.

Wilson, C. (1983). Country summary for Barbados. In J. Wood (Ed.), *Proceedings of Workshop on Biosphere Reserves and Other Protected Areas for Sustainable Development on Small Caribbean Islands* (pp. 44–52). Virgin Islands National Park, St. John, USVI, and United States Department of the Interior National Parks Service, Southeast Regional Office, Atlanta, May 10–12.

Wittgenstein, L. (1958). *Philosophical investigations* (G. E. M. Anscomb, Trans.) Oxford: Basil Blackwell.

Winker, C. (Ed.). (1992). *Cayman Islands yearbook '92 & business directory.* George Town: Cayman Free Press.

Winkler, K. J. (1985, June 26). Questioning the science in social science, scholars signal a 'turn to interpretation.' *Chronical of Higher Education*, pp. 5–6.

Wood, J. (Ed.). (1983). *Proceedings of Workshop on Biosphere Reserves and Other Protected Areas for Sustainable Development on Small Caribbean Islands* (pp. 110–118). Virgin Islands National Park, St. John, USVI, and United States Department of the Interior National Parks Service, Southeast Regional Office, Atlanta, May 10–12.

World Bank. (1972). *Tourism: Sector working paper.* Washington, DC: Author.

World Bank. (1980). *Economic memorandum on the Bahamas* (Report No. 2975-BM). Washington, DC: Author.

World Bank. (1985a). *Dominica: Priorities and prospects for development.* Washington, DC: Author.

World Bank. (1985b). *St. Lucia: Economic performance and prospects.* Washington, DC: Author.

World Bank. (1986a). *The Bahamas: Economic report.* Washington, DC: Author.

World Bank. (1986b). *Barbados economic memorandum.* (Report No. 6509-BAR). Washington, DC: Author.

World Bank. (1986c). *St. Lucia economic memorandum* (Report No. 6385-SLU). Washington, DC: Author.

World Bank. (1988a). *Barbados: The need for economic policy adjustment* (Report No. 7184-BAR). Washington, DC: Author.

World Bank. (1988b). *Caribbean countries: Economic situation, regional issues, and capital flows.* Washington, DC: Author.

World Bank. (1990). *Long-term economic prospects of the OECS countries* (Report No. 8058-CRG). Washington, DC: Author.

World Commission on Environment and Development. (1987). *Our common future.* Oxford: Oxford University Press.

World Tourism Organization. (1980). *Physical planning and area development for tourism in the six WTO regions, 1980.* Madrid: Author.

World Tourism Organization. (1981). *Tourism compendium: 1981.* Madrid: Author.

World Tourism Organization. (1983). *Domestic tourism statistics 1981–82.* Madrid: Author.

Worrell, R. D. (Ed.). (1982). *The economy of Barbados, 1946–1980.* Oxford: Basil Blackwell.

Worrell, R. D. (1987). *Small island economies: Structure and performance in the English-speaking Caribbean since 1970.* New York: Praeger.

Worrell, R. D., & Bourne, C. (Eds.). (1989). *Economic adjustment policies for small nations: Theory and experience in the English-speaking Caribbean.* New York: Praeger.

Wright, R. M. (1985). Morne Trois Pitons National Park in Dominica: A case study in park establishment in the developing world. *Ecology Law Quarterly, 12,* 747–778.

Yapa, L. (1979). Ecopolitical economy of the green revolution. *The Professional Geographer, 31,* 371–376.

Zimmerer, K. (1991). Wetland production and land-holder persistence: Agricultural change in a highland Peruvian region. *Annals of the Association of American Geographers, 81*(3), 443–463.

Zinder and Associates. (1969). *The future of tourism in the Eastern Caribbean.* Washington, DC: United States Agency for International Development

Index

ANNOUNCING:
A NEW SERIES IN TOURISM
TOURISM DYNAMICS:
The Challenges of People and Place

The series is aimed primarily at the undergraduate and graduate market in both academic and professional programs with an additional focus on professionals working in the dynamic fields of tourism and related industries.

Edited by:

Professor Valene L. Smith
Dept of Anthropology, California State Univ.-
Chico Chico, CA 95929
Fax: 916-345-3881,
email: vsmith@oavax.csuchico.edu

Professor Paul F. Wilkinson
Faculty of Environmental Studies York Univ.
4700 Keele Street North York, Ont. M3J 1P3 Canada
Fax: 416-736-5679,
email: eswilkin@yorku.ca

We are seeking manuscripts for possible publication in the international, interdisciplinary series.

SCOPE: **TOURISM DYNAMICS** is an interdisciplinary series focused on the dynamics of tourism as a social, economic and environmental force affecting virtually all of the Earth's people and places.

Tourism represents a complex spatial patterns that incorporates ...

ORIGINS (e.g., the socio-psychological motivations of travellers),

LINKAGE (e.g., advertising and the media, the role of multinational corporations), and . . .

DESTINATIONS (tourist resorts, festivals ranging from the Olympics to the Monterey Jazz Festival, traditional cultural landscapes including Pennsylvania's Amish and Bali's Saweh terraced landscapes) a . . .

RANGE OF SCALES (both origins and destinations) from . . .

GLOBAL (e.g., Disney World) to ...

INTERNATIONAL REGION (e.g., the islands of the caribbean) to . . .

COUNTRY (e.g.,Spain's Mediterranean coast) to . . .

DOMESTIC REGION (e.g., the impact of japanese tourist on Hawaii or the ski resort development in their own country) a range of available . . .

ANALYTICAL TOOLS (e.g., economic,ethnographic policy)

The series, therefore, will concentrate on topics that have a theoretical base and make a scientific contribution, but will also include case examples that are of general, even practical interest.

TOURISM "IS" DYNAMIC

The Series will be held together by that tourism **"IS"** dynamic and that each place and people poses "challenges": how can/does tourism develop, how does it evolve/change in any one area over the passage of time, is it appropriate and sustainable, and what are the impacts upon both land and people caused by tourism?

ANNOUNCING A NEW BOOK SERIES
"TOURISM DYNAMICS"
BOOK TITLES ANNOUNCED FOR 1997:

TOURISM POLICY AND PLANNING:
Case Studies from the Commonwealth Caribbean
Paul Wilkinson, York University, Canada
(H) 1-882345-12-6 $35.00(S) 1-882345-13-4 $26.00 Pub. Date July '97

CASINO GAMBLING IN AMERICA
Origins, Trends & Impacts
Klaus J. Meyer-Arendt, Rudi Hartmand, Mississippi State University, USA
(H) 1-882345-16-9 $35.00 (S) 1-882345-17-7 $26.00 Pub. Date August '97

TOURISM DEVELOPMENT IN CRITICAL ENVIRONMENT
Tej Vir Singh & Shalini Singh, Centre for Tourism Research & Development, India
(H) 1-882345-18-5 $35.00 (S) 1-882345-19-3 $26.00 Pub. Date November '97

TOURISM & GAMING ON AMERICAN INDIAN LANDS
Alan A. Lew, George A. Van Otten, Northern Arizona University
(H) 1-882345-20-7 $00.00 (S) 1-882345-21-5 $00.00 Pub. Date TBA

SEX TOURISM AND PROSTITUTION
Martin Opperman, Waiarki Polytechnic, New Zealand
(H) 1-882345-14-2 $38.00 (S) 1-882345-15-0 $29.00 Pub. Date December '97

EVENT MANAGEMENT & EVENT TOURISM
Don Getz, University of Calgary, Canada
(H) 1-882345-11-8 $74.50 (S) 1-882345-10-0 $59.50 Pub. Date January '97

BOOKS IN PROGRESS: A totally new version of Valene Smith's classic Hosts and Guest. Proposals have been accepted for manuscripts on: island tourism in Thailand, tourism in rural China and in Southeast Asia, tourism on American Indian lands, tourism policy and planning, political economy of tourism in Latin America, economic geography of tourism, tourism in critical environments, and tourism and sustainability.

BOOK PROPOSALS: Please submit your proposal to one of the Editors. Supply an outline of contents, 100 word short scope, sample chapter, a list of contributors if your book is a contributed volume, a list of your publications. Please also supply a statement concerning the books distinguishing features which make the book outstanding.
(H) = Hardbound (S) = Softbound

R INFORMATION PLEASE CONTACT THE PUBLISHER AT:
'ant Communication Corporation
'ale Road, Elmsford, New York 10523 ▪ Fax: 914-592-8981